MW00512438

WILHELM WUNDT IN HISTORY
The Making of a Scientific Psychology

PATH IN PSYCHOLOGY
Published in Cooperation with Publications for the
Advancement of Theory and History in Psychology (PATH)

Series Editors:
David Bakan, *York University*
John M. Broughton, *Teachers College, Columbia University*
Robert W. Rieber, *John Jay College, CUNY, and Columbia University*
Howard Gruber, *University of Geneva*

WILHELM WUNDT IN HISTORY
The Making of a Scientific Psychology

Edited by

Robert W. Rieber

John Jay College of Criminal Justice and the Graduate Center
The City University of New York
New York, New York

and

David K. Robinson

Truman State University
Kirksville, Missouri

In collaboration with
Arthur L. Blumenthal and Kurt Danziger

Kluwer Academic / Plenum Publishers
New York   Boston   Dordrecht   London   Moscow

Library of Congress Cataloging-in-Publication Data

Wilhelm Wundt in history: the making of a scientific psychology/edited by Robert W. Rieber and David K. Robinson.
    p.   cm. — (PATH in psychology)
    Includes bibliographical references and index.
    ISBN 0-306-46599-X
    1. Psychology—History—20th century. 2. Psychology, Experimental—History—20th century. 3. Wundt, Wilhelm Max, 1832–1920. I. Rieber, R. W. (Robert W.) II. Robinson, David Keith. III. Series.

BF105 .W545 2001
150$.92—dc21   2001034436

ISBN 0-306-46599-X

© 2001 Kluwer Academic / Plenum Publishers, New York
233 Spring Street, New York, N.Y. 10013

http://www.wkap.nl/

10 9 8 7 6 5 4 3 2 1

A C.I.P. record for this book is available from the Library of Congress

Printed in the United States of America

Prof. Dr. Wundt, Leipzig

CONTRIBUTORS

Arthur L. Blumenthal, Department of Psychology, Berkeley College, New York, New York 10174

Kurt Danziger, Department of Psychology, York University, Downsville, Ontario M3J 1P3, Canada

Solomon Diamond, Late of the Department of Psychology, California State University, Los Angeles, California 90032

Edward J. Haupt, Late of the Department of Psychology, Montclair State University, Upper Montclair, New Jersey 07043

Robert W. Rieber, John Jay College of Criminal Justice, City University of New York, New York, New York 10019

David K. Robinson, Division of Social Science, Truman State University, Kirksville, Missouri 63501

Miki Takasuna, Department of Psychology, Yamano College of Aesthetics, Tokyo 192-0396, Japan

PREFACE

In this new millenium it may be fair to ask, "Why look at Wundt?" Over
the years, many authors have taken fairly detailed looks at the work and
accomplishments of Wilhelm Wundt (1832–1920). This was especially
true of the years around 1979, the centennial of the Leipzig Institute for
Experimental Psychology, the birthplace of the "graduate program" in
psychology. More than twenty years have passed since then, and in the
intervening time those centennial studies have attracted the attention
and have motivated the efforts of a variety of historians, philosophers,
psychologists, and other social scientists. They have profited from the
questions raised earlier about theoretical, methodological, sociological,
and even political aspects affecting the organized study of mind and
behavior; they have also proposed some new directions for research in the
history of the behavioral and social sciences.

With the advantage of the historiographic perspective that twenty
years can bring, this volume will consider this much-heralded "founding
father of psychology" once again. Some of the authors are veterans of the
centennial who contributed to a very useful volume, edited by Robert W.
Rieber, *Wilhelm Wundt and the Making of a Scientific Psychology* (New York:
Plenum Press, 1980). Others are scholars who have joined Wundt studies
since then, and have used that book, among others, as a guide to further
work.

The first chapter, "Wundt before Leipzig," is essentially unchanged
from the 1980 volume. The late Solomon Diamond did such a tremendous
job researching this early literature that it was never surpassed, not even
by Diamond himself.

The second chapter, "Wundt and the Temptations of Psychology," is
a new one by Kurt Danziger. It is one of the most general and useful
overviews of Wundt's thought and intentions, written by someone who

has looked deeply into philosophical and methodological problems of early psychology and who has communicated his findings more frequently and more clearly than anyone else. We would like to say that this chapter is a culmination of Danziger's studies of Wundt, but he is likely to come up with more later.

Danziger's second contribution, "The Unknown Wundt: Drive, Apperception, and Volition," is a revision of one of his chapters in the 1980 volume. (See his own remarks about that in his footnote.) We wanted to include this essay again, in some form, because when many people began to look at Wundt and early psychology, reading it led them to understand the "real" Wundt (reflected in his own work and writings), opposed to the "structuralist and introspectionist" Wundt of the traditional textbooks in North America.

Next comes a new chapter by Arthur Blumenthal (who explored quite a different theme in 1980), "A Wundt Primer: The Operating Characteristics of Consciousness." Whereas Danziger explores volition, Blumenthal takes a broader look at Wundt's concept of consciousness, including the role of emotions (among other aspects).

Robert Rieber has revised his earlier contribution to offer "Wundt and the Americans: From Flirtation to Abandonment." He sketches several of the ways and reasons why Wundt's work had to be "Americanized" on the Western side of the Atlantic.

David Robinson, who used the 1980 book as a prompt for his doctoral research, elaborates a point emphasized by Danziger, that reaction-time experiments were central to early experimental psychology. "Reaction-time Experiments in Wundt's Institute and Beyond" tries to see just how far, and in what ways, this influence ran.

Edward Haupt also looks at experimentation in detail, particularly at the use of apparatus, and he finds that Wundt's Institute had an early competitor. "Laboratories for Experimental Psychology: Göttingen's Ascendancy over Leipzig in the 1890s" can be read together with Robinson's chapter to provide interesting contrasts in viewpoints and historical interpretation.

The last two chapters are about Wundt's writings and his library. Miki Takasuna tells the fascinating story of Wundt's personal library and why most of it is now in Japan. "Bibliography of Wilhelm Wundt's Writings, Compiled by Eleonore Wundt" reproduces the authoritative listing of all his writings, compiled with accuracy and care by his daughter.

The contributors to this collection do not pretend to cover every aspect of the vast work and complex influence of Wundt on psychology. We also do not speak with one voice. In fact, if you do not find argument and provocation in these pages, then we have failed in our task. Early experimental psychology was a complex enterprise, and the difficulties in interpreting and understanding it do not seem to lessen over time. So we agree on many things, disagree on quite a few things, and discuss all our ideas and readings in a spirit not only of mutual respect, but of outright enthusiasm and love for the productive argument. We think that this approach might help others better to appreciate and to make use of *Wilhelm Wundt in History.*

R.W.R.
D.K.R.

ACKNOWLEDGMENTS: The editorial work on this volume was assisted by Jeanette Mehmert at Truman State University (the bibliography), and by Yaroslav Andreev and Olga Pavelkovskaya at Kherson (Ukraine) State Pedagogical University (word processing). It is a credit to their talents and diligence that none of them was working in their native languages, and yet they all did a marvelous job.

CONTENTS

Chapter 2
Wundt and the Temptations of Psychology 69

Kurt Danziger

Chapter 3
The Unknown Wundt: Drive, Apperception, and Volition . . . 95

Kurt Danziger

Chapter 4
A Wundt Primer: The Operating Characteristics
of Consciousness 121

Arthur L. Blumenthal

edited by David K. Robinson

WUNDT BEFORE LEIPZIG

Solomon Diamond

It is possible to sum up the first 40 years of Wundt's life, in the style of
an introductory textbook of psychology, by saying that he was the son of
a country parson, that he studied medicine at Heidelberg and subsequently served for several years as assistant to Helmholtz at that university, and that he was by profession a physiologist until, in his 40th or 41st
year, he set about writing what Boring (1950) called "the most important
book in the history of modern psychology" (p. 322). All this would be
accurate, but also completely uninformative. The Wilhelm Wundt who is
regularly depicted in much fuller yet still fragmentary accounts is a myth
based on the misconceptions of some of his students, both embellished
and softened by the complementary processes of "sharpening" and
"leveling" that are familiar to all psychologists as phenomena of recall
and rumor and that are unavoidable in that form of information transfer
that we call history. In the case of Wundt, the resulting distortions have
passed acceptable limits. Until we put his career in proper perspective,
our view of the process by which psychology became an experimental
science will be seriously defective.

This chapter has a limited scope. It deals with the first half of Wundt's
life, including the period that Titchener (1921b) aptly called "seventeen
years of depression" (p. 171n)—years during which he worked as a physiologist with only modest success, before the appearance of the *Physiological Psychology* suddenly made him the most prominent figure in an
emerging science. This chapter is motivated by a conviction that it is not
possible to understand the part that Wundt played in the development of
psychology as an independent science without a serious study of his early

career. If Wundt was half so great a force in the history of modern psychology as he is commonly thought to have been, a full-length portrait of him is long overdue. This chapter is a beginning.

Why this task remains to be done sixty years after his death is itself something of an enigma. Before he died in 1920 at the age of 88, Wundt had been honored worldwide for more than four decades as the world's leading psychologist. At that time, it would have seemed safe to assume that his life and work would before long engage more than one enthusiastic biographer. In fact, the closest approach to a full account is that by Petersen (1925), which is explicitly directed primarily to elucidating Wundt's position as a philosopher rather than as a psychologist. One searches the literature in vain for any comprehensive treatment that is written with historical perspective. The imposing presence that overawed his students seems still to inhibit the work of even his most recent chroniclers. Furthermore, some recent articles (Eschler, 1962; Kossakowski, 1966) make such arbitrary selections of facts and quotations as to introduce new distortions.

This situation is in striking contrast to the intensive treatment that has been given to the life of William James (e. g., H. James, 1920; MacLeod, 1969; Perry, 1935), who in much the same period passed through the same progression from physiologist to psychologist to philosopher, and whose name was often linked with that of Wundt during their lifetimes. For example, in 1896, at a time when enthusiasm for the "new psychology" was running high on both sides of the Atlantic, a leading German newspaper reporting on the Third International Congress of Psychology at Munich commented that "the psychological pope of the Old World, Wundt, and the psychological pope of the New World, James, were both distinguished by their absence" (Perry, 1935, Vol. 2, p. 145). There was more than a little truth in this hint of schism in the new faith, but the relative importance of the two leaders in the eyes of their knowledgeable contemporaries was probably correctly reflected in the fact that Villa's Contemporary Psychology (1903) cited Wundt on 95 pages and James on 37.

The scope of this chapter is indicated by its title. Wundt went to Leipzig in 1876, at the age of 44. He was to die at 88. Our intent is to establish a foundation that will permit a meaningful discussion of his work during the second half of his life, but that task is left to future papers, not necessarily by this writer. Readers who are unhappy with some of the interpretations offered will, it is hoped, be stimulated to seek others consistent with the facts, and not simply to asseverate the myth.

A Question of Lifestyle

It is often said of Wundt that he led the quiet, withdrawn life of a scholar and a scientist, in which intellectual pursuits were always dominant. If this were true, it would be oddly out of keeping with his own insistence that his psychology is fundamentally "voluntaristic" rather than intellectual in its orientation and emphasis. He said of himself that his strongest motivations were political and that this was especially true at the high points of his life (1920, p. iv). This statement led Titchener (1920) to comment that "whatever else Wundt learned in the course of his long life he had not learned fully to know himself" (p. 75). It is nevertheless unwise to dismiss Wundt's self-characterization lightly, although we need not limit our conception of political motivation to his definition of it as "concern for the welfare of state and society." We should keep in mind also Spranger's concept of the "political style of life" (usually translated as *political type*) as applicable not only to those involved in "politics" in the narrow sense but also to those who seek to dominate some special field, even if this is done with the intention of benefiting others. Specifically, said Spranger (1925/1928), the term applies to "whoever strives to dominate through knowledge" and by assuming the role of authority (p. 233). That sentence could have been written with Wundt in mind! Both varieties of political interest coexisted in Wundt's complex personality.

Wundt's autobiography is invaluable for our purpose, and on every rereading of it one discovers fresh, illuminating sidelights. However, it is not always accurate in detail, and it shows from time to time the sort of defensiveness that must be expected in even the best-intentioned work of that genre. Specific reference to it will not be made in reporting facts about which there can be no question. Similarly, we shall not clutter the text with references to the many standard biographic sources that have been useful. They are listed separately at the end of the chapter, with an indication of the articles used in each. Throughout, we shall use the unqualified name Wundt only to refer to Wilhelm Wundt, always designating others who bear the same surname by their relationship to him.

Early Childhood and Family

Wundt was born August 16, 1832, at Neckarau, a suburb of Mannheim, which was already an important commercial center, situated as it was at the upper limit of the then navigable Rhine. Neckarau is scarcely two kilometers from the heart of Mannheim and from its great ducal palace, the largest in Germany, with a facade that stretches 600 meters along gardens sloping to the Rhine. Within Wundt's infancy, construction had begun on the harbor facilities that made Mannheim the second greatest inland port of all Europe. In short, Wundt was not born in the rural environment we associate with the term *country pastor*. However, he was only about four years old when his parents moved to Heidelsheim, which he described as "a small town or rather a large village." It was situated about one league (a brisk hour's walk) from the sizable provincial town of Bruchsal, where he later experienced the most traumatic year of his life, his first year of formal schooling away from home. The transfer from Neckarau to Heidelsheim is just the first of a number of facts that show that Wundt's father, despite some fine qualities, was a rather ineffectual person, a circumstance that was not without effect on his son. It was in Heidelsheim that Wundt spent most of his childhood, virtually without peer companionship, though fortunate in attracting the kindly interest of sympathetic adults who also helped to shape his character and interests. (Heidelsheim is not in the vicinity of Heidelberg, where Wundt either studied, taught, or summered for long periods of his life. The similarity in names means only that the common blueberry was plentiful in both regions.)

In Heidelsheim, on the afternoon of the final day of his first year's schooling, he watched from his doorstep as a crowd of peasants erected a "freedom tree" in the public square. Then he saw the burgomaster's house set ablaze by the demonstrators and later—while the local bailiff paced up and down inside the Wundt cottage—he saw them dispersed by a squadron of dragoons. To this childhood experience Wundt immediately added pictures of scenes witnessed in the greater revolution, to which this incident was a minor prelude. Early in 1849, the Republic of Baden was established, and in June of that year, Wundt, not yet 17, from a high vantage point near Heidelberg, watched the distant flashes of cannon that signaled the suppression of that republic by a Prussian army. After the reaction of the 1850s came the liberalism of the 1860s, during which Wundt was active in the Workers' Educational League and served for a time as a member of the Baden diet.

These, except for two early memories that relate to his father, are the events with which Wilhelm Wundt chose to open his autobiography because they were "more vivid in [his] memory than many others." It would be unwise, therefore, as we have said, to dismiss all these experiences as not pertinent to an understanding of his career. If Spranger's definition of the political lifestyle is valid, the priority that Wundt gave to these events (some of which are described in greater detail later) should alert us to the likelihood that coming to terms with power, whether in exercising it or in resisting it, was to be a critical issue in much of his future conduct. Perhaps this was even the root of his later insistence that "will" is the most primitive, most fundamental psychic process.

Wundt (1920, p. 58) tells us that his father, Maximillian (1787–1846), had not become a minister by his free choice but because his older brother had been "untrue" to the study of theology, thus leaving to Maximillian the onus of carrying on the family's long-standing pastoral tradition. Those who worked in that tradition were often simultaneously active in academic life. However, Heidelberg's theological faculty was primarily Catholic in its orientation, and severe limits were placed on advancement for Protestant theologians. From standard biographical sources (including an article by Wundt's daughter [E. Wundt, 1928]), we learn that his paternal grandfather had been a professor, apparently of Baden's history and geography, at the University of Heidelberg, while acting also as pastor of a church at Wieblingen, a small town in the vicinity. The great-grandfather and two great-uncles had also been on the university faculty, one as a greatly honored professor of rhetoric who received attractive offers from other institutions. A son of the latter was for a time on the medical faculty (Stübler, 1926). All these persons were deceased before Wundt's birth, but they left numerous issues, including a cousin named Justus (Bringmann, oral communication, September 2, 1979), who was the "university architect Wundt" who directed the construction of a maternity ward in 1828 and of the university hospital in 1843 (Stübler, 1926).

Wundt mentioned no paternal relative other than the grandfather he never knew and the unnamed uncle who had been "untrue" to theology; his daughter ignored the latter. It would seem, therefore, that the "country pastor" had virtually lost contact with the better-placed members of his family, perhaps because Wundt's father clearly was not an achiever—a fact reflected, as we have already noted, in his transfer from Neckarau to more rural Heidelsheim.

Wundt described him as a jovial and generous person, but generous to a fault: he too readily yielded to parishioners who pleaded hardship in meeting their obligations for support of the church, and hence of the pastor's family, and he displayed embarrassment when his wife tried to stretch their inadequate income by energetic bargaining with

tradespeople—a normal practice of the times. In the end, relatives (doubtless on the maternal side) brought about an understanding that Wundt's
mother would take charge of the family finances, something that could
hardly have taken place unless they had been called on to give some financial assistance. Wundt described his father also as a loving parent who
called him by endearing names and from whom he might expect consol-
ing caresses whenever his mother, who took the more active part in his
early education, administered some painful reproof.

Wundt opened his autobiography with two "earliest memories," both
of which concern his father. The first was of a traumatic tumble down a
flight of cellar stairs, and its recall was always accompanied by a vague
feeling that this had happened while he was attempting to follow his
father into the cellar. In the other, Wundt was roused from a classroom
reverie by a blow on the ear and looked up to see his father glowering
over him. The office of school inspector was an appurtenance to the
position of pastor, and on this day, his father had stepped out of his usual
role of passive observer to become a not-altogether-loving parent. How
shall we interpret these memories? Wundt only said that they show how
the persistence of even very early memories depends on contextual reinforcement. If we look for some more dynamic process as being responsible for their selection from the fullness of a child's experience, we are
struck by the ambivalence that turns a loving father, in each instance, into
a source of pain. Clinically, we know that a boy's identification with such
a father can lead to distrust of himself.

Wundt's relatives on the maternal side played a much greater part in
his life than the Wundts. His mother's grandfather had owned property
and managed church lands in the Palatinate, but after his death and the
unsettling Napoleonic wars her father, Zacharias Arnold (1767–1840), sold
his property and moved to Heidelberg, on the more safely German side
of the Rhine. During Wundt's boyhood, Grandfather Arnold divided his
time between his piano and a roomful of plants in a home that was run
by his youngest, unmarried daughter. While he lived, Wundt and his
parents visited there for a few weeks each summer, providing the young
boy with a masculine model very different from his own father. Wundt
described him as "a man of the greatest precision," who frowned upon
the slightest deviation from the established household order and always
treated his grown sons and daughters as children. He took an active interest in Wundt's education, and during those summer visits, grandfather
and grandson had daily walks together—except when his uncle's daugh-

ters, older than himself, also visited, on which occasions Wundt would be turned over to the care of a servant girl, which cannot have been an ego-building experience. One summer, they went each day to observe the construction of Heidelberg's first railway station, and together they witnessed the departure of the first train to leave that station for Mannheim, with an Englishman in the engineer's cab giving instruction to a German understudy. These vacations were not all amusement. Discipline in the Arnold household was strict, and Wundt recalled especially his terror at being confined in a dark closet as punishment for some infraction—a punishment that "even [!] aroused [his] mother's deepest sympathy" (1920, p. 37).

Wundt's mother, Maria Friederike née Arnold (1797–1868), had acquired a knowledge of French from her childhood governess—an unusual accomplishment in the wife of a country pastor in Baden. She had apparently also acquired some of her father's traits of character. She had two sisters, the unmarried one who ran their father's home and another in whose home Wundt was to live during part of his intermediate schooling. She also had two brothers, both of whom studied medicine at Heidelberg and who started their professional careers teaching there. Johann Wilhelm (1801–1873), after becoming assistant professor of physiology at Zurich, returned to private practice in Heidelberg, where he continued research in physiology, often writing in collaboration with his brother. Wundt spoke of him as having the "nominal title" of professor, without mentioning that he had an active, though short, university career. Philipp Friedrich (1803–1890) became assistant professor at Heidelberg, then went on to full professorships of anatomy and physiology (which were commonly joined in one chair in that period) at Zurich, Freiburg, and Tübingen before returning to end his career with twenty years of service as director of the Anatomical Institute at Heidelberg. He received very special honors at the time of his retirement in 1873 (Hinz, 1961). Each of these persons had some part to play in Wundt's life. Uncle Friedrich's part was especially important and apparently decisive at a critical period. He was also instrumental in bringing Helmholtz to Heidelberg in 1858, a circumstance that cannot have been without influence on Wundt's success in winning the post of assistant to Helmholtz at that time. After the death of Wundt's father, when Wundt was 14, it was the Arnold family that passed on the plans for his education, in addition to providing the role models that obviously helped to determine its direction.

Wundt grew up in effect as an "only child." One sibling died before his birth, another he did not remember, and Wundt was only two years old when the only other survivor, Ludwig (1824–1902), eight years older than himself, was sent to live with their aunt in Heidelberg to attend the gymnasium there. The fact that her husband was an official in the tax service (Fürbringer, 1903) may have played a part in directing Ludwig's university studies and career toward the field of law.

Boyhood and Early Youth

Wundt attended the village school at Heidelsheim for the first two grades. The curriculum of that school would not have prepared him to continue toward a professional career, especially since it lacked the all-important ingredient, Latin. However, when Wundt was eight years old, his father acquired an assistant pastor, and Wundt thereby acquired a tutor, although one who proved to be more sympathetic than efficient. Soon young Friedrich Müller became "closer to [him] than mother or father." During that period, Wundt's only chum was a somewhat older mentally retarded youngster with very defective speech, who waited for him each day outside the Wundt cottage door. An occasional game with other village boys was more a tribulation than a pleasurable experience, and this was true even of the annual Easter egg hunt and the egg-tapping contest that followed it, which he "was not spared." He usually left empty-handed, having lost all his eggs to other boys, who were often less scrupulous about observing the rules.

Wundt sought by preference the less threatening companionship of adults. He was an almost daily visitor at the home of the two spinster daughters and the crippled son of the former pastor. The brother, a book-binder, had a great fund of tales about fictitious adventures that he told with dramatic embellishments in which his sisters participated, even to the point of dressing in costume for their parts. Might this have stimulated Wundt's later active interest in the theater, which led him at one time to write theatrical reviews? He also visited often at the home of a Jewish family with whom his mother had occasional dealings, where the grandmother kept various wares for sale and the husband ordinarily tramped the roads as a peddler, bent under his sack. Sometimes he invited Wundt to the synagogue, or to the Feast of Tabernacles, the harvest festival that is traditionally celebrated in the home under a bower of greenery. Late in life, Wundt "still felt the uplifting impression" he had received when he witnessed the dignified manner in which this peddler then recited the ritual prayers. We must set this memory (on p. 32) alongside another "shadowy recollection" (on p. 199) to appreciate the full impact of this experience on the impressionable boy. His earliest literary project, before he had learned the cursive script, was to write a history that would show what is common to all religions. Thus, the roots of his interest in ethnic psychology apparently ran back to this early warm relationship with members of an alien culture.

Meanwhile, his father's library helped to mature Wundt's early passion for reading, which progressed in time from romantic novels to historical novels to history, and which gave rise to literary aspirations that were destined to go unfulfilled. The precocity of Wundt's literary tastes showed in the fact that when he was about ten, he made his first acquaintance with Shakespeare in translation, which initiated a lifelong enthusiasm.

But possibly the most important consequence of Wundt's lack of peer companionship in his childhood, and one that left its imprint to some extent on all his future life, was his inordinate surreptitious indulgence in daydreams while staring into his open book, pen in hand, without reading a line. Sometimes he "waited longingly" for his tutor to leave to tend to his other duties so that he might then "abandon [himself] to all sorts of imaginary experiences," often taking up on one day where he had left off the day before. (Boring, 1950, took some latitude with this passage, describing Wundt as "longing always for the vicar's return from his parish duties." But though Wundt loved his tutor, he loved his fantasies more. Schlotte, 1956, took even greater liberty, writing that "The boy used a great part of this time to pursue his own thoughts. This habit of directing his attention to his own inner life certainly prepared the ground for the later return of his psychological interests." There is a great difference between introspective analysis and fantasy.) This daydreaming "gradually became a passion" that brought in its wake "an ever increasing inattention to everything going on about [him]," one result of which was that even in his university days, he was a very inattentive auditor, and many lectures that greatly impressed his fellow students "passed over [him] without leaving a trace." Wundt speculated on the influence that such exercise in fantasy, and the general habit of working alone, might have had on his future work habits. Although the thought could not have occurred to him, it seems not unreasonable to regard this facility in daydreams as an incipient stage of what Titchener (1921a) gently described as Wundt's "imperative need to systematize the unripe" (p. 590) or, bluntly stated, his disposition to advance unsubstantiated hypotheses of a scope and grandeur that makes them at times hardly more substantial than daydreams, and tending to serve the same purpose of self-aggrandizement. We suggest, further, that the habitual inattentiveness to which Wundt confessed was not unrelated to his lifelong disposition to disregard hypotheses put forward by others. Within the scope of this chapter, we shall see several instances of how he imposed much harsher criteria on the hypotheses of others than on his own.

Four years after Herr Müller assumed the direction of his education, Wundt entered the Bruchsal gymnasium (high school). A year before that, however, the young vicar obtained his own church at a village not very distant from Heidelsheim. The resulting separation produced in the pupil such "unutterable" desolation that Wundt's parents accepted the tutor's suggestion that the boy be allowed to live with him at Münzesheim for the year remaining before he would be sent off to school. When the time finally came, his parents arranged for Wundt to live with a Protestant family in Bruchsal, which, because it had once been a bishop's residence, was still a predominantly Catholic town. This precaution, and Wundt's gradual weaning from his family, were of no avail. It soon appeared that he was both inadequately prepared for the work expected of him and unable to adjust emotionally to the new situation. He was a timid, frightened youngster who would have found it difficult under the most favorable circumstances to enter into the sort of peer relationships that might have given him emotional support to endure the mistreatments routinely meted out to unsuccessful pupils, which were made all the more damaging by his own feelings that he deserved no better. At one time, he ran home, only to be returned to the school by his determined mother. The year was a total loss academically; and his future—any future beyond, perhaps, one in the postal service, which a "kind" teacher recommended to him as the proper level for his aspiration—was placed in doubt.

Wundt's family—which is to say, the Arnolds—saw to it that he was given another chance. At 13, he joined Ludwig in their aunt's home, to attend the Heidelberg gymnasium and do his studying in the same room with his industrious brother, with no daydreaming nonsense allowed.

Wundt was then of an age when it is not uncommon for adolescent boys to experience a happy change of self-concept when placed in a favorable environment. He formed friendships, entered into the extracurricular activities expected of his age group, and felt himself "as if reborn." Being a year older than most of his classmates, as a result of the Bruchsal fiasco, may have helped him to overcome his feelings of physical inferiority. However, this still does not explain why he acquired close friendships with classmates whose academic performance was as outstanding as his was, and continued to be, mediocre. What was it about Wundt that made this possible?

At this point, we do well to recall Wundt's emphasis on his political interests and his vivid recollections of the Baden revolution. It was in the fall of 1845 that Wundt entered the Heidelberg gymnasium. Early in 1846, Polish peasants in Galicia, who always had the sympathy of Baden's liberals, were in revolt against Austria. (Wundt tells us that the more radical element in Heidelsheim called themselves "Poles" as a residue of their earlier sympathies with Polish peasants in revolt against Russian landlords.) The Galician revolt was suppressed with atrocities that shocked all Europe. By 1847, demands were being voiced throughout Baden to turn the army into a national militia pledged to support the constitution, and to institute various economic reforms. In March 1848, these demands were backed by the Diet, and soon after, the government proclaimed amnesty and promised reforms. In that same month, armed revolution broke out in Vienna. Wundt kept a diary of the revolutionary developments, recording "with immense agitation" such events as the Vienna uprising and the martyrdom of Robert Blum, leader of the Left wing in the Frankfort provisional parliament. Later, there was insurrection in Baden, and a republic was established, but in June 1849, Prussian troops commanded by the future emperor Wilhelm I crushed its army, which was commanded by a Polish general. Wundt, surely standing side by side with his comrades, watched the distant flashes of cannon from a mountaintop near Heidelberg.

"There are today few persons still living," Wundt wrote on almost the first page of his autobiography, "who remember the time when Baden was an independent republic for half a year. Still fewer is the number of those who experienced the preceding decade, at least in part, with clear awareness. I am among those few." There are few circumstances so effective in overcoming introverted isolation as a popular revolutionary movement, which draws people together by common bonds of interest, gives them common heroes, and provides an external focus of attention and never-failing topics of daily discussion. A lively interest in the political events of that period, to which Wundt himself attested, would have fostered the bonding of friendships with classmates who shared that interest. This must have been an important factor in the change that Wundt experienced during this period, which was indeed one of the "high points" of his life, a period in which he felt "as if reborn." (Bringmann, 1975, quite correctly emphasized the importance of the personality changes that Wundt experienced between 1845 and 1874, but he did not, in this writer's judgment, correctly characterize them or adequately explain them.)

Choice of a Career

At nineteen, after six years of normal but unspectacular progress through the gymnasium, Wundt faced the need to select a professional objective. Many generations of Wundts had studied at the University of Heidelberg, and quite a few of that number, including his own grandfather, had served on its faculty. Many, again like his father and his grandfather, had been Protestant churchmen, yet not always by free personal choice. Nor was that choice one to Wundt's liking. He would have preferred a literary career, but he saw that as ruled out by the uncertainties attached to it, especially in view of the fact that his mother, living on the meager pension of a pastor's widow, could give him no financial assistance. (Only at this point in his autobiography do we learn from Wundt that his father had died five years earlier, during his first year at the gymnasium.) The need for assistance meant that whatever choice he made must be acceptable to a family council in which the Arnolds would be dominant. He was disinclined to teaching as a profession because the very school environment was abhorrent to him. Indeed, his overriding motivation was to get away from Heidelberg, from home and city, to become at last an independent person. The reference here to escape from his "parental home" reminds us that Wundt's mother would almost certainly have come to Heidelberg immediately after her husband's death, and that since that time, Wundt had probably been living with her rather than with his aunt, just as he would be doing later as a student and still later as a young faculty member at the university. At this time, he found the arrangement irksome. We must also assume that his desire to get away from Heidelberg was motivated in part by the dread of the inevitable comparisons at a university where many members of his family had held posts of distinction. It is a common syndrome in our own time on much less cause, and it must have played a part in Wundt's motivation, even if unverbalized.

Wundt did escape from Heidelberg, if only for a year, by taking advantage of two more-or-less accidental circumstances. His scholastic record was so mediocre that, despite the special consideration he could expect as the descendant of a long line of pastors, he did not qualify for state aid to attend the university. If this failure disappointed his widowed mother, it seemed a stroke of good luck to him. The loss of a possible state stipend was a misfortune in which he secretly rejoiced, since receiving it would have given him no choice but to attend the University of Heidelberg. However, he still needed a plausible pretext for attending a "foreign" university, in view of the added expense that it would entail. He found this excuse in the fact that one of his uncles, Friedrich Arnold, was then professor of anatomy and physiology at Tübingen, and Wundt reasoned that if he chose medicine as a career, it would seem quite natural that he should pursue his studies there, even though Heidelberg's status in the natural sciences was higher. He therefore announced that to be his intention, and the family council gave its consent on condition that he complete the course within four years, the minimum time required. We may be sure that Wundt's mother asked her younger brother, Friedrich, to keep an eye on his nephew and to see that he did not neglect his studies.

Let us review what we have learned of Wundt's early years. His mother, largely as a result of her upbringing in the Arnold household, was much stricter with him than was his father, and she was probably also more determined to see that he made a mark in the world. He received affection from his father but little guidance. (Wundt's statement that, even if his father had been alive, he would not have interfered with his free choice, can be interpreted in more ways than one.) The lame bookbinder and the Jewish peddler were both father surrogates to some degree, but it was the young assistant vicar who filled this role most nearly, yet ineffectually. The relationships that Wundt established with these men must have been an expression of his own need, not theirs. We would expect, therefore, that as long as his role in life remained uncertain he would seek other father surrogates and suffer disappointments when they failed to live up to his hopes. We shall see that this disappointment clearly happened in his relations with Du Bois-Reymond, probably in his relations with Friedrich Arnold, and possibly in his relations with Helmholtz, although, of course, the manner in which he sought their approbation was quite different from the open hunger of a small boy for simple affection.

Like any child, Wundt also had a need for the satisfaction of mastery. This need was frustrated in his rare contacts with other village boys. It was fulfilled to some degree in his relationship with his mentally retarded playmate, who was so gratifyingly dependent on him, but it was fulfilled to a greater degree in fantasy. We are all entitled to privacy in our fantasies, and we cannot be surprised that Wundt told us nothing about the content of his. However, he did tell us that they were usually accompanied by rhythmic movements of his pen, up and down, and this statement suggests that in them he took active rather than passive roles. The daydreaming boy was father to the man who one day would write to his fiancée, "I am too ambitious to be vainglorious" (Schlotte, 1956, p. 337).

Student Years

If Wundt's mother hoped, when he went off to Tübingen, that he would return a changed person, she was not to be disappointed. Let us look first at that aspect of his experience there that might be called college life. During his final year at the gymnasium, Wundt and several close friends agreed to join a certain student corps (fraternity) when they became university students. He did in fact join the affiliated group at Tübingen, but he found its members less congenial than he had hoped, and he was therefore relieved when it disbanded early in the semester because it had attracted too few members. He then became attached to another corps on a trial basis, but he soon withdrew from that as well "to surrender [himself] to a solitary life" and to a single-minded pursuit of his studies in anatomy. This is the first evidence we have of serious application to any interest not literary. Meanwhile, there were dances, the best being the weekly faculty dance. This was open to fortunate students by faculty invitation, in which respect Uncle Friedrich must have been helpful. There was music and theater—the best in distant Stuttgart, which might be reached on a rare adventure. There were forbidden duels, more exciting than in Heidelberg because, in these narrow streets, the danger that the authorities might appear quite suddenly was heightened. In these, Wundt participated only as a spectator. All these things evidently played a larger part in Wundt's life during the first semester than during the second, when he was caught up in the spirit of his work.

We turn now to the scholastic life. Wundt mentioned attending lecture courses in botany, chemistry, and physics, in all of which the professors were hampered by inadequate, antiquated equipment. The first semester of a course in aesthetics turned out to be the only philosophy course of his entire student career. The professor, he wrote, held his attention only when he dealt with Karl Gutzkow's *Die Ritter vom Geiste*, the influential novel, published in 1850, that depicted "the detrimental characteristics of a police state and its demoralizing influence" and included among its characters "recognizable portraits" of persons who had been active in the Berlin revolution of 1848 (Kurz and Wedel, 1927, p. 698). The fact that Wundt did not continue with that course for the summer semester is less an evidence of disinterest than of his growing passion for cerebral anatomy, which he studied under the guidance of his uncle, Friedrich Arnold. During the entire summer semester, he worked "from early till late," acquiring a knowledge of this special field out of all proportion to his superficial learning of other subjects. This was perhaps the decisive turning point of his career, not because of the relevance of cerebral anatomy to his future interest in physiological psychology, but because for the first time in his life, he experienced the joy of mastery based on his own solid accomplishment. Suddenly, he had become the industrious, seemingly indefatigable Wundt who would be so astonishingly productive in future years. Uncle Arnold deserves most of the credit for bringing this change about. Perhaps in emulation of him, Wundt resolved during that semester that he would make physiology his life's work.

It was the period in which Germany displaced France as the world leader in physiology and changed its nature by the introduction of quantitative methods. Although Arnold was not equipped by his training to participate fully in that advance, he correctly assessed its importance when he explained in his lectures why the kymograph was destined to open new paths of physiological research. (Or perhaps it was really Vierordt speaking through Arnold, who, Wundt observed, "hardly knew how to handle the kymograph." That instrument had been introduced by Carl Ludwig in 1848 as an outcome of his efforts to produce tracings of the pulse, and it was quickly put to further use by Helmholtz in his development of the myograph and in measuring the speed of the nervous impulse. However, it was given its name by Vierordt, then an assistant professor of physiology at Tübingen.)

During the next three years, Wundt completed his medical course at Heidelberg, not Tübingen. A reader who relies solely on the autobiography would conclude that the change came about because Wundt's expenses had been running above his anticipated budget and because facilities in the natural sciences were inferior to those at Heidelberg. There is no mention of the compelling reason for the change: his uncle had accepted a chair at Heidelberg, where for the next twenty years he was director of its Anatomical Institute (Hinz, 1961). The pretext that Wundt had used to attend Tübingen thus no longer existed. However, he no longer needed it, because he had proved his competence to himself and had found a direction for his ambition. At any rate, it was at Heidelberg, if anywhere, that his uncle could now be of help, as he doubtless was from time to time. Among Arnold's students at Heidelberg we find the names—to select only a few well known to psychologists—of Sigmund Exner, David Ferrier, and Krafft-Ebing (Fübringer, 1903).

The first of Wundt's three years as a student at Heidelberg was still chiefly devoted to making up deficiencies in basic sciences because he had given no thought to a scientific career during his gymnasial studies. He took private instruction in mathematics, while pursuing lecture courses in physics and chemistry and a laboratory course in chemistry. His return to Heidelberg coincided with the arrival there of Robert Bunsen, of whom it has been said, in words much like those that have often been applied to Wundt, that his greatness as a teacher "is attested by the scores of pupils who flocked from every part of the globe to study under him, and by the number of those pupils who afterwards made their mark in the chemical world" (*Encyclopaedia Britannica*, 11th ed.). Wundt was very nearly seduced into deserting physiology for chemistry, but he went no farther along that path than to perform a physiological experiment touching on a problem of body chemistry. For several days, he limited his dietary salt intake as much as possible; as a result, he experienced metabolic disorders and an intensified hunger for salt that lasted for some time afterward. He had the immense satisfaction to achieve thereby his first publication (Wundt, 1853) and later to see his work cited in Ludwig's *Textbook of Human Physiology* (1858–1861).

The last two years of his medical study were devoted to the required courses in the various areas of medical practice. Because of his need to compress these courses into a shorter time than customary, he generally took the corresponding lecture and clinical courses simultaneously rather than in the usual successive pattern. Again, he seized an opportunity for experiment by entering a prize contest for experimental study of the effect of sectioning the vagus nerve on the respiratory organs.

At this time, Wundt tells us, he had just begun hearing lectures on pathology and had no training whatever in pathological anatomy. The problem assigned was to study the effect on respiration of sectioning the vagus nerve, and it assumed some practice in vivisection as well as a knowledge of pathological anatomy. Relying for guidance on a textbook, he performed the experimental work in his mother's kitchen, enlisting her as his surgical assistant. It was the custom, Wundt wrote (1920, p. 82ff.), to work on prize problems of the medical faculty

> in the clinic or the institute of the professor who set the problem. Therefore the winner was as a rule known in advance, and my paper, submitted anonymously according to the rules, aroused some measure of surprise to the faculty. It had been prepared in my own study, so that no one outside my home knew anything about it.

Wundt's results nevertheless matched those reached by his leading competitor "with the assistance of his professor," raising a question as to who should be declared the winner. The prize was divided between them. Wundt's paper was also accepted for publication by Johannes Müller (Wundt, 1855), and Müller's letter became a prized possession.

The preceding paragraph is based solely on Wundt's account. The episode takes on greater interest if we add a detail that he omitted: the professor who set the problem that year—and stood ready to give guidance to students working in his laboratory, with a selfless dedication that made him one of the university's best-loved teachers—was none other than Friedrich Arnold (Fürbringer, 1903). It is of course possible that Wundt's "surgical assistant" did not keep the secret from her brother, but that is unimportant. The fact that the paper was accepted for publication attests to its quality. What is important is the proudly individualistic manner in which Wundt carried out his difficult project while rejecting the opportunity to receive guidance. The necessary motivation must have come largely from a desire to gain his uncle's applause. We shall see similar behavior on Wundt's part with respect to two other mentors, Du Bois-Reymond and Helmholtz. In each instance, the relations between Wundt and these older men became strained.

In the summer of 1855, ten years after he had left Bruchsal in disgrace, Wundt passed the state examinations for admission to the practice of medicine. Separate examinations were given in internal medicine, surgery, and obstetrics, and when the names of the successful candidates were published, Wundt's name stood at the top of each list! He modestly explained this result by the fact that because the examinations were devised and graded by practicing physicians rather than by university professors, success depended less on a knowledge of the latest findings than on "a certain superficial skill in expression combined with some knowledge of the history of medicine" (1920, p. 93). He was not alone in regarding the examination practice at this time as superficial (Stübler, 1926). Be that as it may, success brought Wundt face to face once again with the need to make a decision regarding his future course of action.

Postgraduate Training

So far as the "family council" was concerned, once Wundt had passed his examinations they could see no problem: he had qualified for a respected profession, and, therefore, he should practice it and make a decent contribution to the support of his mother. However, although the examination results attested to the fact that he had mastered a great many bookish facts, Wundt felt unprepared for the responsibilities of medical practice. He would have taken a post as a military physician if it were available, on the theory that in times of peace, he could do little harm to healthy young soldiers, but on inquiry, he discovered that openings did not exist. He recoiled from the offer of a position at a health spa, feeling that the social services expected of him would be more onerous than his medical duties in treating the anemic daughters of government functionaries. He was rescued from his difficulty when an acquaintance, who had been working as assistant in a municipal hospital directed by one of the university professors, asked Wundt if he would spell him for six months while he prepared for his own examinations. So Wundt stepped into something like a medical internship early in this century: on call 24 hours a day, in full charge of the women's ward of a public hospital save for the daily visits of the hospital director. The patients included some peasant women, more servants from the town, and a sizable contingent of prostitutes, who were isolated in a separate section but nevertheless saw to it that the ward was never quiet. It was, as Wundt observed, a trying situation for a young doctor, but one from which he could gain a great deal of practical experience. Two special aspects of this hospital experience received repeated mention in Wundt's later writings. Let us call them the *iodine affair* and the *localization problem*.

The Iodine Affair

Wundt's fullest account of this incident appears in his slender book on *Hypnotism and Suggestion* (1892a), which was reprinted in the *Philosophische Studien* the following year and later in his *Kleine Schriften* (Vol. 2) and was also translated into French, Italian, Russian, Bulgarian, and Spanish! In it, Wundt attacked the then-popular notion that post-hypnotic suggestions could provide even more valuable experimental data than the conventional psychological laboratory. In the course of his argument that the suggestibility of the subject invalidates the results obtained under such circumstances, he told at length of an occasion on which he was awakened from a deep sleep by a hospital attendant and summoned to help a patient in great pain. He went about administering a narcotic but instead took the bottle of tincture of iodine, which had much the same appearance but was clearly labeled, and poured a spoonful into the patient's mouth, all the while aware in his somnolent state that it was iodine and yet thinking of it as a narcotic. Fortunately, the patient was more awake than the doctor and instantly spat it out, yet even this action did not fully awaken him, and it was only after returning to his room that he grasped what had happened. Although no harm was done to the patient, the incident revived Wundt's apprehension about entering the practice of medicine. For weeks, as he stated in the autobiography, he was troubled "by doubts whether someone who could commit such an error was competent to practice the medical profession" (1920, p. 99ff.). Wundt's account of this incident leaves little question that his hesitation about entering practice was not based solely on reservations about the training he had received; it was also based, at least in part, on a still-persisting sense of personal inferiority.

The Localization Problem

There were at the hospital, during the period of Wundt's service, some patients who suffered sensory paralysis as a result of leg injuries and the like. In checking on the course of recovery, Wundt made fairly systematic observations on the impairment of localization of touch sensations, and he came to the conclusion that the results could not be harmonized with Weber's theory (E. H. Weber, 1846) that localization is based on a mosaic organization of the sensory innervation of the skin. Indeed, he concluded that the results could not be harmonized with *any* purely physiological hypothesis and that they required a psychological explanation. Thus, said Wundt, it was by experiment that he was led for the first time into thinking about a psychological problem. Why he thought a purely physiological explanation must be inadequate and how he attempted to construct a psychological explanation are matters to be discussed when we deal with his *Contributions to the Theory of Sensory Perception* (1862a).

Wundt's experience in the hospital ward did nothing to reduce either his aversion to the private practice of medicine or his desire to become a research physiologist. On the other hand, the Arnolds were evidently unwilling to subsidize his education further. However, by pooling his own meager resources, including his nest egg of prize money and a small sum that his mother could provide, he had enough to support himself through one semester of residence at some "foreign" university. He gave some thought to going to Zurich, where Carl Ludwig, the inventor of the kymograph, had been professor of anatomy and physiology since 1849, but if he had done so, he would have been disappointed to discover that Ludwig had left Zurich in 1855 to become professor at the Josephinum, a school for military surgeons in Vienna! (This trifling detail is one of several that show that Wundt did his planning, like his work, as an isolate. If he had spoken to his uncle about his plans, he would at least have learned that Ludwig had left Zurich for Vienna. Perhaps he would even have received some financial help. But Wundt, as we shall see again and again, coupled a fierce pride with his sense of inferiority.) Wundt decided in favor of Berlin, where he could maximize the yield of his one short semester by studying under both Johannes Müller, whose letter of encouragement he treasured, and Emil Du Bois-Reymond.

Both men were famous. Müller's *Handbook of Human Physiology* (1833–1840) was, and still is, regarded as the work that marked the transition to physiology as a science, while Du Bois-Reymond's *Researches on Animal Electricity* (1848) had made him the foremost worker in the field of electrophysiology. Only two years later, Müller would be dead at 56, and Du Bois would succeed to his chair. Wundt, perhaps unwisely, undertook to work simultaneously in the laboratories of both men. As it turned out, this meant that he worked along with four others in Müller's laboratory in the mornings, and by himself in the upstairs corridor set aside for Du Bois-Reymond's students in the afternoon.

Müller questioned him about his interests and then proposed that he work on extirpating nerve centers in invertebrates—a project that we may think of as a sort of miniaturization of his student prize work on the effects of interfering with respiratory innervation in mammals. In this case, Wundt wrote, he obtained no results sufficiently noteworthy to warrant publication.

Du Bois set him to measuring the elasticity of muscles, and specifically to checking on the validity of a finding by E. Weber (1846) that the extension of a resting muscle did not vary directly with the load placed upon it, but that successive equal increments of load produce smaller and smaller extensions. Wundt spent the semester wrestling with problems of method and only finished the project several months after his return to Heidelberg. In a paper (Wundt, 1857) submitted in November 1856, he concluded, on the basis of experiments conducted with nerves, tendons, and arteries as well as muscles, (1) that if time is allowed for the tissue to reach its maximum extension, this is proportional to the load, and (2) that within certain (unspecified) limits, this is true for the immediate extension as well. However, the illustrative data provided suggest that Weber's statement was correct for muscle, and later literature has sustained it. One is left wondering why Wundt blurred the issue by stating general conclusions about all "moist, organic tissues" when the matter of concern was the role of elasticity in muscular contraction.

Before the end of the year, Wundt was habilitated as docent at the university. Though he still had not escaped Heidelberg, he had at least escaped the need to practice medicine, and he could go forward with the plan he had stated in a letter written from Berlin to his mother (who apparently still hoped that her son would be a practicing doctor) that "he would teach so that he could remain a physiologist" (Schlotte, 1956, p. 334).

Some Fresh Frustrations

With characteristic lack of caution, Wundt undertook to teach a general survey of experimental physiology in his first semester as a docent, that is, starting in April 1857. It attracted four students. The course was soon interrupted by severe illness that showed itself in a sudden violent hemorrhage. Wundt perceived that his doctors had no hope for his recovery, and this confrontation with death produced in him (as he told it), a "perfect tranquillity" that brought about "a complete reversal of [his] outlook on life" (1920, p. 116ff.). Objectively, we recognize the tranquillity as an effect of the nature of his illness, although this explanation does not elucidate what further effects it may have had on his thinking. Indeed, his new outlook, tinged with religiosity, became explicit only in later retrospect, and by degrees, as a sense that there was an intimate relatedness between his subjective and objective experiences, between the external world and his awareness of it (whence his autobiography derived its title, *Erlebtes und Erkanntes*), and that the true meaning of immortality lay in the uniqueness of personal existence. This new outlook also included, as it ripened, a conviction that scientific knowledge and philosophic knowledge are inseparable. Whether or not these attitudes were ultimately traceable to this traumatic experience, as Wundt implied, they were characteristic of much of Wundt's later work, and the reader must therefore be prepared to accept the fact that Wundt's empiricism, except in his earliest period, had mystical as well as experimental aspects.

Meanwhile, we must not think that this "perfect tranquillity" immediately took hold of his life. Schlotte (1956) found among Wundt's papers the following poem, which can hardly have been written at any other time:

> The world has much of evil in it,
> Much that I don't like a bit,
> Yet of misfortunes only one,
> Nothing but this single one,
> That strikes alike at young and old,
> Against which no defense can hold:
> To lose the best before 'twas won,
> To die before life has begun!

(My rendering is "free" only in the sixth line, where a literal translation would be "against which no power gives protection.") It is hard not to read these lines as a proof that Wundt at 25 was not as philosophically acceptant of death as at 88. Another short poem that Schlotte placed in the same period is no less pessimistic, stating that earth's smallest hamlet has room enough for pain but that the universe has not space enough to hold one untrammeled pleasure. It had to be ambition, not tranquillity, that lifted Wundt from this depression and gave him the resilience soon to produce his first book and to launch a program that would culminate in the second.

By Wundt's account, a full year passed in illness and convalescence before he was able to resume his work. This account cannot be accurate, since the preface to his book (Wundt, 1858b) is dated October 1857, not more than fourteen months at the outside after his return from Berlin, eleven months after submitting his previous publication, and probably not more than six months after the first traumatic episode of his illness. The book's title may be translated as "The Present State of Knowledge Concerning Muscular Action." The subtitle promised a treatment based on the author's own experiments. It was a bold step for a young scientist who was, after all, still a novice in a field in which many distinguished workers were engaged. A reviewer (*Literarisches Centralblatt*, 1858) chided the author for presenting a series of disconnected experiments on the mechanical characteristics of muscular tissue along with some unrelated discussions under a title that promised much more. Nevertheless, the reviewer conceded that the author showed skill and promise, and that if the yield from his experiments was not proportional to the energy expended on them, it might be because it takes luck as well as talent and industry to arrive at noteworthy results.

Needless to say, this assessment of the book's worth fell far below the expectations of its luckless author. More than sixty years later, thirteen pages of Wundt's autobiography expounded the book's merits and excused its failure. He took pride in the fact that his measures of elasticity (on the gastrocnemius of frog) were performed on living animals without disturbing the principal nerves and blood vessels. Although he saw this as an innovation important enough in itself to have attracted attention, a passage in the book shows that he was aware that Schwann had earlier measured the strength of this muscle in living and intact animals, in a procedure that measured the load that the already contracted muscle could bear without further extension, while being stimulated to further contraction. (Schwann's method and results were stated in detail by Müller, 1833–1840, Vol. 2, p. 59ff.) Wundt attributed the lack of response to the book to a conspiracy of silence for which he held Du Bois responsible. After waiting in vain for something more than the original polite note of acknowledgment from his mentor, to whom the book was dedicated, Wundt concluded that Du Bois had probably never read past the introduction, which might have offended him by pointing to the need for something more than atomistic mechanism in dealing with the problems of living organisms. That the bitterness lingered is clear from Wundt's statement that despite this incident, he had friendly relations with many members of the Du Bois school in later years. We shall see later that this was not a general rule.

It is indeed possible to look upon the introduction as possibly the first fruit of Wundt's new outlook on life. It has short opening and closing passages that give a concise statement of the problem he had undertaken and the method he would follow, wholly within the spirit of the new "exact" physiology. Between those passages, set off by horizontal lines, lies an irrelevant discussion of the larger methodological problems of the life sciences generally, the tenor of which may be judged from this passage, to which Du Bois would indeed have taken exception:

> All conceivable atomic movements are, so far as experience shows, reducible to the fundamental laws of mechanics; but such formative forces as have been postulated for organic science would no longer be judged according to mechanical principles. They would be subject to laws the precise formulation of which is still to be discovered. It can by no means be asserted in advance that this is not possible, and therefore this view is not totally unjustified. (1858b, p. 10)

Wundt said that he learned two important lessons from this experience: first, always to give maximum freedom to his students, and second, never to permit himself to become head of a school. These rules, he said, he ever afterward observed! Here we can only repeat what Titchener (1921a) said in a different context: "Whatever else Wundt learned in the course of his long life he had not learned to know himself" (p. 575). It seems clear that Wundt had entertained exaggerated hopes for recognition—both by Du Bois-Reymond personally and by the scientific community generally—of what was in fact a mediocre if not a trivial contribution. In addition, he had allowed his ambition to carry him into generalizations that were not justified by the context and that quite predictably irritated Du Bois. No "conspiracy of silence" was needed to explain the cool reception to his book at a time when memorable advances were being made by the application of "atomistic" methods to the problems of neuromuscular physiology.

Controversy with Hermann Munk

Wundt did not at once forsake this field of work to pursue other interests. In the following year, he published an article (Wundt, 1859) in which he claimed to have discovered a hitherto unreported effect on peripheral nerve of repeated electrical stimulation. He described an increased irritability, which he labeled "secondary modification" to distinguish it from

a contrary effect that was known as *Ritter modification* and that Wundt proposed to call *primary modification*. At this time, Hermann Munk was studying the propagation of nerve currents, and he would not have wanted to
overlook such a phenomenon. To put the matter in perspective, we should
note that Munk was still far from the distinction we now associate with
his name; he was, in fact, seven years younger than Wundt, and in 1859,
he had just received his degree at Berlin at the age of twenty. He was to
spend his entire professional career there, being one of the "two ambitious young Jews" mentioned by William James, in a letter of 1867, as
giving lectures "almost as instructive" as those of Du Bois-Reymond
himself (James, 1920, Vol. 1, p. 121). (The other was Julius Rosenthal, who
graduated the same year and became assistant to Du Bois.)

Munk (1861) analyzed Wundt's claim and concluded that what
he had described was simply a change that takes place in a nerve just
after it is excised and that had already been reported by Pflüger, by
Heidenhain, and by Rosenthal. Wundt had failed to consider the possibility that what he had observed was a time-dependent phenomenon
rather than an effect of stimulation.

Munk's criticism was certainly valid. However, our chief interest is not
in whether Wundt was mistaken but in how he conducted himself in this,
his first professional controversy: he excused his inadequate data by saying
that a full report would be published in a forthcoming textbook of electrophysiology; he resorted to digressions and countercharges; and he
committed the sort of ambiguous shifts of meaning that were to exasperate
his opponents in other controversies throughout his career. Since most
readers will find it difficult to accept this statement without illustration, I
include here Wundt's original definition of secondary modification and the
one he used in a reply to Munk, without any hint of alteration:

> Secondary modification consists in the fact that, after a short application of
> electrical current, irritability for current of that direction is heightened; after
> somewhat longer application, this modification passes through an intermedi-
> ate stage into the commonly observed primary modification. (1859, p. 537)

> This aftereffect consists first in a reduction of irritability to current of the direc-
> tion used (primary, negative modification), but it then passes over into a
> heightened irritability for current of this direction (secondary, positive modi-
> fication). (1861a, p. 782)

How does one conduct a scientific discussion with such an opponent?
Wundt's final sally closed with this insulting paragraph:

Herewith I regard the controversy between Herr Munk and myself as over and done with. I leave unnoticed many details of his article which are irrelevant to the matter and amount to mere verbal fencing. Still less need I waste words over "the greatest possible exactitude and conscientious care" on which my opponent prides himself. Who would be so cruel as to disturb the sweet and innocent pleasure of self-adulation? How lovely it is to wrap oneself in the mantle of an exact researcher . . . and how much more imposing are grandly eloquent phrases than sound proofs, aside from the fact that they are also more convenient! (Wundt, 1862g, p. 507)

Munk, who had already declared the controversy over and done with on his part, was provoked not only to the "concession," as he called it, that if Wundt's "carelessness" led to any more verbal shifts, he was capable of explaining that a healthy man was ready for the madhouse, but also to a detailed critique of Wundt's procedure and a suggestion that Wundt would be well advised to omit "secondary modification" from his promised textbook. In fact, the textbook of electrophysiology never materialized.

Assistant to Helmholtz

By pursuing this revealing controversy to its end, we have broken the chronological thread of our account. Let us go back to 1858. In that eventful year, Wundt not only published his first book but also became assistant to Helmholtz and initiated his career as a psychologist with the first article (1858a) of a series that would lead to his second book (1862a). We shall take up first the history of the assistantship, which has been the subject of a different sort of controversy.

The reader will recall that in 1852, Friedrich Arnold became Heidelberg's professor of anatomy and physiology—two disciplines that, at that time, rarely had separate chairs. Spurred, no doubt, by an awareness that one man could no longer do justice to both disciplines, he persuaded the ministry to establish a separate chair of physiology. With Bunsen acting as intermediary, this chair was offered to Helmholtz (then at Bonn), who accepted after a year's delay, largely to free himself from the need to profess anatomy as well as physiology (Stübler, 1926). At thirty-seven, Helmholtz had already published his epoch-making paper on the conservation of energy, measured the speed of the nervous impulse, invented the ophthalmoscope, and published the first part of the *Physiological Optics*. It is worth noting that his approach to each research problem was essentially mathematical and that this continued to be true throughout his life. The post of assistant to such a distinguished and universally respected scientist should have been a golden opportunity, and yet for Wundt, it turned into a blind alley. Wundt wrote that Helmholtz was so reticent as to be almost unapproachable, and since neither of them had any clear idea at the outset of what the duties of an assistant should be, those duties developed haphazardly, with Helmholtz suggesting at first that Wundt instruct the medical students in microscope technique and later that he assume the direction of a state-mandated course to acquaint all medical candidates with experimental laboratory procedures. After five years (four by his own account), Wundt resigned the post in order to have more time for other things.

A letter that Helmholtz wrote to Wundt, dated May 8, 1858, gives a somewhat different picture. Helmholtz wrote that matters regarding the proposed new Physiological Institute were at last sufficiently defined so that he could offer Wundt the assistantship for which he had entered his application in February. The stipend would be only 300 gulden, because the duties were such as might be assumed by a recent graduate who would regard the experience itself, and access to the facilities of the institute, as constituting a part of his recompense. The appointment would be for only one or two years at a time, but Helmholtz pointed out that it would be to his advantage not to have frequent changes. The duties would include the supervision of student exercises in the physiological laboratory, including microscopic and chemical techniques, as well as demonstrating vivisections and other time-consuming experiments not suited for lecture-hall demonstration. The assistant would also have to be present each day for the several hours when the institute would be open, to give help as needed to those doing research there, although Helmholtz would himself pass through from time to time to discuss projects with individual researchers. It would also be appropriate that the assistant should lecture on microscopic anatomy. (Full text in Schlotte, 1955–56, p. 335ff.)

These stipulations were intended to help Wundt decide if he really wanted the poorly paid position. Stated five months before Helmholtz came to Heidelberg, they cannot be considered vague; and they did rather accurately describe Wundt's future duties. In particular, Wundt's course offerings did include "Microscopic Anatomy with Demonstrations" in the first two semesters of his assistantship, and "Study of Tissues, with Microscopic Demonstrations" in four of the last six semesters (E. Wundt, 1927, p. 67).

On the subject of Helmholtz's reticence and Wundt's activities in the institute as distinct from the student laboratory, at least in the early period of his assistantship, we have an unusually trustworthy witness. Ivan Sechenov worked under Helmholtz for two semesters, starting in the spring of 1859, that is, in Wundt's second semester as an assistant. He described the laboratory as small, with a separate room for Helmholtz but not for Wundt, who shared one room with himself, another Russian named Junge, and two Germans, one an ophthalmologist and another who was busy with the myograph. Of Wundt he wrote,

> Wundt sat the whole year unfailingly at some books in his own corner, not paying attention to anyone and not saying a word to anyone. I did not once hear his voice. (Sechenov, 1945/1952, p. 39)

Equally unfailingly, Helmholtz spoke briefly to each of the four experimenters every morning to inquire about their progress and their difficulties, before disappearing into his own room. (Neither Wundt nor Sechenov mentioned that Helmholtz's first wife died very shortly after he arrived in Heidelberg.)

What Helmholtz modestly omitted from his letter to Wundt was that the major recompense to be taken into account by anyone hiring on as assistant to a distinguished scientist was the opportunity not simply to use the facilities of the institute for research but to benefit from the guidance of its director. This opportunity was one of which Wundt seems never to have availed himself. He prosecuted his research with characteristic proud independence, in that style of "solitary" dedication to his tasks that he himself saw as one of the outcomes of his early habits of study, which had expressed itself at Tübingen in a "surrender to a solitary life" and at Heidelberg, quite dramatically, in the almost secretive manner in which he prepared his entry for the prize competition in his mother's kitchen. All of Wundt's experimental work at Heidelberg seems to have been carried out in his own home, following a pattern that had once been common, but was rapidly being eliminated by the establishment of scientific institutes at the leading universities. (However, Wundt [1862a, p. 202n] acknowledged that it was Helmholtz who suggested that he use projected afterimages to study eye movements and the horopter.) It may be said on Wundt's behalf that the projects in which he engaged came more and more to have a psychological dimension, so that it would not have been possible to carry them out in the same room in which some of the other workers were perhaps performing vivisections on frogs or rabbits. The question that remains is why under these circumstances he continued as assistant for five years. If the pay was poor and the hours long, and if the relationship with Helmholtz lacked any compensating recompense, why did he not resign earlier? Once the question is posed in this form, the answer that suggests itself is that Wundt hoped for some recompense that he never received. This hope need not have been explicit in awareness, but one recalls his need for a father surrogate in boyhood, as well as his disappointing relationship with Du Bois-Reymond, which came to its bitter ending just before Wundt started working for Helmholtz.

Wundt himself said that one reason for the lack of closeness between himself and Helmholtz lay in the fact that their research interests were so similar. We shall reexamine this question later, when we consider the controversy that Hall (1912) started as to whether Helmholtz dismissed Wundt because of his inadequate knowledge of mathematics. However, Wundt seems at times to have been deliberately challenging Helmholtz by choosing to work on problems that Helmholtz already had in hand and then thrusting his own unripe solutions forward as if to declare: "Look at me! Acknowledge me as your equal!" We will see instances of this as we look at Wundt's various publications during the five-year term of his assistantship. For however burdensome his duties may have been, they do not seem to have limited his productiveness.

The Beiträge

Wundt's second book (1862a) consisted of six articles on sense perception plus the famous programmatic introduction, which enunciated the need for an experimental psychology. The first article, written apparently during the period of convalescence from his illness, harked back to his hospital experience of several years earlier, which had convinced him that Weber's anatomical explanation of tactile localization was mistaken. Instead of dealing with this limited problem, Wundt, in characteristic fashion, set it in the much larger framework of perception generally. To this larger question, he propounded a solution combining three elements: Waitz's (1849) Herbartian thesis that space results from our need to organize simultaneous competing ideas into a single experience, Lotze's (1852) theory of local signs, and finally, a Berkeleian reliance on associations cued to eye sensations. But how are these elements used to create the perception of space? He answered,

> This process is unconscious, and we can infer it only from those elements which enter into consciousness. But when we translate it into conscious terms, it takes the form of an *inference*. The *unconscious inference* is the process that joins itself to sensation, giving rise to perception. (1862a, p. 65)

The article contains no intimation that three years earlier Helmholtz (1855/1896) had used the concept of unconscious inference, though not that exact phrase, in discussing the nature of visual illusions. This was no way for an assistant to establish good relations with his new chief. They apparently never spoke together about this subject. After leaving the assistantship, Wundt at least three times asserted his priority to the concept: in his *Textbook of Human Physiology* (1865), in a review of Helmholtz's *Physiological Optics* (Wundt, 1867d), and in a survey article that deals at length with spatial perception (1867b). Without mentioning Wundt, Helmholtz (1868/1896) then asserted his own claim. Later, Wundt (1880, in reply to Erdmann, 1879) said that in 1858 he had not known about Helmholtz's earlier address, but that does not explain how he could have remained ignorant of it for so long afterward. Even if an honest mistake, Wundt's initial use of the concept without acknowledging Helmholtz's priority certainly cast a shadow across their relationship.

In any case, Wundt, in that first chapter, laid the basis for a psychological theory of space perception, not only by asserting the experiential foundations of tactile localization but by insisting that an unconscious logic was needed to make use of the empirical cues. Chapter 2 gave a history of theories of vision. Unimportant in itself, it is notable as Wundt's first historical exercise, the forerunner of the numerous historical interludes that constitute an enduringly valuable feature of the *Principles of Physiological Psychology* in all its editions. Chapter 3, on monocular vision, emphasizes the importance of sensations arising from the muscles of accommodation, and it goes on to say that although accommodation is at first an involuntary act, it becomes largely voluntary in adults, as shown by the fact that it is influenced more by attentional factors than by the physical characteristics of objects in the visual field. (Such "empirical" proofs, without experimental verification, abound.) He also argued that, since directional movement of the eyes is clearly voluntary and is accompanied by conscious sensation, it must be the key to the psychological construction of space. In support of this view, he asserted (quite mistakenly) that we can discriminate "almost infinitesimal differences in degrees of contraction" of the eye muscles (p. 151). Elsewhere, he said that the relative simplicity of the eye muscles offers the best opportunity "to arrive at general laws about the mechanism of voluntary movements" in general, as well as being "the key to an understanding of visual perception, insofar as it rests on a physiological basis" (1862d, p. 11).

Wundt's interest in eye movements, to which he attributed such great significance, is one instance in which he apparently followed the lead of Helmholtz in selecting a problem for investigation. In the *Physiological Optics*, one may read this statement by Helmholtz:

> Professor Junge, of St. Petersburg, working in my laboratory, has endeavoured to determine the centre of rotation of the eye, by observing how much the luminous reflexes in the corneas of the two eyes approached each other when the visual axes were converged from parallelism to a definite angle of convergence. (Helmholtz, 1866/1925, Vol. 3, p. 38)

The reader will recall that Sechenov named Junge as the other Russian present in Helmholtz's laboratory in 1859. Wundt not only picked up the problem but, in his usual style, proceeded at once to use it as the base for an untenable theoretical structure. (Between 1859 and 1862, Wundt read a number of papers on eye movements, chiefly before the Heidelberg Scientific-Medical Association. The titles were given by E. Wundt, 1927. It appears that the substance of these is contained in the discussion of binocular vision in the *Beiträge*.) Instead of working under Helmholtz, accepting a junior position, Wundt chose to pursue the problem independently, and as we shall see, he arrived at mistaken conclusions.

Chapters 4 and 5 of the *Beiträge* deal with binocular vision. They reject the hypothesis of "identity" between corresponding points on the two retinas and offer a new solution to the horopter problem. (See below, under "Controversy with Ewald Hering.") They also describe experiments on such phenomena of binocular vision as contrast effects and stereoscopic fusion, which were not in themselves novel, but about which Wundt argued that they are explicable only if we assume unconscious reasoning. In Chapter 6, Wundt rejected the Herbartian principle that rival ideas exist in consciousness simultaneously and maintained instead that whatever is present in consciousness at a given instant must first have been formed unconsciously into a single percept, as happens in stereoscopic fusion and in the construction of space. We will meet this idea again when we examine Wundt's early experiments and theories on the temporal characteristics of the thinking process, with which he was busy at the same time.

Before closing, Wundt again emphasized the importance of unconscious inference as the basis not only of perceptual processes but of all mental life, including the very fact of consciousness, as arising from a logical differentiation between subject and object. He declared that the elementary laws of logic must play the same leading role in psychology that the concept of the cell plays in our study of the physical organism, and he concluded on an almost ecstatic note that

> psychology is in the fortunate position of being able to guide its research not by an hypothesis but by an empirical fact, and this empirical fact is that the mind is an entity which independently acts and develops in accordance with logical laws. (1862a, p. 451)

Thus, the appeal to unconscious thinking does not in any degree lessen the exclusively intellectualistic emphasis of the book as a whole and in no sense represents an incipient stage of Wundt's future voluntarism.

The Introduction on Method

The six chapters we have been discussing had previously been published as a series of journal articles. In presenting them as a book, Wundt added an introduction that rejected metaphysics as a basis for psychology and asserted the need to go beyond the study of consciousness by using genetic, comparative, statistical, historical, and, above all, experimental method. The stated reason was that only in this way is it possible to discover how conscious phenomena arise as "complex products of the unconscious mind" (p. xvi). He called it a "prejudice" to suppose that experiment cannot deal with the "higher mental activities" (p. xxvii), and he intimated that still unpublished but recently completed experiments clearly demonstrate the psychological law of the unity of ideational content (p. xxviii), which was of course basic to his theory of sense perception. Other experiments had demonstrated two important laws of mental life: (1) that one mental process is dependent on another—this being Wundt's "psychological" restatement of Fechner's "psychophysical" law; and (2) that mental functions develop in accordance with logical principles—this being a generalization based on his theory of perception.

In future years, Wundt would reverse his position on most of these points. He would see experiment not as an essential supplement to introspective method but as a device to control it. He would himself emphatically reject the possibility of its application to higher mental processes, which he would seek to study only through the social history of their products. He would propound an anti-intellectualistic, "voluntaristic" psychology in which logic would not regulate mental development but would arise as a developmental product of more basic psychic processes. Only his assessment of Fechner's findings—an assessment that is demonstrably false in the light of present-day neurophysiology—would remain constant. His possible motivation in this merits some comment.

Wundt was a young man who had recently met frustration in a bold quest for recognition in one field of physiological research and had intensified his efforts in another. He was convinced that by his emphasis on psychological factors in perception he had an important message to deliver. There is no question that he was ambitious, there is much to suggest that he still indulged in daydreams of glory, and there is no fault attaching to either of these traits. On the other hand, his controversy with Munk, which took place in the period between the appearance of Fechner's *Psychophysics* (1860) and his own *Beiträge* (1862a), exhibited a testiness that, to put it mildly, was not altogether admirable. It is apparent that to such a young man, Fechner's great work would appear as a hostile invasion of territory that he had been mapping out for himself. It was not his temperament (as we see from his relations with both Du Bois-Reymond and Helmholtz) to enlist under the banner of another general. While some others questioned the psychological significance of Fechner's findings, Wundt sought to make them conform to his own direction of emphasis by declaring that they had *only* psychological significance; that Fechner had not discovered a *psychophysical* law but had merely given a fresh demonstration of something long recognized, how one psychological process varies under the influence of another. He illustrated this position to his own satisfaction by stating that "everyone has had the experience that the slightest annoyance, which would not be noticed when one is already depressed, is able to totally disrupt a cheerful frame of mind" (p. xxx). To restate this sample of "empirical psychology" in what is at least a framework of "thought experiment," readers may ask themselves whether they would respond with greater irritation to being jostled in a crowd, or to missing a local bus, when in an expansive or a depressed frame of mind, and then try to understand the makeup of a man whose cheery frame of mind can be "totally disrupted" (*gründlich zerstörrt*) by such a minor annoyance. Then, consider further that if this argument was to support Wundt's thesis, what he described must be a universal phenomenon, not an individual oddity or an occasional occurrence.

Controversy with Ewald Hering

Wundt thought that his solution to the horopter problem, on which Helmholtz had been working over a considerable time, merited a separate publication (1862a). This article involved him in a controversy with another young physiologist whose name is now known to all psychologists. Hering (1863) pointed to certain mathematical and conceptual errors in Wundt's article and also questioned the validity of some experimental observations that Wundt had advanced in support of his theory and that Hering found he could not reproduce. Leaving matters of observation aside, although history has shown Hering's acuteness of observation to be quite extraordinary, there could be no question about the errors in mathematics. Wundt had no choice but to concede them, but in retaliation, he seized on what he thought was another such error by Hering. He declared that Hering's solution (to the problem formulated by Wundt) was "unconditionally false" and gave his own correction instead. He then delivered the following jibe:

> If in the future Herr Hering wishes again to devote himself to the praiseworthy business of searching out the errors of calculation in the work of others, it is to be hoped that he will not on those occasions make even coarser errors than those which he wishes to correct. (Wundt, 1863, p. 174)

Hering (1864) replied that Wundt had indeed reached a correct solution by a fortuitous combination of false premises and wrong calculations but that he had failed to reduce his final equation to its simplest terms. If he had known how to do so, he would have recognized that his solution was in fact identical with the one that he called "unconditionally false."

Wundt (1863) also tried to sidestep the original point at issue by declaring it moot because Helmholtz meanwhile had reached a definitive solution to the horopter problem. This vicarious claim was premature. In the end, Helmholtz wrote, "The problem was solved by myself and Mr. E. Hering practically about the same time" (1866/1925, p. 484). Wundt was playing in the wrong league.

The Swiftest Thought

Again, we backtrack a little, to pick up the beginning of another and more interesting aspect of Wundt's experimental and theoretical work in this period. In 1861, German scientists met in congress at Speyer, not forty kilometers by rail from Heidelberg, and Wundt took the opportunity to present two papers, one on eye movements and the other on what the astronomer Bessel had long before called "the personal equation." The latter paper (read September 18, 1861) was reported in the proceedings of the congress in these few lines:

> Dr. Wundt of Heidelberg spoke on the personal difference between visual and auditory observation. He regards this as an absolute magnitude, which is positive or negative because different persons either see first and then hear or the other way around, and from this the speaker explained the difference between Bessel's observations and those of others who, unlike him, would have heard first and then seen. (Quoted, in the original German, by Titchener, 1923.)

It happened that Bessel's former assistant, the astronomer Argelander, was present, and he protested that he, too, "saw first and then heard."

This refutation of an overhasty hypothesis only spurred Wundt to one that was even more ambitious and that was first stated in a family magazine in an article on "The Speed of Thought" (1862b). After summarizing findings on the relative slowness of nervous impulses compared to our intuitive notions of the speed of thought, and after discussing the implications of these data for the thinking process, the article states,

> For each person there must be a certain speed of thinking, which he can never exceed with his given mental constitution. But just as one steam engine can go faster than another, so this speed of thought will probably not be the same in all persons. (p. 264)

But how, it goes on, can we measure the speed of thought in different individuals? Wundt then described a method that anyone can use with the help of a large pendulum clock. (See Figure 1.) Attach a metal crosspiece to the shaft of the pendulum, a knitting needle perhaps, and hang a bell where this crosspiece will strike it as the pendulum swings. This device is labeled a *Gedankenmesser* or *thought meter*. (It may well have been suggested by the pendulum myograph in Helmholtz's laboratory, in which the smoked glass plate on which the tracing was made formed a part of the pendulum, the movement of which triggered switches placed at precisely determined points in the arc of movement in order to open and

Figure 1. The "thought meter." (Wundt, 1862b, p. 264.)

close the electrical circuit as desired.) If we desire to observe the exact position of the pendulum at the moment when the bell rings, said Wundt, we can never do this with complete accuracy. For himself, he found an error of about one-eighth of a second, and he took this to represent the time of his swiftest thought, that is, the shortest time intervening between two successive perceptions. No result was given for any other subject, nor was there any indication that there had ever been another subject. Nevertheless, Wundt stated that the experiment thus provided an important measure of individual differences. In addition, it gave a definitive answer to the age-old question that had puzzled even Aristotle, to wit, whether it is possible to think of two things at the same time. If we could do so, then we would also be able to see the pendulum's position when the bell sounds: "But consciousness holds only a single thought, a single perception. When it appears as if we have several percepts simultaneously, we are deceived by their quick succession" (p. 265).

This account in a popular magazine is the first published account of the complication experiment, which had been the basis for the hypothesis advanced at Speyer, that some persons tend to see first and others to hear first. It was also the basis for the claim subsequently advanced in the *Beiträge* that Wundt had found an experimental proof of the unity of perceptual content. The statement that what we believe to be a single experience consists of confused successive perceptions was suggested by Waitz's discussion of "general feeling" (*Gemeingefühl*). Not so obvious is the source of the notion that the "swiftest thought" is "the natural unit of time," as Wundt would soon be saying. However, it is possible to identify the source of this concept with a degree of probability that approaches certainty.

Starting in 1859, Wundt each year offered a course of lectures on anthropology, defined as "the natural history of man" (E. Wundt, 1927). In the introduction to the *Beiträge*, Wundt had specifically mentioned natural history as an important source of data for a scientific psychology. It is therefore safe to assume that he did not neglect to read that part of Buffon's *Natural History* that is specifically titled "The Natural History of Man." It includes a discussion intended to refute the then-popular fear that the pain experienced even in an instantaneous death may seem to last for a very long time and thus may constitute a sort of infinite torture. Here is a part of that discussion as it was translated by William Smellie, first editor of the *Encyclopaedia Britannica* and a contemporary of Buffon:

> The succession of our ideas is the only natural measure of time, and we conceive it to be shorter or longer in proportion to the uniformity or irregularity of their motions. But in this measure, there is a unit or fixed point, which is neither arbitrary nor indefinite, but is determined by Nature, and corresponds with the particular organization of individuals.
>
> Two ideas which succeed each other must necessarily be separated by an interval; one thought, however rapid, must require some portion of time before it can be followed by another. . . . This interval between our thoughts and

sensations is the unit or fixed point formerly mentioned; and it can be neither
extremely long nor extremely short, but must be nearly equal in duration;
because it depends on the nature of the mind and the organization of the body,
the movements of which must have a determined degree of celerity. (Buffon,
1749–67/1791, Vol. 2, p. 490)

It is all there: the swiftest thought, as measured by the interval between
thoughts, is the natural unit of time, and it varies with the individual constitution. It is clear that Buffon deserves a place in the history of the reaction time concept. Incidentally, *Encyclopaedia Britannica* (11th ed.) says of
Buffon, not of Wundt, that "he was given to excessive and hasty generalization, so that his hypotheses, however seemingly brilliant, are often
destitute of any sufficient basis in observed facts."

Wundt's "Fireside Conversations"

By this time, Wundt had begun to play an active part in the movement for workers' education. He and several other young members of the
Heidelberg faculty gave popular lectures to branches of the Workers' Educational League, not only in Heidelberg but in other cities as well. Wundt
tells anecdotes about occasions when he lectured on the conservation of
"Kraft" (he was surprised to find the auditorium filled with elderly men
and women) and on the theory of evolution (because women were
present, he was not permitted to show pictures of human and ape
embryos). It is likely that other popular lectures are reflected in three
articles that appeared in a magazine called *Fireside Conversations* (*Unterhaltungen am häuslichen Herd*). This magazine had a distinctly liberal orientation, and its editor was Karl von Gutzkow, the author of *Die Ritter
vom Geiste*, the sensational novel that had so intrigued Wundt a dozen
years earlier. Wundt's style in these articles sometimes reminds us of
Fechner's essays published under the pseudonym Dr. Mises, and they
show that Wundt had the skill to present the topics of his own research
in a manner that would attract popular interest.

One article is an essay "On Time," in which Wundt deplored the fact
that we are slaves to artificial time and then wrote,

The first clock was the first policeman, a policeman that thought set up over
itself, and which brought with it all those limitations of personal freedom that
were to follow. . . . A natural instinct leads people to struggle against any
power that tends to repress their independence. We can love everything—
people, animals, flowers, stones—but nobody loves the police! We are also

> engaged, some more, some less, in never-ending conflict with the clock. . . .
> [But] through all this I totally forget that *I* am time; that it is I who sometimes
> flies with the wings of a bird and sometimes creeps like a snail, and that when
> I think I am killing time, I am really killing myself. (1862f, p. 591ff.)

Wundt can rarely have been guilty of that kind of self-destruction.

The other two "fireside conversations" are called "physiognomic
studies," and they are especially worth noting because, like his article on
the speed of thought, they show Wundt as interested at this time in problems of individuality, which are absent from his later psychology. One
(1861b) was based on his work on eye movements, in which he observed
that when our glance moves from one object to another, the eye follows
a straight line if the second object is directly over or under, or directly to
the right or left of the first object. But if the required displacement includes
both vertical and horizontal components, the eye follows not a diagonal
but an arc. Wundt classified persons according to whether the concave or
the convex face of this arc was turned toward the object sought—a crite-
rion that I find difficult to comprehend. Less ambiguous is the statement
that the convex glance begins energetically and then slows down, while
the concave glance starts slowly and then increases in energy. These
movements, he claimed, reveal how the persons who make them perform
every sort of mental and physical task!

The other essay (1862c) began with a discussion of the importance of
tastes and smells in our lives. This is reflected in the figurative meanings
that we give to words like *sweet* and *bitter.* Forming the mouth into the
expression that is ordinarily induced by one of these taste experiences,
even when nothing is being tasted, will, wrote Wundt, bring the actual
sensation to consciousness. Just as the eye movements inform us about
how volitional acts will be performed, the mouth reveals the person's
deeper inclinations and disinclinations.

Early Political Activity

The league was also a forum for political discussion, and Wundt, as
chairperson of the Heidelberg branch, became more and more involved
in political matters. He represented the branch, and sometimes branches
in other nearby cities, in regional conferences, and at one of these he had
the good fortune to meet Friedrich Lange, who about ten years later
would recommend him for the chair of inductive philosophy at Zurich.

(Wundt erred in saying that Lange then occupied that chair; in fact, Lange did not teach at Zurich until 1869.) In 1866, Wundt was elected to represent a Heidelberg district in the Baden diet. Although Wundt said that his service in that body lasted for about four years, this is certainly an error. The occasion for his election was a vacancy caused by the death early that year of his friend Eduard Pickford, an economist at Heidelberg. Petersen (1925) said that the election took place on April 26, and Wundt received 45 of the 51 votes cast. Wundt himself stated (1920, p. 234) that he entered the diet almost immediately after finishing a book published that year (Wundt, 1866a), and that he remembered writing the preface, which is dated September 1866, in the diet chamber. He also stated (1920, p. 30) that his political life ended more or less with the death of Karl Mathy (then president of the cabinet), which occurred February 3, 1868. It thus appears that his intense involvement in government affairs did not last more than 18 months, and there is general agreement that he resigned later that year.

Wundt stated in the autobiography (and also in a letter of 1872 to his fiancée [Schlotte, 1856]) that he resigned because he realized that politics could not be an avocation but required a total commitment that was incompatible with his scientific work. It is worth noting, however, that meanwhile, the Workers' Educational Leagues had become more radicalized, having become absorbed into the Allgemeiner Deutscher Arbeiterverein, which in 1868 became affiliated with the International Working Men's Association. This adherence of the league to a philosophy of class conflict led to Wundt's resignation from it and may have influenced his decision to retire from an active political life.

As a member of the diet, Wundt was affiliated with the dominant Progressive Party. His affiliation with the university made it natural that he should be charged with responsibilities in the field of education, and Wundt did in fact introduce measures dealing both with the secularization of the lower schools and with the abolition of the special legal immunities that students enjoyed, as a result of which, for example, dueling by students was a disciplinary matter for the university although it was a criminal offense for the population at large. His enthusiasm for eventual unity of the German states won him a place on the Peace Commission following the War of 1866 between Prussia and Austria. He referred to these activities in his autobiography, but more interesting to us are the arguments he advanced on certain specific issues.

Krueger (1922) gave the main points of a speech that Wundt made to the Heidelberg branch of the Workers' Educational League in the period just before the seizure of Schleswig-Holstein from Denmark in 1864, by the combined action of Prussia and Austria. Krueger's account is based on an outline of the speech found among Wundt's papers. Wundt stated that the goal of the entire working-class movement was the freedom and independence of the working class and its salvation from mechanization, but that this goal was indissolubly linked to German unity and freedom. German workers must therefore rise above their class interests, to fight with a sense of duty for the honor of the nation. Strength in warfare and soundness of character are independent of privilege, Wundt said, and they have more value than gold and possessions.

Petersen (1925) wrote of arguments that Wundt advanced, in an article in the *Heidelberger Journal* (1866, No. 15), against the agitation of the German Workers Union for universal suffrage. (Note that this article appeared just a week or two prior to his election to the diet, on April 26, by 45 of the 51 votes cast, in an election in which 57 were eligible to vote.) Wundt argued that universal suffrage was acceptable only under conditions of real equality, but that so long as soldiers, servants, and other persons in dependent positions, or those heavily in debt, could be commanded how to cast their votes, the effect would be to give greater advantage to those in control. So long as there was a standing army, it would serve to put these votes at the disposal of the government.

Lectures on Psychology

At the time when Wundt published the popular articles we mentioned previously, and presumably also delivered popular lectures in the same vein, he also for the first time offered a lecture course with the word *psychology* in its title. It should be recognized that prior to 1862, the possibility of giving such a course did not really exist for him. The chair of philosophy at Heidelberg was until that year occupied by the Baron von Reichlin-Meldegg, whom Wundt ridiculed for his superficiality (1920, p. 239ff.), pointing to this course title as evidence: "Psychology, including Somatology and the Study of Mental Disease." On the other hand, it should be noted that since 1856, psychology and psychiatry had been required courses for medical students (Stübler, 1926). Reichlin-Meldegg had in fact shown a pioneering interest in this field by writing many years earlier a two-volume work (1837–1838) with the same title, which was described by Ueberweg (1866/1898, p. 331) as having made "special use of the results of physiological investigations." When Eduard Zeller, whose interest was primarily historical, was named to the chair of philosophy, it became possible for Wundt to lecture on psychology. In the 25 semesters remaining before Wundt left Heidelberg, he lectured on psychology 12 times in all, as follows:

> Psychology from the Standpoint of Natural Science
>> Summer semesters of 1862, 1863, 1864; winter semesters of 1864–1865, 1865–1866, 1866–1867
>
> Physiological Psychology
>> Winter, 1867–1868, 1872–1873
>
> Psychology, including the Study of Mental Disease
>> Summer, 1868; winter, 1868–1869
>
> Psychology
>> Winters, 1869–1870, 1870–1871

The reader will notice that the two offerings of "Physiological Psychology" came five years apart. The occasion for each will be discussed later. The second offering of that course—which was never again repeated in Wundt's lifetime!—was the only course in psychology that Wundt taught during his last seven semesters at Heidelberg. (Data based on E. Wundt, 1927.)

Wundt could never be guilty of writing "too little and too late." His first course in psychology gave birth almost at once to a massive two-volume work, *Lectures on the Human and Animal Mind* (1863–1864). Twice in later years Wundt referred to this work as a "youthful indiscretion"—once in the preface to the drastically revised and much shortened second edition (1892), and again in his autobiography. On the first occasion, he attributed its failings to his inadequate experience at the time in the area of psychological experimentation, while on the second occasion, he regretted chiefly his premature efforts in the direction of ethnic psychology at a time when the necessary materials were not yet available. He also confessed that the treatment of animals was quite superficial and that they were included in the title only because of the current interest in Darwinism.

We shall look at this book first through the eyes of an anonymous contemporary reviewer (*Literarisches Centralblatt*, 1863, 1864). With only the first volume in hand, the work was recommended to laymen as giving a rich, clear, and interesting account of the physiological conditions underlying sensation and perception, although at times, particularly in the areas of optics and acoustics, the author stressed his own work where he might have used the work of others. The author's conclusions are called less clear than these expositions of fact. For example, the statement that "The physical movement in the nerves does not arouse sensation, but is itself sensation" (p. 134) is at odds with the statement that "different sensations are changes in the state of the mind" (p. 298). One is confused, also, by such statements as (1) "Thought is time and time is thought, because the thinking person measures it and thought is the only instrument which measures itself"; (2) "Space is experience and experience is space"; and (3) the implication elsewhere that time and space are identical. Statements about the duration of "the swiftest thought" (in Chapter 3) are found to be inconsistent with others in the discussion of the "personal difference" (in Chapter 23).

Later, the same reviewer summed up the content of the second volume concisely: the author

> deals successively with sensual, aesthetic, intellectual and religious feelings; in the discussion of desire, a few chapters are included on the instinctive behavior of animals and humans and . . . the origin of speech; he then turns to will and the question of free will, and ends with a consideration of the dependence of will and consciousness on the brain.

In fact, the greater part of the volume represents an attempt to write an ethnic psychology, reflecting the influence of Lazarus and Steinthal, who together founded the *Zeitschrift für Völkerpsychologie und Sprachwissenschaft* in 1859. However, the reviewer expressed skepticism about Wundt's confidence that ethnology can inform us better about psychological processes than can the study of individual consciousness. The reviewer also expressed the opinion that "it is convenient, but not very profound, to hide our ignorance about the causes of differences [in mental phenomena] and the laws of their varied formations behind the words *development* and *unfolding*." (Here we may remark that Hans Volkelt, 1922, on the other hand, has seen Wundt's early disposition toward developmental analysis of mental processes as the primary influence that gave rise to his interest in ethnic psychology.) Readers are told that although they will find much that is entertaining in this volume, anyone who wishes to assess the net gain for psychology should read Drobisch's critique of the first volume.

We turn, therefore, to Drobisch (1864). As the dean of Herbartian psychologists, writing in a Herbartian journal, he began by demonstrating Wundt's ignorance of Herbartian psychology. One example of many: Wundt stated that for Herbart the sum of the strength of all ideas into consciousness is a constant, and that this supposition can be experimentally disproved. In fact, that sum, for Herbart, included the strength of unconscious ideas. (Drobisch pointed out that Wundt should not have overlooked this fact, after discussing how the principle of conservation of energy applies to sensations. In later years, Wundt would say that conservation of energy does not apply to psychic causation.) Drobisch then roundly criticized Wundt for his sweeping generalizations based on trivial data, as when he estimated the time of the "swiftest thought" from observations based on only two sense modalities, while neglecting (1) the other senses; (2) successive perceptions involving only one sense; (3) other factors in the complex experimental situation in which the stimuli were presented; and (4) the problem of thought sequences that are not governed by immediate external stimulation. Some other criticisms were that Wundt failed to appreciate the true significance of Fechner's findings and that he was led into absurdities by his fascination with "identity philosophy." "One fresh example is Wundt's statement that "mechanical and logical necessity are not essentially different [because] mechanism and logic are identical." Drobisch's final judgment, that Wundt's attempt to reform psychology was "hasty and premature," was one in which Wundt himself ultimately concurred.

Three Nonpsychological Books

In 1864 (not 1863, as the autobiography states), Wundt relinquished his assistantship (Schlotte, 1956). Whether Helmholtz had requested the resignation is a controversial question that is best examined after we have become acquainted with the work of Wundt's successor in that post. Wundt wrote that he resigned in order to have more time for his own work, but he was also under compulsion to make up somehow for the loss of the small stipend he had been receiving, and the three books that he wrote during the next three years were not of a psychological nature. He was granted the title of assistant professor at this time, but it was an empty title without monetary recompense. (However, the fact that he could list himself on the title pages of these books as "professor" at the prestigious University of Heidelberg did not hurt their sale, and it certainly helped his pride. That he did so without including the modifying word *assistant* [*ausserordentlicher*, literally, "extraordinary"] was a breach of the usual custom.)

Wundt's three earlier books (1858b, 1862a, 1863–1864), each with a different publisher, had all sold very poorly, and for his fourth book, he had to turn to a fourth publisher. The *Textbook of Human Physiology* was indeed a success. The first edition was soon translated into Dutch and Russian, the second (1868) was followed by translations into Hungarian and French, and the fourth and last (1878) by a translation into Italian (E. Wundt, 1927). Perhaps the most distinctive feature of the book was its frequent use of the first-person-singular pronoun, as in "I was the first to. . . ." This phrase occurs so often that an unknowing reader would assume that Wundt was, along with Helmholtz, Du Bois-Reymond, Brücke, and Ludwig, one of the handful of workers who had given shape to the new physiology.

His next book was a venture into philosophy: *The Physical Axioms and Their Relation to the Principle of Causality* (1866a). An anonymous review (*Literarisches Centralblatt*, 1867) was entirely favorable and summarized the book's content as follows:

> First the [six] axioms are defined and it is shown . . . how in the course of time quite contrary views have been held regarding each of them, according to whether the conceptual development was based on empirical or speculative grounds. In a special section, these opposed views are more sharply stated as ontological antinomies. The following chapter shows that the roots of these contradictions lie in different conceptions of causality . . . and (finally) that they are to be regarded altogether as laws derived from ripened experience.

The success of this book surely helped Wundt to obtain a chair in philosophy eight years later.

A third book, the *Handbook of Medical Physics* (1867a), was directed toward medical students who had inadequate preparation in the natural sciences. The idea for it came from the more advanced, pioneering work by A. Fick, which Wundt (1866b) reviewed. In fact, starting in 1866 Wundt became very active as a reviewer of books in physiology and the related sciences, probably chiefly to supplement his income and perhaps because it was the sort of work he could conveniently do in "idle" moments at Karlsruhe, where the diet met. Although these reviews were for the most part short and unsigned, two lengthy signed review articles, one dealing with a work by Helmholtz and the other with a work by Haeckel, deserve our special attention. We shall return to them shortly.

The Complication Pendulum

In the midst of all Wundt's writing, teaching, public lectures, and political activity in the early 1860s, he somehow still found time to continue experimental work with the complication pendulum, the apparatus that he designed to replace the pendulum clock that was his original "thought meter." Although he had made several summary statements about the nature of his work on the speed of thought, no reasonably complete description of it, and no data more precise than that vague "one-eighth of a second," had ever been published. Near the end of the first volume of the *Lectures*, a supplementary note to Chapter 3 promised that the second volume would contain such a report along with a description of an improved apparatus that would make more exact measurements of the speed of ideation possible. But the preface to the second volume ended with a statement that he had decided instead to publish it in a journal article, presumably because of its technical nature. No such article was ever published.

Meanwhile, the astronomer Hirsch had published two reports on experiments using the Hipp chronoscope to measure what he called "physiological time." He explained that his purpose was to provide absolute correction for individual errors in astronomical observations, instead of merely an adjustment based on the "personal difference" between observers, as had been the custom. His first report (Hirsch, 1861–1863; the paper was read in 1862) was based on experiments begun not more than a month after the date of Wundt's paper at Speyer, but there is no evidence that it was in any way stimulated by that paper. Hirsch's paper reported differences in time for manual response (1) to auditory, visual, and tactile stimulation; (2) between observers; (3) in Hirsch's own results when fresh and when fatigued; (4) according to the locus of tactile stimulation and the hand used for response; and (5) according to whether the stimulus was expected or unexpected. A sophisticated procedure for the calibration of the chronoscope is described, and for each series of observations, there is a calculation of the probable error of the mean and the probable error of individual observations. This work was interrupted because Hipp had loaned the chronoscopes to Hirsch for a limited period of time.

The second report (Hirsch, 1863) described an ingenious procedure in which a pendulum moved a simulated star across the meridian of an astronomical telescope, and the time measured was that between the instant of "passage" and the observer's manual response. One finding was that when the "star" moved more slowly, the response time was longer. We cannot but wonder whether the publication of this superb series of experiments did not occasion the delays in Wundt's promised report on his own work.

It was not till several years later that Wundt (1866d) acknowledged that contrary to his earlier views, further experimentation had shown that when a stimulus of one modality, such as sound or touch, occurs during an ongoing series of stimuli of another modality, such as vision (recall Drobisch's comment about Wundt's having neglected other features of the experimental situation!), it will combine with one or another element of that series depending on the tempo of the series, the observer's state of fatigue, and other experimental variables. It is no longer a matter, therefore, of whether a given person "sees first and then hears" or "hears first and then sees" but of which experimental variables favor one result or the other. No data were given. The "natural unit of time" was thus tacitly abandoned and was never mentioned thereafter.

The very brief description of the apparatus used to obtain these results is entirely compatible with the figure of the complication pendulum that was to appear in the first and all the subsequent editions of the *Principles of Physiological Psychology*. The *series* of visual stimuli results, of course, from the movement of the swinging pointer in front of the subdivisions of the scale. The speed of the pendulum's swing is regulated by a movable bob. The pendulum can not only ring a bell at a precise predetermined moment, but it can also produce a tactile stimulus by rotating a small platform on which the subject's finger rests.

Later that year, Wundt published a "popular lecture" on mental measurement (1866c). Pythagoras was honored for discovering the law of relativity in our sensations, and therefore no mention of Weber or Fechner was necessary, but Wundt took personal credit for opening a more important avenue to mental measurement by his discovery that the act of perception consumes more time than that required for nervous conduction between the sense organ and the reacting muscles. It is, he said, as if consciousness needs time to prepare itself to receive the impressions that are brought to it. He called this required time *Auffassungsdauer* or "apprehension time"—not yet apperception time. However, he acknowledged that the method had its limitations because of the fact that not all mental processes take place in consciousness. In closing, Wundt used a simile borrowed from Goethe:

> It is denied us to look behind the loom and see directly how thought is woven from a thousand threads, but we must nevertheless make the attempt to separate the finished tissue from the threads from which it was formed. (p. 412)

Neither article mentions Hirsch's work.

Judgments on Haeckel and Helmholtz

Haeckel's *General Morphology* appeared in 1866. The year before, at 31, he took a chair of zoology especially created for him at Jena. This two-volume work has been called "a landmark in the history of biological doctrine in the 19th century" (*Encyclopaedia Britannica*, 11th ed., article on Haeckel). Haeckel himself would characterize it later (1899, p. 7) as the work in which he drew attention to the fact that the biogenetic law applies to humans as well as to animals and emphasized the logical bond between the transformation of species and the doctrine of anthropogenesis, so that if the former is valid the latter must be so as well, as a special deduction from it. Wundt's critique (1867c) is of particular interest because of the light it throws on his views on Darwin's theory of evolution at this time. He judged that the factual parts of Haeckel's work were more valuable than the theoretical parts, and he chided Haeckel for being less cautious than Darwin in his exclusive emphasis on adaptation as the driving force of evolution. He rejected Haeckel's claim to having shown that morphology could be an explanatory as well as a descriptive discipline. He also rejected Haeckel's antiteleological position and characterized the book as consisting of "random remarks, loose analogies and unfounded hypotheses, in which nothing can be found of principle, or consequence, or thoughtfulness" (p. 17).

It is not irrelevant to draw the reader's attention at this point to the fact that although one often meets quotations from Wundt's later works in which he expressed great appreciation of Darwin's achievement, when these are read in context it will be found that they are always followed by a rejection of the basic concept of Darwinian evolution (which is development in response to blindly operating forces) and by insistence on a view of evolution consistent with German idealistic philosophy and therefore directed primarily by teleological rather than accidental forces.

The year 1866 also saw the completion of Helmholtz's *Treatise on Physiological Optics* with the publication of its third part. This part dealt with the visual perceptions of space, precisely that subject on which Wundt had expended so much of his own effort. It is worth repeating here the paragraph, very nearly the last words in the volume, in which Helmholtz defined the conflict between his own views and those of Wundt:

> In its main features the above presentation of the subject is the same as that which I gave in a popular lecture published in 1855. [This quietly replies to Wundt's repeated claims of priority with respect to unconscious conclusions. One wonders how Wundt could go on after this still ignoring the 1855 address.] It differs in some ways from the more recent works which have been also based on an empirical theory of vision. Thus with reference to the measurement not only of the space-relations on the visual globe but also of the distance of the observed objects, I have not put so much stress on the muscular feeling as Wundt does, because, for the reasons which I have given, I think they must be regarded as quite inaccurate and variable. On the contrary, my method consisted in obtaining the main measurements on the visual globe by making different images fall on the same parts of the retina. Wundt, in particular, has made a very exhaustive study of the relevant psychic phenomena, for which we are much indebted to him. I have called attention to some special observations of his where I differ from him. (Helmholtz, 1866/1925, Vol. 3, p. 558)

The major part of Wundt's review (1867d) was nevertheless devoted to reasserting his claim to priority both for the concept of unconscious conclusions and for the role of muscular sensation in space perception and to insisting on the superiority of his own theories over those of Helmholtz. He wrote that "much as [he] appreciated" the approval that his theory of unconscious conclusions received from its adoption by Helmholtz, he had to disagree with the manner of its application, because Helmholtz used it only to explain visual illusions, whereas he himself had demonstrated that it was essential for a psychological explanation of space perception generally. With respect to the part played by muscle sensations, Wundt conceded that judgments based on these alone are variable, but he nevertheless maintained that the degree of correspondence between the capacity for differentiation between the extent of eye movements and Fechner's findings on differentiation of the magnitude of visual objects constituted convincing proof *("triftiger Beweis")* of their close relationship.

"Physiological Psychology" Arrives

In 1867, Max Leidesdorf and Theodor Meynert launched a quarterly journal of psychiatry that aimed to show "its connections with the morphology and pathology of the central nervous system, physiological psychology, statistics and forensic medicine." The plan was conceived in the spirit of the somatological emphasis that was then dominant in German psychiatry generally, and the use of the phrase "physiological psychology" in its subtitle was not innovative, as we can see from its previous use by Dunn (1858) and Piderit (1863). Wundt was invited to prepare an article on "Recent Advances in the Field of Physiological Psychology" (1867b), and thus, this phrase entered his writing for the first time. It was probably a reading of this article that led William James, who was then attending courses in physiology at the University of Berlin, to write in a letter that at Heidelberg, Hermann Helmholtz (whose name, indeed, was known worldwide) and "a man named Wundt" were working at the beginnings of psychology as a science (H. James, 1920, Vol. 1, p. 119).

Wundt devoted his review chiefly to the areas in which he could claim significant contributions for himself: visual space perception and measurement of the time required for mental operations. However, because of the nature of the assignment he also made extensive mention of the contributions of other workers. With respect to visual space perception, there are references to the work of Aubert, Classen, Delboeuf, Fick, Funke, Helmholtz, Hering, Mach, Panum, Volkmann, and Wittich. With respect to the time of mental operations, there are references to Camerer, Hirsch, Höring (a student of Vierordt), de Jaager (a student of Donders), and Mach. Except for that of Panum, all of the work cited was published between 1863 and 1866. Physiological psychology was obviously a very lively area of research.

Wundt found his task so congenial that he said he would "perhaps" take a later opportunity to make a more complete exposition, and thus, in a sense, this article is the seed from which the *Physiological Psychology* was to grow. Meanwhile, it was doubtless as a direct outgrowth of this article that Wundt lectured on "physiological psychology" in the winter semester of 1867–1868. He was to use this course title only one other time in his entire career: five years later, at the time when he was engaged in writing the book that proclaimed this area to be "a new domain of science."

Research in Neurophysiology

However, something else first had to be cleared from Wundt's agenda. The publication of his *Researches on the Mechanics of the Nerves and Nerve Centers* (1871b, 1876c) shows that he had not given up hope of making a fundamental contribution to the field of neurophysiology, and the rising prestige of the natural sciences at Heidelberg, due to the achievements not only of Helmholtz but also of Kirchhoff and Bunsen, co-developers of spectral analysis, may have helped turn Wundt's mind and efforts again to experiments with nerves and muscles.

Wundt's principal tool in this research was the myograph (Figure 2), and his surprising statement that no other available method could reveal so much about the functions of the nervous system perhaps only betrays an awareness that his methods were antiquated before he was ready to publish the results of his protracted research. The actual results are of little consequence and cannot be summed up in a small space; this discussion is therefore limited to the theoretical structure that Wundt (1876c) built upon these results. To do him justice, one must remember that Waldeyer's neuron theory would not be stated until 1891 and that no one had conceived that central nerve fibers might terminate outside nerve cells rather than within them.

Wundt made three assumptions: (1) that the cells, unlike the fibers, offer resistance to conduction, and that this resistance is greater in one region of each cell than in another; for purposes of convenience, he designated these regions "central" and "peripheral"; (2) that one end of each fiber terminates near the periphery of a cell and that the other end terminates more centrally in another cell; and (3) that these "mechanical" relationships follow different patterns in the sensory and motor tracts. The consequence is something that may be thought of as akin to the physiological gradient hypothesis that Child (1924) advanced half a century later. Child's gradients depend on relative levels of excitation; Wundt's gradients depend on relative strengths of resistance to conduction.

Hall (1912, p. 324ff.) said of this work that it

> deserves to be ranked as the boldest and most interesting hypothesis ever offered to explain quite a large group of facts in a domain where we still have no adequate theory, for Sherrington's conjectures [cf. Sherrington, 1906] are less comprehensive.

But Hall added that "perhaps his rating with contemporary physiologists has not been improved by this work." This theory is stated in the first

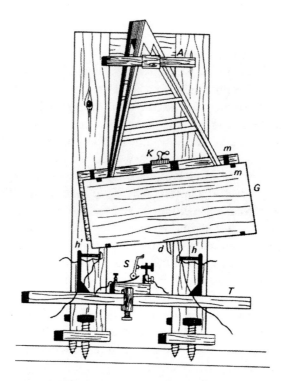

Figure 2. Wundt's pendulum myograph. (Wundt, 1871b, Fig. 1.)

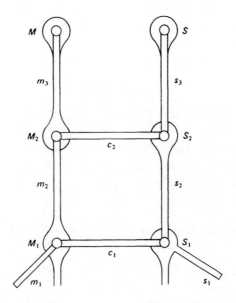

Figure 3. Wundt's schema of central nervous conduction. (Wundt, 1876c, Fig. 41.) See text for explanation.

edition of the *Physiological Psychology* under the running head "Theory of Central Innervation" (pp. 265–271), and even in 1908, in the sixth edition, at a time when the neuron theory was being widely accepted, Wundt said that he thought his hypothesis more plausible (Figure 3).

This research was the basis for the greater part (but not the final section) of Wundt's first publication in English (1876a), where, however, the theory stated above is only intimated (pp. 172–174). The reader who turns to that article can see an example of Wundt's typical hastiness in the related "finding" (p. 167, par. 2), which was acknowledged as an error in the German publication that same year (1876c, p. 18).

Hall, Wundt, and Bernstein

This ambitious hypothesis, based as Wundt said on fourteen years of intermittent labor in the laboratory, forms an appropriate backdrop to a discussion of Wundt's relationship both to Helmholtz and to his own successor in the post of assistant, Julius Bernstein. Hall (1912, p. 311) wrote that Wundt "became for a time assistant to Helmholtz, who later desiring a helper more accomplished in mathematics and physics, sought another in his place." Wundt (1915) published a "correction" to the effect that his duties did not involve such matters. His auto-biography added that an unnamed mathematician friend was amused by the idea that Helmholtz would want such "assistance" (1920, p. 155n). These self-serving statements cannot be taken as refutations. More to the point would be evidence of Helmholtz's satisfaction or dissatisfaction with the manner in which the assistant's instructional duties, which we have seen were not inconsiderable, were carried out at a time when increasing emphasis was being placed on the quantitative aspects of physiology.

We have seen that Wundt got off on the wrong foot with Helmholtz by failing, for whatever reason, to acknowledge the latter's priority in the matter of "unconscious inference," and that this circumstance long hung as a cloud between them. We have seen that Wundt blundered in mathematics. We have read Sechenov's testimony that it was more difficult to communicate with Wundt than with Helmholtz. Now let us go on.

Wundt left the assistantship in 1864, although he wrote that he did so in 1863. The error may have some basis in fact. In 1863, the

Physiological Institute moved from the cramped quarters described by Sechenov to more ample rooms (Hinz, 1961), suggesting the possibility that Helmholtz requested Wundt's resignation during that year because the expansion brought with it greater responsibilities for an assistant. Wundt's replacement, Julius Bernstein, was recommended by Du Bois-Reymond, a circumstance that at once suggests how Hall might have heard the story. Wundt himself said of Du Bois that "he did not hesitate to entrust to his young students things which were at best suitable for the ears of his academic colleagues" (1920, p. 109). It is therefore likely that whatever Helmholtz confided to his friend Du Bois, when he asked him to recommend an assistant, would later have been passed on by Du Bois to his assistants. In the semester before Hall went to Leipzig, he collaborated at Berlin with Du Bois's assistant, Hugo Kronecker, and so close was their relationship that he wrote to William James, "I have stood in much the same terms of intimacy and recipiency as last year to you, and [to him] I am likely to own a scarcely smaller debt of gratitude" (Ross, 1972, p. 81). If Kronecker had any juicy gossip about Wundt, Hall would have heard it before he went to Leipzig.

From these probabilities, we turn to a certainty: that Bernstein was both a better mathematician and a better physiologist than Wundt. Wundt said that one source of difficulty for himself was the coincidence of his research interests with those of Helmholtz. Bernstein's interests were in the same areas: the human senses and neurophysiology. While he served as Helmholtz's assistant, Bernstein (1868a), using the galvanometer that Wundt scorned, established the polarized membrane theory of nerve conduction that lies "at the core of modern theory" (Brazier, 1959, p. 22). He also demonstrated (mathematically!) that if we assume that cortical irradiation of sensory input is limited by local inhibitory processes, and that these are mobilized in direct proportion to the strength of that input, the extent of irradiation will correspond exactly to Fechner's law (Bernstein, 1868b). Wundt dismissed these assumptions as arbitrary. Today, the first is a firmly established fact, and the second must at least be accorded a high probability. Finally, Bernstein (1871) (Figure 4) also applied his theory of irradiation to Weber's two-point threshold, pointing out that the summation of the irradiation fields from two points of the sensory cortex, when they are close together, is unimodal, just as if only one point were stimulated, but that when the two points are sufficiently far apart, the summation becomes bimodal, providing a basis for discrimination. It is

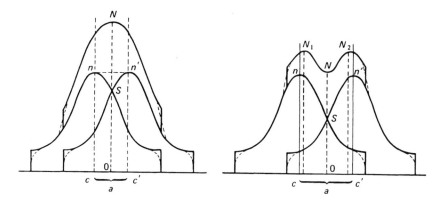

Figure 4. Bernstein's hypothesis relating cortical irradiation and inhibition to two-point tactile discrimination. After Bernstein (1871, Figs. 27 and 28).

clear that Helmholtz had found himself a mathematically adept assistant to replace Wundt and that the coincidence of their research interests did not impede Bernstein's progress. The demonstration that a purely physiological explanation of Weber's findings on spatial discrimination is indeed possible could not have made pleasant reading for Wundt, whose career as a psychologist started from the conviction that such an explanation was not possible.

Bernstein's book on nervous excitation (1871) came out at almost the same time as the first part of Wundt's work on "nerve mechanics" (1871b). Wundt reviewed it anonymously (1871a). After a nonevaluative résumé of Bernstein's experimental findings, the review closed with this passage:

> We shall not enter into the largely theoretical considerations in which the author deals with Weber's touch-circles of irradiation, the psychophysical law, etc., because the factual grounds on which the author seeks to explain the most important laws of the general physiology of the nerves and the senses seem to us inadequate. The hypotheses which he sets up regarding irradiation and sensation-circles can be reduced essentially to those originally assumed by Plateau and by Weber, which, we believe, have been refuted by the modern physiology of the senses.

For quite different judgments on Bernstein's hypotheses regarding Fechner's law and the two-point threshold, see Ward (1876) and Ladd & Woodworth (1911). The account by Boring (1942), in keeping with the practice of American psychologists from about 1910 until about 1960 of denying the reality of cortical inhibition, makes no mention of the active inhibition of irradiation, without which Bernstein's hypotheses are unintelligible.

Academic Mobility

In 1871, Helmholtz left Heidelberg for Berlin to become at last what he had always wished to be, a physicist. Bernstein declined an offer to remain at Heidelberg as assistant professor and the next year, he received the chair that Goltz vacated at Halle. Willy Kühne, another former student of Du Bois, replaced Helmholtz, dashing Wundt's hopes in that regard. However, Wundt was at last assigned specific areas of instruction (anthropology and medical psychology), for which he would receive a guaranteed emolument (Bringmann, 1975). Though modest, it was sufficient to permit his marriage in 1872 to Sophie Mau (1844–1912).

At 40, Wundt had achieved scant professional recognition. He could, and doubtless did, ruefully compare his status with that of his younger cousin Julius Arnold, who in 1870 had been named full professor and director of the Institute of Pathology. Wundt had published seven books, yet no university sought him as a physiologist. He was considered for a chair in philosophy at Jena in 1872, and at Marburg in 1873, but despite supporting letters from Helmholtz (see Schlotte, 1956), he was not offered either post. Lange, who had gone from Zurich to Marburg in 1872, recommended Wundt for the chair in "inductive philosophy" that was still vacant at Zurich, but it is clear that this proposal did not arouse unanimous enthusiasm, since "about a year" passed between the time when Wundt was asked if he would accept such a call and the actual offer (1920, p. 242).

On "a hot summer morning" in 1874, Wundt was house-hunting in Zurich (p. 243). On Whitsunday, 1875, he was in Leipzig on the same errand (Schlotte, 1956, p. 338). It was gratifying mobility for one who had probably never given up hoping to escape from Heidelberg. In 1874, there were 68 medical students at Heidelberg, "more than 200" at Zurich, and 394 at Leipzig (Decaisne, 1876). Equally gratifying was the fact that he had earned recognition as a philosopher and could look forward to forgetting the frustrations of his own career in physiology.

However, before we leave Wundt settled at Leipzig, we must ask what it was about the *Principles of Physiological Psychology* that made the book so successful. I have previously stated my belief that this book benefited from Wundt's reading of Bain's *Senses and the Intellect* (1864), the first psychology book to open with a chapter about the nervous system (Diamond, 1974). Wundt read this book in its second (1864) edition, hence after publication of his own *Lectures* (1863–1864). Also, as mentioned above, his article on "recent advances" in physiological psychology had been an exercise in which he learned to discuss the work of others without necessarily emphasizing his own related achievements and goals. Finally, it is reasonable to suppose that his marriage in 1872 was an even more effectual tranquilizer than his brush with death fifteen years earlier and made it possible for him to drop the role of angry young man. These were some of the factors that enabled Wundt to write a book in which he appeared less as the advocate of his own theories than as spokesman for a broad movement. As Ebbinghaus (1908) later put it, Wundt was the first to graft all the nineteenth-century sproutings of the new psychology (sense physiology, personal equation, psychophysics, brain localization) onto the old, partially withered stock and thus revivify it.

The rapid advancement that came to its author following the publication of the *Physiological Psychology* is the best proof of how ready the world was to receive its message. In the course of time, Wundt substantially modified that message. Our concern now, however, is only with the original edition and how it was perceived at the time. For this purpose, we shall summarize what was said about it by the anonymous reviewer in the *Literarisches Centralblatt* as well as by William James, James Sully, and Friedrich Lange.

What the Reviewers Said

The review in the *Literarisches Centralblatt* (1874) summarized the book's purpose in a paragraph consisting largely of numerous short quotations from its opening pages. It then went on to say that the book

> corresponds exactly to the need created by recent developments in physiology and psychology and the [consequent] lively demand for a *specialized* scientific treatment of the actual relations between body and consciousness.

Final judgment was reserved (in the first part of the review) because the treatment of important issues, and particularly the matter of relationships between consciousness and the organism, would be found only in the second part of the work, which was not yet published. The only specific issue discussed at some length was Wundt's argument against the doctrine of specific energies, and in this connection, attention was drawn to Wundt's failure to acknowledge that much the same argument had been put forward by Horwicz (1872). (Wundt excused himself in the preface to the completed work by saying that Horwicz's book had not come to his attention in time. His unhappiness over this incident may explain the bitterness of the polemic he conducted against an even more significant contribution [Horwicz, 1878], which he might have been expected to greet with some show of hospitality, as in line with his own thinking.)

After seeing the completed work, the reviewer made a judgment that history has confirmed: that by his thorough, scholarly treatment of all the new materials available, Wundt had "defined the scope and tasks of physiological psychology for a long time to come" and that his book would be influential in directing the work of many younger psychologists who shared the same objective. Nevertheless, strong reservations were expressed regarding the final, metaphysical chapter, in which Wundt characterized the mind as "the inner being of the same unity which we apprehend externally as its body." The reviewer also expressed disappointment that greater use had not been made of Darwin's theory of evolution. On the other hand, Wundt's critique of Herbart was seen as useful because it showed the danger inherent in any predominantly philosophical theory of consciousness.

All in all, Wundt was commended for very effectively meeting a current need, providing system where there had been scattered findings, and pointing to profitable lines for further advance. A noncommittal attitude was taken toward Wundt's many theoretical formulations of specific problems. The emphasis on the experimental nature of physiological psychology was seen as part of the program for progress "from the outside in."

James (1875) welcomed the *Physiological Psychology* as representative of that "serious revival of philosophical inquiry" coming from "men engaged in the physical sciences," whose "habits of patience and fairness, their willingness to advance by small steps at a time," gave promise of "results of the highest importance" (p. 195). In view of Wundt's prior record of rushing into print with ill-founded hypotheses, it is ironic that James should refer to him as "perhaps [the] paragon" of "these new prism, pendulum and galvanometer philosophers" (p. 196). The work, he said, "certainly fills a lacuna. . . . If, through a large part of it, the reader finds that physiology and psychology lie side by side without combining, it is more the fault of the science than of the author" (p. 197). "Wundt's book has many shortcomings, but they only prove how confused and rudimentary the science of psycho-physics still is." It is, nevertheless, "indispensable for study and reference" (p. 201).

James made no mention of Wundt's claim that he was defining the limits of a new field of science. The general tone of the review is to welcome not merely this book in itself but the broad movement it represented, a movement of cooperative endeavor between physiologists and psychologists that would surely, in time, provide the data needed as a basis for sound philosophy.

Sully (1876) did accept Wundt's claim to having "defined the boundaries of a new department of research in Germany," and he saw the work as "putting into systematic form the results of a number of more or less isolated inquiries" that "have as their common aim the determination of the exact physiological conditions of a certain group of mental phenomena" as well as the "common presupposition . . . that conscious activity goes on at every point hand in hand with nervous activity" (p. 21). He recalled the historical antecedents of physiological psychology in Germany, designating as early "builders of the edifice of physiological psychology" (p. 26) not only the sense physiologists who were early contemporaries of Wundt but such now-almost-forgotten names as Ritter (who discovered that flexors and adductors respond to stimulation too weak to excite response in extensors and abductors [Gotch, 1900]) and Ehrenberg (presumably mentioned for his early work on the acuity of vision). Sully contrasted the phrase "physiological psychology" with "mental physiology," which was current with English writers, and said that it "seems to lay stress on the fact that a certain portion of the mind is to be built up by an extension of the proper methods of physiological inquiry" (p. 27).

Lange, we know, was so favorably impressed that he recommended Wundt for the chair of inductive philosophy at Zurich. In the first edition of his *History of Materialism* (1866), Lange had coined the phrase "a psychology without a soul," which is now often mistakenly attributed to Wundt. The second edition (appearing 1873–1875) made a number of references to the *Physiological Psychology*, particularly in the chapters on "Mind and the Brain" and "Scientific Psychology." These references always come in the course of discussions of physiological matter, in the narrow sense of that word. To illustrate, I shall outline the discussion in which occurs the fullest reference to Wundt's work. The quotations are from the published English translation (Lange, 1873–75/1881). We begin with a "position statement" by Lange:

> It will always be of service, in order to avoid a relapse into the old psychological ideas and to assist the right view to come to the front, if it is shown how even the complex psychical images can be explained from those simple beginnings with which exact research is now concerning itself. (Vol. 3, p. 152)

On the next page, Wundt is brought in to support this position:

> We possess now, too, at length, in Wundt's admirable "Principles of Physiological Psychology," a work which has already made the new and only fruitful views the basis of a comprehensive treatment of the psychological sphere.

Then, after direct quotation of a dozen lines stressing that "we must necessarily assume that elementary [nervous] forms are also capable of elementary performances only" (Wundt, 1873, p. 226), Lange paraphrased Wundt as follows:

> Everything, observes Wundt farther on, that we call Will and Intelligence resolves itself, as soon as it is traced back to its physiological elements, into nothing but sentient impressions transforming themselves into movements. (p. 154)

Lange was in fact restating the following passage in the *Physiological Psychology*:

> It is clear that the forebrain, in which the most significant functions of the cerebral cortex are concentrated, transforms sensory stimuli into extraordinarily complex movements of many forms. . . . Everything which we call Will and Intelligence resolves itself, as soon as it is traced back to its elementary physiological phenomena, into *nothing but* such transformations. (Wundt, 1873, p. 228—italics added)

In the final paragraph of the chapter, Lange summed up:

> This co-operation of very many, and, individually considered, extraordinarily feeble nerve impulses, must give us the key to the physiological understanding of thinking. (p. 161)

Thus, what Lange found "admirable" in Wundt's presentation was his use of elementary *physiological* facts to explain complex behavior—for to Lange, psychology was not limited to the study of consciousness. His other citations of Wundt's work fit the same pattern.

To summarize: these four expert reviewers agreed that Wundt's work grew out of an existing movement to find physiological foundations for all forms of mental activity, and that the term *physiological psychology* as used by him referred to just such use of physiological findings. This attitude is one that Wundt later characterized as a "widespread misunderstanding" about the nature of the new discipline (1920, p. 197). Did all four writers misperceive Wundt's intention? If so, their reviews demonstrate only so much more conclusively that the great impact of Wundt's book was due to the readiness of readers at the time to welcome a fundamentally physiological approach to psychological problems. However, it is difficult to believe that Wundt would have made his meaning so obscure.

The Inaugurations and Beyond

In his inaugural address at Zurich (1874; I have had access only to the French translation, 1875), Wundt left no doubt that a philosopher, not a physiologist, had come to fill the chair of inductive philosophy. The names of Aristotle, Leibniz, and Locke occurred once each; Fichte twice, Hegel 4 times, Schopenhauer 5, Herbart 8, and Kant 21 times. Those who expected to hear that physiological research on the brain and the senses had significance for epistemology, or that the principle of conservation had a bearing on cosmology, or that Darwinism must modify our notions of man's place in the universe, were surely puzzled by the failure of this "inductive philosopher" to mention the name or work of a single scientist. The door was not slammed shut on such influence, but neither was it opened more than a crack. What was said with assurance was that "all experience is first of all inner experience" and that therefore, the monistic system that modern science requires "can only be idealism" (1875, p. 120). Furthermore, it must be an idealism along the lines initiated by Fichte, holding to the "idea of the necessary development of inner thought" (p. 125). This leaves little room for an "inductive" philosophy.

The inaugural address at Leipzig (1876) had a similar message:

> The more we are inclined today, and rightly, to demand that experience shall have an influence on philosophy, so much the more is it in place to emphasize that precisely in our time philosophy must assert its old influence among the empirical sciences. . . . Nothing can be more mistaken than the widespread opinion that these [empirical and materialistic] views emerged from the development of natural science itself. The standpoint of modern empiricism got its foundation from philosophers. . . . Perhaps the time will not be far distant

when the metaphysics which is now so scorned by empirical investigators will
again be held in some measure of honor. (1876b, pp. 6, 23, 26)

Thus did Wundt enter on the second half of his life span, during which,
through a chain of circumstances that he had helped to set in motion but
over which he had largely lost control, he soon became "an important
rallying point for the generation of young men who saw experimental
psychology as a new avenue to man's self-understanding" (Diamond,
1976, p. 528).

Since the occasions for these two inaugural addresses are certainly to
be counted among the "high points" of Wundt's life, we must ask if the
addresses were inspired by political motives. They were so, in the most
literal sense. The call for adherence to a distinctively Germanic idealism
was in line with the wave of nationalist fervor that swept the universities
in the period following the Franco-Prussian War, when a united Germany
arose under Prussian hegemony. One effect was a relative decline of
enrollment in the natural sciences and a rise in the popularity of the
Geisteswissenschaften or mental sciences. Wundt could enter into this
movement wholeheartedly, for it harmonized with the political program
that he had advocated ten years earlier.

Summary

We have reviewed the first half of Wundt's long life. In his professional work, we have seen evidence of motives incompatible with
genuine scientific dedication. His actions were often directed by personal
ambition. He magnified his own achievements, placed extravagant values
on his own hypotheses, depreciated or disregarded the work of those
whom he regarded as his competitors, and bitterly resented all correction.
The enormous effort he sometimes expended on fruitless efforts to
provide experimental support for overhasty generalizations shows that
he placed more faith in the validity of his speculations than in the force
of empirical evidence. These behaviors are more eloquent than protesta-
tions, and perhaps this is the real meaning of the priority he gave to
"inner" as against "outer" experience and to "will" over intellect.

Since behavior is a function of the situation as well as of the behaver,
new facets of his character might well have appeared following what
Titchener calls his "rapid rise to a position that may almost be called pon-
tifical" (1921a, p. 171n). It is not surprising that he should behave with

kindly paternalism toward the students who revered his authority, or seemed to do so. At the same time, the fierce pride that arose as his compensation for early feelings of inferiority continued to make it impossible for him to deal with professional colleagues as equals. Hall's statement in this regard may be taken as the formulation of hypotheses for testing in an historical study of the later Wundt:

> Perhaps no one ever criticized so many of others' views or was more impatient of criticism or apparently so jealous of those who advanced along his own lines as he. . . . It almost seems as though no one was so generally right in criticizing those who preceded or were contemporaneous with him or so generally wrong in criticizing his own critics and his more independent pupils. He . . . almost seems to wish to be the last in fields where he was the first, instead of taking pleasure in seeing successors arise who advance his lines still further. (1912, p. 419)

If these statements are true, or approximately true, Wundt's actions must often have impeded the progress of experimental psychology. The whole question of his place and his importance in the history of modern psychology, of the relative weight of the beneficial and detrimental effects stemming from his actions, cannot be adequately dealt with simply by expounding his views and comparing them with subsequent developments, as is so often done. It is necessary to face the realities of his character and to ask how they influenced his conduct toward his contemporaries as well as their conduct toward him. That task remains to be done.

References

Bain, A. (1864). *The senses and the intellect* (2nd ed.). London.

Bernstein, J. (1868a). Ueber den zeitlichen Verlauf der negativen Schwankung des Nervenstroms. *Archiv für die gesammte Physiologie, 1,* 173–207. Reprinted in Bernstein, 1871.

Bernstein, J. (1868b). Zur Theorie des Fechner'schen Gesetzes der Empfindung. *Archiv für Anatomie, Physiologie and wissenschaftliche Medicin,* 388–393.

Bernstein, J. (1871). *Untersuchungen über den Erregungsvorgang im Nerven- und Muskelsysteme.* Heidelberg.

Boring, E. G. (1942). *Sensation and perception in the history of experimental psychology.* New York.

Boring, E. G. (1950). *A history of experimental psychology* (2nd ed.). New York.

Brazier, M. (1959). The historical development of neurophysiology. In H. W. Magoun (Ed.), *Handbook of physiology, section 1: Neurophysiology* (Vol. 1). Washington, D.C.

Bringmann, W. G. (1975). Wundt in Heidelberg 1845–1874. *Canadian Psychological Review, 16,* 124–129.

Bringmann, W. G., Balance, W. D. G., & Evans, R. B. (1975). Wilhelm Wundt 1832–1920: A brief biographical sketch. *Journal of the History of the Behavioral Sciences, 11,* 287–297.

Buffon. (1749–1767/1791). *Natural history, general and particular* (9 Vols.) (W. Smellie, Trans.). London.

Child, C. M. (1924). *Physiological foundations of behavior.* New York: Holt.

Decaisne, G. (1876). Les universités de l'Europe en 1876. *Révue scientifique de France et de l'étrangère, 17,* 266–270, 369–375.

Diamond, S. (1974, June 2). The greatness of Alexander Bain. Unpublished invited address, Sixth Annual Meeting of Cheiron, International Society for History of Social and Behavioral Sciences, University of New Hampshire.

Diamond, S. (1976). Wilhelm Wundt. In *Dictionary of scientific biography* (Vol. 14). New York.

Drobisch, M. W. (1864). Ueber den neuesten Versuch die Psychologie naturwissenschaftlich zu begründen. *Zeitschrift für exacte Philosophie, 4,* 313–348.

Du Bois-Reymond, E. (1848). *Untersuchungen über thierische Elektricität.* Berlin.

Dunn, R. (1858). *An essay on physiological psychology.* London.

Ebbinghaus, H. (1908). *Abriss der Psychologie.* Leipzig.

Erdmann, B. (1879). Zur zeitgenössischen Psychologie in Deutschland. *Zeitschrift für wissenschaftliche Philosophie, 3,* 377–407.

Eschler, E. (1962). Ueber die sozial-philosophische Seite im Schaffen Wilhelm Wundts. *Wissenschaftliche Zeitschrift der Karl-Marx-Universität Leipzig, 11,* 737–761.

Fechner, G. T. (1860). *Elemente der Psychophysik* (2 Vols.). Leipzig: Breitkopf und Härtel.

Fürbringer, M. (1903). Friedrich Arnold. In F. Scholl (Ed.), *Heidelberger Professoren aus dem 19. Jahrhundert* (Vol. 2). Heidelberg.

Gotch, F. (1900). Nerve. In E. A. Schäfer (Ed.), *Text-book of physiology* (Vol. 2). Edinburgh.

Haeckel, E. (1899). *Ueber unsere gegenwärtige Kenntniss vom Ursprung des Menschen.* Bonn.

Hall, G. S. (1912). *Founders of modern psychology.* New York.

Helmholtz, H. (1855/1896). Ueber das Sehen des Menschen [Leipzig, 1855]. In *Vorträge und Reden* (4th ed., Vol. 1). Braunschweig: Vieweg und Sohn.

Helmholtz, H. (1866/1925). *Treatise on physiological optics* (Vol. 3) (J. P. C. Southall, Ed.). Optical Society of America.

Helmholtz, H. (1868/1896). Die neueren Fortschritte in der Theorie des Sehens. *Preussischer Jahrbücher, 21,* 149–170, 261–289, 403–444. Reprinted in Helmholtz, *Vorträge und Reden* (4th ed., Vol. 1). Braunschweig: Vieweg und Sohn.

Hering, E. (1863). Ueber W. Wundt's Theorie des binocularen Sehens. *Annalen der Physik und Chemie, 119,* 115–130.

Hering, E. (1864). Zur Kritik der Wundt'schen Theorie des binocularen Sehens. *Annalen der Physik und Chemie, 122,* 476–481.

Hinz, G. (Ed.). (1961). *Aus der Geschichte der Universität Heidelberg und ihre Facultäten.* Heidelberg: Ruperto-Carola (Sonderband).

Hirsch, A. (1861–1863). Expériences chronoscopiques sur la vitesse du différentes sensations et de la transmission nerveuse. *Bulletin de la Societé* [Neuchâteloise] *des Sciences Naturelles, 6,* 100–114.

Hirsch, A. (1863). Ueber persönliche Gleichung und Correction bei chronographischen Durchgangs-Beobachtungen. *Untersuchungen zur Naturlehre des Menschen und der Thiere, 9,* 200–208.

Horwicz, A. (1872). *Psychologische Analysen auf physiologischer Grundlage* (Vol. 1). Halle.

Horwicz, A. (1878). *Psychologische Analysen auf physiologischer Grundlage* (Vol. 2, 2). Die *Analyse der qualitativen Gefühle.* Magdeburg.

James, H. (Ed.). (1920). *The letters of William James* (2 Vols.). Boston.

[James, W.] (1875). [Unsigned review of W. Wundt, *Grundzüge der physiologischen Psychologie*]. *North American Review, 121,* 195–201.

Kossakowski, A. (1966). Wilhelm Wundt und sein wissenschaftliches Erbe. *Wissenschaftliche Zeitschrift der Karl-Marx-Universität Leipzig, 15,* 717–726.

Krueger, F. (1922). Wilhelm Wundt als deutscher Denker. In A. Hoffman (Ed.), *Wilhelm Wundt: Eine Würdigung*. (Beiträge zur Philosophie des deutschen Idealismus, II, 3/4.) Erfurt.

Kurz, H., & Wedel, M. (1927). *Deutsche Literaturgeschichte*. Berlin.

Ladd, G. T., & Woodworth, R. S. (1911). *Elements of physiological psychology* (rev. ed.). New York.

Lange, F. A. (1866). *Geschichte des Materialismus*. Iserlohn, 1866.

Lange, F. A. (1873–1875/1881). *History of materialism* (2nd ed., 3 Vols.) (E. C. Thomas, Trans.). Boston.

Literarisches Centralblatt für Deulschland, 1858, *9*, 395. (Unsigned review of Wundt, *Die Lehre von der Muskelbewegung*.)

Literarisches Centralblatt für Deutschland, 1863, *14*, 773–774. (Unsigned review of Wundt, *Vorlesungen über die Menschen- und Thierseele, I*.)

Literarisches Centralblatt für Deutschland, 1864, *15*, 964–966. (Unsigned review of Wundt, *Vorlesungen über die Menschen und Thierseele, II*.)

Literarisches Centralblatt für Deutschland, 1867, *18*, 1400. (Unsigned review of Wundt, *Die physikalischen Axiome und ihre Bezeihung zum Causalprincip*.)

Literarisches Centralblatt für Deutschland, 1874, *25*, 225–228, 1481–1482. (Unsigned review of Wundt, *Grundzüge der physiologischen Psychologie*.)

Lotze, R. H. (1852). *Medicinische Psychologie oder Physiologie der Seele*. Leipzig.

Ludwig, C. (1858–1861). *Lehrbuch der Physiologie des Menschen* (2nd rev. ed., 2 Vols.). Heidelberg: Winter.

MacLeod, R. B. (Ed.). (1969). *William James: Unfinished business*. Washington, D.C.: American Psychological Association.

McKendrick, J. G. (1899). *Hermann von Helmholtz*. London.

Müller, J. (1833–1840). *Handbuch der Physiologie des Menschen*. Coblenz: Hölscher.

Munk, H. (1861). Ueber die Leitung der Erregung im Nerven, II. *Archiv für Anatomie, Physiologie und wissenschaftliche Medicin*, 425–490.

Munk, H. (1862a). Ueber Dr. Wundt's "Bemerkung u.s.w." *Archiv für Anatomie, Physiologie und wissenschaftliche Medicin*, 145–148.

Munk, H. (1862b). Ueber Herrn Dr. Wundt's Replik. *Archiv für Anatomie, Physiologie und wissenschaftliche Medicin*, 654–660.

[Peirce, C. S.] (1905). [Unsigned review of Wundt, *Principles of physiological psychology*, Vol. 1, 1904; trans. by E. B. Titchener)]. *The Nation, 81*, 56–57.

Peirce, C. S. (1966). *Collected Papers* (Vols. 7–8). Cambridge: Harvard University Press.

Perry, R. B. (1935). *The thought and character of William James* (2 Vols.). Boston: Little, Brown.

Petersen, P. (1925). *Wilhelm Wundt und seine Zeit*. Stuttgart.

Piderit, T. (1863). *Gehirn und Geist: Entwurf einer physiologischen Psychologie für denkende Leser aller Stände*. Leipzig.

Ross, D. G. (1972). *Stanley Hall: The psychologist as prophet*. Chicago.

Schlotte, F. (1955–1956). Beiträge zur Lebensbild Wilhelm Wundts aus seinem Briefwechsel. *Wissenschaftliche Zeitschrift der Karl-Marx-Universität Leipzig, 5*, 333–349.

Sechenov, I. M. (1945/1952). *Autobiographical Notes*. Moscow.

Sherrington, C. S. (1906). *The integrative action of the nervous system*. New Haven: Yale University Press.

Spranger, E. (1925/1928). *Geisteswissenschaftliche Psychologie und Ethik der Persönlichkeit* (5th ed.). Halle. Translated as *Types of men: The psychology and ethics of personality*. Halle.

Stübler, E. (1926). *Geschichte der medizinischen Fakultät der Universität Heidelberg 1386–1925*. Heidelberg.

Sully, J. (1876). Physiological psychology in Germany. *Mind, 1*, 20–43.

T[itchener], E. B. (1921a). [Review of Wundt, *Erlebtes und Erkanntes*]. *American Journal of Psychology, 32,* 575–580.

Titchener, E. B. (1921b). Wilhelm Wundt. *American Journal of Psychology, 32,* 161–177.

T[itchener], E. B. (1923). Wundt's address at Speyer. *American Journal of Psychology, 34,* 311.

Ueberweg, F. (1898). *History of philosophy* (Vol. 2) (Trans. by G. S. Morris, from the 4th German ed.). New York. (Originally published 1866, the 4th German edition in 1871.)

Villa, G. (1903). *Contemporary psychology.* New York.

Volkelt, H. (1922). Die Völkerpsychologie in Wundt's Entwicklungsgang. In A. Hoffman (Ed.), *Wilhelm Wundt: Eine Würdigung.* (Beiträge zur Philosophie des deutschen Idealismus, II, 3/4). Erfurt.

Waitz, T. (1849). *Lehrbuch der Psychologie als Naturwissenschaft.* Braunschweig.

Ward, I. (1876). An attempt to interpret Fechner's Law. *Mind, 1,* 452–466.

Weber, E. (1846). Muskelbewegung. In R. Wagner (Ed.), *Handwörterbuch der Physiologie* (Bd. 3, Abt. 2). Braunschweig.

Weber, E. H. (1846). Der Tastsinn und das Gemeingefühl. In R. Wagner (Ed.), *Handwörterbuch der Physiologie* (Bd. 3, Abt. 2). Braunschweig.

Wundt, E. (1927). *Wilhelm Wundts Werk. Ein Verzeichniss seiner sämtlichen Schriften.* Munich.

Wundt, E. (1928). Wilhelm Wundt. *Deutsches biographisches Jahrbuch, II: 1917–1920.* Stuttgart.

Wundt, W. (1853). Ueber den Kochsalzgehalt des Harns. *Journal für practische Chemie, 59,* 354–363.

Wundt, W. (1855). Versuche über den Einfluss der Durchschneidung des Lungenmagennerven auf die Respirationsorgane. *Archiv für Anatomie, Physiologie und wissenschaftliche Medicin,* 269–313.

Wundt, W. (1857). Ueber die Elasticität feuchter organischer Gewebe. *Archiv für Anatomie, Physiologie und wissenschaftliche Medicin,* 298–308.

Wundt, W. (1858a). Beiträge zur Theorie der Sinneswahrnehmung. I.: Ueber den Gefühlssinn mit besonderer Rücksicht auf dessen räumliche Wahrnehmungen. *Zeitschrift für rationelle Medicin, 4* (3. Reihe), 229–293.

Wundt, W. (1858b). *Die Lehre von der Muskelbewegung. Nach eigenen Untersuchungen bearbeitet.* Braunschweig.

Wundt, W. (1859). Ueber secondäre Modification der Nerven. *Archiv für Anatomie, Physiologie und wissenschaftliche Medicin,* 537–548.

Wundt, W. (1861a). Bemerkung zu den Aufsatz des Herrn Dr. H. Munk "Ueber die Leitung der Erregung im Nerven, II." *Archiv für Anatomie, Physiologie und wissenschaftliche Medicin,* 781–783.

Wundt, W. (1861b). Der Blick. Eine physiognomische Studie. *Unterhaltungen am häuslichen Herd, 1* (3. Folge), 1028–1033.

Wundt, W. (1862a). *Beiträge zur Theorie der Sinneswahrnehmung.* Leipzig.

Wundt, W. (1862b). Die Geschwindigkeit des Gedankens. *Gartenlaube,* 263–265.

Wundt, W. (1862c). Der Mund. Physiognomische Studie. *Unterhaltungen am häuslichen Herd, 2* (3. Folge), 503–510.

Wundt, W. (1862d). Ueber die Bewegung des Auges. *Archiv für Ophthalmologie, 8,* 1–87.

Wundt, W. (1862e). Ueber binokulares Sehen. *Annalen der Physik und Chemie, 116,* 617–626.

Wundt, W. (1862f). Die Zeit. *Unterhaltungen am häuslichen Herd, 2* (3. Folge), 590–593.

Wundt, W. (1862g). Zur "secondären Modification." *Archiv für Anatomie, Physiologie und wissenschaftliche Medicin,* 498–507.

Wundt, W. (1863). Ueber Dr. E. Hering's Kritik meiner Theorie des Binokularsehens. *Annalen der Physik und Chemie, 120,* 172–176.

Wundt, W. (1863–64). *Vorlesungen über die Menschen- und Thierseele* (2 Vols.). Leipzig.

Wundt, W. (1864–1865). *Lehrbuch der Physiologie des Menschen.* Erlangen.

Wundt, W. (1866a). *Die physikalischen Axiome und ihre Beziehung zum Causalprincip. Einer Capitel aus einer Philosophie der Naturwissenschaften.* Erlangen.

Wundt, W. (1866b). [Review of A. Fick, *Die medicinische Physik*]. *Kritische Blätter für wissenschaftliche und praktische Medicin,* 201–202.

Wundt, W. (1866c). Ueber das psychische Maass. Ein populärer Vortrag. *Deutsche Klinik, 18,* 401–403, 409–412.

Wundt, W. (1866d). Ueber einige Zeitverhältnisse des Wechsels der Sinnesvorstellungen. Vorläufige Mittheilung. *Deutsche Klinik, 18,* 77–78.

Wundt, W. (1867a). *Handbuch der medicinischen Physik.* Erlangen.

Wundt, W. (1867b). Neuere Leistungen auf dem Gebiete der physiologischen Psychologie. *Vierteljahrsschrift für Psychiatrie in ihren Beziehungen zur Morphologie und Pathologie des Central-Nerven-Systems, der physiologischen Psychologie, Statistik und gerichtlichen Medicin, 1,* 23–56.

Wundt, W. (1867c). [Review of Haeckel, *Generelle Morphologie der Organismen*]. *Kritische Blätter für wissenschaftliche und praktische Medicin,* 13–17, 41–45.

Wundt, W. (1867d). [Review of Helmholtz, *Handbuch der physiologischen Optik*]. *Deutsche Klinik, 19,* 326–328.

Wundt, W. (1869). Ueber die Entstehung räumlicher Gesichtswahrnehmungen. *Philosophische Monatshefte, 3,* 225–247.

[Wundt, W .] (1871a). [Unsigned review of Bernstein, *Untersuchungen über den Erregungsvorgang im Nerven- und Muskelsysteme*]. *Literarisches Centralblatt für Deutschland, 22,* 1107.

Wundt, W. (1871b). *Untersuchungen zur Mechanik der Nerven und Nervencentren. 1. Abtheilung: Ueber Verlauf und Wesen der Nervenerregung.* Erlangen.

Wundt, W. (1873). *Grundzüge der physiologischen Psychologie* (Introduction. Parts 1 and 2). Leipzig.

Wundt, W. (1874a). *Grundzüge der physiologischen Psychologie* (Parts 3, 4, and 5). Leipzig.

Wundt, W. (1874b). *Ueber die Aufgabe der Philosophie in der Gegenwart. Akademische Antrittsrede in Zürich.* Leipzig.

Wundt, W. (1875). Mission de la philosophie dans le temps présent. *Révue philosophique de la France et de l'étrangère, 1,* 113–124. (Translation of the preceding item.)

Wundt, W. (1876a). Central innervation and consciousness. *Mind, 1,* 161–178.

Wundt, W. (1876b). *Ueber den Einfluss der Philosophie auf die Erfahrungswissenschaften.* Leipzig.

Wundt, W. (1876c). *Untersuchungen zur Mechanik der Nerven und Nervencentren. 2. Abtheilung: Ueber den Reflexvorgang und das Wesen der centralen Innervation.* Stuttgart.

Wundt, W. (1880). Berichtigende Bemerkung zu dem Aufsatze des Herrn B. Erdmann, "Zur zeitgenössischen Psychologie im Deutschland." *Vierteljahrsschrift für wissenschaftliche Philosophie, 4,* 135–136.

Wundt, W. (1892a). *Hypnotismus und Suggestion.* Leipzig.

Wundt, W. (1892b). *Vorlesungen über die Menschen- und Thierseele* (2nd ed.). Hamburg and Leipzig.

Wundt, W. (1915). Eine Berichtigung. *Literarisches Centralblatt für Deutschland, 66,* 1080.

Wundt, W. (1920). *Erlebtes und Erkanntes.* Stuttgart. (Posthumous.)

Standard Reference Works

Numerous factual details have been culled from the following standard reference works. To avoid needlessly cluttering the text, specific references are not made except for quotations. The articles profitably consulted in each are indicated in parentheses.

Allgemeine deutsche Biographie. (Reichlin-Meldegg. Wundt.)

Baedeker, K. *Southern Germany* (13th rev. ed.). Leipzig, 1929.

Biographisches Lexicon der hervorragende Aerzte aller Zeiten und Völker. (Friedrich Arnold.)

Biographisches Lexicon der hervorragende Aerzte der letzten fünfzig Jahren [1880–1930]. (Bernstein. Julius Arnold.)

Deutsches biographisches Jahrbuch. (See E. Wundt, 1928.)

Encyclopaedia Britannica (11th ed.). (Robert Bunsen. Buffon. Carl Ludwig. Karl Mathy. William Smellie. Baden, history. Franco-Prussian War. Schleswig-Holstein Question. International [International Working Men's Association].)

Jewish Encyclopedia. (Bernstein. Munk. Rosenthal.)

Neue deutsche Biographie. (Arnold, Ärzte.)

Acknowledgments

This paper is an expanded version of an invited address to Division 26 of the American Psychological Association, Toronto, Canada, August 29, 1978. In its present form, it has profited from critical readings by Kurt Danziger and William R. Woodward—and would doubtless have profited more if the author were more flexible in his views. —S.D.

2

WUNDT AND THE TEMPTATIONS OF PSYCHOLOGY

Kurt Danziger

Does Wundt Matter?

Not many years ago a prominent contemporary reader of Wundt posed the provocative question: "Why study Wundtian psychology?" (Blumenthal, 1998). For most non-readers of Wundt this is a rhetorical question: There are no good reasons for studying Wundtian psychology now. Anything Wundt wrote or did has long been totally superseded by the onward march of psychological science, which, as everyone knows, owes him respect for just one thing, the founding of the first psychological laboratory. Even that is not so certain—perhaps it wasn't even the first.

Contrary to this ahistorical understanding of science there are those who recognize the importance of tradition in science, as in other fields of human activity, even if only in the special form of "research traditions." In other words, they recognize that progress or the lack of it, in science as elsewhere, depends on the vicissitudes of traditional ways of thinking and working. If that is so, then the study of scientific traditions may not be altogether irrelevant to current scientific practice.

The recognition of traditions in science, however, does not necessarily lead to an enthusiastic study of these traditions by those who follow them. A major reason for this is to be found in the widespread belief that the historical course taken by a discipline such as psychology has been vindicated by success, that presently operative traditions have obviously put us on the right path. Therefore, if we are to look at tradition at all, why bother with any but those that have enabled us to get to where we are today? One could call this the Panglossian approach to the history of discipline because it seems to be based on the implicit belief that the present state of affairs represents the best of all possible worlds. If that is indeed the case, then let us celebrate the historical path that brought us to this happy position, by all means. But anything that deviated from this path deserves the historical oblivion that is its lot.

From this point of view there is certainly no point in studying Wundtian psychology. Between it and the subsequently predominant directions in the discipline's development there was little or no continuity. Apart from his singular lucky decision to promote laboratory studies in psychology, Wundt's path in psychology became for the discipline a path definitely not to be taken. His work, therefore, was either consigned to the dustbin of history, or worse, replaced by strange myths linked to his name.

But suppose we refuse to count ourselves among the numerous followers of Dr. Pangloss. Suppose we leave open the question of what value to assign to the actual development of the discipline. Perhaps it was not for the best, perhaps—to go to the other extreme—it should even be counted a disaster. The operative word here is "perhaps." Prejudging the value of what history has led to always results in bad history. It also results in redundant history; for if the past merely represents imperfect stages along the path to the achievements of the present, why bother with it? But if we suspend judgment on whether the path taken by the majority was the right one or the wrong one, or more likely, something in between, then the work of those who, like Wundt, took another path becomes much more interesting. For it is possible that it may open up perspectives that have been closed off by the biases of the present.

Wundt's psychology is a major occupant of that relatively brief period when the shape of modern psychology was still wide open. Various projects for such a discipline were in the air, Wundt's being the most elaborately developed one. Matters which later became taken-for-granted and implicit were still on the table for explicit discussion. Moreover, although he ended up as a historical loser, Wundt was deeply involved in the process that ultimately led to the formation of the psychology we know. His work is therefore a unique source of insight into the nature of the traditions to which twentieth century psychology was heir.

Figure 1. Wilhelm Wundt circa 1890

Traditions and Their Temptations

The fact that Wundt as an individual was able to play the role he did at a crucial juncture in the history of the discipline was surely linked to his ability to see the subject of psychology in very broad perspective.

Although later psychologists remembered him chiefly for his organization and promotion of laboratory studies, he was much more of a philosopher than a working scientist. Whatever practical work he undertook,
whatever specific hypotheses he developed, they were always embedded
in an elaborate framework of first principles. Not for him the nose-to-the-
grindstone attitude of contemporaries like G. E. Müller who were quite
happy dealing with specific empirical questions without losing any sleep
about the problematic nature of the intellectual context within which such
questions arose. In the long run, however, the broader issues which preoccupied Wundt tend to have a much longer shelf life than the specific
empirical issues that arise in day-to-day laboratory work. As empirical
knowledge advances the latter lose their relevance, except in stagnant
research areas or in work that is going around in circles. On the other
hand, the more fundamental issues that define the field, rather than this
or that question within the field, generally retain their relevance over
much longer periods, even in the face of strong empirical advances.[1]

Here it is useful to make a distinction between the *problems* that
psychologists try to solve and the broader *problematics* within which such
problems arise. The problem, for example, may be that of accounting for
visual size constancy, but formulating this as a problem within a naturalistic psychology implies a problematic of psychological explanation. For
such a psychology only certain kinds of explanation are acceptable, and
within this field of possibilities there are certain predefined alternatives.
In our example these alternatives were traditionally identified as "empiricist" or "nativist" solutions. In other words, specific psychological
problems arise within a certain "problem situation" that predetermines
the formulation of the problem and preselects the range of possible solutions. In this respect psychology resembles other fields dedicated to the
pursuit of "objective knowledge" (Popper, 1972, p. 165).[2] In general, there
tends to be less historical continuity in regard to specific problems than

---

[1]This applies to empirical "findings," not to the research practices and institutional arrangements on which such findings depend. The latter do introduce profound historical
discontinuities (see Danziger, 1990). It is possible to analyze Wundt's role from the perspective of intellectual history, which of course makes light of the very contributions that
disciplinary historians have valued most. Such an undertaking (Hatfield, 1997) tilts the
balance in a direction opposite to that of disciplinary histories, but that is not my purpose
in this chapter. My focus here is on theoretical issues, but this is not to deny that Wundt's
historical role was essentially defined by his contributions on the level of institutionalization and practice.

[2]I prefer to use the term "problematic" rather than "problem setting" to avoid confusion
with Popper's usage that is embedded in a Platonic context of "third world objects." See
also Danziger (1984).

in regard to problematics. Specific problems come and go all the time, but problematics tend to have a longer shelf life. Consequently, redefinitions of problems usually indicate a more profound historical change than the replacement of one solution by another. Moreover, whereas problems are usually formulated with great explicitness, the formulation of problematics varies; some of the most significant problematics remain implicit. That too makes problematics historically more interesting because their study can bring into the light of day matters that would otherwise have remained obscure.

By referring to the broader problem situations surrounding specific problems as "problematics" I am trying to emphasize the potentially open nature of these situations. Certainly, the problem situations of psychology incorporate traditional ways of thinking about its subject matter, but these traditions, though powerful, do not have the force of inevitability. They are, after all, only habits of mind. It is always possible to question them and to construct alternatives to them. It is this questionable nature of the problem situations that is expressed in the term "problematics."

In discussing the relation of Wundt to the traditions of psychology, I propose to focus on his general problematics rather than on his specific problems. The latter are still significant insofar as they throw light on how he saw the problematics of psychology, but in themselves they are essentially of antiquarian interest. Wundt's problematics, however, are another matter. They show a fascinating mixture of continuities and discontinuities both with what came before Wundt and what came after. Some of them are still relevant, for example, the problem of what constitutes a psychological experiment, the nature of causal explanations in psychology, how to incorporate the social aspects of humanity into psychological investigations, how psychology relates to neighboring disciplines, and many others. But at the same time, Wundt's formulation of these problematics, and consequently his choice of solutions, does have a quality of otherness that shows us an alternative path for psychology that once seemed reasonable. If we then ask why we ended up somewhere completely different we are probably on the way to a better understanding of our situation.

Wundt did not invent the problematics that link him to the traditions of psychology. He received them from past discourse and practice and then bequeathed them to his successors in more or less modified form. Perhaps because he found himself at a turning point in the history of the subject he was often more explicit about the nature of these problematics than either his predecessors or his successors. That recognition of the problematic nature of the project of psychology gives his contributions an abiding interest.

When he referred to the way psychology had traditionally defined its subject matter and formulated its theoretical accounts, it was usually with polemical intent. His large textbooks do not function as transmission belts for received doctrines but provide occasions for showing up the root problems of these doctrines. His relationship to what had gone before is therefore decidedly ambivalent. On the one hand, he is clearly indebted to the existing literature on psychological topics. It is his starting point. Without it he would not know where to begin. He therefore recognizes that his predecessors contributed important insights that enabled them to construct a framework within which a productive psychological discourse could now proceed. But, at the same time, he sees dangers in this framework; he sees it as incorporating fundamental errors that must lead psychology in unfortunate directions. These errors, he believes, were not recognized as such by his predecessors; on the contrary, they were regarded positively, even as guarantees of psychology's scientificity.

Wundt therefore tends to write about the foundations of received psychological doctrines as though they constituted a series of *temptations* for the unwary. These doctrines are seductive—they provide an orientation, they introduce order into a bewildering field, they offer the promise of a naturalistic, even a scientific, kind of enlightenment. But beware, their orientation is illusory, their order is skewed, their promise is false. This is because they are built on shaky foundations. Wundt undertakes to identify the individual planks of these foundations and expose their weakness. They are the temptations of psychology, inseparable from its past promise, but potentially misleading and sterile.

From the critical references to his predecessors that are scattered through all of Wundt's major writings on psychology it appears that he saw he own work as a reaction against three kinds of psychology that had flourished before his time. First, there was scholastic faculty psychology which had already been superseded by the other two and whose defects were already well recognized. Of much more immediate concern to Wundt were the more recent psychologies of the British (he always called them the English) associationists and the German Herbartians. These not only happened to be the academically respectable forms of psychology at the beginning of Wundt's career, he also shared with them the basic conviction that, contrary to the scholastic tradition, the basic datum and starting point of psychology lay in the conscious experience of individual human subjects.

Wundt always credited the British associationists with having been the first to develop a psychological system founded on this conviction and with developing a way of talking about psychological phenomena that any later psychological system, including Herbart's and his own, would have to come to terms with. Herbart had made some crucial changes but the very achievements of both these earlier forms of psychology had led to a new set of problems. Their contributions had been indispensable in demolishing the legacy of faculty psychology, but the theoretical constructions with which they replaced the latter were based on fundamental errors and illusions. Because the alternatives they presented were undoubtedly better than faculty psychology one might easily be tempted to swallow their medicine whole, but Wundt considered that dangerous. He therefore returned again and again to the critique of the false assumptions on which his psychological predecessors had built their conceptual edifice. Many who were interested in promoting a naturalistic, a more scientific, psychology had considered these assumptions necessary, but Wundt always treated them as temptations to be avoided. Three of these temptations were particularly powerful; they were the temptations of mechanism, intellectualism, and individualism.

The Mechanistic Temptation

Empiricist philosophers not only insisted on the foundational importance of observable mental life, they also tended to describe this life in a particular way. They adopted an elementaristic language that provided an account of mental life in terms of mental entities variously referred to as "sensations," "impressions," "ideas," and so on. Although mental faculties were not abandoned immediately, their explanatory role was increasingly usurped by hypothetical bonds or links among mental elements. These connections soon became generally known as associations, a term borrowed from social life. In the empiricist explanation of complex mental life the so-called association of ideas came to play a particularly important role. Thoughts, memories, the perception of objects, and other common aspects of mental life were all explained in terms of the formation of associations among simpler mental elements. In this way a rather mechanistic model of mental life had come into being.

Although Wundt fully accepted that psychology had to start with observable mental life and had to avoid explanations in terms of mental faculties, he regarded the mechanistic alternative represented by traditional associationism as a temptation to be avoided. If psychologists began their task by examining what was to be found in individual consciousness some reference to mental elements and their interconnections still seemed to be necessary. Having followed tradition up to this point, however, Wundt pointed to three mistakes of his predecessors that should be avoided. First, one must not imagine that the unifying operations of the mind are ever reducible to relations among elements. Such operations of mental synthesis, as he called them, are *sui generis* and constitute the prepotent factor in mental life. So, far from being dependent on the interaction of elements, such unifying synthetic processes actually determine the course of more elementary processes. Second, one had to avoid treating mental elements as though they had the same kind of objective, corpuscular existence as physical objects. Mental elements were actually events and thus were more like the abstractions of mathematics than the solid atoms in which the physics of the time believed. Third, one must not take the physical world as a model in explaining the interrelationship among the components of mental life. Wundt's posture towards his mechanistic predecessors was determined by these precepts. In this section I shall focus on the first precept, dealing with the fallacy of elementaristic reductionism.

By the early part of the nineteenth century there were two rather different versions of mental mechanics in existence, one based on the classical associationism of Hartley and Hume as systematized by James Mill (1829/1869/1967), the other represented by the German philosopher J. F. Herbart (1824–1825/1890–1892). There were important differences between the two. Following in the footsteps of Leibniz, who had earlier criticized John Locke's empiricist theory of mind, Herbart conceived the elements of mind as units of activity rather than as static contents. They were loci of self-activity as contrasted with the reactive model of mind to be found in classical British associationism. Herbart also saw the elements of the mind as expressions of its underlying unity, a view formulated in terms of the concept of apperception which did not exist within the empiricist tradition.

Although Wundt criticized Herbart severely for his nonempirical approach and for his "intellectualism" (of which more later), he also admitted to the debt he owed his psychological predecessor. Indeed the echoes of Herbart in Wundt's psychology are not hard to detect. He certainly shared Herbart's contempt for the language of mental faculties, a contempt so deep that they both rejected common psychological categories, e.g. memory (Danziger, 2001), as too tainted by faculty psychology to be admitted into a scientific psychology. Herbart and Wundt were in the same camp as staunch upholders of the principle that psychological explanation must be based on the interrelations among mental contents and not on hypothetical "powers" of the mind. In that sense, they followed in the footsteps of the empiricists; in fact they were far more consistent in following this principle than classical empiricists like Locke, or even Hume, who were not above invoking mental powers. However, there was a parting of the ways on the question of how the interrelationship among mental contents was to be conceived. The explanatory language of classical empiricism was the language of associationism; Herbart, however, replaced this with concepts like apperception, assimilation, fusion, and complication, in an attempt to describe mental contents in terms of the self-activity of structures rather than in terms of the links among reactive elements.

Wundt took over these terms from Herbart, but, characteristically, criticizes him for still being too much of an associationist. Apperception, for Herbart, was still reducible to forces of attraction among mental contents, whereas for Wundt (1887, p. 369) it was explicitly an "act of consciousness as a whole" (*Act des Gesammtbewußtseins*). He went on to claim that associations actually depended on such acts of apperception: "Thus association is only possible on the basis of this central unity of our consciousness . . . ideas become connected because the single acts of the representational activity itself, of apperception, are thoroughly interconnected (Wundt, 1887, p. 380)." For Wundt, the contents of consciousness are not elements but compounds that are the product of the apperceptive unity of the mind, not simply of associative connections.

The incompatibility of the associationist and the Wundtian explanatory framework was recognized by both sides at the time. Alexander Bain, the then high priest of associationist psychology, duly criticized Wundt for his inappropriate treatment of "Association" (with a capital "A") and for his emphasis on apperception, which he regarded as just another name for facts that classical associationism had long accounted for (Bain, 1887). Wundt replied that, while he recognized the contributions of the associationists, he thought their psychology inadequate because of their failure to recognize "the essential differences between the apperceptive and the associative course of ideas" (*Vorstellungsverlauf*). He adds: "Among the English (*sic*) psychologists, whose merits I actually fully recognize, I have never found anything comparable to an emphasis on the peculiarities of apperception as contrasted with the associative connection of ideas" (Wundt, 1887, p. 389).[3]

This divergence of explanatory constructs emerges once again in connection with the notorious notion of "mental chemistry," invented by John Stuart Mill to account for the appearance of novel qualities in consciousness on the basis of a combination of elements. The basic idea, though not the name, is actually to be found in the writings of David Hartley to whom Mill, like other associationists, remains indebted. The eighteenth- and nineteenth-century mental philosophers who constructed a psychology of mental contents on the basis of mental elements generally found themselves obliged to account for the appearance of novel contents in terms of some sort of synthetic process.

Insofar as he recognized mental elements Wundt remains part of this tradition, though his treatment of them as subordinate to apperception creates a profound divergence between his account and the associationist one. He readily credited Mill's notion of mental chemistry with providing a striking image for illustrating the fact that the perception of space, for example, involves new qualities not present in its psychological antecedents. But he also pointed out the limitations of the chemical analogy: Mental synthesis is different from physical synthesis because of its "creative" aspect. In the case of physical synthesis, Wundt believed, one could, in principle, predict from the properties of the parts to the properties of their synthesis, but for mental synthesis this would always be impossible (Wundt, 1887, p. 41)[4]. On the unpredictability of mental syn-

---

[3]Some time later Wundt points out that, in his book on *The emotions and the will*, Bain had become "disloyal" by abandoning the systematic associationism of his first book, *The senses and the intellect*. Accordingly, "outstanding representatives of the English associationist psychology, like John Stuart Mill and Herbert Spencer, did not fail to declare *The emotions and the will* to be Bain's weakest work" (Wundt, 1908, p. 155). He seems to be saying: They would, wouldn't they.

[4]On physical synthesis, Wundt's views underwent a subtle change over the years. After the turn of the century he seemed prepared to concede that, in practice ("with our current means"), predictions from the properties of components to those of complexes might often prove impossible. However, this did not affect the contrast with psychic synthesis because natural sciences like chemistry and physiology always had to adopt elementaristic explanation as a regulative principle whereas this principle was not valid for a field like psychology (Wundt, 1908, p. 270ff). In other words, the basis for the distinction is shifted from real world practice to the norms of scientific activity.

thesis Wundt's stance did not change. In the last of his works to be translated into English, a brief popular introduction to psychology, he uses picturesque language: "The psychologist, like the psychological historian, is a prophet with his eyes turned towards the past" (Wundt, 1912/1973a, p. 167). His point is that, for complex psychological resultants, one cannot predict the outcome from a knowledge of the elements—what one can hope for though are retrospective explanations of outcomes in terms of their components. The principle of "creative synthesis" became the conceptual focus of his emphasis on the difference between synthetic processes in the physical and in the mental world. It was a primary example of his central explanatory principle, *psychic causality*.[5] Apperception was the way in which psychic causality manifested itself. Thus, the emergence of unpredictable novel qualities in mental life was ultimately traced to the capacity of consciousness to act as a single unified system.

There was clearly a major rift between two contrasting explanatory schemata for what was being called the New Psychology. On the one hand, there was the bottom-up mechanistic model of elements and their connections which gained plausibility from physical analogies. On the other hand, there were the top-down models which assigned a major role to holistic processes and emphasized the profound differences between the course taken by physical and by mental events. As a laboratory scientist Wundt had of course to deal with physical apparatus and measurements as well as with an analysis of situations into their components. But for him the practical framework of a laboratory experiment was not a conceptual guide for constructing an explanatory scheme. That set him on a collision course with a younger generation of psychologists, some of them his own students, whose more positivist views prompted them to reject what they regarded as Wundt's "philosophical" or "metaphysical" flights into holistic speculation and to throw out his entire explanatory apparatus of apperception, creative synthesis, and psychic causality (Danziger, 1979). Some, notably Titchener, simply reverted to an elementaristic explanatory scheme that was very much in the classical empiricist tradition. From this source we get the decapitated version of Wundt that made its way into the textbooks.[6]

[5]Few of Wundt's extensive discussions of psychic causality are available in English translation. However, his *Outlines of Psychology* (Wundt, 1897) provides an introduction to the topic.
[6]For a corrective, see Blumenthal (1985).

The Temptations of Intellectualism

On the occasions when Wundt discusses the distance that separates him from his psychological predecessors he usually invokes the concept of *intellectualism* to label a complex of mistakes that he is trying to avoid. Opposed to intellectualism is the *voluntarism* of his own approach. This conceptual polarity certainly implies an attempt to emphasize affective rather than intellectual factors in the explanation of mental life, but it also implies much more. For Wundt the term *intellectualism* had a very broad reference, and *voluntarism* had an idiosyncratic meaning not to be confused with the philosophy of the will propounded by someone like Schopenhauer, for example. By comparison with other "voluntarists" Wundt's reasons for adopting this position might well be considered rather intellectualistic, though not in his sense.

Voluntarism, according to Wundt (1897, p. 14), attempts to avoid the mistakes of "intellectualism" by taking volitions as "*typical* for all psychical processes," and maintaining "that all other psychical processes are to be thought of after the analogy of volitions" (p. 15). Why is this so desirable? The reason is, says Wundt in his introductory exposition, that this approach provides us with a kind of antidote against the root error of "intellectualism," namely, treating mental processes as though they were objects rather than events. "Psychical facts are *occurrences*, not objects; they take place, like all occurrences, in time and are never the same at a given point in time as they were the preceding moment" (p. 14). This elementary insight, according to Wundt, is readily available in the case of volitional phenomena where our understanding has not been perverted by the intellectualistic biases of traditional accounts of cognitive phenomena.

In his more extensive (untranslated) treatment of the issue Wundt (1908) discusses further advantages of voluntarism. In particular, he suggests that the fundamental phenomenon of the unity of consciousness can only be explained by the presence of a constant feature which he sees in the "feeling of activity" that characterizes volitional processes. Purely cognitive phenomena are disparate, separated by differences in content. Only affective states have the pervasive quality that is necessary for consciousness to display its characteristic unity, and among these states it is the feelings of volitional activity that have the necessary constancy over time.

In effect, Wundt claimed that Herbart and the British associationists had pointed psychology in the wrong direction by treating mental phenomena as essentially a matter of cognition. This had enabled them to treat mental processes as objects rather than events. Their common currency was the concept of "ideas," or its German rendering as "representations" (*Vorstellungen*), which were the supposed units of mental content. But Wundt had long maintained that if one adopted a psychological point of view, that is, taking conscious contents as they present themselves in immediate experience, then ideas were only significant as mental activity.[7] To treat them as though they were objects meant adopting the point of view of the external world which the content of these ideas represented. As representations of things in the world, cognitions did reflect the permanence, the impenetrability, the clear boundaries of those things. But as psychological events they were nothing but pure activity.[8] To confuse the point of view of the external world with the psychological point of view was, in Wundt's view, the root error of the "intellectualism" of his predecessors (and some contemporaries) which he never ceased to warn against.[9]

But what exactly did Wundt have in mind when he refers to the point of view that is opposed to the psychological point of view? It turns out that he was not thinking of a naive acceptance of the world but of a very specific metaphysical position, namely that necessarily adopted by the natural sciences. These sciences are based on an attitude of observing events as objects in an external world that is quite independent of the observing subject. What they are after is a logically consistent conceptual construction of objective reality, whereas psychology is interested in the analysis and interconnection of the immediately present facts

[7]"den psychologischen Standpunkt, für welchen die Vorstellungen lediglich als geistige Thätigkeiten Bedeutung haben" (Wundt, 1883, p. 506).
[8]"Von der einfachen Empfindung an bis zum selbstbewußten logischen Denkacte ist hier alles reine Thätigkeit." (From the simple sensation to self-conscious logical acts of thought everything here is pure activity.) (Wundt, 1883, p. 506).
[9]From a Wundtian point of view E. B. Titchener's structuralism would represent yet another variety of intellectualism. Titchener took from Wundt the idea that psychological description had to be based on a separation between the reflective and the experiental aspects of consciousness. But by substituting for Wundt's polarity of activity-feeling vs. object perception the polarity of sensory content vs. meaning, Titchener succeeded in standing Wundt's scheme on its head. For Wundt, meaning would be contributed by the subject's affectivity, which is the foundation of the inner life, while sensory content analyzed in static structuralist terms would exhibit the object-like characteristics that Wundt had criticized in the concepts of the traditional empiricist psychology.

of subjective perception (Wundt, 1908, p. 263). The temptation to which intellectualism succumbs is "to overlook the immediate actuality of psychic events by mixing up the standpoint of an objective observation of nature with that of subjective experience" (Wundt, 1908, p. 264). So we find that "the attributes which natural science ascribes to external objects, were transferred to the immediate objects of the 'inner sense,' the ideas.[10] The assumption was then made that ideas are themselves things, just as much as the external objects to which we refer them" (Wundt, 1897, p. 14).

Insofar as cognitions are representations of things that are not cognitions, they provide a misleading foundation for psychology. They tempt us to substitute a description of logical relations among the objects they represent for the study of the activity of representation itself. That, as Wundt repeatedly observes, is exactly what the so-called laws of association did. Similarity, contrast, contiguity in space or in time, are ways of ordering objects conceptually, not principles derived from the study of actual mental activity as it happens. Intellectualism in psychology replicates the point of view of natural science which abstracts from subjective experience. But the price it pays is that it ends up with a science of the interrelationships among reflected objects while the subjective processes of which these reflected objects are the product always eludes its grasp.

What Wundt was trying to work out in his extensive discussions of these issues were principles that should govern the formulation of psychological *theories.* Elsewhere, he discussed methodological issues, such as the role of experimentation or of introspection in psychological investigation. The reconciliation of his theoretical and his methodological precepts was problematical (Danziger, 1988). For example, he explicitly traces the vice of intellectualism to the importation of the perspective of natural science into psychology. Yet his own fame rests on his pioneering work in adopting some of the methods of physiological experimentation for studying psychological questions! How did he live with such an apparent paradox? His answer, very roughly, was to say that experimentation and natural science were OK for investigating relatively simpler psychological phenomena but that they provided an

---

[10]It is worth noting that Titchener did not share Wundt's ambivalence towards natural science. He saw nothing wrong in adopting the perspective of natural science when analyzing inner experience. Many of the profound differences between their approaches to psychological analysis can be regarded as a logical consequence of this root disagreement.

inadequate basis for the conceptual organization of the most important aspects of the field as a whole. His psychological contemporaries and successors generally found his theoretical medicine hard to swallow, though his laboratory methods were much appreciated. Because the two were not tightly interconnected it proved relatively easy to adopt the one and ignore the other.

There is one other aspect of Wundt's critique of "intellectualism" which deserves some consideration. This concerns the problematic of psychological description, or, the questionable relation between actual mental events and the conceptual categories used to describe (and ultimately explain) them. In his recognition of this problematic Wundt was ahead of most of his contemporaries, and it is in this area that his insights appear to have retained a certain relevance.

In questioning the appropriateness of an objectivistic description of mental life Wundt was pointing to a gap between the actuality of the latter and the categories imposed on that actuality for purposes of description and analysis. But this gap is always there, it is not limited to the case of the psychology of "ideas" and their associations. Psychological categories, like sensation, feeling, intellection, or volition, should never be confused with actual psychological events.[11] Such categories are intellectual abstractions whose referents must not be treated as though they were separate entities. At most, they are distinguishable features in a complex process that changes over time. In the course of this change various features appear and disappear and the pattern of their interrelationship changes too.

Wundt suggested that the tendency to describe human experience and behavior in terms of separate independent categories was analogous to the way Newtonian physics had treated the impenetrability and the mutual attraction of bodies as independent properties of matter. But what was permissible in physical science was not permissible in psychology. All that is given to us is the reality of psychological events.

> If our abstracting intellect pulls out components of this reality and subsumes them under class concepts like sensations, ideas, feelings, volitional impulses, it does not follow that such components could actually exist independently of one another separate from the entire context of the reality to which they belong ... because we isolate them they are not therefore parts of reality that occur in isolation. (Wundt, 1908, p. 263f)

[11]Note the similarity to what William James (1890) referred to as "the psychologist's fallacy."

Wundt's strictures against the reification of psychological categories were not limited to the analysis of conscious experience. In fact,
some of the most interesting consequences of his approach appeared
when he turned his attention to the analysis of action. The empiricist-
associationist approach had placed the question of the genesis of voluntary movement on the psychological agenda. In the second half of the
nineteenth century the standard account was that of Alexander Bain[12] who
had regarded voluntary movement as the product of associations between
entities called feelings, sensations, ideas, and movements. But such a
scheme, according to Wundt (1883), converts the concepts of the psychologist into neatly distinct sets of objects that then require yet another
set of reified hypotheses to unite them again. As indicated in the next
chapter, Wundt's account of how voluntary activity emerged out of something more primitive involved a kind of differentiation in which the
potentially identifiable components of an original unity achieve a certain
degree of relative independence. What in the empiricist tradition had been
regarded as a primitive fact, namely, the association between two separate entities, a movement and the idea of that movement, Wundt regarded
as a later product of psychological development. Similarly, movements
and the cognitive representation of their effects only become differentiated in the course of development; they do not start off as distinct entities which then have to become associated.[13]

What Wundt rejected was any form of psychological explanation that
analyses the observed data of experience and action in terms of an interaction among components which are nothing more than the reified categories
of the psychologist. He would certainly have been horrified by the subsequently popular style of research into the "contributions" of various
"factors" (motivational, emotional, cognitive, etc.) to some psychological
outcome. His own attempts at psychological explanation, however, were
much stronger in intention than in execution. They took the form of two
kinds of principles, or "laws," those of relations and those of development.
Creative synthesis, mentioned in the previous section, may serve as an
example of the former; his account of the genesis of voluntary movement

[12]There was a later incarnation in the work of E. L. Thorndike.
[13]Long after Wundt's death it became possible and fashionable to build the assumptions of
associationism into artificial devices. However, the behavior of such devices could help to
decide the adequacy of different theoretical models only where it is possible to build
devices that incorporate the assumptions of fundamentally different theories and then
compare the results.

illustrates his developmental emphasis. The specifics of his so-called laws are of much less interest, however, than the general direction of his attempts at psychological explanation. He came to believe that only two kinds of explanatory account would be adequate to the peculiarities of psychological phenomena, developmental accounts, and accounts that specified the conditions for the appearance of novel phenomena (which is another kind of developmental account). The specifics he offered to fill this prescription were not particularly important historically. It is as an antidote to the temptations of intellectualism that the prescription still retains some interest.

The Temptation of Individualism

No one can doubt Wundt's role as a major champion of a psychological point of view. Historically, this point of view had usually been linked with an individualistic metaphysics based on the conviction that autonomous individuals were the ultimate reality (and the ultimate good) while social life was secondary and derivative. But Wundt's elaborately developed social philosophy was collectivistic rather than individualistic (Kusch, 1999), and this led him to insist that psychology must not succumb to the temptations of individualism.

Almost as soon as he had established his psychological laboratory Wundt (1883, p. 501) was objecting to the tendency to overestimate individual psychology and its methods, which he thought had been particularly widespread among linguists who were looking for a psychological interpretation of linguistic facts rather than drawing psychological conclusions from those facts. Such a tendency implied assumptions about the relation between the individual and the social which Wundt considered to be wrong. He traced these assumptions to a Herbartian psychology which would explain social relationships by analogy to the mechanics of ideas supposedly found in the minds of individuals (Wundt, 1886a). But this analogy is false. For Wundt, the social order represents a level of phenomena that can never be explained in terms of individual psychology. The interaction of human minds produces a new order of phenomena, a process that cannot be discovered by studying them individually. Moreover, the social order is deeply implicated in individual psychology, the separation of the individual from his mental environment (*geistige Umgebung*), he says, is "only an arbitrary abstraction" (Wundt, 1908, p. 293). There are no isolated individual minds, only minds in interaction.

It followed that any psychology which attempted to study, or to the-
orize about, individuals in isolation, any psychology which abstracted
from the social aspect of human experience, was seriously defective.
Beginning with John Locke, there had been a convergence between the
empiricist psychology of "ideas" and a social contract theory of society
which posited the existence of perfectly human, perfectly rational, individuals prior to the existence of a social order. From this point of view the
pursuit of individual psychology without regard for social relations made
perfect sense. The social aspects would most appropriately be added later,
after the psychology of individuals had been worked out. For Wundt, on
the other hand, the social contract theory of society was wrong; he rejected
it as firmly as he rejected the psychology that went with it. Cultural forms,
like language, custom, law and religion, did not have their origin in "a
contract emerging out of the consideration of individual utility" but in
the basically social nature of human beings. The isolated individual
presupposed by social contract theories is a fiction, for the relative
autonomy of individuals is the result of a process of development from
an original state of "shared sensing, willing and thinking" (Wundt, 1886b,
p. 389).

Far from being merely a philosophical dispute, this divergence of
views had serious practical implications for experimental psychology.
Wundt could never agree that the experimental study of individual
psychological functions might suffice for constructing an adequate
account of human psychology. Because he could not conceive of an
experimental study of human social life, and therefore considered
experimental psychology to be equivalent to individual psychology, he
thought it imperative to supplement experimental psychology with the
non-experimental investigation of social psychological phenomena. The
latter was labeled *Völkerpsychologie*, a field that had actually been established by some of Herbart's followers (Danziger, 1983), and to it Wundt
devoted much of his time and energy. So far from regarding its scientific
status as inferior to that of experimental psychology, he eventually
declared it to be the more important branch of the discipline (Wundt, 1906,
preface).

If psychology was not to succumb to the individualistic temptation,
Wundt believed, it would have to recognize that the study of individuals
as individuals would only have a limited role in its investigations. In
particular, it should avoid the illusion that valid knowledge about such
topics as human personality, human thinking or complex affects could

be obtained by abstracting these topics from their social embeddedness. In Wundt's lifetime the issue came to a head when the psychologists of the Würzburg School began to study thought processes experimentally. Wundt (1907b) attacked such an undertaking at great length, objecting, among other things, to the notion that human thinking could be studied as though it were a feature of the individual human mind. He thought there could be no valid account of human thinking independently of the psychology of language, and that, in his view, was a topic for *Völkerpsychologie*, not for laboratory studies.[14]

Wundt's resistance against the temptations of individualism went beyond his general stricture on equating the field of psychology with the psychology of individuals; it also extended to the way in which he conceived the social aspect. I have already mentioned that his social philosophy was organicist. He rejected any account of social life whose intellectual ancestry could be traced to some form of social contract theory. The latter regarded social phenomena as the result of deliberate, reflective, individual action. Contractual relationships provided the model for all social bonds. For Wundt, on the other hand, the social bonds that mattered psychologically were those that found expression in the existence of mental communities formed by shared language, shared customs, and shared myths, a conception that had much in common with the later and more familiar concept of culture.[15] Mental or cultural communities were not formed through deliberate decision making but through spontaneous forms of interaction at a pre-rational level. Such a process could never be studied experimentally, especially as Wundt subscribed to very narrow criteria for an acceptable psychological experiment (Danziger, 1990). But one could study the products of these spontaneous interactions— language, custom, and myth—and draw conclusions about the psychological principles that had been at work in their formation. This constituted the major part of *Völkerpsychologie*, a social psychology of sorts, yet not a social psychology in the sense in which that term came to be understood after Wundt's death.

[14]The papers, totaling some 75 pages, in which Wundt develops his critique of the Würzburg experiments remain untranslated. But, without any identification of the target, there is a brief and greatly simplified summary of parts of this critique in the English translation of his popular introduction to psychology (Wundt, 1912/1973a, p. 147ff).

[15]Wundt (1908, p. 229) distinguished *Völkerpsychologie* from ethnology in that the latter is concerned with the description and comparison of specific communities whereas the former focuses on the general characteristics of language, myth, and custom. On the bizarre misunderstanding of *Völkerpsychologie* by Gordon Allport and others, see Brock (1992).

Insofar as the seeds of twentieth century social psychology existed in Wundt's time he opposed them. For example, he dismissed the individualistic principle of imitation as an important contributor to the genesis of psychologically significant social phenomena. Changes in communal mental products and mental communities were not the result of a process initiated by one individual and then propagated from one individual to another, as Tarde's imitation theory claimed, but depended on the involvement of all, or at least most, of the members of a community (Wundt, 1904, p. 14–15). Experiments on suggestion were psychologically worthless because they did not satisfy Wundt's criteria for psychological experimentation (Wundt, 1893). In any case, the concept of suggestion would have run afoul of Wundt's more general rejection of the idea that inter-individual influences could be treated as external influences on the individual. He regarded this idea as an expression of ethical individualism (Wundt, 1886b, p. 391). Unlike influences in the physical world, which really did impinge on individual bodies from the outside, inter-personal influences were not strictly external but depended on the degree to which individuals shared a common psychological community (Wundt, 1886b, p. 386). John Stuart Mill had been wrong to claim that the methods of the natural sciences were also applicable to the human sciences (Wundt, 1908, p. 80).[16]

Although Wundt's manifest concern to escape the clutches of individualism is real enough, some doubts about the success of his endeavor are not out of place. As noted long ago by Karl Bühler (1927/1978), Wundt's references to the importance of mental communities were largely confined to the more programmatic parts of his writings. When it came to the nitty-gritty of interpreting specific phenomena, especially in the field of language, Wundt tended to fall back on rather individualistic explanations, emphasizing the expressive aspect of language at the expense of its communicative aspect.

This points to a fundamental paradox that runs through Wundt's work in this area, a paradox formed by his simultaneous insistence that the only psychologically real events were conscious experiences and that the human mind was inherently social. Wundt was very clear that only individuals could have conscious experiences and equally clear that most of these experiences were not simply individual achievements but social in character. How did this come about? His attempted answer was in

[16]However, Wundt hastened to add, he could not agree with Dilthey either when the latter claimed that the natural and the human sciences had entirely different logical foundations.

terms of shared experiences in mental communities, but, as he never developed a distinct way of investigating the formation of shared experiences, this answer remained programmatic.[17] His failure in this regard was ultimately due to his participation in a tradition of philosophical idealism which constructed both the social and the individual sides of the relationship in terms of *Geist*, of mind, or of consciousness. Wundt actually lacked the concept of a social environment; the psychologically relevant environment for him was *geistig*, i.e. mental or spiritual. He referred to it as a *Volksseele* (curiously translated as folk soul). On this basis the question of actual social interaction had little significance, and when it was pursued, as it was by Wundt (1921/1973b) in the "language of gestures," it was resolved into a question of duplicating consciousness. This was not the direction in which twentieth-century social psychology was to develop. Obviously, there were some traditional temptations that Wundt did not resist, and this was important for those, like Karl Bühler and George Herbert Mead, who developed their own positions in the course of a critical analysis of Wundt. However, it was not they who gave shape to the traditional disciplinary historiography of psychology in the English speaking countries but men like E. B. Titchener and E. G. Boring, the latter remaining essentially Titchener's disciple in matters historical. From their perspective Wundt's very extensive work on the foundations of psychology, and especially his work on the social aspects of mind, was essentially an embarrassment, for it did nothing to advance the cause of that narrow experimentalism whose champions they were. Such work was either ignored or radically misrepresented. Progress in restoring some balance to the representation of Wundt in the historiography of the discipline has been slow. To some extent, therefore, this legacy must still affect the direction and emphasis of Wundt studies.

Postscript: Pitfalls of Wundt Scholarship

As indicated at the end of the preceding section, the history of Wundt's reception in the secondary English language psychological

---

[17]Even in what was to all intents and purposes the final summary of his position he offered only this definition: "The *Volksseele*, or any other form of collective consciousness, is nothing else than the factual reality of all those psychic processes that arise in a particular community through the interaction (*Wechselwirkung*) of the psychic energies of individuals" (Wundt, 1908, p. 294).

literature has been a singularly troubled one. His position, especially on fundamental issues like those discussed in this chapter, has often been egregiously misrepresented and misunderstood. It is therefore appropriate to note, in conclusion, that there are indeed some formidable barriers to a balanced understanding of his position. Several of these barriers are easily identified.

A first barrier is constituted by much of the older secondary English-language literature which presented an image of Wundt as seen through the prism of a Titchenerian psychology from which it actually differed profoundly. Here one meets the Wundt of textbook myth, the "structuralist," the "introspectionist," the "empiricist" Wundt. More recently, there has been a little house cleaning in this intellectual slum though no one should expect rich insights from this source (Brock, 1993).

If one turns instead to Wundt's own writings, as one should, one meets another barrier. Wundt was notoriously prolific—he would have a strong claim to the prize of being the most published psychologist in history were it not for the question mark that must be attached to his identification as a psychologist. Unfortunately, relatively little of his enormous output was ever translated into English, providing a body of translated texts that, though useful, offers only a glimpse of Wundt's intellectual world.

To make matters worse, what was translated were mostly introductory texts and works for a broader audience, while his major systematic works and the often lengthy theoretical papers directed at specialist audiences were not translated. His more popular (if one can use this term in connection with Wundt) and more elementary writings—generally the ones available in translation—have all the limitations one usually associates with publications of this type. They sacrifice depth in the interests of a simplified, brief exposition, and they are full of provisional and incomplete formulations that can only be identified as such when one knows the systematic work on which they are based. They contain ambiguities and apparent contradictions that can be clarified only by reference to the fuller discussion of the issues to be found elsewhere.

In addition, there are the usual pitfalls of translation. Interpreting the meaning of Wundt's texts for an audience with a different cultural and linguistic background often depends on the precise rendering of certain key terms. This can be hellishly difficult. The translator's choice of one word rather than another can have far-reaching consequences for the way the meaning of the author comes to be understood. For example, as indicated in the following chapter, Wundt accorded the status of *the* fundamental psychological phenomenon to something for which he used the German word *Trieb*, translated as "impulse." Freud used the same term but his translator rendered it as "instinct." One wonders what direction the English-language secondary literature on these authors would have taken had the translators' choices been reversed.

But the difficulties of Wundt scholarship are not entirely a matter of translation. Some of them are intrinsic to the original texts. Wundt was virtually encyclopedic in his writings with the result that he would often discuss topics in different contexts and therefore arrive at somewhat different formulations. That can make it difficult to extract the definitive Wundt position on specific issues. He also changed his mind about some issues, though he was sometimes reluctant to admit that he had done so. His ideas did not stand still over the period of a very long and very productive life (van Hoorn & Verhave, 1980), so that one can easily be misled by concentrating on a particular phase in his intellectual trajectory. This applies particularly to Wundt's early writings. As is often the case, his first attempts at working out a position of his own are not representative of his more mature views. When he was about thirty years old he published two books that contained what he was later to refer to as his "sins of youth," *Beiträge zur Theorie der Sinneswahrnehmung* (1862), and *Vorlesungen über die Menschen- und Thierseele* (1863), works that expressed a number of views which differed quite profoundly from the views that characterized the psychological system of the Wundt who trained a generation of psychologists after his appointment at Leipzig University.[18] Even the Leipzig Wundt continued to revise his views on some rather fundamental issues (see Diamond, 1980).

In the face of these complexities it is easy to lose sight of the wood for the trees. The fact that Wundt's views did not stand still does not mean that they varied at random. In fact it is not difficult to detect certain consistent trends and patterns in the development of his ideas. For example, Wundt shows an unmistakable tendency to become gradually less sanguine about the prospects and scope of experimentation in psychology. Correspondingly, his psychological explanations tend to deviate more and

---

[18]In the case of the latter work a completely revised edition appeared almost thirty years later, and this was translated into English. The original version of the former work, however, continued to be cited without qualification as an expression of Wundt's "program." For analyses of Wundt's early work, see Graumann (1980), and Richards (1980).

more from the models provided by nineteenth-century natural science. As his views mature they also become more idiosyncratic, more characteristically "Wundtian." Over the years, a distinctive system of thought takes shape, as some of the interests that are present from the beginning achieve greater and greater prominence while others wither. All of Wundt's writings would be of potential interest if one were attempting to trace the path of his intellectual development, and earlier writings would be relevant if one were investigating their specific historical period. But an appraisal of something that can justifiably be called "Wundtian psychology" has to be based largely on the work he produced at the height of his influence during the last two decades of the nineteenth and the first decade of the twentieth century.

Historical studies pursued by active practitioners of a discipline often suffer from a tendency to look for precursors of present day viewpoints or anticipations of current theoretical positions. That is quite understandable if one's primary engagement is with today's issues, but it does not make for very good history. Whether Wundt is cast aside because he offends current orthodoxy or whether he is admired because some of his ideas are seen as sympathetic to modern projects, the aim of the exercise remains justificationist, his name is used to justify situations that developed long after his death. This kind of historiography may have some ornamental or rhetorical value, but it remains trapped within the parameters of the present and therefore cannot supply what only good history can deliver, namely, an illumination of the present through its confrontation with the otherness of the past. In relation to the psychologies of today Wundt's psychology has a quality of otherness that is potentially its most valuable feature. Paying attention to this otherness just might enhance awareness of current biases and preconceptions.

References

Bain, A. (1887). On association controversies. *Mind, 12,* 161–182.

Blumenthal, A. L. (1985). Wilhelm Wundt: Psychology as the propadeutic science. In C. Buxton (Ed.) *Points of view in the modern history of psychology* (pp. 19–49). New York: Academic Press.

Blumenthal, A. L. (1998). Why study Wundtian psychology? In R. W. Rieber & K. D. Salzinger (Eds.) *Psychology: Theoretical-historical perspectives* (2nd ed.) (pp. 77–87). Washington, DC: APA.

Brock, A. (1992). Was Wundt a "Nazi"? Völkerpsychologie, racism and anti-semitism. *Theory and Psychology, 2,* 205–223.

Brock, A. (1993). Something old, something new: The reappraisal of Wilhelm Wundt in text-books. *Theory and Psychology*, 3, 235–242.

Bühler, K. (1927/1978). *Die Krise der Psychologie*. Frankfurt: Ullstein.

Danziger, K. (1979). The positivist repudiation of Wundt. *Journal of the History of the Behavioral Sciences*, 15, 205–230.

Danziger, K. (1983). Origins and basic principles of Wundt's *Völkerpsychologie*. *British Journal of Social Psychology*, 22, 303–313.

Danziger, K. (1984). Towards a conceptual tramework for a critical history of psychology. In H. Carpintero & J. M. Peiro (Eds.) *Psychology in its historical context*, pp. 99–107. Valencia: Universidad de Valencia.

Danziger, K. (1988). Wilhelm Wundt and the emergence of experimental psychology. In G. N. Cantor, J. R. R. Christie, & R. C. Olby (Eds.) *A companion to the history of modern science* (pp. 396–409). Chicago: University of Chicago Press.

Danziger, K. (1990). *Constructing the subject: Historical origins of psychological research*. New York: Cambridge University Press.

Danziger, K. (2001). Sealing off the discipline: Wundt and the psychology of memory. In C. D. Green, M. Shore, & T. Teo (Eds.) *The transformation of psychology: Influences of 19th century philosophy, technology, and natural science*. Washington, DC: APA.

Diamond, S. (1980). Selected texts from writings of Wilhelm Wundt. In R. W. Rieber (Ed.) *Wilhelm Wundt and the making of a scientific psychology* (pp. 155–195). New York: Plenum Press.

Graumann, C. F. (1980). Experiment, statistics, history: Wundt's first program of psychology. In W. G. Bringmann & R. D. Tweney (Eds.) *Wundt studies* (pp. 33–41). Toronto: C. J. Hogrefe.

Hatfield, G. (1997). Wundt and psychology as science: Disciplinary transformations. *Perspectives on Science*, 5, 349–382.

Herbart, J. F. (1824–1825/1890–1892). *Psychologie als Wissenschaft, neu gegründet auf Erfahrung, Metaphysik, und Mathematik*. In K. Kehrbach (Ed.) *Joh. Fr. Herbart's sämtliche Werke*, Vols. 5&6. Langensalza: Beyer.

James, W. (1890). *Principles of psychology*. New York: Holt.

Kusch, M. (1999). *Psychological knowledge: A social history and philosophy*. London: Routledge.

Mill, J. (1829/1869/1967). *Analysis of the phenomena of the human mind*. New York: Kelley.

Popper, K. R. (1972). *Objective knowledge: An evolutionary approach*. Oxford: Oxford University Press.

Richards, R. J. (1980). Wundt's early theories of unconscious inference and cognitive evolution in their relation to Darwinian biopsychology. In W. G. Bringmann & R. D. Tweney (Eds.) *Wundt studies* (pp. 42–70). Toronto: C. J. Hogrefe.

van Hoorn, W., & Verhave, T. (1980). Wundt's changing conceptions of a general and theoretical psychology. In W. G. Bringmann & R. D. Tweney (Eds.) *Wundt studies*. Toronto: C. J. Hogrefe.

Wundt, W. (1862). *Beiträge zur Theorie der Sinneswahrnehmung*. Leipzig: C. F. Winter.

Wundt, W. (1863). *Vorlesungen über die Menschen- und Thierseele*. Leipzig: Voss.

Wundt, W. (1883). *Logik, Vol. 2: Methodenlehre*. Stuttgart: Enke.

Wundt, W. (1886a). Über Ziele und Wege der Völkerpsychologie. *Philosophische Studien*, 4, 1–27.

Wundt, W. (1886b). *Ethik: Eine Untersuchung der Tatsachen und Gesetze des sittlichen Lebens*. Stuttgart: Enke.

Wundt, W. (1887). *Grundzüge der physiologischen Psychologie*, Vol. 2. (3rd ed.). Leipzig: Engelmann.

Wundt, W. (1893). Hypnotismus und Suggestion. *Philosophische Studien*, 8, 1–85.

Wundt, W. (1897). *Outlines of psychology.* (Transl. C. H. Judd). Leipzig: Engelmann.

Wundt, W. (1904). *Völkerpsychologie,* Vol. 1. (2nd ed.). Leipzig: Engelmann.

Wundt, W. (1906). *Logik,* Vol. 1. (3rd ed.). Stuttgart: Enke.

Wundt, W. (1907). Über Ausfrageexperimente und über die Methoden zur Psychologie des Denkens. *Psychologische Studien, 3,* 301–360.

Wundt, W. (1908). *Logik,* Vol. 3. (3rd ed.). Stuttgart: Enke.

Wundt, W. (1912/1973a). *An introduction to psychology.* New York: Macmillan. (Reprinted by Arno Press).

Wundt, W. (1921/1973b). *The language of gestures.* The Hague: Mouton. (Translated from *Völkerpsychologie,* Vol. 1, ch. 2, 4th ed.).

3

THE UNKNOWN WUNDT
DRIVE, APPERCEPTION, AND VOLITION

Kurt Danziger

Introduction

The version of the following chapter that appeared in the original edition of this volume required very few changes because the historiographic issues it was intended to address have not changed in any fundamental way.[1] The chapter was intended to help fill some of the major gaps that existed in the English language secondary literature on Wundt. Although some progress has been made in filling these gaps, the contents of this chapter should still prove useful for readers without access to the primary German-language sources.

One gap in the secondary literature concerns the historical contextualization of Wundt's texts. Too often, Wundt's views have simply been attributed to him as an individual without any regard for the fact that they were deeply embedded in a discourse to which he was far from being the only contributor. The question of psychology as a natural science provided a partial exception to this isolating treatment, in that Wundt's voice was recognized as only one among many. But this was not the only

---

[1] The original title, "Wundt's theory of behavior and volition," did need changing, however. The use of the term "behavior" in connection with Wundt is of course anachronistic. He did not use the term, nor did he have the concept of "behavior" in the twentieth-century sense (Danziger, 1997). Although I knew this at the time, I decided the anachronism was justifiable in the interest of making Wundt more accessible to twentieth-century readers. I now consider this decision to have been misguided. The new title, as well as the corresponding changes in the text, reflects the terms that were central to Wundt's own treatment of the topics discussed here.

historically significant discourse in which Wundt was one participant among others. The wide range of his interests ensured that there were many, and it is hardly possible to understand his contributions without knowing something about the discursive currents of which these contributions formed a part. I have attempted such a contextualization of some of Wundt's views in the next section and also in the last section.

A second gap concerns the relationship between Wundt's program of experimental work and his broader theories about the nature of psychological processes. American textbook accounts of Wundt's reaction time experiments, in particular, tended to present them as essentially empirical exercises without much concern for the rich theoretical background to which they owed their significance. In the present chapter this issue is addressed in the section *The Apperception Concept and the Experimental Context*.

In works that pay some attention to Wundt the theorist, one can often notice a further, particularly striking, gap. In the more traditional psychological literature on Wundt there was a marked tendency to consider his contributions almost entirely in terms of problems of sensation and perception or, at most, in terms of general problems of cognition. That was a function of historians' biases and interests rather than any reflection of Wundt's own position. For Boring (1942), who constituted the most influential traditional source, the area of sensation and perception was of supreme interest; it was the one area that merited a major historical text on the same level as his more general *History of experimental psychology*. However, this special concern with sensation and perception was not merely an expression of the particular research interests of one individual. More significantly, the concentration of historical interest on this area made it possible to use historical studies to project an image of psychology as an experimental discipline whose more recent historical development could be construed to show the kind of cumulative linear progress that was accepted as the hallmark of the natural sciences (O'Donnell, 1979).

One consequence of this limited approach to the history of psychology was the relative neglect of a topic that was in fact the subject of considerable interest in the century preceding World War I: the explanation of human and animal movement and action. Although behaviorism changed the parameters of the discussion, it did not invent the topic which was one of profound importance for nineteenth-century psychology. The earlier part of the century had brought those physiological discoveries that firmly established the existence of a type of animal movement that depended only on identified sensorimotor arcs in the nervous system and did not involve the intervention of mind. This approach led to a sharp distinction between voluntary movement on the one hand and various types of involuntary movement on the other. The problems created by this stark dualism provided the instigation for much theoretical discussion and a considerable amount of laboratory work during the second half of the nineteenth century. In that historical context such issues were generally presented in terms of the topic of volition.

This is the period during which the concept of volition was increasingly discussed in naturalistic rather than moralistic terms. While ethical implications were still present, questions such as that of the relationship between voluntary and involuntary movement or that of the determinants of volitional processes were not in themselves ethical but psychological questions. Nineteenth-century psychologists often presented their attempts at explaining action, as distinct from passive responding, in terms of the concept of volition. This concept covered a great deal of what would later be discussed in terms of the psychology of drives and motives. As we will see, Wundt played a significant role in preparing for this change.

Wundt's Opposition to the Theories of Lotze and Bain

In order to understand the nature of Wundt's contribution to this field, it is necessary to examine its relationship to the work of his predecessors. When Wundt began to concern himself with the explanation of human and animal movement, he had to come to terms with the solutions to the problems that had been proposed in the 1850s by two highly influential scholars: Lotze and Bain. Within three years of each other, these philosopher-psychologists had published accounts of the genesis of purposive behavior, which, though they bore the distinguishing marks of different intellectual traditions, had important common features. To some extent, this convergence was due to the fact that they were both clearly indebted to the earlier work of the physiologist Johannes Müller, who had been the first to attempt a reconciliation between traditional doctrine of the will and early nineteenth-century discoveries on the neurophysiology of reflex action.

What was common to these mid-nineteenth-century attempts to explain human and animal movement was the split between two levels of functioning, the voluntary and the involuntary. The latter depended on physiological mechanisms that did not involve subjective deliberation and choice. Several types of such involuntary movement were recognized at this time. In addition to simple or combined reflex movement instigated by a sensory stimulus, there was the "expressive" movement produced by the internal excitation characterizing emotional arousal. Finally, there was the kind of involuntary movement for which the term *ideomotor activity* later became popular, that is to say, a movement produced automatically by the representation or idea of that movement, as in hypnotic states or in spontaneous imitation. By this time, therefore, there had emerged a systematic appreciation of a range of human behavior that did not involve the operation of the will. While there had been earlier speculation in this area, there was now solid and systematic evidence that seemed to demand an essentially physiological account of the generation of these various kinds of involuntary movement.

But this development created a hiatus between one part of human behavior that was involuntary and another part that still involved the operation of subjective purpose and choice, in the language of the time, the will. How was this gap to be bridged? Lotze and Bain both adopted a genetic perspective in response to this problem: involuntary movement must exist prior to voluntary movement, and the latter must be regarded as an acquisition, the product of a process of learning. This proved to be one of the most important basic propositions in the history of psychology. Bain's (1855, 1859) account of this learning process contained the germs of much more modern formulations. He held that some of the purposeless spontaneous movements would accidentally lead to feelings of pleasure and some others to feelings of pain. If this process occurred repeatedly, these feelings would become associated with the movements that led up to them, so that the idea of pleasure would in future tend to produce movements that were previously followed by the experience of pleasure. As feelings become associated with certain situations, the basis exists for the production of appropriate movements that have previously led to pleasurable results in a particular situation. This process is the origin of voluntary activity, according to Bain.

Lotze's (1852, pp. 287–324) account is somewhat different. There is a bidirectional link between actual movements and the mental representation of these movements, so that while movements produce their mental representations, the latter can also produce the movements themselves. There is a complex apparatus of involuntary movements reflexly coordinated with a variety of physical stimuli. As these involuntary movements occur, they are subjectively represented, thus informing the mind of the possibilities of movement open to it. The mind thus learns to produce movements voluntarily by evoking the appropriate movement representations. While the views of Bain and Lotze entail different embryonic theories of motor learning, they clearly share a common perspective on the relationship of involuntary and voluntary activity: the latter arises on the basis of the former as a result of some kind of learning process.

It was precisely this supposition that Wundt refused to accept— first of all, because it seemed to him to imply a metaphysical dualism he would rather avoid. If movements originally run off without the intervention of the mind and mental processes only come to intervene causally in this mechanism at a later stage, then one is back at a Cartesian conception of physical and mental causes. However subtly the mental agency is introduced, it remains a mystery how it is able to intervene effectively in what has up to this point been a purely physical process (Wundt, 1885). Second, the Lotze-Bain notion of voluntary activity as a learned acquisition seemed to Wundt to conflict with everyday observation of the learning process. When a person acquires a new skill, the process commonly observed is the reverse of that postulated by the view Wundt criticized. It is in the early stages of learning that the exercise of volition is at its height, only to subside when the skill has been learned and the acquired movements run off quite automatically. Wundt did not deny the existence of the opposite process, that is, the case where automatic movement patterns become integrated into complex voluntary movements; what he rejected was the exemplary or paradigmatic status of this case for the development of voluntary movement in general. The common case seemed to him to be rather the one where an initially voluntary activity becomes automatized as a result of practice (Wundt, 1883).

Wundt was able to make use of the much discussed experiments on the behavior of spinal frogs to strengthen the plausibility of his point of view. Pflüger (1853) had demonstrated that the behavior of such laboratory preparations showed peculiarly adapted characteristics. For example, the brainless frog makes wiping motions with its leg when the side of its body is stimulated with acid, but when the leg on the stimulated side is amputated, the frog apparently attempts to reach the spot with the opposite leg. Pflüger felt that such seemingly purposeful behavior required us to suppose that some form of mental activity must be involved even at the spinal level, which, according to the accepted view, involved nothing but simple reflex arcs linking specific stimulus areas with specific responses. Lotze (1853) took issue with Pflüger's interpretation from his own point of view, which was based on the unity and indivisibility of the mind. For Lotze, there could be no spinal mind, and the apparent purposefulness in some of the behavior of spinal laboratory animals must simply be taken as evidence that the purely physical machinery of reflexes was more complex than previously supposed. Pflüger's experiments only served to reinforce Lotze's dualistic model, which envisioned a mind that learned to control a complex apparatus of involuntary activity. Any remaining doubts about the existence of mental processes at the spinal level were probably dispelled by the later experiments of Goltz (1869), which showed how completely nonresponsive, and of course nonadaptive, the behavior of spinal frogs could be if the physical conditions did not activate the machinery of their reflexes. Such animals would, for example, sit quietly while the temperature was gradually raised to the point at which their death occurred.

The Pflüger-Lotze controversy was an important landmark in the history of nineteenth-century attempts to explain the difference between action and movement. It stimulated considerable research and discussion. Wundt grappled with its implications as early as his *Lectures on the human and animal mind* (1863, Lecture 57), though he had revised his position by the time the *Grundzüge der physiologischen Psychologie* appeared. He did not accept the relative adaptiveness of reflex behavior at the spinal level as evidence of mental activity, but he did see it as evidence of a process of automatization of originally voluntary activity that must have taken place in the course of evolution. The very inconsistency of the adaptiveness of the behavior of the spinal animal, totally nonadaptive under some conditions though strangely adaptive under others, pointed to a phylogenetically earlier stage, bits and pieces of whose adaptive acquisitions had passed into the inherited organization of later generations. In the words of the English translation of the second edition of the *Lectures*: "The purposive character of the reflexes becomes then readily intelligible, if we regard them as resulting from the voluntary action of previous generations" (Wundt, 1894a, p. 227). What Wundt contributes to this debate is a phylogenetic perspective clearly indebted to the idea of natural evolution.

On the level of individual development, the situation is somewhat complicated by the fact that individuals do have a range of inherited reflex reactions in their repertoire. But Wundt did not believe that these mechanisms played any significant role in the development of adapted voluntary behavior. As the latter is clearly a later accomplishment, the question arises of what its precursors might be in the development of the individual. Wundt excluded reflexes, and he also excluded Bain's notion of "spontaneous" vital activity as including nothing that is not better represented by the more precise terms *reflex* or *automatic movement*, the latter being the product of central physiological excitation. For Wundt, the primitive antecedent of complex voluntary action must have two characteristics that all these automatic mechanisms do not have: consciousness and direction. If these characteristics were not already present at the most primitive level of behavior, their appearance in the course of development became an unresolvable mystery that Wundt refused to accept.

From Impulse to Choice: The Development of Volitional Activity

The psychological tradition to which he was heir provided Wundt with an alternative concept of primitive forms of activity: the concept of impulse or drive. Drives, as conceived by Wundt and an older German psychological tradition, were a characteristic of human and animal organisms that simultaneously involved both mind and body, both direction and force. The German word is *Trieb*, which nowadays may be translated as "drive," a term that was introduced into English-language psychology in the twentieth century.[2] Wundt's contemporaries translated it as "impulse," so this usage is partly retained in the present discussion. However, it should be noted that the lack of an English equivalent for *Trieb* created problems for translators which they sometimes solved in ways that created traps for the unwary reader. How, for example, was the English-speaking reader to guess that the term *impulse*, to be found in Wundt's translated work, and the term *instinct*, to be found in Freud's translated work, were both versions of the identical German term, *Trieb*?

---

[2]However, it must be emphasised that *Trieb* and "drive" have very different psychological and historical connotations. "Drive" was introduced into English-language psychology by R. S. Woodworth in 1918. He was almost certainly unaware of the historical significance of *Trieb* and was inspired rather by mechanical models (see Woodworth, 1918; Young, 1936; Danziger, 1997).

This term had been used by Reimarus (1760) in the eighteenth century to refer to animal instinct, but it had also been given a metaphysical meaning by the philosopher Fichte (1817). By the middle of the nineteenth century, most of the German philosopher-psychologists used the term, and for some, it was the basis of psychology. For example, at the time that Wundt was beginning to interest himself in psychology, the use of *Trieb* as *the* basic explanatory category of psychology was being propagated by the now forgotten introspectionist, Karl Fortlage, whom Wundt later credited with "some fine comments," although he disapproved of his methods (Wundt, 1888). For Fortlage and others, the drive concept referred to a specific union of four components: a feeling of pleasure or unpleasure (*Unlust*, the same term that Freud used); a striving toward or away from some condition; a temporal relationship between a present negative and a future positive state; and specific movements that tend to eliminate the negative or to achieve the positive state (Fortlage, 1855, Vol. 1, p. 301). Drives form the elementary units underlying the life of the mind and of the body. They constitute a union of mental and physiological events at the most basic level. For Fortlage, the role of drives was all-pervasive; there were unconscious drives, and cognitive activity was seen as the product of drive inhibition.

Wundt (1879) did not accept these propositions, but he did agree on the fundamental status of affect and impulse. He combined this affirmation with a strong developmental perspective. In his view, drives provided the origin of a process of psychological development in the course of which differentiated psychological functions appeared. Thus, it was not reflexes that provided the foundation on which adapted voluntary action was based, but drives. At the time that Wundt developed his theory, Kussmaul's (1859) systematic studies of the behavior of neonates were well known. Wundt (1880) suggested that the neonatal responses described by Kussmaul were of three types: (1) "automatic movements," mostly of the limbs and the trunk, produced by central physiological excitation; (2) true reflexes produced by specific sensory stimulation, as in the startle reaction and in the movement of the eyes in response to light; and (3) "impulsive movements" (*Triebbewegungen*), which included sucking movements and the responses to sweet and sour tastes. The last differed from the first two in that the response was more than simply a reaction to antecedent conditions: it included an aspect of "striving," that is, a directional component expressing either the acceptance or the rejection of the stimulus by the organism. It was these impulsive movements that constituted the basis for the development of complex voluntary activity, because only they involved the crucial component of "volition."

The concept of volition was so central to Wundt's thought that he came to identify his psychological system as *voluntarism*. But, as already indicated in the previous chapter, his use of such terms was idiosyncratic. Volition, in Wundt's sense, did not necessarily involve an act of conscious choice or decision. In fact, he criticized Lotze for limiting the operation of the will to such cases. For Wundt, the act of choice constituted only a special case of "volitional activity"; it was a product of a psychological development in which volition first appeared in simpler forms. The primitive manifestation of what Wundt called will occurs in the form of drives. This is the basis on which the later forms of volition (i.e., choice and decision) develop. For a contemporary understanding of Wundt's psychology, it is useful to bear in mind that what he meant by *voluntarism* was not something that referred to the act of will in the narrow sense but something that had a great deal in common with what were later to be referred to as *dynamic approaches* to psychology. In other words, Wundt's psychology was one that emphasized the primacy of affective-motivational processes and regarded them as the indispensable foundation for the explanation of psychological events.[3]

Like most of his other theories, Wundt's views on volition were subject to periodic revision. However, once he had developed the independent position of his mature years, these revisions did not affect his fundamental views, and it is with these that we are concerned here. There is, however, a real structural difference between the revisions of his views during the period of intellectual gestation in his early years and the later revisions. In the early works, the main features of what was to become Wundt's characteristic approach are often only intuitively indicated, together with much intellectual baggage that was dropped subsequently. Gradually, the main outline of his views was stated more clearly and explicitly, and, after a certain point, the revisions affected only relatively specific aspects, leaving the framework largely intact. In the case of his theory of volitional activity, that point was clearly reached with the second edition of the *Grundzüge der physiologischen Psychologie* in 1880. In regard to this fundamental aspect of Wundt's thinking, the first edition of 1873–74 was still a transitional work, and many of the major changes that Wundt made in the second edition concern the topic of volition. These

---

[3]See the section on "Intellectualism" in the previous chapter.

changes also involved a completely new restatement of his fundamental
ideas on psychology in the concluding section of the work. After 1880, he
undertook no changes of comparable magnitude. Therefore, in order to
avoid unnecessary confusion, we will take the second and the very similar
third edition (1887) of the *Grundzüge* as the main basis for the following
exposition of his views. These were the editions that coincided with the
first flourishing of the program of experimental research on reaction times
that was stimulated by Wundt's theories of volitional activity, and they
were also the editions that his most important critics and commentators
generally referred to.[4]

Wundt regarded all drives as being affective in nature. This affect
imparts direction to the impulsive movement, manifesting itself either as
a striving against, or a striving for, some state of affairs. Subjectively, this
manifests itself in feelings of aversion or of desire produced by some insti-
gating condition. These feelings exist before there is any knowledge of
drive goals, that is, of the conditions that will satisfy the drive and alle-
viate the affect. Such knowledge, Wundt agreed, is the result of learning.
But the basis for this learning does not lie in the setting up of associations
between the two separate processes of movement on the one hand and
feelings of pleasure or pain on the other.[5] The original movements, being
impulsive movements, are already accompanied by an affective component. It is only later that feelings gain a temporary and limited independence from the motor component by a process of differentiation set in
motion by the inhibition of the movement component due to internal or
external factors.

As previously indicated, Wundt insisted that psychological categories, such as sensation, feeling, and volition, should never be confused
with the actual psychological process itself.[6] Such categories are intellectual abstractions whose referents exist, not as separate entities, but only
as components in a complex process of differentiation of an original unity

---

[4]The views which Wundt expounded in these volumes also formed the basis for the treatment of the relevant topics in the second edition of his *Lectures on human and animal
psychology* (1892, transl. 1894) which are available in English translation. This is a useful
source provided the following caveat expressed in the translators' preface is borne in mind:
"Its (i.e. the volume of *Lectures*) comparatively popular and introductory character will, it
is hoped, render it especially acceptable to those beginning the study of psychology,
to whom the technicalities of the author's *Grundzüge* would present very considerable
difficulties. . . ." (Wundt, 1894, iii).
[5]See the section on "The Mechanistic Temptation" in the previous chapter.
[6]See the section on "Intellectualism" in the previous chapter.

designated as *Trieb*, i.e. drive or impulse: "The course of both general [i.e., phylogenetic] and individual development shows that drives are the fundamental psychic phenomena from which all mental development originates" (Wundt, 1880, Vol. 2, p. 455). This is true also of the development of cognition:

> The psychic synthesis of sensations always involves the contributing fact of movement that is produced under the influence of sensory stimulation, originally as impulsive movement accompanying the sensation. The spatial and temporal order of ideas originates in this connection. The apperception of ideas is originally tied inseparably to movements corresponding to the ideas. Only gradually internal separates from external volitional activity through the temporary inhibition of the external component of impulsive activity, so that apperception remains as an activity that has become independent. Thus psychological development is essentially based on the separation of the initially joined parts of an impulsive activity. Once separated, these components experience independent development, and when they are once again linked with movements, new, more complex forms of impulse emerge out of them. (Wundt, 1880, Vol. 2, p. 456)

Originally, then, sensation, affect, and movement are linked in an undifferentiated complex. When the movement component is inhibited (because physical or physiological conditions prevent its execution or, more generally, because incompatible movement tendencies are aroused), the sensory and affective components continue on their own and gain a degree of independence. This development provides the basis for the formation of new connections among the three components. Links between movement images and the actual movements that correspond to them were also not primitive but could arise only when these components had emerged out of a less differentiated stage. Such developmental processes resulted in a gradual transition from a state of affairs where a given set of stimulus conditions inevitably produces a particular kind of impulsive action, to one where it arouses a multiplicity of response tendencies. Wundt referred to this as the transition from simply determined to multiply determined volitional activity.

A final aspect of this development involves the association of movements with their external effects insofar as the effects become cognitively represented. This is a later development because at the level of pure impulsive movements, there is no anticipation of results. The simultaneous cognitive availability of a multiplicity of movement and effect images makes possible the characteristic feature of fully formed voluntary activity, the act of choice. While the intensity of the affective component would usually be reduced in the course of the development of volitional activity, that component never disappears. There was no such thing as a purely rational choice in Wundt's system.

It should perhaps be emphasized that the act of choice was, for Wundt, a link in a network of causal determination and did not imply a freedom of the will in any absolute sense. Voluntary activity was always determined by psychological causes. Wundt did not believe that the will operated by fiat, though the network of determinants in which the act of volition was embedded was one of psychological rather than physical causes. While all volition depended on "the supply of innervation energy available in our nervous system" (Wundt, 1887, p. 483), the specific course of volition was a matter of a "psychic causality" in which the general dispositions developed in the course of the individual's life played a major role.

The development of voluntary action out of an original level of undifferentiated drive activity represents only one side of Wundt's treatment of the psychology of action and movement. In the discussion of his objections to the older theories of Bain and Lotze, it was mentioned that Wundt not only rejected the idea that reflexes or automatic movements generally formed the basis for the development of voluntary action, but that, on the contrary, he also maintained that such automatic behavior mechanisms were in fact the product of changes in activities that had started off by being volitional in nature. In the case of the innate reflexes, he regarded this process of change as having taken place in the course of phylogenetic development. But he applied the same analysis to the development of acquired automatic reactions in the course of individual development. The effect of repeated practice on a voluntary action is first to make it return to the level of a simply determined volitional activity; that is to say, a specific set of response tendencies comes to predominate, thus eliminating the element of choice. The process is therefore the reverse of that involved in the genesis of voluntary action.

But the process of automatization can go further and result in the formation of completely automatized habits, a development that may also occur when the starting point is not voluntary action but simple drive activity. The essential condition for this process of automatization is always the repeated exercise of the motor activity, and its explanation is entirely physiological; the repeated passage of a nerve impulse through particular pathways results in a relative lowering of thresholds, thus increasing the facility with which the impulse travels these pathways in the future (Wundt, 1880, Vol. 1, p. 269).

It is clear from all this that Wundt emerged with a theory of volitional change that provides for a duality of processes that move in opposite directions.[7] The one process results in simplification and automatization, the other in greater complexity and autonomy. The one is a process of training and habit formation, the other a process of psychological development.[8]

Wundt's theories in this area diverged critically from the conception of human activity that had emerged in Britain around the middle of the nineteenth century, the main contributors being Bain, Spencer, and Carpenter. In Wundt's view, their approach was characterized by too heavy reliance on two principles: the principle of training or habit formation and the principle of utility. Neither of these found favor with Wundt, and insofar as Darwin (1872/1965) employed these same concepts—for instance, in his notion of "serviceable associated habits"—he, too, became the target of Wundt's criticism. As far as the concept of habit training was concerned, Wundt objected that it represented a preoccupation with external conditions while neglecting internal psychological conditions. In any case, we have seen that for Wundt, development was a matter of the differentiation, or else the simplification, of complexes rather than the combination of originally separate entities.

The questions raised by the principle of utility were even more far-reaching. According to the utilitarian school, behavior changes as a result of a selection process which favors activities that have been useful to the individual; such activities may then continue to be reproduced by force of association even when their original usefulness is over. Wundt (1900, Vol. 1, p. 68ff.) objected first of all to the tendency to apply this principle universally, suggesting rather that there are large areas of activity where it is simply irrelevant. Second, he criticized the tendency of proponents of the utility principle to substitute their own perspective for that of the individual (or the organism or the culture) under study. The effects that were supposed to determine changes in activity were generally the effects that were clear to the outside observer, but this did not

[7]See the illustrative diagrams in *Grundzüge der physiologischen Psychologie* (1903, vol. 3, p. 312) and *Völkerpsychologie* (1900, vol. 1, p. 34).

[8]A third process appears to be involved in the development of so-called expressive movements which are first evoked by relatively simple sensory stimuli and later come to be evoked by complex situations and ideas. Here Wundt's explanation becomes associationistic: Any conditions that arouse an affective response similar to the original one will also tend to arouse the movement that is tied to it. He (Wundt, 1900, Vol. 1, p. 112) referred to this phenomenon as the "association of analogous feeling."

mean that they functioned as motives for the individuals involved in the change.

Third, Wundt saw in the utility theory a major example of what he referred to as "intellectualism," a type of psychological theorizing that never failed to evoke his disapproval. As outlined in the previous chapter, "intellectualism" involved the tendency to explain mental life in terms of essentially cognitive processes, like the association of ideas, while neglecting the special character and underemphasizing the role of the affective and dynamic (volitional) processes that Wundt regarded as basic. More specifically, the utility theorists tended to explain adaptive conduct in terms of individuals' intellectual anticipation of the effects of their actions. Wundt, on the other hand, regarded actions that fitted this model as a relatively advanced product of a psychological development that depended essentially on the vagaries of affectively charged drives. While the utility theorists tended to equate motives with intellectually perceived ends, Wundt distinguished sharply between motives, which were the actual determinants of action, and anticipated effects, which might or might not become motives, depending on the affective situation.

In his later writings, Wundt increasingly conceptualized the individual-environment relationship in terms of his principle of the *heterogony of ends* (Wundt, 1903, Vol. 3, p. 787). This principle expressed, first, the fact that individual goals change as a result of action on the environment. Second, it attributed this change to the fact that the individual's actions on the environment generally have unintended consequences. Insofar as the effects produced differ from the effects intended, the latter would become modified. New goals would arise because of the unintended side effects of voluntary movements. Vague though it is, this principle is of interest for two reasons. First, it shows that Wundt regarded change at the level of voluntary action as essentially a matter of what would later be called motivational learning. Second, it illustrates Wundt's belief that at this level it was not success that provided the essential condition for learning but the absence of success. What he presented was an incipient theory of behavior change that differed rather fundamentally from the selection-by-utility model of the mid-nineteenth-century British psychologists.

The total pattern of Wundt's various discussions of the psychology of action and movement is clearly such as to exclude the concept of *behavior* in the abstract and hence to exclude the possibility of general laws of behavior change. Wundt's theories in this area presuppose the existence of various types of movement that differ not only in complexity but also in kind. The principles involved in the modification of movements vary with the nature of the movement. But the different categories of movement also develop out of each other, so that the theory also has to be concerned with the principles involved in these developments. In the course of replying to criticism, Wundt (1883) referred to his theory of volitional action as a "genetic" theory.[9] Compared with most other theories of the time it certainly was that. The reason that it did not do much to advance "genetic" perspectives in psychology was that the empirical methods that Wundt advocated—at least, on the level of individual psychology—were totally unsuitable for throwing light on developmental hypotheses. Nevertheless, there were aspects of his theories that were relevant in an experimental context, and it is these that will be considered next.

The Apperception Concept and the Experimental Context

Apart from his more general developmental theories, Wundt also developed a more specific model of the psychological processes involved in the production of overt action patterns. His explanation was mentalistic in the sense that the operation of dynamic-volitional processes was described in categories that were taken from mental life rather than from biology or from some psychophysically neutral language that did not exist in his time. Thus, he described the functioning of the dynamic principle in human behavior in terms of the concept of *apperception*, which involves the focalization of some content in consciousness.[10] Wundt's model of mental functioning is that of a field in which there is always a polarity between the central part (the *Blickpunkt*) and the periphery (the *Blickfeld*), that is, between the focal point and the rest of the field. This polarization is the product of the apperceptive process, which is a fundamental active principle that is responsible for the fact that all experience is structured. Apperception, however, was for Wundt a manifestation of volition. It was the dynamic principle that gave direction and structure both to experience and to movement.

Apperception was a central process that operated in two directions. On the one hand, it operated on sensory content producing the complex

[9]Wundt and his translators employed "genetic" in the sense of "developmental."
[10]By the time Wundt appropriated it, the apperception concept had already had a long history (see Baldwin, 1901, vol. 1, p. 61; Boring, 1950; Danziger, 1987).

forms of perception and ultimately of ideation. This aspect of apperception is relatively well known. But for Wundt, this was only half the story.
Apperception also operated on the motor apparatus. Just as the contents
of the cognitive field were structured in terms of focus and periphery, so
the field of skeletal movements involved some that were apperceived and
others that were peripheral at any particular time. Just as the apperception of perceptual content imposed form and direction on perceived
figures, so the apperception of movements of the individual's own body
imposed the selective inhibition of motor centers (see the diagram in
Wundt, 1904, p. 318). In Wundt's terms, an apperceived movement constituted a volitional action. In this case, he spoke of an "external" form of
volitional activity, as contrasted with the "internal" form in which some
ideational content is apperceived. In either case, apperception operates as
a patterning principle.

In the third edition of the *Grundzüge der physiologischen Psychologie*,
Wundt (1887, Vol. 2, pp. 263, 472) introduced an important distinction
between what he called "impulsive apperception" and "reproductive
apperception." The former involves the motor direction of the apperception process, the latter a cognitive direction. In impulsive apperception,
the central dynamic process affects the motor apparatus directly, so that
the apperceived movement is actually carried out. In the course of the
developmental process previously described, movement images are eventually formed by the differentiation and recombination of movement
sensations. Subsequently, these movement images may be recalled in a
process of reproductive apperception, where it is the idea of the movement rather than the movement itself that moves into focus. Thus, unlike
impulsive apperception, reproductive apperception does not involve the
actual carrying out of the movement but only the memory of the movement. In applying this distinction to the scheme of development, it is clear
that the most primitive level of activity involves impulsive apperception,
where the central excitation discharges directly into certain patterns of
motor activity. This is what happens in what Wundt called "impulsive
movements" (*Triebbewegungen*), as in the sucking of the infant. But such
motor activity leads necessarily to the formation of motor images (no
matter how rudimentary) which can then be recalled by reproductive
apperception. This process makes possible the cognitive fusion, analysis,
and recombination of motor images and creates new movement possibilities, which in turn may become the focus of impulsive apperception.
Wundt thought that the simultaneous arousal of two or more motor

patterns played an important role in the cognitive elaboration of move-ments leading to the development of increasingly complex patterns.

Unlike others who theorized about the genesis of voluntary action at this time, Wundt applied certain aspects of his theory in an experimental context. In doing so, he initiated a development whose consequences went far beyond anything he had foreseen or intended. Wundt found the experimental vehicle for demonstrating certain implications of his theory in the reaction time studies that had been conducted in the 1860s and 1870s by Donders, Hirsch, Exner, and von Kries. What Wundt added to these studies was not so much a matter of technical innovation as a matter of theoretical perspective. The earlier studies had been conducted from a physiological perspective and published in physiological journals. By putting the reaction time experiment in the context of a theory of apper-ception as volition in action, Wundt transformed it into an experiment that was conducted in order to throw light on issues that were primarily psychological and not physiological. The reaction time studies conducted during the first few years of Wundt's laboratory constitute a unique early example of a coherent research program, explicitly directed toward psy-chological issues and involving a number of interlocking studies (Cattell, 1886; Friedrich, 1883, 1885; L. Lange, 1888; N. Lange, 1888; Merkel, 1885; Tischer, 1883; von Tschisch, 1885). Wundt's apperception concept pro-vided a theoretical framework that transformed what would other-wise have been a collection of isolated studies into a coherent program that demonstrated the practical possibility of systematic psychological research.

One of the first examples of the experimental implications of Wundt's theoretical schema was provided by the distinction between sensory and muscular reaction times. As indicated above, Wundt's theory involved a bidirectional operation of apperception, either on sensory content or on the motor apparatus. He also saw in voluntary attention a means of manipulating the apperceptive process experimentally. Thus, by instruct-ing the subject to concentrate either on the stimulus or on the response, the two directions of apperception could be differentially strengthened. The expectation was that reaction times would be longer in the former case than in the latter because the apperception of the movement would have to be interpolated before an actual movement could take place. This theory provided an explanation for the laboratory findings of some of Wundt's students that sensory reaction times were longer than muscular ones (L. Lange, 1888).

When one compares successive formulations of Wundt's theories of volitional activity after 1880, it becomes apparent that his conceptualization was subject to considerable modification and sharpening in the light of experimental results. His earlier formulations provided a general impetus and direction for the experimental work rather than a set of specific hypotheses. Later on, Wundt conceived the idea of using the two kinds of reaction time as a way of studying experimentally some of the characteristics of the two directions of psychological change that he had distinguished theoretically. In his view, the muscular type of reaction offered opportunities for studying the automatization process, while the sensory type made it possible to study the development of multiply determined voluntary actions out of simple ones (Wundt, 1897, p. 199ff.). For instance, when the muscular reaction was subjected to conditions of prolonged practice with constant interstimulus intervals, the response latency could be reduced to zero or the reaction would even occur before the presentation of the stimulus or in response to an extraneous stimulus. These observations were taken as evidence of the automatization process. On the other side, variations in experimental conditions were used to complicate the cognitive task in the sensory type of reaction, requiring the subject to discriminate between stimuli, choose among alternative movements, and so on. For Wundt, this was a way of studying some of the factors involved in the transition from the simple to the complex type of voluntary activity, i.e., the process that was opposite to automatization.

By the time the Leipzig laboratory was in its second decade, the accumulation of experimental data and a changing climate of opinion produced a gradual eclipse of Wundt's theoretical formulations (Danziger, 1990). But this eclipse should not lead us to underestimate their historical importance. It was Wundt's theory of volitional activity that provided the set of specifically psychological issues that transformed some rather pedestrian physiological studies into a research program with extraordinary implications. Employing the much abused term *paradigm* in the rather specific sense of "exemplar," one might say that the linking of the reaction time experiment with the apperception concept provided psychology with an early experimental paradigm of its own. In Wundt's own estimation, this had been a productive link:

> Just as the introduction of the experimental method is the most obvious external criterion which distinguishes the new from the old psychology, so it might be said that, for the views which have emerged under the influence of this

method, the concept of the will has become the central problem toward which
all the other main problems of psychology are eventually oriented. (Wundt,
1906, p. 342)

Some Early Reactions to Wundt's Theories

Initial reactions to Wundt's theory of "volitional activity," were
mixed. Philosophers of the old school did not like it, but among those who
were interested in a naturalistic approach to psychology, there was a more
positive response. Julius Baumann (1881) wrote an extremely long-
winded philosophical critique of Wundt's ideas in this area, to which
Wundt replied in his own journal, the *Philosophische Studien* (Wundt,
1883), to be followed by further comments on Baumann's part (Baumann,
1883). Apart from taking Wundt to task for his idiosyncratic use of the
term volition, which was justified, Baumann objected to Wundt's "Dar-
winistic" way of treating the human will as part of a natural order that
embraced reflex, impulsive, and voluntary action in a single continuum
of development. Baumann took his stand on the philosophical tradition
from Kant to Lotze, according to which human volition stood above
nature. Wundt counterattacked by charging that metaphysical theories
about *the* will as an independent entity were simply based on a reification
of abstractions derived from a particular analysis of our behavior. His
theory, Wundt explained, was meant to do justice to two basic sets of
observations: that consciousness is always active and not merely a passive
mechanism of registration, and that consciousness is always associated
with movements in the physical world.

Wundt fared much better at the hands of G. H. Schneider, a follower
of Haeckel and an ardent champion of Darwinian naturalism. Schneider
(1879, 1880) had been a pioneer of comparative psychology in Germany
and subsequently (1882) attempted to show that human voluntary activity could be explained as an adaptive development, without recourse to
metaphysical concepts of will. In this attempt, he made considerable use
of Wundt's formulations regarding the role of apperception and the developmental interrelationship of impulsive, reflexive, and voluntary activity.
His disagreement with Wundt on one point is of some interest. Wundt
had expressed the belief that "internal" apperception (i.e., the focalization
of some psychic content) was primary and that "external" (i.e., motor)
apperception was secondary. Schneider (1882, p. 308ff.) argued very

convincingly that, biologically, this relationship must be reversed, a motor direction of the central psychophysical apperceptive process being primary. Several years later, Wundt (1897, pp. 183–184) seems to have reversed his position on this point. But at other times, he seems to have suggested that neither internal nor external volitional action may claim priority. Here, his notorious slipperiness becomes apparent. The philosopher Wundt and the scientist Wundt did not always speak with the same voice.

However, during the 1880s, it was Wundt the scientist who was at the height of his influence. His account of the interrelationships among the various types of movements carried all the more weight as the Leipzig reaction time experiments opened up prospects for the empirical investigation of issues that had hitherto been reserved solely for speculative treatment. The new style of psychological textbook usually took its cue from Wundt's *Physiological Psychology* in its relatively naturalistic treatment of the topic of volition. One finds echoes of Wundt's theory in the work of Sully (1884) in England and to a lesser extent of Ladd (1887) in the United States.

But the reaction was not long in coming. In 1888, a young German scholar by the name of Hugo Münsterberg entered the psychological scene with a monograph on volitional activity that was explicitly at variance with Wundt's view. The core of Münsterberg's position was the doctrine of sensationalism, the principle that all contents of consciousness were reducible to sensation. Ideas were complexes of sensations and feelings were qualities of sensation. This was simply a way of expressing a model of the mind as essentially a registering mechanism. There was no room here for the impulsive-affective aspect of mind that played so large a role in Wundt's theory. Another aspect of sensationalism that brought it into sharp conflict with Wundtian psychology was its emphasis on the peripheral rather than the central origin of psychological processes. From Münsterberg's point of view, all movement was ultimately reflex movement. In the course of individual development, these movements became adapted to securing beneficial effects for the organism, but this was a purely physiological process that did not involve any causal role for so-called impulsive or apperceptive mental processes. The mental aspect of movement was simply the sensation or idea of movement: the mind registered, but it did not activate.

Münsterberg's position was unusual among German academics. Philosophically, he partly returned to the fold by a peculiar dualism that had room for a world of "eternal values," but in practice, this stance made no difference whatever to his psychology. In the course of his subsequent North American career, Münsterberg's ideas on the explanation of human and animal movement fell on fertile soil. But for Wundt, Münsterberg's theories came to function as a kind of "antipole," the opposition to which helped to define and clarify the essential features of his own position. The monographs of the 1890s (Wundt, 1891, 1894b) in which he reverted to issues in this area, as well as the later editions of the *Physiological Psychology*, were extremely critical of the position adopted by Münsterberg and reaffirmed the primacy of central impulsive processes.

The young Münsterberg had found a powerful patron in the person of William James, who arranged for him to direct the Harvard Psychological Laboratory. Given James's intense irritation with Wundt and his style (James, 1894), Münsterberg's disagreements with the oracle of Leipzig certainly did not hurt his chances. But for us, the differences of substance that divided Wundt and James are more instructive than the incompatibility of their intellectual styles. One source of their differences probably lies in the incompatibility of James's commitment to a form of the doctrine of the freedom of the will and Wundt's determinism.

For Wundt, and those influenced by him, central impulsive-affective processes formed a sufficient and entirely natural basis for the development of voluntary action. For James, the natural component of these processes was defined in terms of sensory feedback from the organic changes of emotion or from the kinesthetic stimulation produced by movement of the skeletal musculature. While sensations could reflexly produce movement, they could not choose among themselves. For choice, an additional mental function, the will, was necessary: "Will is a relation between the mind and its ideas" (James, 1890, Vol. 2, p. 559). For Wundt, on the other hand, will was a psychophysical process already involved in an affective-motor discharge; it was not something added at the level of choice among *ideas* of action, the latter being seen as a product of psychological development. Wundt tried to argue for a continuity of psychological processes from impulsive motor discharge to voluntary selection among ideas; James tried to argue for discontinuity.

It is this fundamental divergence that makes their well-known difference about "feelings of innervation" intelligible. This was the question of whether what James called "the mental determination of a voluntary act" involved not only a kinesthetic memory image of the act but also an awareness of outgoing motor impulses. When one examines their respective comments on the matter, it becomes very obvious that this issue was far more important to James than it was to Wundt. There is a striking discrepancy between James's lengthy and passionate discussion of the matter and Wundt's relatively brief and rather noncommittal comments (James, 1890, Vol. 2, pp. 492–521; Wundt, 1880, Vol. 1, pp. 372–378). What is even more significant for an understanding of the underlying issues is the fact that while for James, this was a key problem in the psychology of *volition*, Wundt treated it solely as a problem in the psychology of *sensation* (with implications for perception) and did not discuss it in the context of volition. While in the context of the special problem of muscular sensation Wundt was for a long time prepared to recognize the existence of feelings of motor innervation *in addition* to kinesthetic sensation, this recognition had no bearing on his theory of volition because the latter was for him a question of *impulse* and not of sensation at all. His theory was that all volitional activity had its basis in a central psychophysical process that manifested itself subjectively as feeling and objectively as movement. The nature of the experienced feeling would vary with the type of volitional activity. For example, the so-called feeling of activity (*Tätigkeitsgefühl*) was characteristic of the highest level of volitional activity, namely, voluntary activity, and simpler forms of volitional activity involved cruder affective components. All these affective processes involved central neurophysiological changes, but whether the outgoing motor impulse was part of these was a highly specific question that seemed to Wundt to be devoid of theoretical implications for his general position (Wundt, 1891).

What separated Wundt and James was the more general question of whether "volitional" processes were present in all directed motor activity, as Wundt held, or whether they operated only on the level of a mental choice among ideas, as James maintained. In order to support the latter position, James had to show that the mental side of movement consisted only of sensations or ideas of movement, for in the last analysis, the existence of an affective motor consciousness would have made voluntary choice a matter of conflict among competing impulses. Now, while the notion of a free choice among ideas was plausible, the notion of a free choice among affects was not. If the will was to be free and moreover open to ethical considerations, it had to be conceived of as operating on the level of ideas rather than of affects. Far from being merely a philosophical squabble about words, this difference between James and Wundt entailed diverging implication for any empirical research program in the area of volitional activity. The Jamesian model suggested that research efforts ought to concentrate on investigating the genesis of those sensori-motor mechanisms that provided the foundation on which the will performed its work. The Wundtian model, on the other hand, encouraged research on the affective aspects of volitional activity, a trend begun by Wundt in the 1890s and continued after his death by the so-called second Leipzig school.

While certain general features of Wundt's and James's explanations of human behavior continued to exert their influence on the development of psychology, the specifics of both their theories quickly fell victim to the powerful wave of positivism that swept over experimental psychology in the early years of the twentieth century (Danziger, 1979). However, in both cases, there were also internal reasons that would work against these theories in a research context. In Wundt's case, vagueness and inconsistency on crucial points often offended his critics. Nevertheless, his theories were fruitful enough over a considerable period, and it is by no means obvious that they were any more vague or any less consistent than many of their replacements in the first half of the twentieth century.

But Wundt did create some rather substantial difficulties for himself. Not the least among these arose out of his insistence that those affective processes that played such a key role in his explanation of volitional activity had to be *conscious* processes.[11] This meant that he was never prepared to consider the role that latent affective dispositions might play in behavior. The difficulty was compounded by his rigid views about the nature and scope of psychological experimentation (Danziger, 1990). As valid experimentation depended for him on the strictest objective control and/or monitoring of mental processes, the largest area of voluntary behavior was considered forever beyond the reach of laboratory methods (Wundt, 1907). In effect, Wundt painted himself into a corner. On the one hand, he proclaimed that the key to the explanation of purposive behavior lay in the processes of impulse and affect. But only the conscious aspects of these processes had psychological reality, and these were precisely the aspects that largely resisted experimental investigation. Wundt's only way out was to say that the problem could not be solved on the level of individual psychology but required a new approach altogether, that of *Völkerpsychologie*, or the psychological study of cultural products.

---

[11]This insistence was characteristic of the Leipzig Wundt. Earlier on, he had held different views (see Richards, 1980).

However, the cultural studies that increasingly preoccupied Wundt in his later years had only limited relevance for the exploration of the dynamic causes of individual activity and development. The unsolved problem that Wundt had bequeathed to later generations of psychologists could be confronted only by penetrating the frontiers that Wundt had attempted to set up for psychological method and theory. Nevertheless, his own work involved directions that pointed beyond those frontiers and sowed seeds that were sometimes fruitful in unexpected ways.

References

Bain, A. (1855). *The senses and the intellect*. London: Longmans, Green.

Bain, A. (1859). *The emotions and the will*. London: Longmans, Green.

Baldwin, J. M. (Ed.) (1901). *Dictionary of philosophy and psychology*. New York: Macmillan.

Baumann, J. (1881). Wundt's Lehre vom Willen und sein animistischer Monismus. *Philosophische Monatshefte, 17*, 558–602.

Baumann, J. (1883). Nochmals Wundt's Lehre vom Willen. *Philosophische Monatshefte, 19*, 354–374.

Boring, E. G. (1942). *Sensation and perception in the history of experimental psychology*. New York: Appleton-Century-Crofts, 1942.

Boring, E. G. (1950). *A history of experimental psychology* (2nd ed.). New York: Appleton-Century-Crofts.

Cattell, J. M. (1886). Psychometrische Untersuchungen. *Philosophische Studien, 3*, 305–336, 452–492.

Danziger, K. (1979). The positivist repudiation of Wundt. *Journal of the History of the Behavioral Sciences, 15*, 205–230.

Danziger, K. (1987). Apperception. In R. L. Gregory (Ed.), *The Oxford companion to the mind*. Oxford: Oxford University Press, 1987.

Danziger, K. (1990). *Constructing the subject: Historical origins of psychological research*. New York: Cambridge University Press.

Danziger, K. (1997). *Naming the mind: How psychology found its language*. London: Sage.

Darwin, C. (1872/1965) *The expression of the emotions in man and animals*. Chicago: University of Chicago Press, 1965.

Fichte, J. G. (1817). *Die Thatsachen des Bewusstseyns*. Stuttgart: Cotta.

Fortlage, K. (1855). *System der Psychologie*. Leipzig: Brockhaus.

Friedrich, M. (1883). Über die Apperceptionsdauer bei einfachen und zusammengesetzten Vorstellungen. *Philosophische Studien, 1*, 39–77.

Friedrich, M. (1885). Zur Methodik der Apperceptionsversuche. *Philosophische Studien, 2*, 66–72.

Goltz, F. L. (1869). *Beiträge zur Lehre von den Functionen der Nervencentren des Frosches*. Berlin: A. Hirschwald.

James, W. (1890). *The principles of psychology*. New York: Holt.

James, W. (1894). Professor Wundt and feelings of innervation. *Psychological Review, 1*, 70–73.

Külpe, O. (1888–1889). Die Lehre vom Willen in der neueren Psychologie. *Philosophische Studien, 5*, 179–244, 381–446.

Kussmaul, A. (1859). *Untersuchungen über das Seelenleben des neugeborenen Menschen.* Leipzig: Winter.

Ladd, G. T. (1887). *Elements of physiological psychology.* New York: Scribner.

Lange, L. (1888). Neue Experimente über den Vorgang der einfachen Reaction auf Sinneseindrücke. *Philosophische Studien, 4,* 479–510.

Lange, N. (1888). Beiträge zur Theorie der sinnlichen Aufmerksamkeit und der activen Apperception. *Philosophische Studien, 4,* 390–422.

Lotze, R. H. (1852). *Medicinische Psychologie oder Physiologie der Seele.* Leipzig: Widmann.

Lotze, R. H. (1853). Pflüger's Die sensoriellen Functionen etc. *Göttinger gelehrte Anzeigen, 3,* 1737–1776.

Merkel, J. (1883). Die zeitlichen Verhältnisse der Willenstätigkeit. *Philosophische Studien, 2,* 73–127.

Münsterberg, H. (1888). *Die Willenshandlung, ein Beitrag zur physiologischen Psychologie.* Freiburg: Mohr.

O'Donnell, J. M. (1979). The crisis of experimentalism in the 1920's. *American Psychologist, 34,* 289–295.

Pflüger, E. (1853). *Die sensorischen Functionen des Rückenmarks der Wirbelthiere nebst einer neuen Lehre über die Leitungsgesetze der Reflexionen.* Berlin: Hirschwald, 1853.

Reimarus, H. S. (1760). *Allgemeine Betrachtungen über die Triebe der Thiere, hauptsächlich über ihre Kunsttriebe.* Hamburg: Bohn.

Richards, R. J. (1980). Wundt's early theories of unconscious inference and cognitive evolution in their relation to Darwinian biopsychology. In W. G. Bringmann & R. D. Tweney (Eds.) *Wundt studies* (pp. 42–70) Toronto: Hogrefe.

Schneider, G. H. (1879). Zur Entwicklung der Willensäußerungen im Thierreiche. *Vierteljahrsschrift für wissenschaftliche Philosophie, 3,* 176–205, 294–306.

Schneider, G. H. (1880). *Der thierische Wille.* Leipzig: Abel, 1880.

Schneider, G. H. (1882). *Der menschliche Wille.* Berlin: Dümmler, 1882.

Sully, J. (1884). *Outlines of Psychology.* London: Longmans, Green, 1884.

Tischer, E. (1883). Über die Unterscheidung von Schallstärken. *Philosophische Studien, 1,* 495–542.

von Tschisch, W. (1885). Über die Zeitverhältnisse der Apperception einfacher und zusammengesetzter Vorstellungen untersucht mit Hülfe der Complicationsmethode. *Philosophische Studien, 2,* 603–634.

Woodworth, R. S. (1918). *Dynamic psychology.* New York: Columbia University Press.

Wundt, W. (1863). *Vorlesungen über die Menschen- und Thierseele.* Leipzig: Voss.

Wundt, W. (1879). Über das Verhältnis der Gefühle zu den Vorstellungen. *Vierteljahrsschrift für wissenschaftliche Philosophie, 3,* 129–151.

Wundt, W. (1880). *Grundzüge der physiologische Psychologie* (2nd ed.). Leipzig: Engelmann.

Wundt, W. (1883). Die Entwicklung vom Willen. *Philosophische Studien, 1,* 337–378.

Wundt, W. (1885). Zur Lehre vom Willen. In *Essays.* Leipzig: Engelmann.

Wundt, W. (1887). *Grundzüge der physiologischen Psychologie* (3rd ed.). Leipzig: Engelmann.

Wundt, W. (1888). Selbstbeobachtung und innere Wahrnehmung. *Philosophische Studien, 4,* 292–309.

Wundt, W. (1891). Zur Lehre von den Gemüthsbewegungen. *Philosophische Studien, 6,* 335–393.

Wundt, W. (1894a). *Lectures on human and animal psychology* (2nd ed.) (Trans. Creighton and Titchener). New York: Macmillan.

Wundt, W. (1894b). Über psychische Kausalität und das Princip des psychophysischen Parallelismus. *Philosophische Studien, 10,* 1–124.

Wundt, W. (1897). *Outlines of psychology* (Trans. C. H. Judd). Leipzig: Engelmann.

Wundt, W. (1900). *Völkerpsychologie*, Vol. 1. Leipzig: Engelmann.

Wundt, W. (1903). *Grundzüge der physiologischen Psychologie* (5th ed.). Leipzig: Engelmann.

Wundt, W. (1904). *Principles of physiological psychology* (Trans. E. B. Titchener, Part 1 of 5th German ed.). New York: Macmillan.

Wundt, W. (1906). Die Entwicklung des Willens. In *Essays* (2nd ed.). Leipzig: Engelmann.

Wundt, W. (1907). Über Ausfrageexperimente und über die Methoden zur Psychologie des Denkens. *Philosophische Studien, 3*, 301–360.

Young, P. T. (1936). *Motivation of behavior: The fundamental determinants of human and animal activity*. New York: Wiley.

4

A WUNDT PRIMER
THE OPERATING CHARACTERISTICS OF CONSCIOUSNESS

Arthur L. Blumenthal

Presentations of Wundt

It was a well-known title in its day: *Grundzüge der physiologischen Psychologie.* When it first took shape in 1873, tentative yet bold, it ignited a theme that had been ready and waiting for someone who could bring it off. Spirited reviews appeared in journals everywhere. Students flocked to study with its author. That early rush to join in the book's pronouncements and promises should continue to arouse our curiosity, even today. But subsequent collisions of ideologies and clashes of cultures were, inevitably, to consign the old book to the less frequented corners of library shelves. Lost from view now, as well, is the old German parochialism of the title's adjective *physiologische* in its 1870s local German usage. That adjective once referred to a methodology rather than a program of reducing psychological processes to physiological mechanisms. The methodology so implied was *laboratory experimentation*, newly successful and lauded in German physiology laboratories.[1] *Grundzüge*, when translated literally, means "main features" or "characteristics." After sorting out the title's meaning as

---

[1] See the 1894 edition of the *Grundzüge*, Vol. 1, p. 9. Here Wundt explains that this old-fashioned usage of *physiologische* to mean "experimental" had, by 1894, gone out of style and therefore might cause some misinterpretation of his basic system of thought as being a physicalistic or neurologically oriented form of psychology—quite different from his intentions. But Wundt noted that his book had attained a strong identity with its old title and therefore he should not change it. In the following century, that title did confuse, as Wundt had feared, many a psychology historian in the English-speaking world.

Figure 1. Wilhelm Wundt circa 1870

a treatise on experimentation, we find, however, that the book is weighted with theory and philosophy, even to the point of overshadowing its depictions of "characteristics of experimental psychology."

Yet that old title, if not the contents that lie behind it, is still ceremoniously trotted out and celebrated in today's historical treatments of modern psychology. Ostensibly, this fame can be attributed to its history-making announcement of the founding of a new science. A century later, student readers of this field would scarcely realize that the author of the 1873 *Grundzüge* literally meant a NEW science—or that it was to be the addition of another level of phenomena in the series *physics, chemistry, biology*, that next level being mental processes, or *psychology*. Nor would they read of the details in that enterprising proposal. Instead, they received descriptions of the number of pages and words that the old

Grundzüge contained, the revisions it went through, the time taken to write it, the author's capacity for work, the attempts to translate it, the famous students who studied it, and similar historical "data." Surely, the overweening presentation of superficial information shows that pagecounting historians were not studying the seminal work of Wilhelm Wundt, founder of the first formally recognized psychology research center which remained active until bombed out of existence in the heart of Leipzig in the winter of 1943.

The reasons for the neglect are many. Only in part are they reflections of the contentious upheavals in psychological thought that rippled across the twentieth century. The wars, the cultures, the nationalities, the politics, the language differences, some poor translations, are all elements of the story. Wundt had not translated well into the Anglo-American tongue nor into the culture. His poorly rendered *Outlines of Psychology* was distributed afar, though now it is scarcely readable for anyone except the dedicated antiquarian. It omits the famous Leipzig laboratory data and gives, instead, long convoluted phenomenological descriptions of experience. With a lack of attention to style, it had been written in haste, on the spur of the moment, for introductory students. Wundt's papers in his journal for research findings and theoretical essays, *Philosophische Studien*, show a different writer who is engaging and who laces his thoughts with wit and sarcasm. But those essays remain untranslated.

Certainly not the least reason for neglect of the whole Wundtian *corpus* is the challenge of sheer quantity. Wundt's academic career was huge—sixty years of productivity, 17,000 students, the all-time winner in the academic ritual of "publish-or-perish." Who could be surprised that the later recollections (Wundt memorial publications), appearing in several countries shortly after his death, suggest the fable of the blind men feeling different parts of an elephant? One need mention only those dozens of American college boys who sailed off for a year or two at Leipzig in the late nineteenth century. They were armed merely with a semester or two of college German and an American small-college degree—hardly a match for the formidable academic preparation of German *Gymnasium* students.

What could those American innocents have understood as they listened to Wundt's polysyllabic philosophical lectures or as they paged through his massive *Grundzüge*? When they returned home, often weary and culture-shocked, they certainly gave different and conflicting accounts of their experiences. In the catastrophic atmosphere of anti-German prejudice sweeping their nation at the outset of World War I, some of them surfaced as pundits on the "evils" of Wundt's mind and of his culture. An independent observer of this, the distinguished American journalist H. L. Mencken, who was fluent in German language and philosophy, made the following mid-1920s observation on the discomforts that many a German-trained American professor may have experienced when facing the challenge of translating the works of German academics:

> The average American professor is far too dull a fellow to undertake so difficult an enterprise. Even when he sports a German Ph.D. one usually finds on examination that all he knows about modern German literature is that a *Mass* of Hofbrau in Munich used to cost 27 *Pfennig* downstairs and 32 *Pfennig* upstairs. The German universities were formerly very tolerant of foreigners. Many an American, in preparation for professoring at Harvard, spent a couple of years roaming from one to the other of them without picking up enough German to read the *Berliner Tageblatt*. Such frauds swarm in all our lesser universities, and many of them, during the war, became eminent authorities upon the crimes of Nietzsche and the errors of Treitschke. (Mencken, 1955, 110–11)

To that profound observation we could add, with supportive citations, that many a patriotic American academic also became an overnight authority on the "crimes and errors" of Wundt.

The first commanding historical chronicler of Wundt, for the English-reading audience and subsequently for other languages, was E. G. Boring (1929, 1950) who fashioned his remarkably personalized survey in the mid-1920s. It was dedicated, as he said, to the veneration of great personalities. With modesty, Boring acknowledges in a *Preface* his inadequacies for the task. But by the time of the appearance of the expanded 1950 edition, no such modesty was necessary. The chapter on Wundt, however, was republished unchanged in 1950.

Boring was the leading page-counter. Some years after his death a few critics ventured the ungrateful impression that he had spent more time counting the pages Wundt wrote than he spent reading them. When it comes to primary sources—quotations directly from Wundt—Boring gives practically none at all. Instead, he offers allusions to the recollections of his celebrated teacher, the charismatic English-bred E. B. Titchener. These citations are often in the form of "Titchener said . . . about Wundt." Now Titchener, as we should recall, spent the mandatory eighteen months in Leipzig to pick up the then easily obtained German doctorate. But we should also notice that he was a follower of Wundt's arch intellectual opponents, the positivists Mach and Avenarius

(Danziger, 1979, and Kusch, 1995, review that schism). Not surprisingly, but still little known, Wundt was later to make efforts to keep Titchener off the editorial boards of journals (see Robinson, 1989), and Wundt wrote disparaging remarks about Titchener's "introspectionist-structuralist" school of psychology. He says, for example,

> Introspective method [*introspektive Methode*] relies either on arbitrary observa-
> tions that go astray or on a withdrawal to a lonely sitting room where it
> becomes lost in self-absorption. The unreliability of this method is universally
> recognized. . . . Clearly, Titchener has himself come under the influence of the
> deceptions of this method. (Wundt, 1900, 180)[2]

Other Leipzig Ph.D.'s who stayed close to Wundt had similar reactions. Interestingly Titchener's fellow countryman, Charles Spearman at London University, also a Leipzig psychology Ph.D., wrote the following evaluation of Titchener:

> My negative reaction reached its highest intensity to that very remarkable, and
> I believe, ill-fated man Titchener. . . . He has been the author and champion of
> a peculiar method of introspection. . . . Introspection degenerates into a sort of
> inward staring. . . . The ensuing harm was rendered still worse by his doctrine
> of "structuralism". . . . But Titchener had such extraordinary abilities and such
> an impressive personality, that these doctrines of his seem to have blocked the
> advance of psychology for many years. And even when they themselves even-
> tually collapsed, it was only to give birth to reactionary extravagancies nearly
> as bad. Among these may be counted the initial excesses of Behaviorism, as
> also a part of what passes under the name of the doctrine of Gestalt. . . . I am
> brought back to Wundt with his epoch-making introduction of the experi-
> mental method. To him and to Galton I certainly owe more than to anyone
> else. (Spearman, 1930, 331–333)

Within the accumulated historical scholarship of this field there are today serious reasons for calling the Boring-Titchener account of founding-father Wundt into question. Not long after Wundt stepped off the arriving train in the Leipzig *Bahnhof* in 1875, his system of

---

[2]Wundt called his experimental method "Selbstbeobachtung" which is now translated, ironically and confusingly, as "introspection." But Wundt's intended experimental method was
the use of reaction-time measurements, Fechnerian psychophysical experimental procedures, discriminative responses, measurable reaction patterns for assessing emotional
states, measures of the capacities of short-term storage, and similar techniques. He certainly did discuss, casually, private subjective experiences, but did not count that as scientific data. Danziger (1980a) has helped untangle the confusion over introspection in the
Wundtian literature. (Unless otherwise noted, translations in the present chapter are
by A. L. Blumenthal.)

thought grew to fulfill its new name as "the *voluntarist* school" (a logical title for his teachings as will be shown below). That title remained in place throughout the remainder of his life, and so it must now seem to be another sign of lapses in historical scholarship when textbooks, especially in the English language, began to refer to Wundt's school as *structuralism*. That was the name Titchener had coined to describe his own proprietary and different system after he arrived at Cornell. One can now imagine the anti-Titchenerian bones of Wundt rolling in the grave when American textbooks began to make Wundt out to be a Titchenerian structuralist.

Unwitting misinterpretations of Wundt, later in the twentieth century, unmistakably served a pedagogical purpose that was not uncommon in the patterns of intellectual history. That purpose was to justify and elevate later schools of thought. As often happens, such movements of interpretation will lead to negative *ad hominem* characterizations of one old master or another, helping to swing opinion in the direction of newer schools of thought. Those accounts become entrenched in textbooks resisting revision. Late-twentieth-century re-orientations in psychology known as the "cognitive revolution" did, however, create an atmosphere open to re-examinations of Wundt (see, for example, Baars' explanation in *The cognitive revolution in psychology*, 1986).

Serious re-examinations of Wundtian psychology began in the 1970s. The rediscovery of a large body of Wundtian work in psycholinguistics in the late 1960s (Blumenthal, 1970) brought invitations from the American Psychological Association's primary journal, *American Psychologist*, to publish "A reappraisal of Wilhelm Wundt." In 1979 that Association's journal for book reviews, *Contemporary Psychology*, initiated a series of reviews of historically significant works with an opening article on Wundt entitled "The founding father we never knew" (Blumenthal, 1975, 1979). Those historical profiles were the antithesis of the then standard textbook descriptions of Wundt. Considerable controversy ensued which led to a literature of contentious re-examination. In 1979 a centenary celebration of the founding of Wundt's first formal laboratory took place in Leipzig and was a stimulus for further re-examinations (Meischner & Metge, 1980). By the beginning of the twenty-first century most textbooks on psychology's history have radically revised the portrayal of Wundtian psychology that had prevailed fifty years earlier.

Wundt's "Actuality Principle"—The Heart of Controversy

When introducing his "new science," Wundt requires our acceptance of *consciousness* as a natural reality. Subjective experience is a fact, just as factual as the alternations between sleep and wakefulness. How it is to be studied systematically is another question. This proposal had, of course, always flown in the face of the physicalist trend in positivist philosophy and of the anti-mentalistic trend of behaviorism. Though not placating those detractors, Wundt readily acknowledged that the methical, scientific study of consciousness and subjectivity is a monumental challenge but maintained that one doesn't give up on something *real* only because it is difficult, as his life story illustrates. History provides examples of supremely difficult questions that were faced squarely with determination, and faced successfully.

As noted above, Wundt placed his subject matter in line to be another level following upwards in the series of sciences, *physics, chemistry, and biology*. Differences of considerable substance, however, separate this next level from the others. Physical sciences are about objects and energies conceptualized by physical scientists. Consciousness is not a thing-like physical concept. Rather, it is an immediate and transient *process*, the investigation of which amounts to no less than the study of *subjectivity*. Consciousness is a continuous flow, a constant unfolding of experience, which according to Wundt's findings cannot be separated into discrete "faculties" as had been done in ancient times. This argument became known as Wundt's *principle of actuality*.

Wundt's teams of laboratory workers found that unique operating characteristics of consciousness are describable, thus, in their view, bringing the goals of his new science within reach. Investigations eventually flowed from the Leipzig laboratory. The findings included the limitations on mental capacities, on spans, on the timing of the temporal flow, on the nature of selective attention and short-term memory. The number of attentional fixations that could be captured from one momentary field of short-term memory storage was always limited to approximately six or seven. The variations in qualities of experience, of sensation and emotion, were unraveled as multidimensional quality spaces. Out of the syntheses of affective qualities came the urges and tensions that produce volitional action (i.e. motivated behavior), the study of which showed how they fluctuate, as variations in forms of self-control, from the effortful to the automatic. These findings were offered in support of a theoretical system that was spread broadly to adjacent disciplines at the end of the nineteenth century, even, for one example, into psychiatry where it formed the basis of Emil Kraepelin's (1917) theory of schizophrenia. Kraepelin had been an early student of Wundt's, and his account of schizophrenia is based on the Wundtian descriptions of processes of central selective attention. In brief, schizophrenia is described as the breakdown or distortion of attention deployment.

It is clear that Wundt's psychology emerges in its lasting form in the *second* edition of his *Grundzüge* (1880). Other significant changes also came in later editions. The original 1873–4 edition had been still too tentative, programmatic, and thus markedly different from later editions. That first edition should not now be recommended to anyone but the specialized historian of Wundt's intellectual development. The 1880 and later editions were, further, fitted out with the many more pages of objective replicable experimental data on subjective processes for which the whole project represented by this book won its recognition.

Concerning the factual basis of his subject matter, Wundt held firmly to the view that mental processes are the *activity* of the brain. Activity is not substance. He fatefully referred to this view as "parallelism," which he put forward in *opposition* to mind/body dualism. Historical accounts have often overlooked his intention to keep that concept of "parallelism" distinct from mind/body dualism (e.g., Boring, 1950, p. 333). Later construals of Wundt as a mind/body dualist may well have deflated the interest of a few students who might otherwise have been curious about what went on in that old Leipzig laboratory.

In contrast to Wundt's parallelism, a *pure materialism* (i.e., describing psychological processes *only* as neural structures or brain chemistry) often appeared in the scientific community in Wundt's day. But that approach threatens, warned Wundt, to degenerate backwards into mind/body dualism. It does so whenever we push the pure physicalist viewpoint toward explaining consciousness. As with Descartes, he says, this type of thinking eventually conceptualizes some "mind-stuff" by analogy to concepts of matter, even though the "mind-stuff" be given a more modern scientific-sounding incarnation. When examined systematically, the operating characteristics of consciousness do not fit, argues Wundt, with the axioms of physical science. It is the point he made in the casting of his core principle of *creative synthesis*, the founding principle of the theoretical system. It states that qualities of immediate experience are constructions that are not found in the examination of the objects of the physical sciences.

The Principle of "Creative Synthesis" (Schöpferische Synthese)

In later writings Wundt referred to this core principle as "the principle of creative *resultants*," a terminological variation on *synthesis*. Given the length of his career as theoretician, it is a wonder that his system remained as consistent as it did with so little terminological variation. As Freud always revolved around the key notion of *repression*, as Skinner always revolved around the key notion of *reinforcement*, so Wundt revolved around his key notion of *creative synthesis* which was first articulated in 1862, used continually, and cited as his most central idea when dictating deathbed memoirs in 1920.

In this psychology of emergent mental phenomena, *colors, touches, musical tones*, and the *words of speech* are not taken to be the *decoding* of stimulus input nor the reception and storage of something sent in from the outside. Rather, colors, tastes, touches, etc. are the brain's subjective *reactions* to events in our sensory systems. That reaction is what Wundt called the "creative synthesis." Sense organ and neural events may be described endlessly in terms of physics and chemistry, but such descriptions do not include (do not produce for us) the actual psychological qualities known as "sweet," "sour," "heavy," "dark blue," "dazzling crimson," "sharp," "painful," or "meaningful." To get those qualities you must have a living brain, one that is awake, conscious, and attentive, i.e., a brain that is reacting and having experiences. A key feature of Wundt's findings is that these mental capacities are generative, or creative, in every aspect.

When the theory matured in the decade after his move to Leipzig, a more pronounced emphasis on principles concerned with emotion, motivation, and volition appears and begins to compete with that of "creative synthesis" at the center of it all (in the second edition of the *Grundzüge*, 1880). The German word *Trieb*, used in the sense of "impulse" or "urge," becomes as prominent as *Synthese:* "The course of both general and individual development shows that desires or urges (*Triebe*) are the fundamental psychological phenomena from which all mental processes derive." (1880, vol. 2, 455) If that move hadn't occurred, the theory might always have been described, basically, as *constructivism* rather than as *voluntarism*. But the later principles of volition incorporate *creative synthesis*.

All these trends in Wundt's thought were the substance of his career-long refutations of *mechanistic associationism* as reflected especially in British psychology and philosophy following Locke and Hume, and as it had preceded him in Germany in the form of Herbart's "mental mechanics." Here again we are forced to correct Boring (1929, 1950) who would portray Wundt as a classical Humean and Herbartian associationist. Wundt's fundamental criticism of associationist theory was that it is based on analogies to physical objects. Psychological processes are not, says Wundt, "billiard-ball ideas" rolling around on a mental table top, bumping into each other—as depicted, he said, in the theories of the associationist psychologists. He argues further as follows: "There are absolutely no psychological structures that can be characterized in their meaning or in the value of their contents as the sum of their elemental factors of the mere mechanical results of their components." (Wundt, 1908, vol. 3, 276) Here is an autobiographic summary of how Wundt came to, and expanded on, these views which are germinal in the development of his whole theoretical system:

> If I were asked what I thought the value for psychology of the experimental method was in the past and still is, I would answer that for me it created and continues to confirm a wholly new view of the nature and interrelations of mental processes. When I first approached psychological problems, I shared the general prejudice natural to physiologists that the formation of perceptions is merely the work of the physiological properties of our sense organs. Then through the examination of visual phenomena I learned to conceive of perception as an act of *creative synthesis*. This gradually became my guide, at the hand of which I arrived at a psychological understanding of the development of the higher functions of imagination and intellect. The older psychology gave me no help in this. When I then proceeded to investigate the temporal relations in the flow of mental events, I gained a new insight into the development of volition . . . an insight likewise into the similarity of mental functions which are artificially distinguished by abstractions and names—such as "ideas," "feelings," or "will." In a word, I glimpsed the indivisibility of mental life, and saw its similarity on all its levels. The chronometric investigation of associative processes showed me the relation of perceptual processes to memory images. It also taught me to recognize that the concept of "reproduced" ideas is one of the many fictions that has become set in our language to create a picture of something that does not exist in reality. I learned to understand that "mental representation" is a process which is no less changing and transient than a feeling or an act of will. As a consequence of all this I saw that the old theory of association is no longer tenable. It must be replaced by the notion of relational processes involving rudimentary feelings, a view that results in

giving up the stable linkages and close connections of successive as well as
simultaneous associations. (Wundt, 1894, 122–124)

The *creative synthesis* principle was continually being expanded.
Wundt and his followers worked to define the conditions under which
the emergent, qualitatively different, phenomena of immediate experience arise: mental states are context dependent; they typically take the
path of least effort in their constructive acts; they fluctuate through opponent processes as when a pleasant experience is always more pleasant
if preceded by a painful experience, or when a sweet substance tastes
sweeter if preceded by a bitter substance. The whole mental state
(*Gesamtvorstellung*) is typically more than the sum of its parts. Consciousness was found to be a two-stage process: (1) a large-capacity,
short-term memory (once called the *Blickfeld*), and (2) a narrow-capacity
focus of selective attention (often then called *apperception*) under voluntary (effortful) control; it moves through the field, or *Blickfeld*, of short-
term memory. The first psychology doctoral dissertations completed
in the Leipzig laboratory had been on that topic of selective attention
(*apperception*).

A remarkable effort, remarkable at least for its magnitude, was the
series of interlocking laboratory studies that progressed for approximately three decades through the Leipzig laboratory. Its purpose was to
describe the temporal flow of, and the momentary capacities of consciousness. Most all of this was accomplished by assistants and advanced
students. Perhaps the best example is the work of the one who stayed with
Wundt for the longest period in the formal position of *Assistant*, or the
administrative assistant in charge of the experimental laboratory. That
person was Wilhelm Wirth, whose book, *Die experimentelle Analyse der
Bewusstseinsphänomene* (*Experimental analysis of the phenomena of consciousness*, 1908), is a prime example of the fruits of that laboratory.[3]

In his Leipzig years Wundt was not an active experimenter. He
remained always and primarily in the role of *theoretical* psychologist.

---

[3]It was a bitter disappointment for Wirth when he was not appointed as Wundt's successor
(See Robinson's account, 1987). But Wirth was a pure experimentalist, whereas Wundt had
always been primarily a theorist. At the close of his life, Wundt appointed the highly theoretical Felix Krueger to be his successor. Not only was Krueger qualified as theoretician,
he also promised to continue to develop Wundt's axiom that psychologically we are first
and foremost *emotional* creatures. Krueger lectured on this at Columbia University in the
mid-1920s. Susan Langer was his student there and carried forward some of his teachings
in her later writings in philosophy.

During the laboratory's most productive years he expended an enormous effort to extend the theory to the foundations of other disciplines in the social sciences from the study of moral development to that of history. These extensions were in general called *Völkerpsychologie* (cultural psychology). Standing out from them all as the most successful is the work in psycholinguistics.

The Influential Wundtian School of Psycholinguistics (Sprachpsychologie)

By many accounts the most successful expansion of Wundtian psychology was in the area of psychology of language. An elaborate linguistic theory, derived from psychological principles, was the result. At the start of the twentieth-century Wundt had a wide following here, for he had written extensively on language in the late nineteenth century in scattered places. His first lecture at Leipzig when he arrived there in 1875 was on the psychology of language. His first extensive writing on language appeared in his *Logik* of 1883. These interests concerning all aspects of linguistics and language performance were eventually pulled together to form the first two books of his *Völkerpsychologie* series (1900), that part entitled *Die Sprache (Language)* which was revised in 1904 and then revised again and much expanded in 1911–12.

The key to understanding Wundtian linguistics, and controversies once swirling around it, is that the syntax, the sound systems, and all structures in language are seen as taking their particular form by virtue of the operating characteristics of underlying universal mental processes. America's most influential linguist in the first half of the twentieth century, Leonard Bloomfield, based his first and widely followed linguistics textbook on Wundtian psychology (Bloomfield, 1914) as did many other language scholars of that time. By the 1930s, however, American linguists had converted to behaviorism, and Bloomfield's 1933 second edition dropped the Wundtian psychology to replace it with a stimulus-response conditioning model. Surveys of the Wundtian-era psycholinguistics can be found in Blumenthal (1970, 1974).

In any Wundtian analysis of language, mechanisms of attention, short-term memory, cognitive temporal limits, and constraints on self-control underlie language form. The fundamental unit of language is found to be the *sentence*, and "sentence" in this case means a special *mental* state—the result of the ability of the central focal attention process to subdivide and segregate global mental impressions into parts and qualities and relations between them. Neither words, nor any other linguistic structure, have meaning unless related to some underlying (mental) sentence.

A binary principle operates in sentence structure due to the nature of attentional focusings which divide the momentary content of consciousness into a focused aspect and a background from which that aspect is selected. That bifurcation then becomes the *subject* and the *predicate* division of sentences. Further attentional focusing may produce further binary subdivisions into other parts of speech. For the fluent speaker much of this process becomes automatized as a refined skill, such skill development being a major part of Wundt's account of volitional processes. The purely linguistic aspect of this work was the study of the layers of syntactic structuring that unfold in the transformation of the initial mental content into sentence patterns and then into the sound system of the language.

The analysis of slips and lapses in speech (particularly the voluminous studies conducted by Merringer and Mayer, 1895) was one of the productive empirical ways, endorsed by Wundt, of studying the intricate language performance processes. Even the careful observation of hesitations in spontaneous speech can be used as signs of the underlying mental activity involved in the production of the syntactic structure of sentences.

The unfolding of the language capacity in the stages of language acquisition in children, heavily studied in Wundt's day, was found to be another source of evidence concerning the mental mechanisms of language. One of the best examples of research on child language acquisition, from that time, was the book *Die Kindersprache* (1907) by Clara and William Stern. Language acquisition, in the Wundtian account, begins in emotional gestures and sounds even before the first true words develop. What the adult may hear as the child's first word represents only a more refined movement of the emotional expression system. It is the increasing ability of the child to focus its attention on emotional urges that leads to the beginnings of the underlying mental activity of sentence formation.

Wundt's work on the psychological roots of syntactic structure reached a level of considerable complexity. One product of that work was the invention, in the *Logik* of 1883, of the tree diagram for the description of syntactic structure—a type of diagramming which became a standard for language scholars in the following century. The image of a tree had long been in use as a metaphor for all sorts of thought. But Wundt's so-called tree diagrams of sentences were different, resembling more a pyramid shape. These diagrams of sentence structure start, at the top, with the general sentence thought (S), then subdivide with two lines running downward to indicate the division of the *subject* and *predicate*. Those two parts may then be further subdivided into other parts of speech each of which could be further subdivided and so on. This maintains, throughout, the binary principle that again reflects the focus vs. background operations of selective attention.

All of this particular Wundtian work appeared within the context of the type of controversy typical of his entire psychological and social thought—opposition to an atomistic associationism, which would explain language in a "bottom-up" fashion as the compounding of speech elements into larger structures. For Wundt, in sharp contrast to such views, language structure and performance can be grasped only from a "top-down" point of view. Here is the essential argument in the Wundtian psycholinguistic theory from his *Sprachpsychologie*, the chapter on *Satzfügung* (roughly meaning "sentence structure" or more literally "sentence arrangement or articulation"). These points are the essential principles on which Wundt's linguistic work hinges:

> The sentence . . . is not an image running with precision through consciousness where each single word or single sound appears only momentarily while the preceding and following elements are lost from consciousness. Rather, it stands as a whole at the cognitive level while it is being spoken. If this should ever not be the case, we would irrevocably lose the thread of speech. . . . The claim that the sentence is a "chain of word concepts" is as psychologically untenable as that it is merely a "chain of words." On the contrary, it is the dissection of a totality present as a whole in consciousness. If one characterizes this as a linking process, then the outer grammatical form is taken as the inner mental form. And it is thus assumed that the outer form is from moment to moment a faithful picture of the psychological process underlying it. This of course it is not. The outer form is only the result of the process. It is, moreover, an end product which shows by its nature that the psychological factors determining a grammatical utterance are themselves distinct from the utterance. The sentence as an *inner* psychological construction must have a simultaneous nature in addition to the sequential one. Without this quality it could not be a coherent totality. (Wundt, 1911, 243–244)

A considerable "cognitive load," or performance load, is involved the act of speaking or of writing. It is basically the mental act of converting a mental simultaneity (an image, a whole mental impression) into the sequentialities of the language code. This is a feat of high skill that depends entirely on the operating characteristics of selective focal attention, short-term memory, and on the processes of self-control mechanisms, many of which must become automatized in language performance before language usage can be fluent and articulate.

Wundt's primary *Assistent* in psycholinguistics was Ottmar Dittrich, who headed a psycholinguistics research group in the decade before the World War. His own *Grundzüge der Sprachpsychologie* appeared in 1903 and *Die Probleme der Sprachpsychologie* in 1913. Though influential in Europe, Dittrich's continuation of Wundtian psycholinguistics remains almost wholly unknown in the English-speaking community. However, in 1933 a book by the Viennese professor of speech pathology Emil Froeschels appeared in English under the title *The psychological elements of speech*; it included a long appendix written by Dittrich. That appendix gives a sample of the depth and complexity of Dittrich's work on syntactic structure.

The Emotion System

In histories of psychology we are accustomed to reading of contrasts between traditions of thought called *rationalism* and *romanticism.* The former assumes humans to be first and foremost thinking, calculating, or computing creatures. Emotion from that viewpoint is often seen as a breakdown or disruption of the psychological machinery. A major influence in rationalist psychological theory in early nineteenth-century Germany had been Johann Herbart, who robustly represented that school of thought. In criticisms of Herbart and his many followers, Wundt used the term "intellectualism" rather than rationalism as he disputed their supremely *mechanistic* theories of mental processes, action, and society.

Romanticism in present-day psychology is most often understood to mean, of course, the "depth" psychologies of the psychoanalytic traditions in psychiatry, though it has much older roots. In this view humans, or even all living creatures, are taken to be first and foremost emotional beings. All action and mentation is seen as originating in primal emotional states. Emotion precedes cognition, and therefore rational thought processes become the fragile veneer overlying more fundamental emotional-motivational mechanisms. In late-twentieth-century American psychology, a debate concerning the relative priority of cognition and emotion was noisily revived, as any reader of an introductory psychology text should know.

Wundt was one of the purer representatives of the romanticist tradition. As dictated by his overall theoretical axioms, he was also quick to refute physicalistic explanations of emotion, and that meant, of course, the James-Lange theory that ascended so quickly in popularity within the new behaviorism as to mask the Wundtian alternative. James and Lange argued that visceral bodily reactions (glandular and muscular actions) are the substance of emotion (though experimental evidence for that view was lacking). American writers obviously bypassed Wundt's critiques of the James-Lange theory, even though Wundt makes essentially the same points against James and Lange that were brought out in Walter Cannon's widely read experimental studies of emotion three decades later (Cannon, 1927). Wundt summarized his observations as follows:

> ... when Lange and James make these [physiological] phenomena the exclusive *causes* of the emotion, when they describe the emotions as psychical processes which can be aroused only through expressive movements, we must reject their paradoxical view for the following three reasons: *First*, the definite outer symptoms of emotions do not appear until such time as the psychical nature of the emotion is already clearly established. The emotion, accordingly, precedes the innervation effects which are looked upon by these investigators as causes of the emotion. *Second*, it is absolutely impossible to classify the rich variety of psychical emotional states in the comparatively simple scheme of innervation changes. The psychical processes are much more varied than are their accompanying forms of expression. *Third*, and finally, the physical concomitants stand in no constant relation to the psychical quality of the emotions. This holds especially for the effects on pulse and respiration, but is true also for the pantomimetic expressive movements. It may sometimes happen that emotions with very different, even opposite kinds of affective contents, may belong to the same class so far as the accompanying physical phenomena are concerned. (Wundt, 1907, 195–196)

Cannon's program of experimentation and subsequent critiques of the same James-Lange theory duplicate the earlier Leipzig findings. The largest compendium of experimental research on emotion from the Leipzig laboratory is found in a book by Wundt's student Alfred Lehmann, *Die körperlichen Äußerungen psychischer Zustände* (*The bodily expression of psychological states*, 1899).

Wundt uses the terms "feelings," "moods," and "emotions" but only to refer to different levels of intensity, not different categories. His discussions of sensory qualities, belabored in his later *Grundriß* (*Outlines*), shades gradually into descriptions of affective and aesthetic qualities of experience. Reactions to music and rhythms were a favorite example. When reactions to single sound pitches are studied, they are discussed in terms of sensory qualities. But when pitches are combined simultaneously, such as when the notes *c*, *e*, and *g* are sounded together on the piano producing a musical cord, then descriptions refer to a creative synthesis occurring in experienced affect—a pleasant musical quality may emerge in consciousness. These elemental and transient aesthetic experiences are called "feelings." When such feelings last for longer periods of time, Wundt refers to them as "moods." When the combinations of notes and chords on the piano keyboard are extended into musical compositions, then more intense affective experiences may arise which he refers to as "emotions."

In Wundt's view all mental states move constantly through fluctuating fields of changing emotional, or mood, or feeling qualities. When those qualities take especially intense or pressured forms, they are goads to action (actions of movement or of mind), and then they are called "motivations" or "volitions." This is the point of entry into the other major Wundtian theoretical development—the analysis of self-control or volition—the topic for which the whole of the Wundtian school of thought received its designation as "the voluntarist school."

Because of seemingly endless variations in emotional and aesthetic experiences, Wundt argues that it would be hopeless to attempt any taxonomy of emotions. Rather we must describe emotions in terms of quality-dimensions which allow for infinite variability. He argues that all emotional experience is *bipolar*; each emotional state or quality has its opposite. This could account for a number of findings such as cyclical mood swings and cyclical changes in aesthetic preferences (later formalized as Wundt's *principle of development toward opposites*).

The Wundtian studies of emotion-qualities were therefore an early exercise in multidimensional scaling inspired in part by the methods of Fechnerian psychophysics. Through various avenues of experimental data, naturalistic observation, logic, and pure speculation, Wundt settled on the famous three dimensions of emotional quality that were to reappear repeatedly in the hands of later researchers. Prominent examples, all independent of and far removed from Wundtian influence, include Schlosberg's (1954) cluster analysis of facial expressions of emotion, Osgood, Suci, and Tannenbaum's (1957) factor analysis of emotional expression in language, and Bales and Cohen's (1979) factor analysis of emotional interactions in group dynamics. High agreement appears in the three underlying quality dimensions that these investigators found, though they struggled at some points to give names to the dimensions as Wundt may have himself. But the later terminologies match those of Wundt fairly well.

The *first* and obviously most discussed variation in emotional states is what Wundt called the dimension of "pleasure-displeasure." There is little disagreement on this, though it may sometimes be referred to as "positive vs. negative affect," or "high vs. low evaluation." The *second* dimension is the "arousal" dimension, or "high vs. low arousal," "activity vs. passivity," "high vs. low excitation," or "high vs. low activation." More of a struggle can be sensed in the naming of the *third* dimension that came out of these scaling or factor-analysis results. The descriptive terms are "concentrated vs. relaxed attention," "strain vs. relaxation," "high vs. low control," "high vs. low potency," and "dominance vs. submissiveness."

Much of Wundt's discussion of emotion takes on the character of a psychology of aesthetics, or perhaps better, an *aesthetics of everyday experience*. He suspected that subtleties of affect are characteristic of all experience, from elemental sensations to abstract problem solving. Consciousness, as he speculated, must ceaselessly be colored by fluctuating affective states. Therein is the tension that occurs when we struggle to remember a name, the unpleasant discord of inarticulate speech, or the flow of feeling accompanying the quick solution to a complex problem. For Wundt this view of mental processes was no less than necessary for the motivational/volitional aspect of his psychological theory.

The Volition System

It was a telling mark of twentieth-century historical scholarship in psychology: not until the year 1980 did a historical investigator of Wundtian psychology, namely Kurt Danziger (1980b), publish the first in-depth account in English of the development of Wundt's treatment of volition and motivation. A briefer and less detailed account had appeared embedded within a 1970 paper by the philosopher Theodore Mischel, but since it was in a philosophy journal it went unnoticed by psychologists. Little noticed minor accounts had also appeared in English early in the century. Danziger summarized most of the twists and turns, debates and revisions, that flowed from Wundt's theorizing over the four decades of experimentation and theory-construction (practically all of which is still available only in German).

The reaction-time research program at Leipzig was exceptional in that it gained much attention in the West (though perhaps not given the intended Wundtian interpretation). Actually, the program's main purpose was to analyze volition, or as the Wundtians often phrased it, the study of "decision and choice." This work was open to misinterpretation in the English-language community because the basic Wundtian theory of the central processes of self-control had rarely been imported into the English-language literature. It had been influential in some other regions, particularly the Belgium-French psychological literature under the guidance of Albert Michotte at Louvain. An Irish student, E. B. Barrett, completed an early doctoral dissertation under Michotte's guidance and published it as a book, *Motive-force and motivation-tracks* (1911). It presents a broad picture of the voluntarist school and its many satellites at the turn of the century, particularly the experimental work that came from the many variations on this theme.

Modern psychology has witnessed many forms of "control theory." There are, for example, conceptions of machinelike (cybernetic) control systems based on sensory feedback principles, or "behavior shaping" where the stimulus control is that of the environmental contingencies following behaviors, or instinctual control in which the innate control process is released by some triggering stimulus. All those examples are forms of stimulus/sensory control. There is a crucial fundamental difference in Wundt's control theory that is rooted in his theory of emotion described above. It is his position that emotions (and "feelings" or *Gefühle)* are NOT external stimulus activity—are not sensations. Emotion is entirely the product of the central nervous system in Wundt's account. This distinction is important. It places Wundt, again, squarely in the internalist camp in the spectrum of psychological theories. The strictly internal controlling emotional forces—the controls of mental processes and behavior—are seen as ever-present, fluctuating, features of consciousness and of consciousness alone.

Apperzeption, the old Leibnizian term that runs ceaselessly through all of Wundt's works, is his name for the process of selective focal attention. An act of "selection" is always indicated in his usage of that term, and "selection" implies a "selector" who is doing the selecting.

The "activity" and the "agent" are cast as qualities of emotional fluctuation. For Wundt, then, volition and motivation are other terms for emotion. A volitional or motivational state is an internal emotional condition, or some sequence of experienced emotional contrasts. Volitional states, of course, take many forms, from pure *impulses* to complex *decisions* that may follow a period of mood swings in processes of deliberation. Simultaneous affective states may sometimes be in conflict, or different urges may be present or rapidly alternating, which is the state of motivational conflict.

In retrospect one clearly important aspect of this volitional theorizing and the data it generated was the light shed on the development of deliberate attention-controlled voluntary processes into processes that are automatic. The great value of that development for human life is that it frees up the focus of attention for some new control action while earlier, once effortful actions, are now running automatically. A number of operating characteristics distinguish controlled from automatic behavior, as Wundtian investigators were to learn. Voluntary action (mental or behavioral) is slow, effortful, better remembered, generally a serial process. Involuntary is faster, less conscious, or not conscious at all, and has little or no sense of effort associated with it. In this view, therefore, "controlled or voluntary" is the more primal, the initial state, which may later develop into automatic mechanisms.

Of course, instinctual and automatic behaviors appear at the beginning of an individual's life. Here Wundt is at pains to speculate that this behavior must have been, at early stages of evolution, also under voluntary or effortful control. Through the long expanse of evolutionary time, that behavior would have become encapsulated in the evolutionary process to become a part of the innate control systems in more highly evolved life forms. Thus he writes,

> It is not improbable that all the reflex movements of both animals and men originate in this way. As evidence of this we have, besides the above described reduction of volitional acts through practice to pure mechanical processes, also the *purposeful character of reflexes*, which points to the presence at some time of purposive ideas as motives. (Wundt, 1907, 214)

In highly evolved organisms, as Wundt argues, pure impulses or drives can be brought back under attentional control and thus again are conscious volitions.

In modern control theories in psychology most examples are expressed in terms of external behaviors. Wundt lays stress on the fact that the principles of self-control apply equally and follow the same principles in the operations of the stream of consciousness—in *perception*, *memory*, *imagination*, *dreaming*, and especially, for Wundt, in the case of *thinking*. The development of logical thought, he argues, is the highest form of self-control attained by the human brain.

The critical resultant of the *automatization* of activity (mental or otherwise) is that we are then free to turn to the control or development of other actions. This has long been studied in the case of motor skills. In piano playing, for one example, we can observe how the skilled player develops an ability to play the music and to talk to anyone nearby at the same time. Wundt's psychology stresses that this is not limited to motor skills but that such a pattern of skill development can take place in all mental operations. With the automatization of habitual patterns of thought, or of imagery, mental reactions then fade from awareness, and again this produces a savings of considerable efficiency for mental operations. The process of producing grammatical sentences, for example, becomes largely automatic, allowing us to focus more of our attention on the subject matter we are talking about or on the responses of the listener we are talking to. For another example, we would find it tedious and debilitating to learn higher levels of math if we had never mentally automatized the elementary rules of algebra. For another example, we also may experience functional autonomy even in the case of motivations, and so even the reasons or goals of some of our actions may fade from consciousness as they become habitual. With this general capacity for the automatization of mental processes, today's attention-demanding actions may become tomorrow's automatic activities, thus offering the potential for continually freeing up the human mind to experience and create new things.

The automatization of actions mental or otherwise is, however, a double-edged sword. Rapid articulate speech, for example, is a largely automatized process, but when we focus too intently on some motive or extraneous thought while speaking, we are in danger of losing control of the articulation process. It is as if the automatic control schema is rather like a decaying short-term memory image that must be periodically refocused to keep it running properly. Otherwise we experience "lapses" or "slips" in our speech when the automatic control process breaks down at some point.

Final Days

Looking back over the breadth of Wundt's life and thought, we can see the movement of a spirit of optimism in the form of a faith in the creative capacities of human consciousness which include its ability for endless advance and endless constructions. That optimistic spirit took to its wings even in his last and melodramatic writings during the dark days in Germany following the World War, as shadows of cultural pessimism spread across the landscapes of art, science, and philosophy.

At that moment, when he was losing his once formidable ability to defend himself intellectually, Wundt was hoisted up as the archetypal tribal father by virtue of the length of his career and the length of his publications. In that role he was a target for the spears and arrows of a new generation, chafing at his long dominance and eager to claim his territory for its own. He was then cast as the icon of a dead and failed past, and so his name became an epithet that served as a springboard for new movements. Inspired by behaviorist reformulations of psychology and by other social/cultural clashes, rejections of Wundt then reached, in some circles, high levels of vitriolic intensity that lasted well past mid-century.[4]

As the darkness closed in on Wundt's last days, and on the final days of what had been a great era in his nation's history, the optimism of Wundt's once gilded age shines in the last utterances of his memoirs (Wundt, 1920) and the last pages of his *Völkerpsychologie*. He proclaims a faith in the positive, creative, and moral powers of the human mind that he saw leading inevitably to a better future. It was this same spirit that animated his perennial involvement in politics that had, for most of his life, brought progressive political reformers to his dinner table. But still in those last days we find him thrust back into his customary role of being at odds with many of his contemporaries when ominous movements, political and intellectual movements that he feared, began to take shape in his bleeding nation and in a changing world.

References

Baars, B. (1986). *The cognitive revolution in psychology.* New York: The Guilford Press.
Bales, F., & Cohen, S. (1979). *Symlog: A system for the multiple level observation of groups.* New York: Free Press.

[4]One of the most remarkable efforts in that vein came from Diamond (1980).

Barrett, E. (1911) *Motive-force and motivation-tracks.* London: Longmans, Green.

Bloomfield, L. (1914). *Introduction to the study of language.* New York: Holt.

Bloomfield, L. (1933). *Language.* New York: Holt.

Blumenthal, A. L. (1970). *Language and psychology: Historical aspects of psycholinguistics.* New York: John Wiley and Sons.

Blumenthal, A. L. (1974). An historical view of psycholinguistics. In T. Sebeok (Ed.), *Linguistics and adjacent arts and sciences.* The Hague: Mouton.

Blumenthal, A. L. (1975). A reappraisal of Wilhelm Wundt. *American Psychologist, 30,* 1081–1088.

Blumenthal, A. L. (1979). The founding father we never knew. *Contemporary Psychology, 24,* 547–550.

Boring, E. G. (1929). *A history of experimental psychology.* New York: The Century Co.

Boring, E. G. (1950). *A history of experimental psychology.* New York: Appleton-Century-Crofts.

Cannon, W. (1927). The James-Lange theory of emotions: A critical examination and alternative theory. *American Journal of Psychology, 39,* 106–124.

Danziger, K. (1979). The positivist repudiation of Wundt. *Journal of the History of the Behavioral Sciences, 15,* 205–230.

Danziger, K. (1980a). The history of introspection reconsidered. *Journal of the History of the Behavioral Sciences, 16,* 241–262.

Danziger, K. (1980b). Wundt's theory of volition and behavior. In R. W. Rieber (Ed.), *Wilhelm Wundt and the making of a scientific psychology.* New York: Plenum. Revised in this book: The unknown Wundt: Drive, apperception, and volition.

Diamond, S. (1980). Wundt before Leipzig. In R. W. Rieber (Ed.), *Wilhelm Wundt and the making of a scientific psychology.* New York: Plenum. Reprinted in this book.

Dittrich, O. (1903). *Grundzüge der Sprachpsychologie.* Halle, Niemeyer.

Dittrich, O. (1913). *Die Probleme der Sprachpsychologie.* Leipzig: Quelle and Meyer.

Froeschels, E. (1933). *The psychological elements of speech.* Boston: Expression Co.

Kraepelin, E. (1917). *Lectures in clinical psychiatry.* New York: Wood.

Kusch, M. (1995). *Psychologism: A case study in the sociology of philosophical knowledge.* London: Routledge.

Lehmann, A. (1899). *Die körperlichen Äusserungen psychischer Zustände.* Leipzig: Engelmann.

Meischner, W., & Metge, A. (1980). *Wilhelm Wundt—Progressives Erbe, Wissenschaftsentwicklung und Gegenwart.* Leipzig: Karl Marx Universität.

Mencken, H. L. (1955). *Prejudices.* New York: Vintage Books.

Merringer, R., & Mayer, C. (1895). *Versprechen und Verlesen: Eine psychologisch-linguistische Studie.* Stuttgart: Göschen.

Mischel, T. (1970). Wundt and the conceptual foundations of psychology. *Philosophical and Phenomenological Research, 31,* 1–26.

Osgood, C., Suci, G., & Tannenbaum, P. (1957). *The measurement of meaning.* Urbana: University of Illinois Press.

Robinson, D. K. (1987). Wilhelm Wundt and the establishment of experimental psychology, 1875–1914: The context of a new field of scientific research. Doctoral dissertation, University of California, Berkeley.

Schlosberg, H. (1954). Three dimensions of emotion. *Psychological Review, 61,* 81–88.

Spearman, C. (1930). Autobiography. In C. Murchison (Ed.), *A history of psychology in autobiography* (Vol. 1). Worcester, MA: Clark University Press.

Stern, C., & Stern, W. (1907). *Die Kindersprache.* Leipzig: Barth.

Wirth, W. (1908). *Die experimentelle Analyse der Bewußtseinsphänomene.* Braunschweig: Vieweg.

Wundt, W. (1862). *Beiträge zur Theorie der Sinneswahrnehmung.* Leipzig: Winter.

Wundt, W. (1873–4). *Grundzüge der physiologischen Psychologie* (1st ed.). Leipzig: Engelmann.

Wundt, W. (1880). *Grundzüge der physiologischen Psychologie* (2nd ed., Vol. 2) Leipzig: Engelmann.

Wundt, W. (1883). *Logik*. Stuttgart: Enke.

Wundt, W. (1894). *Grundzüge der physiologischen Psychologie* (3rd ed.). Leipzig: Engelmann.

Wundt, W. (1900). *Die Sprache*. Leipzig: Engelmann.

Wundt, W. (1907). *Outlines of psychology* (2nd ed., trans. C. H. Judd). Leipzig: Engelmann.

Wundt, W. (1908). *Grundzüge der physiologischen Psychology* (5th ed., Vol. 3). Leipzig: Engelmann.

Wundt, W. (1911–12). *Die Sprache* (3rd ed., 2 Vols.). Leipzig: Engelmann.

Wundt, W. (1920). *Erlebtes und Erkanntes*. Stuttgart: Kröner.

5

WUNDT AND THE AMERICANS
FROM FLIRTATION TO ABANDONMENT

Robert W. Rieber

In 1920, no less than G. Stanley Hall had the following to say about Wilhelm Wundt:

> Wundt has had for decades the prestige of a most advantageous academic chair. He founded the first laboratory for experimental psychology, which attracted many of the most gifted and mature students from all lands. By his development of the doctrine of apperception he took psychology forever beyond the old associationism which had ceased to be fruitful. He also established the independence of psychology from physiology, and by his encyclopaedic and always thronged lectures, to say nothing of his more or less esoteric seminary, he materially advanced every branch of natural sciences and extended its influence over the whole wide domain of folklore, mores, language, and primitive religion. His best texts will long constitute a thesaurus which every psychologist must know. (p. 6)

Following his marvelous tribute, Hall reversed Hamlet's reproach to his mother, by demonstrating that he must be kind only to be cruel. Hall went on in the next paragraph to contrast Wundt with Freud, demonstrating the gross limitations of Wundt's narrow approach to the understanding of the human mind. He proceeded to warn his readers with an almost foreboding prophecy of what is to come: "We cannot forebear to express the hope that Freud will not repeat Wundt's error in making too abrupt a break with his more advanced pupils like Adler or the Zurich group." Of course, this warning did not prevent this break from becoming a reality (Rieber, 1998b).

145

Figure 1. G. Stanley Hall

In his book *Life and confessions of a psychologist* (1923) G. Stanley
Hall listed several factors responsible for the decline of psychology
during his period. The first of these factors Hall pointed out to be
"the fact that Wundt for so long set the fashion here, served his appren-
ticeship in physics and physiology instead of biology (which would
have been a better propaedeutic); hence his disciples have little use for
evolution or the genetic aspect of psychic powers and activities" (p. 9).
Much earlier in his academic career, especially when he was professor
of psychology and pedagogy at Johns Hopkins University, Hall was
much more sympathetic to Wundtian psychology and was responsible
for the publication of, and wrote an introduction to, a book entitled
Habit and its importance in education (Radestock, 1886), an essay in pedagogical psychology translated from the German of Dr. Paul Radestock.
This book is basically a summary of both Wundtian and other related
theories, as well as applications for teachers. Although it is rather
doubtful that Wundt officially approved of this work, the book is
nevertheless highly appreciative of and influenced by the Wundtian
psychology of the period and is equally well endorsed by G. Stanley
Hall.

The question arises as to why Hall and many others (e.g., Münsterberg,[1] Baldwin, and Cattell[2]) were unhappy about Wundt's influence on American psychology. Obviously, the full answer to this question would require more intensive investigation; our intention is not to take on this task but simply to provide a short survey of Wundt's influence on the development of American psychology and to indicate why these researchers came to criticize their erstwhile master.

Our objective is to achieve this task in such a way as to demonstrate how Wundt and his ideas were both assimilated and dramatically transformed through a process that we shall refer to as the *Americanization of psychology*.

The Americanization Process

In order to aid an understanding of the meaning of the concept of Americanization, we provide a brief description of the groundwork

[1]Hugo Münsterberg received his Ph.D. under Wundt at Leipzig in 1885. According to Boring (1950), Münsterberg, while still in Germany, had deviated from the Wundtian psychology of the time. This deviation resulted in some major disagreements and debates between Münsterberg and the Wundtians in Leipzig. William James admired Münsterberg's early separation from Wundtianism and called him to be in charge of Harvard's psychological laboratory in 1892. Münsterberg was one of the major forces that facilitated the Americanization of psychology during his period. He was the first psychologist to apply psychology to the law in his classic book *On the witness stand* (1908) and, thereafter, to industry, medicine, and education. The first textbook with the term "applied psychology" in the title was written by him in 1914, *Psychology: General and Applied*. There is no mention of any tension between Münsterberg and Wundt in Margaret Münsterberg's book, *Hugo Münsterberg: His Life and Work* (1922). Any reference that Mrs. Münsterberg made to the relationship between Wundt and Münsterberg was always couched in a positive vein. It is not clear whether this omission was a sensitive and tactful consideration on the part of Mrs. Münsterberg or simply an indication that the differences between Wundt and Münsterberg were so minor as not to interfere with an ongoing friendly relationship. (For more specific details regarding the differences between Münsterberg and Wundt, as well as between William James and Wundt, see chapters by Danziger and Robinson in this book.) Nevertheless, it appears that Münsterberg's work in psychology—at least, during his American period—was more characteristic and compatible with American philosophic and psychological trends. Furthermore, it could be characterized as a variation on the theme of pragmatism and particularly applied psychology.

[2]In discussing a comparison of Wundt's and Galton's influences on American psychology, Solomon Diamond (1998) regarded Galton's influence as having been greater, even though historians have given more recognition to Wundt. Diamond went on to make it clear that the early bearers of Galton's influence on Americans were Cattell and Jastrow, but the methods originated by Galton—including test batteries, word association, the questionnaire, twin comparison, classification based on the normal distribution, and especially correlation and regression techniques—have been prominent in the development of American psychology.

for this process. The groundwork for psychology before the Civil War was largely shaped by the mental and moral philosophers and the religiously oriented colleges and universities in New England. Rieber (1998a) has provided a pertinent discussion of his period and how such men as Thomas Upham and Francis Wayland contributed to this development. As a system rather than for its content, the mental and moral philosophy of the pre-Civil War period was new and different, containing the essence of the American dream as we know it even today. Tarnished though this dream may have become, it has not been altogether replaced, perhaps because nearly all belligerents in our psychosocial controversies still subscribe to its basic premises.

A brief definition of this dream is essential to our understanding of the groundwork for psychology in America. This groundwork included a belief in equal opportunity and the right of everyone to participate in the shaping of his own life and destiny. This belief was basically compatible with the democratic government of agrarian capitalism during the pre-Civil War period and with the industrial capitalism of the post-war period. All scientific discoveries were valued because they were seen as applied to the good of each and every individual and to the nation as a whole.

The second important part of the groundwork consisted of the belief that every individual had the capacity to change for the better in accordance with his needs and desires—the "do-it-yourself" philosophy embodied in the children's story of the little red hen. This aspect of America's character was seen not as some arbitrary and capricious activity but as a more serious behavior directed toward the benefit of all mankind. Therefore, any application of the science of the human mind was fundamental to the Americanization process. Education, of course, was a necessary and important instrument for the cultivation of both body and mind. The family as an institution played a key role in providing the discipline and moral training, as well as the knowledge and skill required by the growing society.

A third and important part of this groundwork was religious faith and lifestyle, extremely varied, but usually true to the ethnic origins of the founders. The Deity was to be appreciated not only through the study of the Scriptures but also through the accurate study of nature—the work of the Creator. This attitude provided for the connection between the belief in the value of the inner life of the individual and the importance of self-knowledge. All these beliefs were brought to America in their rudimentary forms by the Puritans and have remained alive, in some measure, to the present day.

The above-mentioned factors were responsible for the easy assimilation and transformation of phrenology and mesmerism, Darwinism, Wundtian psychology, psychoanalysis, and many other related fads or movements into American thought. To a considerable extent, however, Wundtian psychology was shaped or Americanized to make it conform to this pre-existing framework.

The Functionalist-Structuralist Debate

The functionalist-structuralist debate in American psychology at the turn of the century has been written about by many scholars, for example, Krantz (1969), Boring (1969), and Rychlak (1977). Heidbreder (1969) gave a fine description of this controversy in the following manner:

> Functionalism *did* make its appearance as a psychology of protest. Its leaders *did* oppose the school that was then the establishment in American psychology: the classical experimentalists, essentially Wundtian in outlook, who saw as their basic and immediate scientific task the introspective analysis of conscious experiences under experimentally controlled conditions. These were its psychologists who, during the ensuing controversy, came to be called structuralists. And the functionalists *did* place more emphasis on the study of behavior than the classical experimentation has accorded it. Without denying introspection a legitimate and useful role, the functionalists in their own researches drew heavily on behavioral data. Influenced as they were by Darwinian theory, they undertook investigations that required that most, and in some cases all of the empirical data be obtained from the study of behavior—researched in developmental psychology, in educational and other forms of applied psychology, and in animal psychology, to mention a few examples. (p. 177)

In relating to the functionalist-structuralist debate, Rychlak (1977) made some important points. For instance, it was actually the philosopher William Caldwell who prompted Titchener to write his famous 1898 paper entitled "The Postulates of a Structural Psychology," which appeared in the *Philosophical Review*. Titchener employed the functionalist-structuralist dichotomy in two ways. First and most importantly, he considered functionalism second-class and subordinate to structuralism. Second, he used a teleological description, thereby identifying all functionalists as teleologists. The basic assumptions of this structuralist position were that sensations and affections are elements of the mind and that they are incapable of being derived from one another. Moreover, they are subject to determination by the factors of intensity and quality. The temporal aspects of mental life were also very important to Titchener, because he was not willing to conceive of emotions and sensations as being free of some form of temporal order. Even though Caldwell and, to a certain extent, Mary Calkins were sympathetic with the early Titchenerian attempt to define structuralism, they were not at all happy with the way that Titchener developed this structural or content psychology during the early 1900s. As Rychlak (1977) pointed out, "They were humanists wanting to see a role for intentionality by way of self-direction in the psychology of their time."

Calkins (1906) even accused Angell of having defected to the structuralist position in his emphasis on the importance of the physical basis of behavior. However, Angell (1906) was quick to point out that the functionalists at Chicago were not at all sympathetic with the Wundtian methodology of a "direct observation of inner experience."

Another aspect of this tension between functionalism and structuralism concerned the Darwinian theory of evolution. Angell made it perfectly clear that the functionalists of the Chicago school wished to study the mind in its relationship to the biological foundations of the organism in terms of both phylogenetics and ontogenetics. The differences between Darwin and Wundt and their effect on the Americans are discussed later in this chapter along with the contributions of James Mark Baldwin.

Psychological functionalism was involved in what one might call a common-law marriage with biology (and physiology) and, therefore, could not see itself as an ally to Wundtian psychophysical parallelism. As Rychlak (1977) points out, the often-cited historical debate between functionalism and structuralism was "no confrontation at all in one aspect and a misfired polemic in another." Rychlak went on to say:

> It [the functionalist-structuralist debate] was begun by a humanist, who found the Newtonian interpretations of science brought to this country by Wundt's students lacking in something vital to man's conceptualization. Titchener lost the totality (the one) in the constitutive total of basal elements (the many), and yet this self-organizing principle of mental life is most characteristic of the human experience. Rather than a full airing of the introspective-versus-extraspective *theoretical* slant implied, what developed was a temporary quibble over the rules of *methodological* procedure. (pp. 140–147)

Wundtian Influence and James Mark Baldwin

One very important endeavor in Wundt's scientific work was to study the facts pertaining to the nature of the human organism, to isolate

Figure 2. James Mark Baldwin

these facts by observation, and to measure them in terms of intensity and duration, that is to say, to study the psychic compounds formed by and revealed to us by our "introspective experience." It was through the form of *representation* and *emotions* that Wundt attempted to fix the empirical laws of the mind and their relationship to the body. This interest in representations was more than likely one of the things that attracted James Mark Baldwin to Wundtian psychology early in his career. Baldwin's frequent citations of Wundt in his *Handbook of Psychology* (1889) demonstrated Wundt's importance to Baldwin at that point in time.[3]

But, alas, Wundt's importance to Baldwin did not last very long, for in the *History of Psychology* (1913), Baldwin has only a few references to Wundt and in his only discussion of Wundt, in a footnote, adds insult to injury by pointing out that "this work [the *Völkerpsychologie*] is less effective because of the writer's tendency to abstract classification and schematicism" (p. 16). This extraordinary, deliberate abatement of

[3]There were many textbooks in psychology at the turn of the century. One very interesting and important text—J. Clark Murray's entitled a *Handbook of Psychology* (1888), which was successful both in Canada and in the United States—demonstrates the influence of Wundt on Canadian psychology and contains many references to Wundtian and other related ideas.

Wundt clearly demonstrates Baldwin's desire to forget him and to help others do the same, especially since Baldwin devoted whole sections to such important scholars as Herbart, Lotze, Helmholtz, Spencer, James, Fechner, and Ribot.

Baldwin's importance in American psychology during his early period is described in a very important paper by Wozniak (1998), in which Wozniak argues a position that is basically compatible with the point of view of this chapter: namely, that Baldwin's most powerful influences stemmed not from Wundt and the Europeans but from more indigenous influences in America, represented by the American mental and moral philosophy movement during the middle of the nineteenth century. Nevertheless, Baldwin's references to Wundt in his *Handbook* (1889) constitute the largest number of references to any one author in that work.

Baldwin quoted Brentano's criticism of psychological theories that do not include an appreciation of the unity between body and mind. Brentano (cited in Baldwin, 1889) pointed out that "Wundt, for example, forfeits unity in the mental life and finds three problems on his hands instead of one. First to account for the purely mental, second to account for the psychophysical, and third to account for this duality." Baldwin continued his critique of Wundtian psychology by pointing out the narrow and limited importance that Wundt gave to the concept of the unconscious. Furthermore, still in a critical vein, Baldwin then discussed the concept of association of ideas with a fascinating diagram of the German approach (see Figure 3), putting Wundt in his proper place, as it were.

A similar criticism of Wundt's use of the association of ideas was given by Royce (1903) in his discussion of the general laws of docility. Here, Royce referred to Wundt's fictitious mental elements and criticized

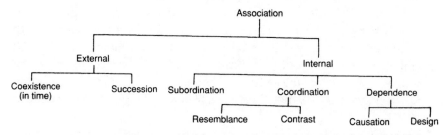

Figure 3. The prevailing German classification of the principles of association followed by Herbart, Wundt, Taine, and Trautscholdt. (From J. M. Baldwin, *Handbook of psychology: Sense and intellect*, New York, 1889.)

Wundt for his narrow volitional approach to the understanding of the mind. Though Royce took issue with the Wundtian tri-dimensional theory of emotion, he had the following to say:

> In view of the facts which constitute Wundt's admittedly still incomplete evidence for his three "directions" of feelings, and in view of the really very large body of inexact but impressive evidence on the subject which the literature of the emotions seems to contain, I am disposed to regard it as decidedly improbable that the dual theory of the feelings gives an adequate account of the phenomena. (p. 177)

Wundt and Darwinism in America

In the latter half of the nineteenth century, an influential movement advocating the theories of Darwin and Spencer developed in America. This Americanization of evolutionary theory had a considerable impact on intellectual, scientific, and pedagogical thought during that period. The movement was mainly led by the American scientist and editor Edward Livingston Youmans.[4]

Many works of English and European scientists were either reprinted or translated by American publishers during the period between 1860 and 1890. It should be noted that, during this period, very little importance was give to Wundt in America, and, conversely, Darwin and Spencer received only brief mention in passing in the writings of Wundt. As Blumenthal points out (1980), referring to Hofstadter's analysis, Social Darwinism à la Spencer "fell from American popularity very quickly" (p. 128). In some measure this may have been the case. Nevertheless, Darwin's and Spencer's influence on scientific thought in general and on scientific psychology in particular continued in the decades to come, and remnants of this development can still be seen even in today's psychology.

[4] E. L. Youmans was the catalytic agent for the connection between John Fiske and Herbert Spencer. He developed a close association with both of these men during the late 1860s and the 1870s. His close association with D. Appleton & Co., a prominent American publishing firm of the time, helped popularize evolutionary theory in America. With the creation of the journal that Youmans edited for many years, entitled *Popular Science Monthly*, and a most influential group of books, entitled the *International Scientific Series*, Youmans arranged for the publication and the simultaneous translation into English and other languages of important scientific works by authors from England and other European nations. Youmans corresponded and worked with many of the most distinguished European scientists, and Wilhelm Wundt was conspicuously absent from this list.

The difference between Darwin and Wundt alluded to earlier centered mostly on Wundt's criticism of Darwin's theory of emotional expression.[5] Emotions, according to Wundt (1907) are capable of being divided into three classes: (1) purely intensive symptoms; (2) qualitative

---

[5]Solomon Diamond has been good enough to translate for us an interesting passage in which Wundt discusses Darwin's theory of expressive movements. He has also written the paragraph of comment at the end of this footnote. At several points, where Wundt is restating Darwin's theory, the German words have been left in the text and Darwin's own words are given in brackets.

Darwin subsumes all expressive movements of animals and humans under three general principles, which are however essentially different from those which have been stated above. He calls the first principle of zweckmäßig associerter Gewohnheiten [serviceable associated habits]. Certain complicated behaviors, which unter Umstanden [under certain states of the mind] were of direct or indirect use, are supposedly performed as a consequence of habit and association even when they are not useful. The second principle is that of Gegensatz [antithesis]. When certain mental states are connected with particular habitual behaviors, the opposite states are supposed to become connected with the opposite behaviors by the mere fact of contrast. Finally, according to the third principle, some acts are from the first caused by the constitution of the nervous system, independently of the will and [omitted: to a certain extent] of habit. I cannot conceal the fact that to me these three laws seem to be neither correct generalizations of the facts nor capable of embracing them adequately. Naturally, real or apparent usefulness can be observed in expressive movements, to a certain extent, because they are originally reflexes and as such they are subject to the law of purpose and adaptation. They are this, however, at least for individuals, because of the constitution of the nervous system. Darwin's first and third principles therefore coincide at this point. As to why such purposive reflexes are also transferred to other stimuli, when there is no longer any question of their being useful, Darwin's rules provide no explanation. The factors that come into play here are in part the law of association of analogous sensations, and in part the law of the relation of movements to sensory ideas, and neither of these is included in Darwin's statement. The law of contrast is an obvious makeshift to meet this situation. If one expressive movement is to arise by contrast with another, some psychological basis for this must be discovered. Such a basis will, however, always bring us back again to the principles of expression which we formulated above, and thus to a *positive* reason for the movement in question. For example, if a dog that is expressing affection for its master displays a posture that is just the opposite of the one it takes when it approaches another dog with the intention of fighting (cf. Darwin, 1872, p. 51ff.), the reason lies partly in the fear of its master which shows itself in the crouching attitude; that is, in movements which have their basis either in sensory analogies or in the connection of these movements with ideas. Aside from this inadequate psychological development of his theory, Darwin does have the merit of having collected an extraordinarily rich set of observations and of having given numerous examples which prove the importance of heredity in this area. (Wundt, 1874, pp. 856–857)

Wundt's *Grundzüge* was to substitute "principle" for "law" where the latter word occurs in sentences 7 and 12 as translated (but not in sentences 8 and 13!). This substitution was introduced in the third edition, when Wundt (1887, vol. 2, pp. 514–515) also added a paragraph stating that even his own "principles" of expressive movement (previously

expressions of feelings: these are mimetic movements; and (3) expression of ideas: these are generally pantomimetic movements. Wundt's critique of Darwin centers mainly on Wundt's claim that Darwin had subsumed all expressive movements of humans and animals under three general principles that were different from the principles that Wundt postulated. This is a rather good illustration of how Wundt rejected Darwin's theory, giving him credit for being a good observer and nothing more and thus rejecting all that was really essential to the Darwinian position.

Edward Wheeler Scripture: The Yale Laboratory and the New Psychology

The last of the important figures in our discussion who studied under Wundt, and who was strongly influenced by him, was Edward Wheeler Scripture. After studying with Wundt, Scripture held his first job at the Yale Psychology Laboratory under the supervision of George T. Ladd. The general conclusion that Scripture took from his studies at Leipzig to his position at Yale was that statements were dependent on reliable measurements and, correspondingly, that statements without measurements were of little value; he adhered to the principle: "If it can't be measured, then it can't be any good." His time at Yale was a chaotic period for Scripture. For almost a decade, Scripture was in conflict with Ladd. This conflict dealt with intradepartmental and philosophical struggles, essentially focusing on philosophical-theoretical versus laboratory psychology, and it led to the termination of the services of both men. Carl E. Seashore (1930), a student of Scripture's while at Yale, commented on this conflict, saying, "the president should have recognized in Scripture the new approach to mental science of which Scripture was champion. Instead, he threw the baby out with the bath."

---

called laws) were purely descriptive, because any causal explanation of movements must be in physiological rather than psychological terms. In the fifth edition, in broader context, Wundt (1902–1905, vol. 3, p. 689) stated further that the principle of natural selection is a teleological rather than a causal concept, and that by describing as "accidental" the variations on which natural selection operates, Darwin had expressly foregone any attempt at causal explanation. All in all, this is a good example of how Wundt often acknowledged Darwin's acuity as an observer, but consistently rejected Darwinian theory.

In some measure, the Yale conflict stemmed from a dispute over Wundt,[6] although personality conflicts played a major part as well. Although Scripture was basically a "Wundtian," nevertheless, he was gradually contributing to the Americanization process as previously described. An important aspect of this development was particularly evident in James Rowland Angell's review (1895) of Scripture's *Thinking, feeling, and doing*, particularly as it is a partial reflection of the functionalist-structuralist controversy that has been previously described. Angell attacked Scripture for gross carelessness in his use of quotation marks by saying:

> In Chapter XXI, Dr. Scripture has the occasion to quote Wundt's human and animal psychology in these passages. The English varies widely from that of Creighton's and Titchener's translation of this work. But throughout nearly the whole of Chapter XVII where the author vaguely states that he follows Wundt the English is not only a translation of the German but is furthermore identical with that of the published translation just mentioned (pp. 606–607).

Scripture's involvement in the Americanization process led to the applications of quasi-Wundtian methods in industrial psychology (e.g., time-motion studies; see Gilbreth, 1916) and clinical applications in the area of communication disorders (Scripture, 1912).

Carl E. Seashore was strongly influenced by his teacher, Scripture, as is evident from at least two of his works. Seashore's book, the *Psychology of music* (1933), more than likely had its origins through Scripture because

---

[6]Ladd, who is best known for his *Elements of physiological psychology* (1887), acknowledged the importance of Wundt's work as a tool in helping him produce his textbook. Nevertheless, Ladd's early training at Andover Theological Seminary instilled in him a powerful and lasting appreciation of early-nineteenth-century mental and moral philosophy. Boring (1950) indicated that Ladd, like James and others, stressed the importance of the concept of self within psychology, thus making consciousness a matter of activity, namely, the activity of a self. Therefore, Boring considered Ladd basically a functional psychologist. Clearly, this difference must have been one of the sources of tension between Scripture and Ladd when they were both at Yale. In the revised edition of the *Elements of physiological psychology*, prepared in collaboration with Woodworth, the authors, in their introduction, pay a token tribute to Wundt but are quick to point out, "In brief, it may be said that introspective psychology, important as its results have been and indispensable as its method is, has shown its incompetency to deal with the many and most interesting inquiries which it has itself raised." The authors go on to say, "We may affirm with Wundt without fear of successive contradiction: 'psychology is compelled to make use of objective changes in order by means of the influences which they exert on our consciousness to establish the subjective properties and laws of that consciousness.' (Quote taken from "Über psychophysischen Methoden," Philosophische Studien [1881], Heft 1, p. 4.)" (Ladd & Woodworth, 1911, p. 10).

of his dispute with Carl Stumpf (one of Brentano's students). Wundt's students taught that melodies were actually constituted of elemental sounds and that tunes were patterns of combinations of these sounds. Stumpf argued that Wundt's data contradicted what a trained musician's ear would discover to be important to the melody. As a result, Stumpf disagreed with Wundt's findings and criticized him for not supplying us with an explanation that was truly reflective of what musical experience actually was. Additionally, Seashore's earlier book, entitled *Elementary experiments in psychology* (1908), was considered a manual for the instructor and clearly was in the tradition of other works of the period that were written by Wundt's students, such as Titchener's *Experimental psychology* (1901), Witmer's *Analytical psychology* (1902).

By far the most loyal American student of Wundt was Charles Herbert Judd, who took over at Yale when both Ladd and Scripture were fired. At least during the first ten years or so of the new century, Judd represented his master in Leipzig with the greatest of fidelity. Three English editions of Wundt's *Outlines of psychology* were translated and prepared by Judd with the cooperation of the author, as the title pages specifically indicate. They were printed in Leipzig by Wundt's publisher—an unusual arrangement, but one that gave Wundt complete assurance that the final copy would be exactly the way he wanted it. This example serves as an important contrast to all the translations of Wundt prepared by Titchener and his associates, none of which were translated with the cooperation of the author, as were the Judd translations. After Wundt's death, Judd was the only American psychologist to recognize the *Völkerpsychologie* and to alert the American readers to its importance (Judd, 1926).

Judd remained a loyal Wundtian until very near the end of Wundt's career, but by then it became apparent that application, particularly in the area of educational psychology, was both important and inevitable in American psychology. Thus, even the most faithful of all the American Wundtians had eventually to succumb to the Americanization process.

As we can see from the information provided in this essay, the American psychologists' relation to Wundt may be exemplified best as an affair that ran its course from flirtation to abandonment. This brief but intense relationship, especially through the political polemics and the tensions that came out of the functionalist-structuralist controversy, opened the door to two potentially powerful but nevertheless sleeping tigers, that is, positivism and behaviorism. A flicker of light in the form of a more dynamic, humanistic psychology was quickly blown out, along with the remnants of the Wundtian "structuralism," as the second decade of the twentieth century proceeded to build a new psychology that would hope to be as truly scientific as chemistry and physics.

Addendum

As we conclude this chapter, we go back to a statement by G. S. Hall, with whom we began. Hall (1912), as if he were looking for the new psychological superman, has this to say:

> Perhaps what is now needed is another Wundt with another life . . . perhaps it is a bold synthetic genius who will show us the way out . . . It would seem as if laboratory psychology in this country was now sufficiently developed so that it should be less dependent upon the new departures made in Germany. The present impasse is the most challenging opportunity ever presented to psychologists. In this crisis our need is a new method, point of view, assortment of topics and problems. These, I believe, geneticism is very soon to supply. Meanwhile, we may have at least for a time to follow Wirth's call to go back to Wundt. (p. 456–457)

It now appears, even after approximately eighty years, as if history has heeded Hall's prediction. For Michael Cole (1996), and many others cited by him in his book, have decided to explore the territory (unwittingly or not) that Wundt opened:

> On the whole I am enormously impressed with the quality of Wundt's thinking about the choices that faced psychology if it wanted to become an autonomous science at the end of the nineteenth century. In proposing a dual science he was incorporating a long history of thought about *Homo sapiens'* dual nature and the means by which the resulting hybrid could be rigorously investigated. Moreover, his analysis maps nicely onto divisions within the discipline between those who seek to make a natural sciences approach extend to all of psychology and those who seek a second psychology, of which various forms of cultural psychology are one manifestation. (p. 326f)

To conclude, I ask you to consider the following: if Wundt had visited America, he might not have had to say about Cattell, James, and others, "ganz amerikanisch." And if Boring had gone to Germany, he might have written a very different (more contextual) history of psychology. But they didn't.

References

Angell, J. (1895). A review of *Thinking, feeling, and doing* by E. W. Scripture. *Psychological Review, 1,* 606–609.

Angell, J. R. (1906). *Psychology.* New York: Henry Holt.

Baldwin, J. M. (1889). *Handbook of psychology: Sense and intellect.* New York: Henry Holt.

Baldwin, J. M. (1913). *History of psychology.* London: Watts & Co.

Blumenthal, A. L. (1980). Wilhelm Wundt and early American psychology: A clash of cultures. In R. W. Rieber (Ed.), *Wilhelm Wundt and the making of a scientific psychology* (pp. 117–135). New York: Plenum.

Boring, E. G. (1950). *A history of experimental psychology* (2nd ed.). New York: Appleton-Century-Crofts.

Boring, E. G. (1969). Titchener, meaning, and behaviorism. In D. Krantz (Ed.), *Schools of psychology: A symposium.* New York: Appleton-Century-Crofts.

Calkins, M. W. (1906). A reconciliation between structural and functional psychology. *Psychological Review, 13,* 61–81.

Cole, M. (1996). *Cultural psychology: A once and future discipline.* Cambridge: Belknap Press of Harvard University Press.

Diamond, S. (1998). Francis Galton and American psychology. In R. W. Rieber & K. D. Salzinger (Eds.), *Psychology: Theoretical and historical perspectives* (2nd ed., pp. 89–99). Washington, D.C.: APA.

Gilbreth, F. W. (1916). *Fatigue study.* New York: Sturgis & Walton.

Hall, G. S. (1912). *Founders of modern psychology.* New York: Appleton.

Hall, G. S. (1920). Preface to the American edition. In Sigmund Freud, *A general introduction to psychoanalysis.* New York: Edward L. Bernay.

Hall, G. S. (1923). *Life and confessions of a psychologist.* New York: D. Appleton.

Heidbreder, E. (1969). Functionalism. In D. Krantz (Ed.), *Schools of psychology: A symposium.* New York: Appleton-Century-Crofts.

Judd, C. H. (1907). *Psychology: General introduction.* New York: Scribner's.

Judd, C. H. (1926). *Psychology of social institutions.* New York: Macmillan.

Krantz, D. L. (Ed.). (1969). *Schools of psychology: A symposium.* New York: Appleton-Century-Crofts.

Ladd, G. T. (1887). *Elements of physiological psychology.* New York: Scribner's.

Ladd, G. T., & Woodward, R. (1911). *Elements of physiological psychology* (rev. ed.). New York.

Münsterberg, H. (1908). *On the witness stand: Essays on psychology and crime.* New York: McClure.

Münsterberg, H. (1914). *Psychology: General and applied.* New York: D. Appleton.

Münsterberg, M. (1922). *Hugo Münsterberg: His life and work.* New York: D. Appleton.

Murray, J. C. (1888). *Handbook of psychology.* Boston: Cupples & Hurd.

Radestock, P. (1886). *Habit and its importance in education: Essay in pedagogical psychology* (F. A. Caspari, Trans.). Boston: D. C. Heath.

Rieber, R. W. (1998a). The Americanization of psychology before William James. In R. W. Rieber & K. D. Salzinger (Eds.), *Psychology: Theoretical and historical perspectives* (2nd ed., pp. 191–213). Washington, D.C.: APA.

Rieber, R. W. (1998b). Assimilation of psychoanalysis in America: From popularization to vulgarization. In R. W. Rieber & K. D. Salzinger (Eds.), *Psychology: Theoretical and historical perspectives* (2nd ed., pp. 355–395). Washington, D.C.: APA.

Royce, J. (1903). *Outlines of psychology.* New York: Macmillan.

Rychlak, J. F. (1977). *The psychology of rigorous humanism.* New York: Wiley.

Scripture, E. W. (1895). *Thinking, feeling, and doing* (1st ed.). New York: Meadville, Flood & Vincent.

Scripture, E. W. (1907). *Thinking, feeling, and doing* (2nd ed.). New York: G.P. Putnam & Sons.

Scripture, E. W. (1912). *Stuttering and lisping*. New York: Macmillan.

Seashore, C. E. (1908). *Elementary experiments in psychology*. New York: Henry Holt.

Seashore, C. E. (1930). In C. Murchison (Ed.), *History of psychology in autobiography* (pp. 225–297). Worcester, Mass.: Clark University Press.

Seashore, C. E. (1933). *Psychology of music*. New York: McGraw-Hill.

Titchener, E. B. (1901). *Experimental psychology: A manual of laboratory practice*. New York: Macmillan.

Witmer, L. (1902). *Analytical psychology*. New York: Gin & Co.

Wozniak, R. (1998). Thought and things: James Mark Baldwin and biosocial origins of mind. In R. W. Rieber & K. D. Salzinger (Eds.), *Psychology: Theoretical and historical perspectives* (2nd ed., pp. 429–453). Washington, D.C.: APA.

Wundt, W. (1907). *Outlines of psychology* (3rd English ed.) (C. H. Judd, Trans.). Leipzig: Wilhelm Engelmann.

6

REACTION-TIME EXPERIMENTS
IN WUNDT'S INSTITUTE
AND BEYOND

David K. Robinson

Kurt Danziger (1980d) observed, "The reaction-time studies conducted during the first few years of Wundt's laboratory constitute the first historical example of a coherent research program, explicitly directed toward psychological issues and involving a number of interlocking studies" (p. 106). Wilhelm Wundt argued that these experiments investigated "purely psychological" phenomena, whereas much work in psychophysics and sensory physiology did not.

To make psychology an experimental science, Wundt needed to conceive a research program that justified experimental psychology as a separate discipline. He had been making arguments for such a new discipline since his first treatise on psychology (1862); in the 1880s an international community of researchers joined him in the effort. Up to this point psychology was a (generally minor) part of philosophy, and psychophysical methods generally were interesting only to the physicists and sensory physiologists who used them in their research. To establish a separate experimental discipline of psychology, Wundt proposed a theory of mind that supported a well-defined, quantitative, and easily reproducible experimental methodology. Such a program was fully operational in the Leipzig Institute for Experimental Psychology during the 1880s.

The Heart of the Work of the Leipzig Institute in the 1880s

What kinds of experiments were carried out in Wundt's Institute? And what were they intended to prove or discover? Edwin G. Boring (1950) offered the following survey of the Institute's publications, particularly in the journal Wundt edited. He began with the remark that Wundt actually

> defined experimental psychology for the time being, because the work of this first laboratory was really the practical demonstration that there could be an experimental psychology . . . Practically all the work from the Leipzig laboratory was published in the *Philosophische Studien* (1881–1903) and there is not very much in this journal that did not come either directly from Leipzig, or from Wundt's students so soon after leaving Leipzig that they still represented the intentions of Wundt. (p. 339)

"Practically all the work from the Leipzig laboratory" refers to the five or so doctoral dissertations from Wundt's Institute each year, as well as research reports by more advanced researchers. Many dissertations that Wundt sponsored were not published in *Philosophische Studien*, but nearly all the experimental ones were.

Following the general remarks, Boring proceeded to classify 109 experimental articles in Wundt's first journal into four categories: (1) more than one-half on sensation and perception, with the proportion increasing toward the end of the series; (2) one-sixth on reaction times, concentrated in the period before 1890; (3) one-tenth on attention and feeling, especially in the 1890s; and (4) somewhat less than one-tenth on association. Dividing the first category further, he found that vision received the lion's share, nearly a quarter of all the experimental studies in the journal. The next most important area of sensation was auditory perception. In the area of tactile sensation, so important in the history of psychophysics (the Weber law, etc.), there were only a few studies. A couple of researchers published on sense of taste, and there were no articles on the sense of smell. A sixth sense, the "time sense," was represented by three different researchers' studies of the perception or estimation of time intervals.

As a specialist in sensory perception, Boring strongly identified with the Wundtian experimental tradition. Although he suggested that reaction-time experiments were part of the core of the work of the early Institute, he concluded that this line of research ultimately failed when it proved impossible to measure separately the times required by discrete mental functions (1950, p. 342). The failure was by no means total, as Metge (1983) has argued, and Boring neglected to emphasize how important this "failed program" was to the development of laboratory psychology.

A separate discipline of psychology needed an area of study that it could call its own. When Wundt came to Leipzig, studies of sensation and perception were primarily identified with physiology, and Wundt would change that identification only partially. Research on sensation and perception in the Leipzig Institute, in the large picture, was preliminary or ancillary to investigations of complex central-nervous processes. Reaction-time experiments sought to measure those processes directly. Leipzig researchers worked in hot pursuit of the parameters and laws of mental chronometry, and Wundt's theory of mental processes implied that reaction-time experiments could serve as the model for investigating many mental phenomena, including attention, will, association, feeling, and emotion.

The "failed" program of reaction-time studies provides a very good historical probe into early experimental psychology. It defined the "social structure of psychological experimentation" in Leipzig (Danziger, 1990). Moreover, prominent experimental psychologists (e.g. Münsterberg, Külpe, Titchener) formed their particular styles of experimentation, at least partly in response to the problems (and their solutions) that arose in Leipzig reaction-time work.

Reaction-Time Studies before the Leipzig Institute

Woodworth (1938, pp. 298–339) gives a useful review of the origins of reaction-time studies. Astronomers, trying to gain ever more accurate simultaneous measurements of position and time for a given celestial event, came up against the phenomenon of the personal equation in the early nineteenth century. No matter how careful the observers, they could differ in reporting a given event by as much as a half-second. This dilemma interested Wundt during his earlier career as a physiologist, and his "complication experiment" sought to explain the discrepancies and develop some standard measurement of reaction times. By 1866 Wundt was taking credit for the discovery that the observed time of a reaction was significantly greater than the time required for a nervous impulse to travel from sense organ to the brain plus that required to travel back to the reacting muscle (Diamond, 1980, p. 49). In other words, a good chunk of the time was taken up by *central* nervous processes. For a young physiologist declaring a new scientific psychology, that was a crucial finding. It only remained to discover a way to investigate those central processes experimentally.

At about this time such investigations were made possible by the appearance of an accurate instrument to measure the "speed of thought." The Swiss astronomer Adolph Hirsch (1830–1901) began doing experiments with a chronoscope (a very accurate stop-clock) which had been developed by his precision mechanic, Mathias Hipp (1813–1893). The Hipp chronoscope (see Figure 2) registered time intervals to the one-thousandth second. With minor improvements, it remained a standard piece of apparatus in psychology laboratories for at least fifty years after Hirsch published his reaction-time measurements (1861–63, 1863; see also Sokal, Davis, & Merzbach, 1976).

Hirsch determined the times for some simple reactions, in which the subject signaled, e.g. pressed a telegraph key, upon perceiving a stimulus:

visual stimulus	200 ms (milliseconds)
auditory stimulus	150 ms
electric shock	140 ms.

It was of great interest to astronomers that visual perception required more time; astronomical photography was then in its infancy, and precision-timed observations still required eye-ear coordinated reports.

At Utrecht, the physiologist Franciscus Cornelis Donders (1818–1889) proposed a way to measure the time taken by different mental functions. His technique, the "subtraction method," was essentially this: find the time for a simple reaction to stimulus (such as those Hirsch did); run another reaction which is set up in the same way but which involves a more complicated mental process; then subtract the first time from the second to get the "physiological time" required by that additional mental process. The first presentation of such experiments was the medical dissertation of J. J. de Jaager (1865/1970), a student of Donders, although the teacher usually gets the credit for beginning systematic reaction-time measurements.

Donders's experiments (1868/1969) rely on the assumption that each part of the reaction (sensation, perception, discrimination, choice, reaction movement) takes a specific amount of time; "physiological time" for particular mental processes can be determined if experiments are devised in which there is first no such process and then that process is simply "inserted." The additional time is the time required by that particular mental process. Donders proposed three types of reactions that, taken together, could measure times for "choice" and "discrimination."

Speech sounds served as stimuli and reactions. These were recorded on a chronograph, consisting of a kymograph (moving drum) and a tuning fork marking its regular vibrations on the drum; the set-up allowed small time differences to be measured. Donders's first reaction, the a-reaction, was the simple response to stimulus. The b-reaction required sensory discrimination and then motor selection in signaling the choice. The c-reaction required sensory discrimination but, according to Donders, no motor selection.

The experiment used five syllables, something like "ka, ke, ki, ko, ku." For the simple reaction, the a-reaction, the stimulus was always "ki," and the response was also "ki." For the "choice reaction," the b-reaction, the stimulus was any one of the five syllables; the subject responded by speaking the same syllable. The subject had to make a sensory discrimination and then a motor selection in order to produce the correct response. For the c-reaction, the stimulus was again any of the five syllables, but the subject was instructed to respond only when he heard "ki." Donders thought that this last reaction involved sensory discrimination but no motor selection, no choice. Donders found these average results:

> a-reaction 197 ms
> b-reaction 285 ms
> c-reaction 243 ms

Using the subtraction method, sensory discrimination time (c-a) was 46 ms, and pure choice (b-c) took 42 ms.

Wundt eagerly grasped this quantitative handle on mental processes. The time intervals were very small, considering the crude technology that measured them, but the subtraction method promised to produce time measurements for mental processes. Conscious mental actions had become the focus of Wundtian psychology, and the reaction-time experiment was the raison d'être of the Institute when the work began there in 1879.

One active participant in the program, James McKeen Cattell (1888), made a point to correct a common misperception and to distinguish psychometry from psychophysics: "We are naturally glad to find it possible to apply methods of measurement directly to consciousness; there is no doubt but that mental processes take up time, and that this time can be determined. The measurements thus obtained are not psychophysical, as those which we have been recently considering, but purely psychological" (p. 45). Whether or not they directly addressed the reaction times, many of the crucial (and controversial) problems in early experimental psychology actually grew out of reaction-time work in Leipzig; this was the experimental ground upon which Wundt staked his theoretical claims and set his students to work. Innovations and improvements in psychological experimentation by other researchers often originated in a criticism of Wundt's approach.

Reaction-Time Studies in the Leipzig Institute

Wundt altered the Donders experiment, for practical and theoretical reasons. He accepted the subtraction method but preferred to use the Hipp chronoscope rather than the chronograph (on the latter, see Haupt's chapter in this book and Figure 1); direct readout was more convenient for repeated series of experiments than time-consuming measurements and conversions of line-lengths on the drum. (See Figure 2, a set-up for an auditory reaction.) In addition to this technical change, Wundt's reaction-time experiment incorporated an important conceptual difference.

Wundt's theory of mental processes involved a stricter distinction between choice and discrimination. In the first edition of *Grundzüge* (1874, pp. 744–745), Wundt expressed doubts about Donders's classification. To him, both the b-reaction and the c-reaction involved choice. In the case of the b-reaction the choice was between different muscular responses; in the c-reaction the choice was to respond or not to respond. In the second edition of *Grundzüge* (1880, Vol. 2, pp. 247–256), published shortly after advanced students began to work in the Leipzig laboratory, Wundt formally introduced his pure discrimination reaction. In such a reaction there were different possible stimuli, and the subject signaled (always using the same muscular movement) as soon as he "recognized or identified" the stimulus given. This d-reaction involved discrimination (*Unterscheidung*) but not choice (*Wahl*).

Although the d-reaction would appear to be little more than an interesting thought experiment—there being no external way to know exactly when recognition occurs—this was in fact the actual discrimination

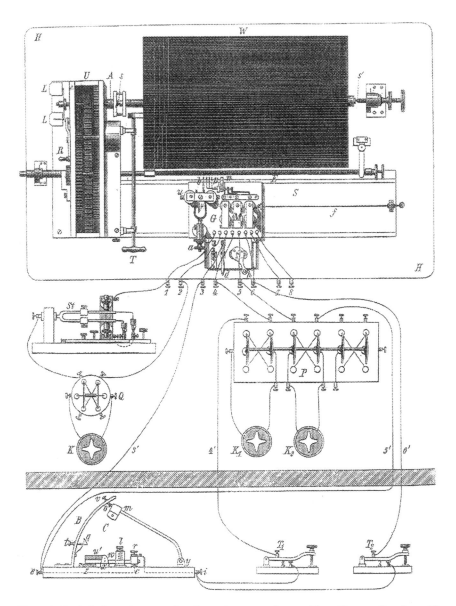

Figure 1. Ludwig Lange's setup, showing a chronograph assembly, with recording drum W and tuning forks at G and St. (Lange, 1886b, p. 458)

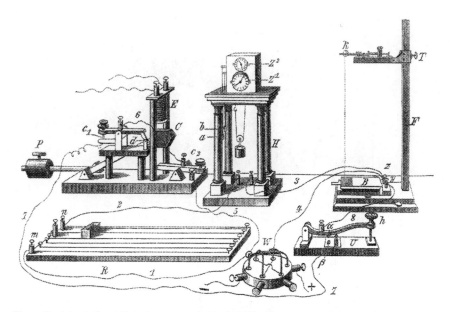

Figure 2. A typical reaction-time set-up in the Leipzing Institute, with auditory stimulus *F*, Pohl's see-saw switch (*Wippe*) *W*, *Kontrollhammer* *C*, Hipp chronoscope *H*, rheostat *R*, and response key *U*. (Wundt, 1902–1903, Vol. 3, p. 388)

experiment used in Wundt's Institute. It may be that Wundt's strict theoretical requirements resulted in more flexibility in experimental controls, but he was, in any case, pioneering new territory.

A purely *psychological* experiment, employing the advanced instrumentation of current physical and physiological research, was largely undefined in the 1870s and 1880s. Wundt believed that experiments on purely psychological phenomena were possible and that psychological experiments would necessarily involve subjective elements that physiologists (particularly those of the reductionist persuasion) generally tried to exclude. This was precisely why a special science of experimental psychology, in addition to and distinct from physiology, was needed. Experimental psychology depended upon refined techniques that Wundt variously referred to as self-observation (*Selbstbeobachtung*), inner observation (*innere Beobachtung*) and inner experience (*innere Erfahrung*). Although Wundt's English-language translators commonly used "introspection" to refer to his experimental methodology, the term has been used too loosely. "Self-observation, controlled by experiment" is perhaps the best description of Wundt's method (cf. Danziger, 1980a).

Wundt was no novice at physiological experimentation, so his faith in the d-reaction reveals a strong theoretical commitment. The sharp distinction between discrimination and choice corresponded with Wundt's five-part model for mental reaction. The schema was the centerpiece of the work of the early Institute, and not only of reaction-time studies. Especially in the 1880s, this litany began nearly every paper from the Leipzig Institute:

> (1) sensation, the movement of the nerve impulse from the sense organ into the brain;
> (2) perception, the entry of the signal into the field of consciousness (*Blickfeld des Bewußtseins*);
> (3) apperception, the entry of the signal into the focus of attention (*Blickpunkt des Aufmerksamkeits*);
> (4) act of will, in which the appropriate response signal is released in the brain;
> (5) response movement, or more precisely, the movement of the response signal from the brain to where it initiates muscular movement.

Wundt contended that steps one and five are purely physiological, whereas the three middle steps are psychophysical, i.e. they involve processes that "have both a physiological and a psychic side" (1880, Vol. 2, p. 221). Any mental reaction could involve all five steps, and there was no direct way to measure separate times for the three middle steps. However, well-constructed experiments using the subtraction method could give estimates of "time of apperception" (discrimination time) and "time for an act of will" (choice time). The subjects in these experiments had to be trained in self-observation in order to report these psychic events. Figure 3 shows Wundt's schematic of his apperception theory (for more discussion of the figure, see Diamond, Balvin, & Diamond, 1963, p. 162; and Woodward, 1982).

Wundt's first doctoral students in the Institute used the discrimination reaction in the way just described. In one study using visual stimuli, the simple reaction consisted of pressing a key upon perceiving a flash of light. In another reaction, Wundt's d-reaction, one of two different images was suddenly illuminated before the subject: either a white circle on black background or a black circle on white background. The subject pressed the key as soon as he decided which one he was seeing. Initial illumination started the Hipp chronoscope running, and the pressing of the key stopped the dial, giving time elapsed for the entire reaction.

Wundt and two of his doctoral students, Max Friedrich and Ernst Tischer, did the experiments together. One served as the subject, as

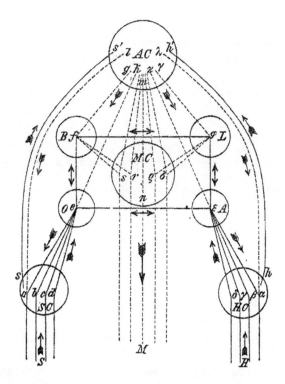

Figure 3. Wundt's schema for the "hypothetical connections of the center of apperception" *AC*, the site of discrimination and choice. The motor center *MC* is the reflex center; *SC* is the vision center; *HC* represents the hearing center; *B, L, A,* and *O* are "intermediate centers." (Wundt, 1902–1903, Vol. 1, p. 324)

another initiated the reaction by illuminating the image and the third recorded the times. Then they alternated roles. This was the classical Wundtian experimental set-up: subject (*Reagent*), experimenter (*Experimentator*), and observer (*Beobachter*), respectively. Needless to say, all three had to have a clear understanding of what it meant to "recognize" a black or a white circle, and they had to be consistent in their performance of this recognition. In these early experiments, they trained until average reaction time was as short as possible, and mean variation was minimized for each reacting subject.

The d-reaction seemed to give reasonable results in the first several studies, summarized in the second edition of *Grundzüge* (1880, Vol. 2, pp. 219–327). The simple reaction took from 132 to 226 ms, in fair agreement with Donders, and "recognition" added from 50 ms (Friedrich's average

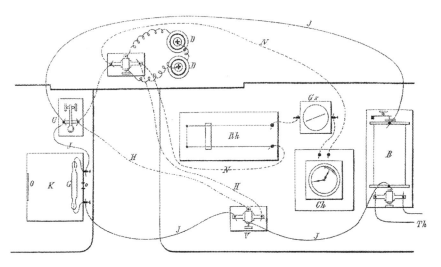

Figure 4. Max Friedrich's setup for visual reaction-time studies, showing batteries *D*, light source *G*, observed stimulus *O*, response key *U*, and Hipp chronoscope *Ch*. (Friedrich, 1883, p. 45)

time) to 79 ms (Wundt's). With four different colors the recognition time increased, from Tischer's average of 73 ms to Friedrich's 157 ms. Figure 4 shows Friedrich's laboratory set-up for experiment with visual stimuli.

Similar experiments gave choice times. First was the simple choice, to react or not react to the stimulus, e.g., press the key for the white circle but not if it is the black one that appears. (This was the reaction which Donders had claimed involved no choice.) Reaction time averaged between 368 ms and 455 ms, whereas discrimination without the simple choice averaged from 185 ms to 303 ms for the three subjects. Therefore, extra time taken to make the simple choice ranged between 152 ms and 184 ms for these subjects.

There could also be choice between different movements: press a key with the right hand if the image is white, a different key with the left hand if black. This choice time was somewhat longer (thus agreeing with Wundt's five-stage theory), averaging between 188 ms to 331 ms more than the time for the simple discrimination reaction.

A summary of the results:

1st experiment: simple reaction   132–226 ms
                   discrimination, 2 stimuli 50–79 ms more
                   discrimination, 4 stimuli 73–157 ms more

2nd experiment: reaction with discrimination,
                  but no choice   185–303 ms
                  simple choice   152–184 ms more
                  multiple choice 188–331 ms more

Wundt and his students recognized that individual differences and external conditions (distractions, fatigue, etc.) could affect the outcome of a
reaction, but their main goal was to establish base averages for the different mental functions.

With confidence that they had a way to measure indirectly the
time required for two parts of Wundt's five-phase reaction, the Leipzig
psychologists undertook to determine the extent to which more complicated tasks called for extra action by the apperception (in recognition)
and/or the will (in choice). Max Friedrich's doctoral dissertation
(1883; also Behrens, 1980a; 1980b), recognized as the first dissertation
in experimental psychology, found that time of apperception increased
with complexity of stimulus, i.e. it took more time to "recognize" a
string of six digits than just one or two, and that practice could shorten
discrimination time, but not simple reaction time to any appreciable
extent.

Another early doctoral dissertation was Martin Trautscholdt's study
of time of association (1883). Association, according to Wundt's theory,
was a particular action of the apperception, a successive focusing of attention on different thoughts. The subject in this experiment was instructed
to signal the moment an idea, produced by an association with the stimulus, appeared in consciousness. Subtracting this time from "recognition
time" for the stimulus itself, it was determined that the association part
of apperception added 706 to 874 ms to reaction time (Wundt, 1880, Vol.
2, pp. 279–291).

The investigations employing the subtraction method looked promis-
ing, but too much depended upon separate measurements of discrimination time, measurements which proved to be very unstable. In the first
volume of *Philosophische Studien*, where Friedrich's and Trautscholdt's dissertations appeared, Ernst Tischer's dissertation (1883) on discrimination
of sounds already pointed to some difficulties. Auditory stimulus, as
Hirsch had noted earlier, gave substantially shorter reaction times than
visual stimulus. Occasionally discrimination time seemed to be zero, that
is, the time required simply to react to an acoustical stimulus was
equal to the time required to react when the stimulus was "recognized."

Likewise, Emil Kraepelin's article (1883) on the effects of drugs on these reaction times found that discrimination time was an unreliable concept, particularly when the subject was under the influence of drugs or alcohol. It was becoming apparent that the discrimination reaction required practice and expertise of such a special and fragile nature that it was uncomfortable, to say the least, to base a whole line of research on it.

An ambitious American student added significantly to the discredit of the discrimination reaction. James McKeen Cattell (1860–1944) made considerable improvements to reaction-time measurements; then he essentially abandoned the discrimination reaction. Early in his work at Leipzig, he determined that the magnetic mechanism on the Hipp chronoscope engaged the time dial faster than it disengaged. The delay in stopping the dial caused overall reaction times to be measured as greater than they should have been. Cattell (1886–88) invented a device to engage and disengage the timer equally, a mouth key for verbal response, and a gravity chronometer (*Fallapparat*) which improved experiments involving visual stimuli. In this device, a gate would drop, starting the Hipp chronoscope running and revealing the visual stimulus (a word, figure, etc.); the reacting subject pressed a key, stopping the chronoscope. Time elapsed was thus registered. This arrangement produced reaction times shorter than the sudden illumination used in Friedrich's experiment, because abrupt change in light level required extra accommodation by the eyes (Wundt, 1902–03, Vol. 3, p. 476).

Since Cattell's improvements lessened measured reaction times, he had problems keeping enough slack for a distinct discrimination time. Another doctoral student who shared Cattell's critical view of the d-reaction was Gustav Berger, Cattell's closest colleague in the Institute and at times his paid personal assistant and translator. Berger's dissertation (1886) concentrated on the simple reaction and questioned the methodological status of the choiceless discrimination reaction: the motor response which actually stopped the chronometer did not depend upon perception, something with a physical correlate, but rather upon apperception, a "psychophysical event" which (at least until the electronic devices of the mid-twentieth century) could not be registered independently. There was no sure way to check for false reactions or otherwise be certain when apperception occurred.

Cattell and Berger apparently lost faith in Wundt's five-phase schema for mental action. In one of his occasional critical outbursts, the bright young American in Leipzig wrote to his parents:

> Wundt's laboratory has a reputation greater than it deserves—the work done in it is decidedly amateurish. Work has only been done in two departments—the relations of the internal stimulus to the sensation [i.e. psychophysics], and the time of mental process [reaction times]. The latter is my subject—I started working on it at Baltimore before I had read a word written by Wundt—what I did there was decidedly original. I'm quite sure my work is worth more than all done by Wundt and his pupils in this department, and as I have said it is one of the two departments on which they have worked. Mind I do not consider my work of any special importance—I only consider Wundt's of still less. The subject was first taken up by Exner, and Wundt's continuation of it has no originality at all; and being mostly wrong has done more harm than good. (Cattell to parents, 22 January 1885; Sokal, 1981, p. 156)

Cattell's bragging to his parents undoubtedly involved a certain amount of perfunctory denigration of his teacher, but in fact he had some reason to brag.

Cattell's mechanical ingenuity was supplemented by his keen thinking. He compared Wundt's ideas on the reaction-time experiment to what he knew about other studies and found Wundt's view to be wanting. Exner's emphasis on the effects of attention, or preparation for a reaction, figured into Cattell's reaction studies already in his first semester in the Institute, from November 1883 to March 1884 (Sokal, 1981, pp. 98–105).

Sigmund Exner (1842–1926), a physiologist in Vienna who had studied in Heidelberg under Helmholtz and Wundt's uncle, Friedrich Arnold, apparently coined the term "reaction-time experiment." He found that for simple reactions, preparation was the only thing that was voluntary; the reaction itself was involuntary, simply a reflex chain set in motion by the perception of the stimulus (Exner, 1873; 1874; 1875). Wundt argued that Exner used incorrect values for the different speeds of nerve impulses in sensory, spinal, and motor areas and that Exner simply underestimated "psychophysical time"—the time Wundt ascribed to the central nervous processes of perception, apperception, and will (Wundt, 1880, Vol. 2, p. 225n4). Cattell, however, judged that Exner was more correct than Wundt about the overall times and the effects of preparation.

The whole program, reaction-time research as a way of demonstrating and investigating Wundt's schema for mental processes, was about to fall apart. Yet Wundt was ready to accept the results of experimental research, and he must have been pleased by the improvements in the instruments. He gave Cattell the honor of being his first Institute Assistant, though Cattell was unpaid and apparently did not have the extensive responsibilities for training students that later assistants had.

It was, in fact, Cattell's replacement, the next Institute Assistant, who came forth with an idea that revitalized Wundt's program and opened up areas for new research, and for new controversies.

Ludwig Lange's Approach: Muscular vs. Sensorial Reaction

Ludwig Lange (1863–1936) was one of the most interesting and most tragic of Wundt's students. The son of the professor of classical philology at Leipzig, he had his early education at the famous Thomasschule. He began university studies, first with a semester at Leipzig University, then two semesters in Gießen, then back to Leipzig. He concentrated on mathematics and physics, but he also studied philosophy, attending Wundt's lectures on logic, ethics, history of philosophy, and psychology. Lange was one of several mathematics students, like Max Friedrich, who were attracted to research in the early Institute.

In 1885, Lange's father died, and Wundt took the young man under his wing. Lange attained the doctoral degree in 1886, and his three historical-epistemological articles on the law of inertia (1885a, 1885b, 1886a) appeared in Wundt's journal. Much later these studies attracted the attention of the famous physicist, Max von Laue (1948), who wrote a biographical piece on Ludwig Lange.

Although Lange's first writings were not on experimental psychology, Wundt chose him to succeed Cattell as Institute Assistant. Lange was the first paid assistant, also the first to have the doctoral degree already in hand. During 1885–86, as Berger and Cattell pursued Wundt's experimental program with great accuracy, and in the process undermined the theory behind reaction-time studies in the Institute, Lange came up with a way to save Wundt's model. His experiments were reported in the 1887 (third) edition of the *Grundzüge* and appeared in an article in Wundt's journal, "New experiments on the process of the simple reaction to sense impressions" (Lange, 1886b). This article introduced the *Kontrollhammer* for calibrating the Hipp chronoscope (see Haupt's chapter in this book; also see Figures 5 and 6), and it made a theoretical distinction that served as the basis for many future publications in experimental psychology.

Lange claimed that simple reactions were of two very different types: "sensorial" or "muscular," depending upon whether the subject directed attention toward the stimulus or toward the reacting movement. The sensorial reaction was a "complete" reaction, whereas the muscular reaction

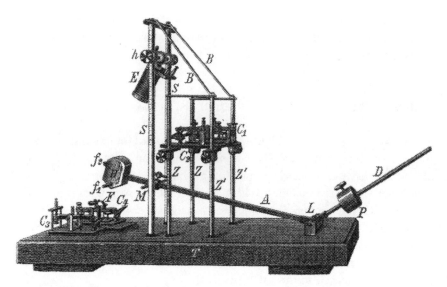

Figure 5. *Kontrollhammer*, for calibrating the chronoscope. (Wundt, 1902–1903, Vol. 3, p. 397)

was "shortened"—as it were, preparation by directed attention could short-circuit apperception and will in Wundt's schema of mental processes. The purely muscular reaction was nothing more than a "brain reflex."

The experiment to show the distinction between the two types of reactions required the subject to assume certain mental attitudes of preparation. For the muscular reaction he was to concentrate on the response movement and not to think at all about the stimulus. The sensorial reaction required more difficult preparation. As Robert Woodworth (1938) explains it, the subject had "to avoid altogether all preparatory innervation of the movement, but to direct the whole preparatory tension towards the expected sense impression, with the intention, however, of letting the motor impulse follow immediately on the apprehension of the stimulus, without any unnecessary delay" (p. 306). The subject practiced to acquire one or the other extreme of attitude. The muscular attitude was easier to assume, but it also produced many premature and false reactions, which did not occur in the sensorial reaction. The muscular and sensorial reactions were the extremes; in any given, unpracticed reaction, attention lay somewhere between the two attitudes. Lange thus accounted for the problematic findings of Tischer, Kraepelin, Cattell, and Berger, and at the same time he opened up a line of reaction-time research on attention.

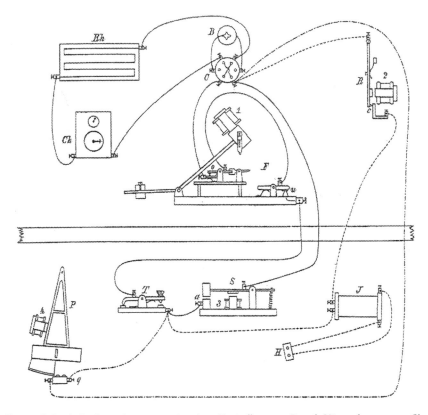

Figure 6. Ludwig Lange's set-up, showing *Kontrolhammer F* and Hipp chronscope *Ch.*
(Lange, 1886b, p. 482)

Lange and two colleagues in Wundt's Institute did simple reactions
to acoustic and cutaneous stimuli and found that the muscular reaction
took about 125 ms, whereas the sensorial reaction took approximately
100 ms longer. (See Figure 7.) Lange interpreted the muscular reaction
as action through prepared reflex (à la Exner) and the sensorial reaction
as involving the full five steps of Wundt's schema, including the three
psychophysical actions. To continue studies of apperception and will, one
had only to make sure that subjects did only sensorial reactions.

Lange himself could not stay to carry out this effort. Mental illness
(perhaps manic-depression; see Robinson, 1987, pp. 106–109) forced him
to leave the Institute, even though Wundt had intended for him to remain
as Assistant, and he spent the rest of his rather long life as a mental

	Sensorielle Reaction			Muskuläre Reaction			D	Reagent
	M	mV	n	M	mV	n		
Schall	216	21	26	127	8	24	89	N. Lange
＞	235	24	24	121	9	28	114	Belkin
＞	230	33	19	124	9	27	106	L. Lange
Elektr. Hautreiz. .	213	25	19	105	6	25	108	N. Lange
Lichtreiz	290	28	20	.172	8	24	118	L. Lange
＞	291	39	20	182	13	25	109	G. Martius

Figure 7. Table of sensorial and muscular reaction times for sound (*Schall*), electric stimulus, and visual stimulus (*Lichtreiz*). The differences are given in column *D*. (Wundt, 1902–1903, Vol. 3, p. 414)

invalid. When E. B. Titchener (1921) arrived in Leipzig a couple of years later, he heard rumors that "strenuous objection was made to the new laboratory on the grounds that continued self-observation would drive young persons to insanity" (p. 178n34). Maintaining the "sensorial attitude" while doing discrimination experiments must have been demanding and tedious. The subject had to concentrate on *not* anticipating the response movement, since one naturally tended to drift toward that state of preparation during a series of repeated reactions. Lange's problems had become the stuff of gossip and rumors against Wundt, but Lange clearly had weak physical and mental health before he came into the Institute. Nevertheless, the sad developments must have given Wundt some cause to think about possible problems with psychological experiments.

But the work continued. The sensorial reaction offered renewed opportunity for investigations and time measurements of conscious mental processes: apperception, choice, even associations. Exner's notion of willful preparation followed by essentially unconscious reaction by reflex was not the stuff of psychological research, not as Wundt had envisioned it anyway. Wundt wanted direct experimentation on conscious mental functions. To a large extent, it was in efforts either to reject or defend Wundt's reaction-time research that an international community of experimental psychologists found its identity. (For example, see Jastrow's 1890 summary of reaction-time work for American psychologists.) Many of them first experienced this community in the Leipzig Institute for Experimental Psychology.

Social Organization of Research in the Leipzig Institute; The Set-Up for Experiments

The Leipzig experiments just reviewed began in 1879. Their research set-up already had its final form, where the human players were concerned. Although instrumentation developed and theories were altered, the social organization of research remained remarkably stable and represented particular goals, as Danziger has argued (1990). It is worthwhile to take a closer look at the Wundtian experimental set-up, since it, like instrumentation, was more directly transferable to other institutions and to other cultural environments than were the theories and philosophical framework which reigned in the Leipzig Institute.

Ten years after official establishment of the Institute, an occasion arose which called for Wundt to reflect upon his accomplishment. For the 1893 Columbian Exposition in Chicago, an international celebration of industry and science, German academics prepared a volume designed to put the best of their universities forward to the world. Wundt contributed an article, "Experimental psychology and psychophysics" (1893b). That such a chapter would be included in such a volume is a measure of the importance attached to the development of Wundt's line of research. Sixteen years later, when Leipzig University celebrated the 500th anniversary of its founding in 1409, Wundt (1909) had another opportunity to sketch a history and a description of his Institute.

Both sketches describe the same set-up for psychological experimentation. That stability was a result of Wundt's many years of preparation before coming to Leipzig. As assistant in Helmholtz's physiological institute in Heidelberg, Wundt had ably routinized the work there. He did a similar job in Leipzig, even before the educational ministry formally established the Institute in 1883. When Külpe assumed the position, the Institute Assistant began to run routine operations for Wundt, much as Wundt had done it for Helmholtz.

Wundt's most detailed description of the organization of the Institute's work appears in the 500th-anniversary sketch. The Institute, he wrote, had two functions: to give an introductory course in the methods of experimental psychology, usually taught by an Institute Assistant, and secondly, to carry out original research.

> The plan for the research projects is determined in a special assembly of all participants on the opening day of each semester. The director distributes the topics to be worked on, those to be continued from the previous semester as well as those newly chosen. In the case of the latter, consideration is given to the special wishes of particular older members who are interested in a certain theme. Then the members are divided into groups, each of which is occupied with a special topic. Participation in a group is voluntary, and each member is allowed to participate in several groups, as time and schedules allow. This group structure is as a rule necessary for psychological experiments, because it is best if the observer and experimenter are different persons; moreover, it is desirable that results from a single observer should be controlled by those from the others. It can also happen with complicated experimental set-ups that it is necessary for different parts of the apparatus to be handled by different experimenters. There are very few tasks that are suitable for just one person with the combined job of observer and experimenter.
>
> After the participants have been divided into separate groups, the schedule for the semester is determined, as well as the distribution of work space for the different groups at their different times. After groups are constituted, a leader is designated for each one. This is usually an older member of the Institute who has proved himself in previous semesters by helping in others' projects. The leader assembles the results of the experiments and, in the case that they are suitable, prepares them for publication. Whether results are published or not, the protocols of the experiments always remain the property of the Institute. (Wundt, 1909, pp. 131–132)

Unlike the control conditions that prevail in today's experimental psychology, all actors typically knew all the roles and simply rotated through all the positions: subject (*Reagent*), experimenter (*Experimentator*) and observer (*Beobachter*). The alternation of roles in the Institute had obvious pedagogical advantages, but Wundt's words make clear his conviction that the arrangement also had scientific value. His description clarifies the need for different observers, but it was also important that observers served as subjects in their own experiments as well. In the Leipzig set-up for psychological experiments, the subject had to know as much about the experiment as the experimenter or the observer, in order to be sure he was doing the reaction correctly. Reaction-time experiments, for example, depended upon consistency in the reporting of "recognition." For experiments in his Institute, Wundt insisted that subjects be trained, perhaps even, as Cattell recalled, "that only psychologists would be the subjects in psychological experiments" (B. T. Baldwin, 1921, p. 156).

Exceptions to the institute-centered experiment only proved the rule in Leipzig. Cattell preferred to set up his experiments in his apartment, where work would not be limited to the hours the Institute was open. However, he also disagreed with Wundt on the need for the third person; he and his friend Berger worked together, without the separate observer (Sokal, 1981, pp. 127, 139). Their line of thinking and their experimental results challenged and even slightly altered Wundt's design of the reaction-time experiment, but Wundt did not change his fundamental theory of mental processes nor his requirements for the experimental set-up in the Institute.

Although most psychologists now reject essential aspects of Wundt's set-up for psychological experiments, its advantages in early laboratories should not be overlooked. Like any standard method, it achieved a certain stability of results and gave a clear point of departure for critics. It was also easily transferable. Even foreign students and visitors who had little understanding of, or interest in, German idealistic philosophy and Wundt's larger theoretical concerns could understand the function of the apparatus and the operation of a research team.

Enthusiastic adoption of Wundt's techniques, without due attention to his underlying theory and intent, spelled conflict down the road; but no alternative theoretical position really threatened Wundt's way of doing things during the 1880s, and Wundt at the time seemed happy to let a thousand flowers bloom. He had, so he claimed later near the end of his life, never intended to be "head of a school." He only wanted to establish a research program for the experimental investigation of conscious mental processes.

Leipzig Psychology Spreads in Europe, 1885–1895

As Wundt's international students began to take his methods home and begin laboratories and institutes for psychology there, the reaction-time work figured very prominently in the process. A key figure was George Dwelshauvers (1866–1937), an ardent promoter of experimental psychology both in Belgium and in France. After receiving the doctorate in Brussels and then working in Wundt's Institute, he returned to the Belgian capital in 1889, intending to open a psychological institute and to let the true way of experimental psychology rescue his "extremely unphilosophical country" from the "ridiculous masquerades" of the "spiritualists, positivists, and materialists" (G. Dwelshauvers to Wundt, 6 October 1889, Archive of Leipzig University, Wundt Nachlaß, Nr. 1131; 22 December 1889, Nr. 1134).

While in Leipzig Dwelshauvers shared in the excitement of Ludwig Lange's new methodology for the reaction-time experiment. With five experimental subjects, he investigated the effects of different time intervals in which attention prepared for the muscular and for the sensorial reaction. The preparation signal and the stimulus were both acoustical. Dwelshauvers alternated preparation times of 0, 1.5, 3, and 6 seconds and obtained results that "fully supported Lange's distinction." The shortest sensorial reaction took an average of 60 ms longer than the longest muscular reaction. The shortest reactions occurred after preparation time of 1.5 seconds, and subjects reported that the 6-second preparation was "unpleasant and tiring" (Dwelshauvers, 1891, pp. 226–229). There were some preliminary observations concerning practice, use of different time intervals between experiments, and subjects' own assessments of their performance.

Dwelshauvers presented his laboratory study for habilitation in philosophy at Brussels, but the faculty rejected it. Apparently the "spiritualists, positivists, and materialists" among the philosophers did not see the usefulness of his work (Martius, 1891a). His initial failure to win friends for experimental psychology meant that his laboratory in Brussels, begun by 1890, had to limp along for a while. By 1893, however, it had four rooms and some financial support, as Belgian universities became increasingly receptive to the new field (Dwelshauvers to Wundt, 3 August 1893, Archive of Leipzig University, Wundt Nachlaß, Nr. 1139; cf. Sahakian, 1968, p. 524).

Dwelshauvers's articles, books, and lecture tours did much to promote interest in experimental psychology in Belgium and also, to some extent, in France. He joined Désiré (later Cardinal) Mercier, professor of philosophy at Louvain University, in the effort to make the new psychology a bridge between Catholic Thomist philosophy and modern science (Misiak, 1980). They sent young researchers to study with Wundt, including F. V. Dwelshauvers (cousin to George), Albert Michotte (who became the most prominent Belgian psychologist of his time), and Armand Thiéry (a canon who obtained his doctoral degree with Wundt in 1895) (Misiak & Staudt, 1954, pp. 34–110).

By the late 1890s the Belgian followers of Wundt had strong professional commitment, some backing from senior colleagues, and support in the developing educational institutions. German cultural and philosophical traditions there were probably not as strong as the French, but there were Belgians who understood German idealism better than the

Americans psychologists, and the neo-Thomists in particular were anxious to make use of certain aspects of German thought.

Considering the ideological issues often associated with the study of the mind, it seems odd that Wundt's style of psychology enjoyed earlier reception in Catholic Belgium than in Scandinavia. Scandinavia's first experimental psychologist, Alfred Lehmann (1858–1921), promised to give Leipzig psychology a strong start to the north, but local academic politics worked against him.

After completing his doctoral dissertation, a study of physical aspects of color aesthetics, in Copenhagen in 1884, Lehmann spent a year in Wundt's Institute, where he developed a psychophysical method for investigating the color contrast of visual brightness (1886). Back in Copenhagen he erected, at his own expense, one of the first psychophysical laboratories outside of Germany, where he began experiments to challenge the theory of association expounded by Denmark's reigning philosopher, Harold Höffding (1843–1931).

Höffding posited that immediate recognition by similarity was fundamentally different from association by contiguity of ideas in consciousness. Lehmann, more in keeping with Wundt's notion of association as an act of apperception, did experiments to show that all associative processes were essentially contiguous focussings of attention, that there was no distinct act of associative recognition. The Lehmann-Höffding debate appeared in Wundt's journal (Lehmann, 1893; Höffding, 1892). Höffding quickly tired of public debate with Lehmann, but he may have used his influence to slow the academic advancement of his opponent: Lehmann did not become full professor in Copenhagen until late in his career, in 1919 (Nilsson, 1980).

Another study by Lehmann became very important to the work in Leipzig: bodily correlates of emotions, specifically pulse and breathing. Again Lehmann essentially supported the Wundtian notion of active and creative apperception against the theory of another of his countrymen. The Copenhagen pathologist Carl Lange (1834–1900) published a study of vasomotor reactions accompanying emotions and claimed, reversing the usual supposition, that mental states of emotions were responses to bodily occurrences, themselves brought about by reflex actions (1885/1887). Lehmann's experiments attempted to prove that emotions originated in the mind and then were expressed in certain parts of the body (1892). His study influenced Wundt's theory of emotion, which was the basis of much of the work of the Leipzig Institute, beginning in the 1890s.

Although Lehmann had the professional commitment and the Danes certainly shared German cultural and intellectual traditions, the institutional and collegial supports for experimental psychology were not immediately forthcoming. Lehmann's polemics against his countrymen in support of his German teacher may have contributed to his lack of academic status and to his isolation in Copenhagen. Experimental psychology in Scandinavia had to wait a generation or more before it had any distinct organization, even though Scandinavian philosophers and physiologists contributed relevant work to the field. For example, Tigerstedt and Bergqvist (1883), physiologists in Stockholm, rendered a masterful review of visual reaction-time work, up to and including Friedrich's dissertation.

Reaction-time studies also dominated early Russian experimental psychology, which was taken up mostly by young psychiatrists there. V. M. Bekhterev was an early visitor to Wundt's Institute, and V. F. Chizh revisited the complication experiment using the new reaction-time apparatus (Tschisch, 1885). The first psychological laboratory in Moscow published extensive summaries of the Leipzig reaction-time experiments, complete with illustrations of the apparatus (Tokarskiy, 1896). St. Petersburg "reflexology" and the Georgian school of "set theory" were both well informed by the foundational work in Leipzig.

Münsterberg's Dissent

The first among Wundt's doctoral students to attain an academic position and concentrate on experimental psychology was Hugo Münsterberg (1863–1916). He was also the first among Wundt's doctoral students seriously to challenge his teacher's views in print. Not surprisingly, their relationship has been the subject of considerable discussion and occasional controversy.

Born to a prosperous Jewish merchant family in the northern port of Danzig, Münsterberg studied French in Geneva then began medical studies in Leipzig in 1882, at age nineteen. He quickly gravitated toward the new psychology and completed the doctorate in philosophy under Wundt in 1885. It was in Leipzig, according to one writer, that young Münsterberg began his dispute with Wundt on whether the sense of effort in a muscular action originates in a signal from the central nervous system toward the muscles (Wundt's view) or in sensations developed in the muscles themselves (Münsterberg's). Since they disagreed, so the story goes, Wundt advised Münsterberg not to do an experimental study for the doctoral degree (Roback, 1952, pp. 212–233). Münsterberg's dissertation, "The theory of natural adaptation in its development, use and meaning, with particular reference to psychophysical organization [Die Lehre von der natürlichen Anpassung in ihrer Entwicklung, Anwendung und Bedeutung mit besonderer Berücksichtigung der psycho-physischen Organisation]," was not an experimental study, but it was certainly related to psychology. Wundt signed off on the dissertation in 1885, but it was not published in *Philosophische Studien*.

Münsterberg decided not to finish his medical education in Leipzig. Instead he went to Heidelberg, where he completed the medical doctorate in 1887. Moving on to Freiburg, he habilitated as *Privatdozent* that same year, started teaching philosophy, married, and began a family. He also set up his psychological laboratory in two large rooms of his home. Münsterberg's was probably the fourth German laboratory to train students in experimental psychology (following those of Wundt, Ebbinghaus, and G. E. Müller). Though only a *Privatdozent*, Münsterberg was nevertheless able to support his research through his personal inheritance. His resources—combined with his ambition—enabled him to do work in psychology that was independent of Wundt and much broader in scope than the work of Ebbinghaus or even G. E. Müller. Münsterberg hired a mechanic to build apparatus of his own design or adaptation. When Theodore Flournoy was appointed to a new professorship of physiological psychology in Geneva in 1892, he ordered duplicates of all of Münsterberg's equipment (Krohn, 1892).

Münsterberg's publications directly challenged Wundt's psychological theories. His habilitation essay (1888) supported Carl Lange's theory of emotions (rather than that of Lehmann and Wundt) and extended it to a general theory of will. Münsterberg opposed Wundt's notion that a psychic element could be created in the central nervous system; he saw no need to posit anything more fundamental than sensations and nervous reflexes in reaction to them. Münsterberg published a series of studies, *Beiträge zur experimentellen Psychologie* (1889–92), which supported the views set forth in the habilitation essay with experimental studies, all more or less directed against Wundt's doctrine of central control of mental processes. These studies established Münsterberg as an experimenter of considerable ability. These Freiburg studies attracted considerable attention—in Leipzig, in Göttingen (see Haupt's chapter in this book), and even in North America.

Münsterberg's energy and intellectual capacity helped make him a successful lecturer in Freiburg. He was appointed *Professor Extra-ordinarius* in 1891 and taught many topics in philosophy, in addition to psychology. He also took interest in the French work on hypnosis and gave a course of lectures on the topic. This last bit of research fore-shadows Münsterberg's interest in applied psychology, an interest that grew after he arrived in the United States. By contrast, Wundt's reaction to the increased attention to hypnotic experiments was an essay (1893a) arguing that hypnotic suggestion was not an experimental method which could give precise information about the subject's mental processes. Such experiments did not meet his criteria for experimentally controlled self-observation, since, *inter alia*, roles were not interchangeable (Danziger, 1980c).

In a letter to him, William James praised Münsterberg as "the ablest experimental psychologist in Germany" and asked him to come to Harvard for three years and direct a new psychological laboratory (James to Münsterberg, 21 February 1892; quoted in Keller, 1979, p. 25). James realized that the new discipline was outstripping his own amateurish efforts in the laboratory (Harper, 1950), and he was attracted by the young man's originality in experimentation. He wrote to his (apparently doubt-ful) Harvard colleague Josiah Royce:

> It is in the laboratory that he appears at his best, and that best is *very* good. His indefatigable love of experimental labor has led him to an extraordinarily wide range of experience, he has invented a lot of elegant and simple appara-tus, his students all seem delighted with him, and so far as I can make out, everyone recognizes him to be, as a *teacher*, far ahead of everyone else in the field, whatever you may think of his published results. (James to Royce, 22 June 1892; quoted in Keller, 1979, p. 26)

James also convinced himself that there was ample flexibility in Münsterberg's philosophical position. Although thoroughly sensational-istic, if not materialistic, in his psychological theories, Münsterberg had, like the pluralist James, a more idealistic expression in other areas of phi-losophy. It was precisely this kind of division of intellectual turf that Wundt disliked.

James was finishing his *Principles of Psychology* (1890) as Münsterberg began publishing his *Beiträge*. Remarkably, James's text also presented a five-stage description of reaction, though it differed from Wundt's model in that it, like Münsterberg, put more emphasis on physiological processes. Whereas Wundt had two "physiological" stages (at beginning and end), and three "psychophysical" stages in between, James identified four purely physiological stages, with only one psychological stage in the middle:

1. The stimulus excites the peripheral sense organ adequately for a current to pass into the sensory nerve;
2. The sensory nerve is traversed;
3. The transformation (or reflection) of the sensory into a motor current occurs in the center;
4. The spinal cord and motor nerve are traversed;
5. The motor current excites the muscle to the contracting point.

As far as James was concerned, Wundt had no empirical justification for dividing the central step into separate acts of perception, apperception, and volition. Furthermore, according to James, Ludwig Lange's experiments showed that sensorial reactions were too "excessive" and "untypical" to be of much value to experimental psychology. Only times for muscular reaction should be used for quantitative comparisons, James concluded, and he took Wundt's acceptance of Lange's muscular-sensorial distinction to mean that "Wundt has himself become converted to the view which I defend" (James, 1890, Vol. 1, pp. 88–94).

James was mistaken, of course, to write that Wundt had given up the distinction between perception, apperception, and choice, and their accessibility via the sensorial reaction. Wundt retained his reaction model, even though he eventually had to admit the difficulty in measuring the duration of any separate stage (Wundt, 1894). Moreover, Wundt continued to regard the sensorial reaction as the most important type for the study of mental action. In his view, the muscular reaction was only a lower limit, an automatic reaction that had little to do with most of the mental processes he wished to investigate.

James took a different approach altogether. He argued that reflex actions could be characterized definitively by physiology's quantities of intensity and time; acts of volition, however, were beyond the reach of exact measurement. In Wundt's view, James made the concept of "volition" too narrow and used "reflex" too liberally. Wundt, with his voluntarist psychology, tended not to account actions to reflex if he could argue that central nervous processes played a role. To his way of thinking, James excluded from experimentation any process that was at all psychological, and only allowed measurement of physiological processes.

Although they had some disagreements later, James and Münsterberg's mutual opposition to Wundt initially made them very compatible ca. 1890. James and his friend, Carl Stumpf, had already decided that Wundt was their opponent in psychology and philosophy, and a formidable one. They found encouragement in Münsterberg's defection to their side (James to Stumpf, 6 February 1887; in H. James, 1920, Vol. 1, pp. 262–264). James had formulated his conceptions of habit and "ideomotor action" in parallel with, though without knowledge of, Carl Lange's theory of emotions, which became known as the James-Lange theory of emotions (James, 1884). So Münsterberg's treatise on the will also happened to support James. Both had employed an extended concept of reflex (Woodward, 1984; Danziger, 1980b).

Münsterberg became a prominent experimental psychologist, and, like Wundt, a successful organizer of psychological laboratories for training and research, first briefly at Freiburg and then impressively at Harvard. However, his theoretical views put him outside of Wundt's circle. The theoretical differences between Wundt and Münsterberg involved differences in their visions for the field of psychology. In America Münsterberg became a major proponent of applications of psychology to law, commerce, and industry. In Germany, Wundt generally opposed the development of applications by academic psychologists.

After three successful years at Harvard, Münsterberg came close to becoming a professor in the German-language Swiss university in Zurich. He failed to receive the appointment, whereas an important student of Wundt's, Ernst Meumann, was able to capture the position for experimental psychology. Münsterberg agreed to stay at Harvard, but often sailed to Germany for vacations and sabbaticals. He even visited Wundt a few times (M. Münsterberg, 1922, pp. 105, 155–156). Indeed, their personal relations were neither as unfriendly as is commonly supposed, nor as strained as those between Wundt and James; and they were certainly less hostile than Wundt and Stumpf were to one another. Responding to Münsterberg's congratulations on Wundt's seventieth birthday, only ten years after Münsterberg went to Harvard, Wundt noted that their views in philosophy had much in common, and he even found value (albeit negative) in Münsterberg's work in psychology:

Even though our views on psychology differ today as much as ever, you can be assured that whenever I look back on my life, as these last days have prompted me to do, I appreciate that I owe much not only to those who stood by me as like-minded colleagues—I also owe much to those whose strict criticism of my opinions made it necessary for me to prove better that which I believed I had discovered; to secure better, if possible, that which was uncertain; or where a view became untenable, to admit as much, and readily concede. Among those whose opposition has been useful to me many times in this respect, you, honored colleague, are of the first rank (Wundt to Münsterberg, [August] 1902; quoted in Schlotte, 1955–56, p. 347).

In spite of his success at Harvard and his contributions to the development of American psychology, Münsterberg never became an American, either officially or at heart. His feverish efforts to win American sympathy for the German cause in the Great War helped bring on a stroke. Münsterberg died quite young, at 53, one morning during his lecture.

Wundt's Allies in Germany: Kraepelin and Martius

Although experimental psychology was part of philosophy, the most distinguished of the Germans who worked in Wundt's Institute in its early years was a young psychiatrist, Emil Kraepelin (1856–1926). He became interested in Wundt's work even before he came to Leipzig in 1878 to become assistant in the psychiatric clinic of Paul Flechsig. He experimented occasionally in Wundt's Institute and also conducted psychological studies in the clinic. He collaborated with Wundt on the beginning of Wundt's journal, *Philosophische Studien*. Wundt, however, advised Kraepelin not to leave the field of psychiatry for psychology (Fischel, 1959; Wirth, 1927; Kraepelin, 1983/87).

Kraepelin used Wundt's experimental method to test the effects of alcohol, morphine, and other substances on mental processes, particularly reaction time (1883). Also in 1883, he published his *Compendium der Psychiatrie*, which introduced the nosology of mental disorders (e.g., the distinction between neurosis and psychosis) that became a basis of modern psychiatry. This important book went into several enlarged editions during Kraepelin's lifetime.

Attracted by the notion that experimental investigations would help to distinguish normal and pathological mental states, Kraepelin kept up his contact with the work in Wundt's laboratory, even after he left Leipzig in 1886. He contributed a total of seven articles to *Philosophische Studien*.

Besides his study of the effects of drugs on simple reactions, these included critical studies on psychophysical methods. He also defended the program for reaction-time studies, as it faced some criticism. (Kraepelin & Merkel, 1894). Kraepelin began his own journal in 1896, published by Wundt's publisher, Engelmann, and named it *Psychological Writings* (*Psychologische Arbeiten*). Kraepelin's journal featured, as the title of his lead article specified, "The psychological experiment in psychiatry" (1896). He continued laboratory research at Dorpat (1886–1890), Heidelberg (1890–1904), and Munich (1904–1926), and was the leading German psychiatrist of his generation.

Even with Kraepelin's early participation, and even with Ludwig's Physiological Institute, Flechsig's *Nervenklinik*, and other medical facilities nearby, psychology in Leipzig was essentially philosophical, certainly during Wundt's lifetime. Kraepelin's interests were exceptional for Leipzig psychology. Had this prominent psychiatrist stayed and worked in proximity with Wundt, experimental psychology in Leipzig may not have kept its focus on normal psychology.

Another German, who also came early to Wundt with doctorate already in hand, was Götz Martius (1853–1927). Although he later slipped into obscurity (but see Wirth, 1928), Martius was a significant personality in early experimental psychology, and he was an early champion of Wundt's program for psychological research. He also introduced several others to the field, some of whom became important figures in German psychology.

Martius took his doctoral degree in philosophy in Bonn in 1877, then he spent several years working as a schoolteacher and tutor. The financial circumstances of his marriage made it possible for him to return to Bonn University, where he habilitated in philosophy in 1885. In 1887 he took a semester's leave to go work in Wundt's Institute. He returned to Bonn with a set of Leipzig instruments and planned, with his friend and colleague Theodor Lipps, to start a laboratory.

Martius probably began working with his apparatus at his own home in Bonn. His first experimental study appeared in Wundt's journal in 1889, and soon Martius's plans for a laboratory at Bonn University came to fruition, when the new professor of physics, Heinrich Hertz, gave him the use of unneeded rooms inherited from Clausius. Martius used his new laboratory space to challenge the Münsterberg experiments that undermined the essential distinction between muscular and sensorial reactions and, by extension, Wundt's theory of mental processes. Before he proceeded, though, Martius made sure he was not usurping Leipzig territory: "I would like very much to know whether someone in Leipzig is undertaking this work, or whether you, honored Herr Geheimrat, intend to give this work to someone. In that case I would turn to something else" (Martius to Wundt, 23 May 1889, Archive of Leipzig University, Wundt Nachlaß, Nr. 1314). Münsterberg had recently taken his doctorate with Wundt, so it may be that Wundt was reluctant to criticize these experiments himself and it was convenient that Martius volunteered his services. When Martius's study appeared in *Philosophische Studien*, Wundt also contributed a critical review of the general concepts behind the work of Münsterberg, Carl Lange, and others who rejected his doctrine of the central origin of feelings and emotions (Wundt, 1891).

Martius began his forthright defense of Wundt by reviewing Ludwig Lange's treatise on muscular and sensorial reactions. He noted that he had assisted Lange with these experiments in Leipzig. Then Martius reviewed the first issue of Münsterberg's *Beiträge zur experimentellen Psychologie*. Experiments presented there showed that some individuals, when doing more complicated discrimination and choice reactions, took longer in the muscular mode than in the sensorial. Wundt's approach insisted that complex reactions were possible only in the sensorial mode; in his theory of mental processes, a muscular reaction could not involve complicated discrimination or choice, because apperception and will (the psychophysical phases of the process during which discrimination and choice occur) are short-circuited in the muscular reaction. Münsterberg broke down the sensory-muscular distinction because he wanted to show that there was "no clear boundary between psychophysical and physical processes; multiple choice reactions can be brain reflexes too" (Münsterberg; quoted in Martius, 1891b, p. 168).

One of Münsterberg's experiments on choice called for movement of each of the five fingers according to a different stimulus, e.g. numbers one through five, five grammatical cases, five professional occupations. Subjects did muscular reactions (directing attention to finger movement) and then sensorial reactions (directing attention to the spoken stimulus). Münsterberg found that the muscular reaction could take longer. Martius admitted that this was an occasional result, though he could not confirm the regular, large differences that Münsterberg reported.

The main problem with Münsterberg's work, Martius contended, was that the reactions under study were not muscular reactions of the type specified by Ludwig Lange and Wundt. The direction of attention (preparing the apperception) is not simply toward one movement. There are five, and there cannot (so the Wundtians argued) be five separate ideas in the focus of consciousness at one time. Secondly, in Münsterberg's 'muscular' reactions, attention is actually not directed toward the movement, but rather toward the coordination of the category and the movement. Such a complicated process must involve apperception and cannot short-circuit it. Martius showed that Münsterberg's unambiguous results could be obtained by doing the muscular reactions first, and then the sensorial reactions, with the subjects thus more practiced.

At this opportune point in his criticism of Münsterberg, Martius explained the Wundtian methodology for psychological experimentation:

> Another remark, valid for all psychological experiments, should not be suppressed. Münsterberg simply sat at his clock and took readings while running the experiments; others reacted. That is a mistake that will be detrimental anywhere in experimental psychology. Psychology, also experimental psychology, is based on inner observation (*innere Beobachtung*). Even the measurement of mental processes cannot be carried out without the help of inner experience (*innere Erfahrung*), which alone can control what process is to be measured. Someone who just brings in other persons and makes observations on them has no certainty whatever that the processes being measured are those that he ordered or those that he desires. Only by doing the reaction himself can he have this assurance. This is valid everywhere in psychology, but particularly in subtle processes like those of psychometry; it is more important with complex reactions than with the simple ones. If self-observation (*Selbstbeobachtung*), or inner experience (*innere Erfahrung*) does not remain the decisive factor in psychology, then the door will be opened to the most extravagant fancies. Without the constant restriction and supervision by inner experience, experimental psychology would do more harm than good. The dependability of inner experience proves itself time and again; on it alone rests the future of scientific psychology. (Martius, 1891b, p. 178)

The reaction-time experiment functioned as the medium for controversies in experimental psychology, making possible quantitative investigations of mental processes and, more importantly, giving some sort of common basis for comparing very different theoretical approaches to their explanation. It is interesting that Martius emphasized the social arrangement of Wundt's psychological experiment and attributed Münsterberg's "misleading" results to his failure to adhere to that arrangement.

Besides Martius and Lipps, at least one other psychologist, a prominent one, began his research career in Martius's laboratory in Bonn. Karl Marbe (1869–1953) studied in Freiburg and became acquainted with Münsterberg's work, but it was Martius who really attracted him to psychology. Marbe recalled his arrival in Bonn during summer-semester 1890: "At that time Martius was making all sorts of reaction experiments, in which I helped him, and which increased my interest in modern psychology" (Marbe, 1936, p. 188). Marbe spent additional semesters with Martius but eventually diverged from the views of both Martius and Wundt. Ironically, Marbe was one the Germans who developed applied psychology, more of a Münsterberg than a Martius, as it turned out.

In 1893 Martius was appointed *Professor Extraordinarius* in philosophy at Bonn. He no longer published in Wundt's journal; instead he contracted with Wundt's publisher Engelmann to begin a journal to report his work and that of his students. He named it *Contributions to Psychology and Philosophy* (*Beiträge zur Psychologie und Philosophie*). Martius managed to produce only one volume between 1896 and 1905: eleven lengthy articles (including a manifesto-like introduction), all but four of them written by Martius himself. The last three articles were based on research carried out in Kiel. Martius had been called to a full professorship there in 1898 and started a psychological institute the next year.

After having produced a dozen studies in experimental psychology between 1889 and 1905, Martius stopped publishing altogether. In his autobiography, written late in his life, he explained that he became disillusioned with Wundt's program for psychophysical investigation of subjective processes, and he admitted that his university lectures and not his publications gave the best account of his philosophical views (Martius, 1922). Perhaps Martius identified too closely with Wundt early on and neglected to make his own way in philosophy and theoretical psychology. The same could not be said of Wundt's most influential student, Oswald Külpe (1862–1915), the third assistant in Wundt's Institute.

Külpe's Rejection of the Subtraction Method

The reaction-time experiment was arguably the most integral part of the research program in the first decade of the Leipzig Institute, when that institution was the unchallenged leader in the field. These experiments purported to investigate "purely psychological" phenomena. Külpe, however, came to the conclusion that the subtraction method, as used in Leipzig, could not analyze complex reactions. In the 1890s, moreover, authors writing for the new *Zeitschrift für Psychologie und Physiologie der Sinnesorgane* devoted almost no attention at all to reaction-time work.

We have seen how Cattell and others in the Leipzig Institute reduced measured reaction times to such an extent as to cast doubt on Wundt's five-stage model: sensation, perception, apperception, volition, and reactive impulse. Ludwig Lange then came to the model's rescue by distinguishing two different types of reactions, muscular and sensorial. In the shorter muscular reaction, the subject attended to the reactive movement; in the longer sensorial reaction, attention focused on the stimulus. According to Wundt's theory, the muscular reaction was only possible in simple reactions; it was essentially a reflex that short-circuited the psychic stages in his model. A sensorial reaction might be either simple or compound, i.e., involving one or several psychic actions such as discrimination, choice, or association. As long as Wundt continued as director, the Institute continued to recognize the distinction between the sensorial and the muscular reaction.

With the acceptance of the sensorial-muscular distinction, the role of attention became very important, since attention either to the stimulus or to the response movement distinguished the two types. Consequently, Leipzig researchers began investigating and timing fluctuations (*Schwankungen*) of attention (for example, these three studies in a single volume of Wundt's journal: Eckener, 1893; Pace, 1893; Marbe, 1893; see also the general treatise by Heinrich, 1895). Külpe, seeking an elegant approach to the problem, noticed certain constant departures from simultaneity when subjects attempted to react with both hands at once. He tried to discover how different types of expectation or attention produced preferences of one hand over the other, and how these preferences changed with changes in preparation. By determining variable factors of preparation, Külpe hoped to understand their role in these reactions, especially in the more variable sensorial type.

But Külpe was unable to bring his research to the desired conclusion. He was able to show that variation of attention was the most significant factor—more important than intensity and clarity of the stimulus, or than the external conditions for the reacting movement. However, he did not get very far in his study of preparation and its effects on attention. He finished only two sections of a planned three-part study (Külpe, 1891–92; cf. Titchener, 1892, pp. 219–221). About the same time, Külpe prepared for publication, in 1893, his *Grundriß der*

Psychologie. Although the textbook is notable for many departures from Wundt's teachings, in the general direction of Machian positivism, the most interesting part for our purposes is section 70, "The analysis of compound reactions," which rejects the subtraction method: a cognition reaction is not simply the simple sensorial reaction plus a new mental act.

The time required for a distinct mental action in a compound reaction, Külpe argued, could not be derived by simple subtraction. The problem was that addition of a mental task (e.g., discrimination, choice) inevitably required different mental preparation, and preparation was the most important factor in such reactions. Time required for a compound reaction minus time for a corresponding simple reaction could not equal time for the added mental act, because the preparation for the compound reaction determined an entirely different mental course for the reaction. Külpe's psychology textbook treated such compound reaction-time experiments with a tone of apology, and did not even mention his own aborted work on preparation and attention (1893/95, pp. 406–445 of the English edition).

To be sure, Külpe continued reaction-time work, but as he developed his own institute in Würzburg, he allowed his students (including Marbe, Ach, and Karl Bühler) to take their theories and methodologies in new directions, far afield from the Wundtian models. Nevertheless, the famous Würzburg "thought experiments," often called "imageless thought" in the literature, can be considered outgrowths of Wundtian reaction-time work (Mack, 1993). Indeed, the seminal work for the whole direction was Ach's work on volition and thinking, which devoted an appendix to the detailed workings of the Hipp chronoscope (Ach, 1905). The questioners usually recorded the time elapsed between the prompt and response, even if they did little to interpret the times.

Before Külpe's critique of Leipzig reaction-time work in 1893, Münsterberg had already argued for disposal of the sensorial reaction and its alleged psychic actions altogether. He claimed that the muscular reaction was just as useful for studying compound reactions as for simple ones. William James in America favorably received Münsterberg's reaction-time work and its theoretical implications. Although James and Münsterberg had little use for the sensorial reaction, other psychologists in North America took more interest in it. In fact, a debate on the sensorial-muscular distinction helped to distinguish an important American school of psychology, functionalism.

Structuralism and Functionalism

E. B. Titchener at Cornell surveyed reaction-time experiments in 1895. He essentially agreed with his friend Külpe, that the subtraction method was flawed, but insisted that muscular and sensorial reaction-types were still useful tools for the analysis of mental action (Titchener, 1895a). J. Mark Baldwin (1895) at Princeton, on the other hand, saw the muscular-sensorial distinction as a way to characterize different "types" of individuals. Using unpracticed subjects, he found that some people were disposed to react "sensorially" whereas others tended to react in the "motor" fashion.

There was a debate on the purpose of the reaction-time experiment. Baldwin (1896) claimed that individual differences were the important facts of nature that the psychologist should study. Titchener (1895b; 1896) argued that the goal of psychological science was the discovery of the laws of the generalized mind, and he defended the Wundtian use of practiced subjects to exhibit sensorial and motor attitudes in a way that minimized individual differences.

James R. Angell, together with one of his colleagues at the University of Chicago, analyzed the Baldwin-Titchener debate. "Reaction-time: A study in attention and habit" begins with these words: "It is not without grounds that experimentation upon reaction-time has been called the *Lieblingsgegenstand* [favorite topic] of experimental psychology. The facts appear so simple and the interpretation so illusive that ingenuity has seemed piqued anew each time the matter has been opened" (Angell & Moore, 1896, p. 245). Further experiments led these authors to the conclusion that both sides were correct: Baldwin's unpracticed subjects demonstrated that there could be sensorial and muscular *subjects* in reaction-time experiments, while Titchener's practiced subjects showed the distinction between sensorial and muscular *reactions*. Angell, John Dewey, and others at the "Chicago school" urged psychologists to stop fighting over fundamental theories of mind and to develop models better adapted to the practical problems that psychologists might address and help to solve.

It was Titchener (1898; 1899) who first articulated the structuralist and functionalist approaches to psychology. He defended the structuralist approach, identifying it with Wundt's, and argued that the functionalists were premature in their efforts, because not enough was yet known about the structure of mental action. The reaction-time experiments thus played an important role in distinguishing the major schools of American psychology at that time, the structuralists and the functionalists. The distinction might well have emerged in the discussion of some other issue, but at the time there was nothing more fundamental to psychological studies than reaction-time experiments.

Wundt's Tri-Dimensional Theory of Emotions

In Leipzig, reaction experiments had meanwhile taken an entirely different direction: the registration of physiological correlates of emotions. Physiologists and psychologists, such as Angelo Mosso, Max von Frey, and especially Alfred Lehmann, published experiments in support of Wundt's "central" theory of emotion against the "peripheral" theory of Carl Lange, William James, and Münsterberg, who considered emotions to be artifacts of reflex rather than of will. Danziger (1980d), comparing Wundt and James on volition, concludes that they basically differed on "whether 'volitional' processes were present in all directed motor activity, as Wundt held, or whether they operated only on the level of a mental choice among ideas, as James maintained" (p. 111). Wundt found centrally originating impulses to be involved in many more behavioral phenomena than James would allow, and Wundt's model kept emotional responses and acts of will within the province of experimental psychology, whereas James separated them from that discipline.

In pursuit of the connections between feelings and willful action, the Leipzig laboratory studied changes in pulse rate in reaction to suggestions or experiences that evoked emotional responses. The pulse varied by weakening (*geschwächt*) or strengthening (*verstärkt*); it might also either accelerate (*beschleunigt*) or slow down (*verlangsamt*).

As a result of pulse measurements in a variety of circumstances, Wundt outlined his system of "simple feelings." He decided that a stronger and slower pulse was associated with the feeling of pleasure (*Lust*), a weaker and faster pulse with displeasure (*Unlust*). A stronger and faster pulse indicated relaxation (*Lösung*), whereas weaker and slower pulse meant tension (*Spannung*). A stronger pulse with no change in pace was associated with excitement (*Erregung*), and a weaker one at the unchanged pace indicated composure (*Beruhigung*).

Wundt thus organized "simple feelings" into three fundamental modes: pleasure-displeasure (*Lust-Unlust*), tension-composure (*Spannung-Lösung*), and excitement-composure (*Erregung-Beruhigung*). In addition to pulse, Leipzig researchers worked to correlate responses of respiration, blood pressure, and even pupil dilation with these modalities. With analyses of these bodily correlates, they tried to represent common, everyday feelings and emotions (i.e., compounds feelings) in terms of the elementary modes of feeling. For example, joy has strong components of pleasure and excitement, but first tension then relaxation. Anger has displeasure, excitement, and an ambivalence in the tension-relaxation modality.

Wundt's tridimensional theory of feelings first appeared in his general textbook of psychology in 1896. Although the textbook was popular, Wundt's theory of feelings did not have many supporters outside of his associates in Leipzig. Certainly this research program was, by this time, not so widely influential and fruitful as the earlier reaction-time studies had been. As Wundt and his associates expounded this their next major theory, Machian positivists among European psychologists, and the quite similar functionalists in America, agreed to exclude (or certainly to downplay) such grand theoretical questions. For them the important thing was simply to find experiments that "worked."

Reaction Times after 1900

The impact of the new positivism on experimental psychology was not at all to Wundt's liking. The relaxation of theoretical requirements allowed technically or physiologically oriented experimentalists in Germany to claim psychology as their domain, even when their work often supported no general psychological theory. Wundt complained about such "technicians" but could do little to stop the spread of their influence, especially as they received support from G. E. Müller, Stumpf, and even Külpe.

Experimental psychology grew up within philosophy in Germany and therefore was vulnerable to trends in philosophical thought. When Wundt was on the leading edge of the trend in the 1870s and 1880s, his research program prospered. In that environment of scientism, a physiologist such as Wundt, or a specialist in psychophysics such G. E. Müller, could even become professor of philosophy at a major German university. By 1894, Wilhelm Dilthey's criticism of his Berlin colleague

Ebbinghaus signaled a change in the attitude that philosophers had toward the role of natural-scientific experiment in their field. Partly in response to the philosophers' qualms, but mostly as a result of their own philosophical positivism, younger specialists in experimental psychology were inclined to dispense with grand theories of mind.

Even in *Philosophische Studien*, Wundt's house publication, reaction-time studies became quite rare for a while after 1896, as studies of emotions appeared in greater number. But then an interesting thing happened in Wundt's second journal, *Psychologische Studien* (10 Vols., 1905–1918), which published only work from the Leipzig Institute. In these volumes, reaction-time studies proliferate once again, featuring the sensorial reaction, sometimes using the subtraction method, and often linking reaction-time work with Wundt's theory of emotions. Probably, the key figure in this revival was another Institute Assistant, Wilhelm Wirth (1876–1952), who first took the post in 1900 and worked as a psychologist in Leipzig in one capacity or another for decades. Wirth is best known for his work in psychophysics, but in his important early treatise (1908, 389–443), he uses his careful experimental methods to defend Wundt and to attack his critics, including Külpe. Once Wundt retired in 1917, however, Wirth was shifted to his own Psychophysical Institute and had less influence on the general direction of psychology in Leipzig.

To gauge the interest in reaction-time studies in twentieth-century North America, we can look at the three editions of Woodworth's famous textbook. We have already noted that Woodworth (1938, pp. 298–339) originally devoted an important chapter to reaction-time methods. The chapter remains, though it was moved to the front and shortened a bit, in the second edition (Woodworth & Schlosberg, 1954, pp. 8–42). In the 'third edition of Woodworth' (Kling & Riggs, 1971), the preface notes that the chapters on "reaction time, attention, emotion . . ." have been dropped, to make room for "new material" (p. vi).

Using citation analysis, Elizabeth Goodman (1971) concluded that interest in the mental reaction times waned until cognitive psychologists began to take an interest in the topic again, starting in the 1950s. Although Michael Posner (1978) is indeed concerned with reaction times, and mentions Helmholtz and Donders, he makes no reference to the work of Wundt or Ludwig Lange in this area. The greatest interest in reaction times currently can probably be summed up by the title of a textbook that Posner co-authored, *Human Performance* (Fitts and Posner, 1967). Psychologists and psychiatrists will use reaction times to learn about human capacities (and infirmities); they are less likely to use the experiments as Wundt did, as the central testing ground for his general theory of mind.

References

Ach, Narziß. (1905). *Über die Willenstätigkeit und das Denken: Eine experimentelle Untersuchung mit einem Anhange: Über das Hipp'sche Chronoskop.* Göttingen: Vandenboeck & Ruprecht.

Angell, J. R., & Moore, A. W. (1896). Reaction-time: A study in attention and habit. *Psychological Review, 3,* 245–258.

Baldwin, B. T. (Ed.). (1921). In memory of Wilhelm Wundt. *Psychological Review, 28.*

Baldwin, J. M. (1895). Types of reaction. *Psychological Review, 2,* 259–273.

Baldwin, J. M. (1896). The 'type-theory' of reaction. *Mind (New Series), 5,* 81–89.

Behrens, P. J. (1980a). An edited translation of the first dissertation in experimental psychology by Max Friedrich at Leipzig University in Germany. *Psychological research, 42,* 19–38.

Behrens, P. J. (1980b). The first dissertation in experimental psychology: Max Friedrich's study of apperception. In W. G. Bringmann & R. D. Tweney (Eds.), *Wundt studies, a centennial collection* (pp. 193–209). Toronto: Hogrefe.

Berger, G. O. (1886). Über den Einfluß der Reizstärke auf die Dauer einfacher psychischer Vorgänge mit besonderer Rücksicht auf Lichtreize. *Philosophische Studien, 3,* 38–93.

Boring, E. G. (1950). *A history of experimental psychology* (2nd ed.). New York: Appleton-Century-Crofts.

Bringmann, W. G., Bringmann, N. J., & Ungerer, G. (1980). The establishment of Wundt's laboratory: An archival and documentary study. In W. G. Bringmann & R. D. Tweney (Eds.), *Wundt studies, a centennial collection* (pp. 123–157). Toronto: Hogrefe.

Cattell, J. M. (1886–88). Psychometrische Untersuchungen. *Philosophische Studien, 3,* 305–335; 4, 241–250.

Cattell, J. M. (1888). The psychological laboratory at Leipsic. *Mind, 13,* 37–51.

Danziger, K. (1980a). The history of introspection reconsidered. *Journal of the History of the Behavioral Sciences, 16,* 241–262.

Danziger, K. (1980b). On the threshold of the new psychology: Situating Wundt and James. In W. G. Bringmann & R. D. Tweney (Eds.), *Wundt studies, a centennial collection* (pp. 363–379). Toronto: Hogrefe.

Danziger, K. (1980c). Wundt's psychological experiment in the light of his philosophy of science. *Psychological Studies, 42,* 109–122.

Danziger, K. (1980d). Wundt's theory of behavior and volition. In R. W. Rieber (Ed.), *Wilhelm Wundt and the making of a scientific psychology* (pp. 89–115). New York: Plenum Press. Revised in this book: The unknown Wundt: Drive, apperception, and volition.

Danziger, K. (1990). *Constructing the subject: Historical origins of psychological research.* New York: Cambridge University Press.

de Jaager, J. J. (1865/1970). *De physiologische tijd bij psychische processen.* Utrecht: P. W. Van de Weijer. Translated: Reaction time and mental processes. In J. Brozek & M. S. Sibinga (Eds. & Trans.), *Origins of psychometry.* Nieuwkoop, Netherlands: de Graff.

Diamond, S. (1980). Wundt before Leipzig. In R. W. Rieber (Ed.), *Wilhelm Wundt and the making of a scientific psychology* (pp. 3–70). New York: Plenum Press. Reprinted in this book.

Diamond, S., Balvin, R. S., & Diamond, F. R. (1963). *Inhibition and choice: A neurobehavioral approach to problems of plasticity in behavior.* New York: Harper and Row.

Dilthey, Wilhelm. (1894). Ideen über eine beschreibende und zergliedernde Psychologie. *Sitzungsberichte der Akademie der Wissenschaften zu Berlin,* 1309–1407.

Donders, F. C. (1868/1969). Die Schnelligkeit psychischer Process. *Archiv für Anatomie und Physiologie,* 1868, 657–681. Translated: On the speed of mental processes. *Acta psychologica, 30,* 412–431.

Dwelshauvers, G. (1891). Untersuchungen zur Methodik der activen Aufmerksamkeit. *Philosophische Studien, 6,* 217–249, 226–229.

Eckener, H. (1893). Untersuchungen über die Schwankungen der Auffassung minimaler Sinnesreize. *Philosophische Studien, 8,* 343–387.

Exner, S. (1873). Experimentelle Untersuchungen der einfachsten psychischen Processe. *Pflügers Archiv für die gesamte Physiologie, 7,* 601–660.

Exner, S. (1874). Experimentelle Untersuchungen der einfachsten psychischen Processe. *Pflügers Archiv für die gesamte Physiologie, 8,* 526–537.

Exner, S. (1875). Experimentelle Untersuchungen der einfachsten psychischen Processe. *Pflügers Archiv für die gesamte Physiologie, 11,* 403–432, 581–602.

Fischel, W. (1959). Wilhelm Wundt and Emil Kraepelin, Gedanken über einen Briefwechsel. In E. Engelberg et al. (Eds.), *Karl-Marx-Universität Leipzig, 1409–1959: Beiträge zur Universitätsgeschichte* (pp. 382–391). Leipzig: Verlag Enzyklopädie.

Fitts, P. M., & Posner, M. I. (1967). *Human Performance* (Basic Concepts in Psychology Series). Belmont, CA: Wadsworth.

Friedrich, M. (1883). Über die Apperceptionsdauer bei einfacher und zusammengesetzten Vorstellungen. *Philosophische Studien, 1,* 39–78.

Goodman, Elizabeth S. (1971). Citation analysis as a tool in historical study: A case study based on F. C. Donders and mental reaction times. *Journal of the History of the Behavioral Sciences, 7,* 187–191.

Harper, R. (1950). The first psychological laboratory. *Isis, 41,* 158–161.

Heinrich, W. (1895). *Die moderne physiologische Psychologie: Eine historisch-kritische Untersuchung mit besonderer Berücksichtigung des Problems der Aufmerksamkeit.* Zurich: E. Speidel.

Hirsch, A. (1861–63). Expériences chronoscopiques sur la vitesse des différentes sensations et de la transmission nerveuse. *Bulletin de la société des sciences naturelles, Neuchâtel, 6,* 100–114.

Hirsch, A. (1863). Ueber persönliche Gleichung und Correction bei chronographischen Durschgangs-Beobachtungen. *Untersuchungen zur Naturlehre des Menschen und der Thiere, 9,* 200–208.

Höffding, H. (1892). Zur Theorie des Wiedererkennens: Eine Replik. *Philosophische Studien, 8,* 86–96.

James, H. (Ed.). (1920). *The letters of William James* (Vol. 1). Boston: Atlantic Monthly.

James, W. (1884). What is emotion? *Mind, 9,* 188–205.

James, W. (1890). *Principles of psychology* (2 Vols.). New York: Holt.

Jastrow, J. (1890). *The time-relations of mental phenomena.* New York: N. D. C. Hodges.

Keller, P. (1979). *States of belonging: German-American intellectuals and the First World War.* Cambridge: Harvard University Press.

Kling, J. W., & Riggs, L. A. (1971). *Woodworth & Schlosberg's experimental psychology* (3rd ed.). New York: Holt, Rinehart, and Winston.

Kraepelin, E. (1883). Über die Einwirkung einiger medicamentöser Stoffe auf die Dauer einfacher psychischer Vorgänge. *Philosophische Studien, 1,* 417–462, 573–605.

Kraepelin, E. (1896). Der psychologische Versuch in der Psychiatrie. *Psychologische Arbeiten, 1*, 1–91.

Kraepelin, E. (1983/87). *Lebenserinnerungen* (H. Hippius, G. Peters, & D. Ploog, Eds.). Berlin: Springer-Verlag. Translated by C. Wooding-Deane as *Memoirs*. Berlin: Springer-Verlag.

Kraepelin, E., & Merkel, J. (1894). Beobachtungen bei zusammengesetzen Reactionen: Zwei brieflichen Mittheilungen an den Herausgeber. *Philosophische Studien, 10*, 498–506.

Krohn, W. O. (1892). Freiburg. *American Journal of Psychology, 4*, 587.

Külpe, O. (1891–92). Ueber die Gleichzeitigkeit und Ungleichzeitigkeit von Bewegungen. *Philosophische Studien, 6*, 514–535; *7*, 147–168.

Külpe, O. (1893/95). *Grundriß der Psychologie, auf experimenteller Grundlage dargestellt.* Leipzig: Engelmann. Translated by E. B. Titchener as *Outlines of psychology, based upon the results of experimental investigation.* London: Swan Sonnenschein.

Lange, C. G. (1885/1887). *Über Gemüthsbewegungen: Eine psycho-physiologische Studie* (H. Kurella, Trans.). Leipzig: T. Thomas. Danish original: *Om sindsbevaegelser: Et psyko-fysiologisk studie.*

Lange, L. (1885a). Ueber die wissenschaftliche Fassung des Galilei'schen Beharrungsgesetz. *Philosophische Studien, 2*, 266–297.

Lange, L. (1885b). Nochmals über das Beharrungsgesetz. *Philosophische Studien, 2*, 539–545.

Lange, L. (1886a). Die geschichtliche Entwicklung des Bewegungsbegriffes und ihr voraussichtliches Endergebniss. *Philosophische Studien, 3*, 337–419, 643–691.

Lange, L. (1886b). Neue Experimente über den Vorgang der einfachen Reaction auf Sinneseindrücke. *Philosophische Studien, 4*, 479–510.

Lehmann, A. (1886). Über die Anwendung der Methode der mittleren Abstufungen auf den Lichtsinn. Philosophische Studien, 3, 497–544.

Lehmann, A. (1892). *Die Hauptgesetze des menschlichen Gefühlsleben.* Leipzig: O. R. Reisland.

Lehmann, A. (1893). Kritische und experimentelle Studien über das Wiedererkennen. *Philosophische Studien, 7*, 169–212.

Mack, Wolfgang. (1993). Die Würzburger Schule. In H. Lück & R. Miller (Eds.), *Illustrierte Geschichte der Psychologie* (pp. 50–53). Munich: Quintessenz.

Marbe, K. (1893). Die Schwankungen der Gesichtsempfindungen. *Philosophische Studien, 8*, 615–637.

Marbe, K. (1936). Karl Marbe. In C. Murchison (Ed.), *A history of psychology in autobiography* (Vol. 3, pp. 181–213). Worcester, MA: Clark University Press.

Martius, G. (1889). Über die scheinbare Größe der Gegenstände und ihre Beziehung zur Größe der Netzhautbilder. *Philosophische Studien, 5*, 601–617.

Martius, G. (1891a). [Review of Dwelshauvers]. *Zeitschrift für Psychologie und Physiologie der Sinnesorgane, 2*, 130–132.

Martius, G. (1891b). Über die muskuläre Reaction und die Aufmerksamkeit. *Philosophische Studien, 6*, 167–216.

Martius, G. (1922). Götz Martius. In R. Schmidt (Ed.), *Die Philosophie der Gegenwart in Selbstdarstellungen* (Vol. 3, pp. 99–120). Leipzig: Felix Meiner.

Metge, Anneros. (1983). The experimental psychological research conducted at Wundt's Institute and its significance in the history of psychology. In G. Eckardt & L. Sprung (Eds.), *Advances in historiography of psychology* (pp. 43–49). Berlin, GDR: Deutscher Verlag der Wissenschaften.

Misiak, H. (1980). Leipzig and Louvain University in Belgium. *Psychological Research, 42*, 49–56.

Misiak, H., & Staudt, V. M. (1954). *Catholics in psychology: A historical survey.* New York: McGraw-Hill.

Münsterberg, H. (1888). *Die Willenshandlung: Ein Beitrag zur physiologischen Psychologie.* Freiburg: Mohr.

Münsterberg, H. (1889–92). *Beiträge zur experimentellen Psychologie* (4 vols.). Freiburg: Mohr.

Münsterberg, M. (1922). *Hugo Münsterberg, his life and work.* New York: D. Appleton.

Nilsson, I. (1980). Alfred Lehmann and psychology as a physical science. In W. G. Bringmann & R. D. Tweney (Eds.), *Wundt studies, a centennial collection* (pp. 258–268). Toronto: Hogrefe.

Pace, E. A. (1893). Zur Frage der Schwankungen der Aufmerksamkeit nach Versuchen mit der Masson'schen Scheibe. *Philosophische Studien, 8,* 388–402.

Posner, M. I. (1978). *Chronometric Explorations of Mind.* Hillsdale, NJ: Lawrence Erlbaum.

Roback, A. A. (1952). *History of American psychology* (2nd ed.). New York: Collier.

Robinson, D. K. (1987). Wilhelm Wundt and the establishment of experimental psychology, 1875–1914: The context of a new field of scientific research. Doctoral dissertation, University of California, Berkeley.

Sahakian, W. S. (Ed.). (1968). *History of psychology, a source book in systematic psychology.* Itasca, IL: F. E. Peacock.

Schlotte, F. (1955–56). Beiträge zum Lebensbild Wilhelm Wundts aus seinem Briefwechsel. *Wissenschaftliche Zeitschrift der Karl-Marx-Universität Leipzig, gesellschafts- und sprachwissenschaftliche Reihe, 5,* 333–349.

Sokal, M. M. (Ed.). (1981). *An education in psychology: James McKeen Cattell's journal and letters from Germany and England, 1880–1888.* Cambridge: MIT Press.

Sokal, M. M., Davis, A. B., & Merzbach, U. C. (1976). Laboratory instruments in the history of psychology. *Journal of the History of the Behavioral Sciences, 12,* 59–64.

Tigerstedt, R., & Bergqvist, J. (1883). Zur Kenntniss der Apperceptionsdauer zusammengesetzter Gesichtsvorstellungen. *Zeitschrift für Biologie, 19,* 4–44.

Tischer, E. (1883). Über die Untersuchungen von Schallstärken. *Philosophische Studien, 1,* 495–542.

Titchener, E. B. (1892). The Leipzig School of experimental psychology. *Mind (New Series), 1,* 206–234.

Titchener, E. B. (1895a). Simple reactions. *Mind, 4,* 74–81.

Titchener, E. B. (1895b). The type-theory of the simple reaction. *Mind, 4,* 506–514.

Titchener, E. B. (1896). The "type-theory" of simple reaction. *Mind, 5,* 236–241.

Titchener, E. B. (1898). The postulates of a structural psychology. *Philosophical Review, 7,* 449–465.

Titchener, E. B. (1899). Structural and functional psychology. *Philosophical Review, 8,* 290–299.

Titchener, E. B. (1921). Wilhelm Wundt. *American Journal of Psychology, 32,* 161–178.

Tokarskiy, A. A. (Ed.). (1896). *Zapiski psikhologicheskoy laboratorii psikhiatricheskoy kliniki Imperatorskogo Moskovskogo Universiteta.* Moscow: N. N. Kushnerev.

Trautscholdt, M. (1883). Experimentelle Untersuchungen über die Association der Vorstellungen. *Philosophische Studien, 1,* 213–250.

Tschisch [Chizh], W. (1885). Über die Zeitverhältnisse der Apperception einfacher und zusammengesetzter Vorstellungen, untersucht mit Hülfe der Complicationsmethode. *Philosophische Studien, 2,* 603–634.

von Laue, M. (1948). Dr. Ludwig Lange, 1863–1936 (Ein zu Unrecht Vergessener). *Die Naturwissenschaften, 35,* 193–203.

Wirth, W. (1908). *Die experimentelle Analyze der Bewußtseinsphänomene.* Braunschweig: Friedrich Vieweg.

Wirth, W. (1927). Nachruf für Emil Kraepelin. *Archiv für die gesamte Psychologie, 58,* 1–32.

Wirth, W. (1928). Götz Martius. *Archiv für die gesamte Psychologie, 61,* 513.

Woodward, W. R. (1982). Wundt's program for the new psychology: Vicissitudes of experiment, theory, and system. In W. R. Woodward & M. G. Ash (Eds.), *The problematic science: Psychology in nineteenth-century thought* (pp. 167–197). New York: Praeger.

Woodward, W. R. (1984). William James's psychology of will: Its revolutionary impact on American psychology. In J. Brozek (Ed.), *Explorations in the history of psychology in the United States* (pp. 148–195). Lewisburg, PA: Bucknell University Press.

Woodworth, R. S. (1938). *Experimental psychology*. New York: Henry Holt.

Wundt, W. (1862). *Beiträge zur Theorie der Sinneswahrnehmung*. Leipzig: C. F. Winter.

Wundt, W. (1874). *Grundzüge der physiologischen Psychologie*. Leipzig: Engelmann.

Wundt, W. (1880). *Grundzüge der physiologischen Psychologie* (2nd ed., 2 Vols.). Leipzig: Engelmann.

Wundt, W. (1891). Zur Lehre von den Gemüthsbewegungen. *Philosophische Studien, 6*, 335–393.

Wundt, W. (1893a). Hypnotismus und Suggestion. *Philosophische Studien, 8*, 1–85.

Wundt, W. (1893b). Psychophysik und experimentelle Psychologie. In W. Lexis (Ed.), *Die deutschen Universitäten (für die Universitätsausstellung in Chicago 1893 unter Mitwirkung zahlreicher Universitätslehrer)* (Vol. 1, pp. 450–457). Berlin: A. Asher.

Wundt, W. (1894). Zur Beurtheilung der zusammengesetzten Reactionen. *Philosophische Studien, 10*, 485–498.

Wundt, W. (1896/97). *Grundriß der Psychologie*. Leipzig: Engelmann. Translated by C. Judd as *Outlines of psychology*. Leipzig: Engelmann.

Wundt, W. (1902–03). *Grundzüge der physiologischen Psychologie* (5th ed., 3 Vols.). Leipzig: Engelmann.

Wundt, W. (1909). Das Institute für experimentelle Psychologie. In *Festschrift zur Feier des 500 jährigen Bestehens der Universität Leipzig, vol. 4: Die Institute und Seminare der Philosophischen Fakultätan der Universität Leipzig, Part 1: Die philosophische und die philosophisch-historische Sektion* (pp. 118–133). Leipzig: Rektor und Senat der Universität.

7

LABORATORIES FOR EXPERIMENTAL PSYCHOLOGY

GÖTTINGEN'S ASCENDANCY OVER LEIPZIG IN THE 1890S

Edward J. Haupt

Introduction: Did Wundt's Laboratory Lead the Experimental Movement in Psychology in the Early 1890s?

The early 1890s were a critical time for the development of experimental psychology. Wilhelm Wundt, Georg Elias Müller, Carl Stumpf, and Alexis Meinong were the only *Ordinarius* (full) professors in German-speaking countries who ran laboratories that practiced the discipline, and Meinong's laboratory was founded only in 1894. While American laboratories already outnumbered the German ones, the American laboratories were not yet producing studies that signaled advances through novel experiments. In 1894, Wilhelm Dilthey launched his attack on the possibility of an experimental psychology. Of the three *Ordinarius* professors who had trained the most personnel for the new movement, only Jürgen Bona Meyer still held his chair in Bonn. Franz Brentano, while still active in Vienna, had lost his professorship in 1879, because the former priest was forced to assume Saxon citizenship in order to marry Ida von Lieben. Rudolf Hermann Lotze, the senior of this important trio, had died in 1881. By 1894, conservative critics were attacking experimentalist philosophers for being insufficiently devoted to the elimination of the socialist virus spreading amongst university students (Kusch, 1995, pp. 161–177). The experimentalist movement needed clear direction on how to go about its work, and on which equipment and methods produced consistent and accurate results in all the laboratories which shared a commitment to the primacy of experimental results; such clarity of purpose and product would serve as protection against external attacks.

A great deal has been written about Wundt's founding of a psychology laboratory in Leipzig in 1879. He was not then the only psychological experimentalist, and indeed his main activity as a working experimenter lasted only a brief time during his *earliest* years, particularly in the early 1860s at Heidelberg. At Leipzig Wundt certainly sponsored the development of experimental psychology, but he himself remained, in his primary work, a theorist, and he then gave at least equal emphasis to the non-experimental methods of logic, sociological research, historical research, philosophical analysis, and linguistics. Stumpf had been actively experimenting since 1873; Hermann Ebbinghaus had begun his Berlin memory experiments (1885/1909) shortly after New Year's in 1879, earlier in the year than Wundt had assembled his doctoral students for the Winter Semester of 1879; and it is reported that G. E. Müller was carrying out weight-lifting psychophysical experiments in 1879 (Henri, 1893). Even so, the early 1890s would seem to be the time when Wundt's laboratory was clearly in the lead. Research that had made much use of reaction-time measurement was then declining at Leipzig just when Wundt published his theory of emotions. Then his students began to turn toward the measurement of emotional reactions. American and other foreign students were still coming to his lectures in great numbers, some of them completing their dissertations on work done in the Leipzig Institute for Experimental Psychology. By 1897 Wundt would have special new laboratory facilities built for the use of his assistants and students. Also in 1897, Oswald Külpe, who had completed his doctorate and *Habilitation* with Wundt and had served as his second paid *Assistent*, was chosen to be *Ordinarius* professor in Würzburg, thus becoming the first student of the three initiators of experimental psychology (Wundt, Stumpf, Müller) to achieve that rank. And in this period, some of Wundt's students were already returning to the United States and starting the laboratories from which North American experimental psychology grew.

However, in the early 1890s, there was a major alternative to Wundt's workplace. Indeed, in 1887, G. E. Müller (*Ordinarius* in philosophy at Göttingen) had begun memory experiments after the fashion of Ebbinghaus and, since 1879, had been carrying out weight-lifting experiments.

In the period before 1895, there were only two established laboratories for experimental psychology headed by *Ordinarius* professors, those of Müller and Wundt. There were, to be sure, other psychology laboratories, but in 1894, they were either very new or were not headed by an *Ordinarius* (Meinong's laboratory started in 1894; Stumpf started his Berlin laboratory in the fall of 1894, but sought minimal financial support; Ebbinghaus had only been *außerordentlicher Professor* in Berlin but was moving to an *Ordinarius* position in Breslau; Götz Martius in Bonn was still *Privatdocent* but would be *außerordentlicher* by 1895).

In fact, American laboratories and journals cannot be considered to have been well established by 1894, either. William James brought Wundt's student Hugo Münsterberg over from Germany to put Harvard's laboratory on a solid footing. As for journals, only the *American Journal of Psychology* existed before 1894, under the problematic leadership of G. Stanley Hall. American laboratories, while becoming numerous, were not well established and looked to German sources for guidance, as Krohn's reports (1892, 1893b) indicate. By 1900, only seven American universities offered a doctorate in psychology (Rice, 2000), while in Germany, Ebbinghaus, Külpe, Friedrich Schumann, and others had completed *Habilitation* (and thus had become university faculty members) based on experimental work. Thus the German laboratories of the early 1890s still provided the most important direction for the development of an experimental psychology, not only in the German-speaking world, but also in France, Russia, England, and the United States.

Four of the newly minted North American professors of the time are more appropriately classified as Europeans. In chronological order of their arrival in the New World, they are Edward Bradford Titchener at Cornell (1892); Hugo Münsterberg at Harvard (1892, 1897); August Kirschmann at Toronto (1893); and Max Meyer at the University of Missouri (1900). Thus, while Americans were not sought for European positions, European training for Americans was very desirable, and North American universities were actually importing Europeans to teach psychology.

Kirschmann, for example, was extremely well prepared to set up a laboratory in Toronto. He had been *Assistent* to Wundt in Leipzig, but more importantly, he had learned his craft under Külpe and had published a dissertation that included Kirschmann's laws, which are still identifiable in publications on perception (Gordon, Shapley, & Israel, 1999). As a result of severe anti-German prejudice at the time of the World

War Kirschmann returned to Germany impoverished, eventually to be supported and employed by Wundt. There is a Toronto web site (Pantalony & Creelman, 1997) that honors Kirschmann, who, of all the Europeans who were imported to the North American continent, may well have had the best training in experimental technique.

It is thus clear that during the early 1890s, and perhaps for a bit longer, European laboratories still led their American counterparts. The most advanced work was still produced in just two laboratories: the one in Leipzig and the one in Göttingen.

"Göttingen . . . Second Only to Leipzig": I Don't Think So!

In order to evaluate laboratory practice in the early 1890s, we can assess contemporary reports of the reputation, equipment, and experimentation carried out in the two most prominent German-speaking laboratories of the time, those of Wundt and G. E. Müller. This work is comprised of three components, each occasioned by a different sort of evidence. The first component analyzes the published reports of two visitors to these laboratories, one of them American, the other French. The second component compares the equipment manufacturers related to the two laboratories. The third component describes a controversy over the measurement of reaction time in the two laboratories and its resolution. Such a controversy is particularly important since reaction time measurement was central to the early phase of the rather diverse work in Wundt's Institute for Experimental Psychology in Leipzig.

From this survey of the products of the two laboratories, I will argue that the technical achievements of Müller's laboratory in the decade of the 1890s far outstripped those of Wundt's laboratory and contributed key components to the discipline of experimental psychology. Thus, I will implicitly also argue against Ash (1980), who suggests that poorly funded German laboratories, such as these two, could not accomplish much in the way of building a new scientific discipline. The title of this section comes from Edwin G. Boring's (1950, p. 374) editorializing on William O. Krohn's (1893b) conclusion that G. E. Müller's laboratory was "the best for research in all Germany." Boring amended Krohn's remark, somewhat disingenuously, claiming that Müller's laboratory, however superior, was "second only to Leipzig." Such a comparison requires some discussion of the nature of laboratories.

What Is a Laboratory?

The use of the word "laboratory" suggests two kinds of meanings: one is the official designation of the establishment; a second meaning refers to the quality of the research carried out there and the importance of that research for the discipline. The first, the establishment of terminology, is easier, since it is merely a matter of understanding the conventions of language; the second meaning is more complex, a matter of characterizing the scientific culture in which the establishment plays a role.

In the German language, there are at least three terms that might be translated as laboratory: *Labor*, *Laboratorium*, and *Institut*. Each term has a very different meaning. A *Labor* is what Americans might call an instructional session, a class in which basic laboratory technique is taught. In Germany, such classes grew out of the model of the privately financed teaching laboratory of Justus Liebig in Gießen in the 1840s, where chemical and pharmacological technique was taught. Gustav Magnus, the physicist in Berlin, also pioneered such classes, paying for them from his own ample funds. Wundt's work with a group of doctoral students, starting in 1879, certainly counts as a *Labor*, and Wundt had also taught laboratory techniques in an official *Institut* for physiology during his earlier years at Heidelberg (Wundt, 1910).

Laboratorium corresponds much better to our normal sense of a place where scientific activities are carried out. Unfortunately, in German, the word is usually used in a general or unofficial way and thus does not indicate institutional support. Aside from the general meaning of the word, it has little specific institutional meaning.

Institut, the German form of Institute, has a more specific meaning, one which can be justified by reference to governmental acts of naming a building, or a set of rooms, the "Institute for the Study of . . .." (For philological disciplines, such as Greek or archeology, such an establishment was more often called *Seminar*.) Designation as *Institut* usually means that the supervising governmental unit (for Müller, the Prussian *Kultusministerium*; for Wundt, the Saxon *Kultusministerium*) has declared the site a significant one for the production of research and knowledge in its area of scholarship. The close governmental supervision of German universities contrasts sharply with the American situation, where the early development of psychology laboratories took place principally in private universities, such as Johns Hopkins, Clark, Harvard, Yale, Chicago, and Stanford.

The use of terminology could be misleading or confusing: for example, in articles appearing in *Zeitschrift für Psychologie und Physiologie der Sinnesorgane*, G. E. Müller labeled publications from his set of rooms, "aus dem Göttinger psychologischen Institut," starting in 1889, even though the Prussian government did not officially change the name from *Seminar* to *Institut* until 1922. Wundt, however, had the official designation of an institute as early as 1883 (Robinson, 1987, pp. 73–76).

Clearly the term *Institut* signals official recognition, where German government support is concerned. The historian of science, however, might be more concerned with the intellectual achievements of the laboratory, whether or not it is also an institute, so further words about the scientific culture of laboratories are in order.

In his important study of the activity of science, Thomas Kuhn (1970) notes that most laboratories are engaged in "normal science," although some may, at special times, make major, even revolutionary, breakthroughs. It seems to me that, to the extent that a laboratory does something important for a particular natural science, the laboratory must produce, or somehow address, alternative theoretical models. (Hofstadter, 1981, discusses the connection between alternative models/images and cognition, à la Escher.) The psychologist, as natural scientist, will then show the different model versions to a set of observers. If the observers' responses fail to conform to the model/theory, then that model, at least in that specific form, must be rejected. So, in its essential nature, the laboratory is an organization of one or more persons who attempt to find new models that reveal essential properties that can be tested, and who subsequently attempt to test them. A laboratory, for most purposes, cannot stand alone, but must have the assistance of other laboratories in determining which models can survive. Along these lines, I will show that it was Müller's laboratory, with its insistence on falsification-based experimental design, that provided the model for other German-speaking laboratories in Berlin, Bonn, Breslau, Würzburg, and Graz, far more than Wundt's laboratory did in Leipzig.

Although it is admittedly difficult to determine the relative status of the two laboratories, I will show that Wundt's laboratory was founded on demonstration apparatus adapted to experimentation, while Müller's laboratory selected its equipment specifically for experiments. Those experiments provided the most important models for psychological science in the 1890s and afterward. I will thus argue that Krohn was correct in his assessment of the Göttingen laboratory—"the best for research in all Germany"—and not Boring—"second only to Leipzig."

For the comparison of the equipment, there are two reports, written at about the same time, which describe the two laboratories. The equipment lists they give will be supplemented by descriptions of the equipment from the catalogs of Zimmermann (1903) and of Spindler & Hoyer (1908/1921); these catalogs contain the most extensive lists and descriptions of early psychological equipment yet found. The comparison will show that Müller's laboratory was far stronger in terms of precision equipment and adequate methodology than Wundt's.

Krohn and Henri as Evaluators of Laboratories

Before I compare the equipment, I would like to indicate the relevant intellectual backgrounds of the laboratory visitors. The two visitors/reporters were William O. Krohn, who became the founder of the psychology laboratory at the University of Illinois, and Victor Henri, Alfred Binet's assistant and collaborator in Paris (see Nicholas, 1994, for a short biography of Henri). Krohn's survey has been widely cited; it appeared in two parts (1892, 1893b), the part on Göttingen being published separately later, because someone had borrowed it at the time Krohn sent in the first part. The other survey, by Henri (1893), is less well known to American readers, but it offers far more detailed information on the two laboratories.

Krohn had recently finished a doctorate at Yale under George Trumbull Ladd, a few years before Wundt's student Edward Scripture became instructor of experimental psychology there (1892). Ladd, even though he published *Physiological Psychology* (1887), was never himself an experimentalist, although he was a strong supporter of Wundtian psychological theory. Krohn gave his dissertation the title, "The ethics of modern pessimism" (1889). His experience with experimental psychology may have been confined to "An experimental study of simultaneous stimulation of the sense of touch," work carried out in the laboratories of Clark University and subsequently published (1893a). In this study the accuracy of simultaneous stimulation at fixed distances is indexed by percentage correct. Krohn apparently did not use the threshold methods then commonly used in German psychophysical studies.

Krohn wrote the descriptions of the German laboratories as he was taking a yearlong grand tour of Europe. He visited laboratories of experimental psychology in Germany prior to becoming Professor of Psychology and Pedagogy and setting up a psychological laboratory at the University of Illinois, one of the early psychology laboratories at a public university. Most of Krohn's later work concentrated on child study, consistent with his role as professor of pedagogy. There is no particular evidence of strong natural-science training in Krohn's history, and Krohn published nothing further that involved experimental psychology.

Victor Henri had already had university-level instruction in mathematics and natural science at the University of Montpellier before moving to Paris in 1892, where he became a student of Théodule Ribot, the professor for experimental psychology at the Collège de France. Henri also assumed the role of voluntary assistant to Alfred Binet, the unpaid director of a physiology laboratory devoted to experimental psychology. Several years after describing the laboratories, Henri completed a doctorate in G. E. Müller's laboratory on the psychophysics of touch and then returned to Paris to become assistant to the physiologist D'Astre. Henri was later to show his significant achievements in natural science by his selection as professor of physical chemistry at the Swiss Federal Technical University (ETH Zürich). Thus, if preparation and later achievement are any indication, Henri should be judged, compared to Krohn, as the far-more-competent and better-prepared observer of scientific laboratories.

In 1891–92, when Krohn visited both Leipzig and Göttingen (the latter was apparently the last stop before returning to the United States), Leipzig certainly had the longer history as a psychological laboratory. It had greater resources and was first officially funded in 1883; Henri (p. 608) reports that the laboratory was started already in 1878. It included apparatus that Wundt had begun to assemble at Heidelberg in the 1860s. Müller's annual budget at this point was only 500 RM (500 Reichsmark was approximately $100), whereas Wundt had a budget of at least 1200 RM per year (Robinson, 1987, p. 74).

In 1875, Wundt moved to Leipzig from Zurich (where he worked for only one year), carrying crates full of physiological and psychological equipment with him. At Leipzig he received a small lecture room for the storage and use of the equipment (Wundt, 1920, p. 291). This equipment had been acquired mostly in Heidelberg where he had been *außerordentlicher Professor* for psychology. Many of Wundt's students in Leipzig wrote non-experimental dissertations, but by October 1879, certain of his doctoral students were doing experiments for their dissertations; the equipment included a Hipp chronoscope and many of the other instruments that characterized the famous Leipzig experiments. During 1883, Wundt attained regular budgetary support and started his journal, the *Philosophische Studien*. Therefore, by 1892, when Krohn visited, this level of support had thus been in place for almost ten years.

In contrast, Henri (1893, p. 618) reports that G. E. Müller started to carry out experiments in 1879, supporting all his work himself until 1887. It may well be that, during the period from 1879 to 1887, Müller had little more than the set of Fechner weights which their constructor had given Müller in recognition of the importance of Müller's *Zur Grundlegung der Psychophysik* (1878). In 1887, Müller made the first major addition to his apparatus when he acquired the first memory drum (Haupt, in press) which he had commissioned from the Leipzig precision-manufacturing firm of Baltzar and Schmidt. Müller was about to pay the 400 RM for that apparatus himself, but then the usually ungenerous Prussian Ministry of Education provided 600 RM and the designation of "provisional philosophical seminar" as a budget category; this unusual generosity might possibly have been connected with commemoration of the 150th anniversary of the founding of the formerly Hannoverian university. Müller had requested that his establishment be called a *Laboratorium*, but the Berlin bureaucrats insisted on *Seminar*, a term that was more often given to extra facilities for fields other than natural sciences. By way of contrast, we can note that some early American laboratories had budgets of $1000/year (about 5000 RM) during the 1890s. William James spent $2700 between 1891 and 1892 (Albrecht, 1960, p. 134), so American funding clearly far outstripped Prussian parsimony.

The time of Krohn's visit to Göttingen was the Summer Semester (i.e., late spring) of 1892, and Müller had two *Assistenten* at the time, although neither received a salary. Friedrich Schumann (assistant 1887–94) had just had his *Habilitationsschrift* successfully evaluated (Schumann, 1892) and would receive a stipend for the year 1892–93. Alfons Pilzecker, having completed his doctoral dissertation in 1889, was apparently still present and, by this time, had started the memory work that would lead to the famous study that he co-authored with Müller, the first supplementary volume of the *Zeitschrift für Psychologie und Physiologie der Sinnesorgane* (Müller & Pilzecker, 1900). Müller, however, had only two dissertation students in spring 1892, one of them probably Adolf Jost, who would publish his dissertation on the relative strength of older associations in 1897.

According to Henri, the reason for the small number of students at Göttingen was that it was much more difficult there to gain approval for a subject for a doctoral dissertation than it was at Leipzig. In addition, other "voluntary" students were not allowed to use the equipment, as was presumably the case in Leipzig if the appropriate fees were paid (Henri, 1893, pp. 619–620). And so there were only two students at the time Henri visited the laboratory: Jost, and possibly Henri also counted Pilzecker as a student. Since relatively few students were present, other (non-psychology) students, visitors, and even Müller's wife, Käthe, served as subjects in many of the experiments.

The Leipzig Institute for Experimental Psychology, by this time, had two paid *Assistenten*, Oswald Külpe and Ernst Meumann, although Meumann was being paid directly by Wundt. An *Assistent* was usually a person who had completed the doctorate and seemed likely to have a university career. The position of *Assistent* permitted a person to teach laboratory courses under supervision; it provided a salary and came with the expectation that the holder of the position would write a *Habilitationsschrift*, whose successful evaluation would permit the scholar to give lectures in a university as *Privatdocent*. In addition to the two *Assistenten*, according to Henri's report, there were twenty-five active students who had to pay 25 RM each year for use of the Institute's library. Thus the income for Wundt's library alone clearly exceeded the entire budgetary support for the Göttingen laboratory, and the number of *Versuchspersonen* (subjects) available for psychological experiments is clearly greater. Müller had few students before 1900 and charged no fee for the use of his library, which was designated as the *Philosophisches Seminar*.

The Equipment of the Laboratories

Though I am arguing that G. E. Müller had the superior laboratory for exact research, this was not obvious to the observers in 1892/93. Their surveys of laboratory equipment generally found Wundt to be better equipped. Still, I note certain details that show how Müller, within the possibilities of his means, often made more judicious choices in apparatus.

1. *Color studies*. Both laboratories had rotating wheels of different sizes for color mixing, a spectroscope (for separating the colors based on

wavelength), a heliostat, and a series of prisms. Müller, however, had a group of Hering demonstration apparatuses, presumably including the color mixing apparatus (Henri, 1893, p. 618). As Turner's (1993) analysis shows, the Hering apparatus was more flexible than the one by Helmholtz. Since Wundt did not have a Helmholtz apparatus at the time, and color experiments were apparently not yet given much emphasis in the Leipzig lab, Müller's lab must be judged superior for color, space, and lightness perception, at least in 1892/93.

2. *Other vision work.* Both laboratories had darkness chambers, and thus could carry out color and lightness research at different levels of illumination, as well as record dark adaptation curves.

3. *Psychophysics and presentation of short time intervals.* For further characterization of the equipment of the two laboratories, we can compare their studies of the psychophysics of short time intervals (*Zeitsinn*). Henri (1893, p. 619) describes two devices that Schumann crafted in Göttingen for the study of short time intervals, the subject of his *Habilitationsschrift*, approved in early 1892. The first apparatus described by Schumann (1892) has a single axis, driven by a clockwork motor, with three wheels attached to it. Each wheel has a number of adjustable platinum points attached to the periphery. The spacing of these points and the rotation speed of the axis controls specification of the time intervals. The electrical contacts permit a battery to cause a telephone speaker to sound for a specified time.

The lack of precision of this *Zeitsinn* apparatus (note that it is substantially similar to Meumann's, described below) prompted Schumann to devise another. Poor precision is an intrinsic result of the use of the spring in the clockwork motor, since such spring motors always start at maximum speed and slowly decrease in speed. Schumann's second device has one disk and six contacts, driven by a Helmholtz-style electromagnetic motor, furnished with a regulator, which presumably controls the speed at a constant value. Henri comments that the precision that was obtainable with this apparatus, with typical error less than a millisecond, allowed this apparatus to control a Hipp chronoscope.

Schumann's *Zeitsinn* apparatus can be contrasted with those in the Leipzig laboratory (Henri, 1893, p. 613); these are similar to the older apparatus of Estel, with an improvement by Meumann. The Estel apparatus has a clockwork mechanism assisted by weights. The Meumann *Zeitsinn* apparatus has a Baltzar clockwork (spring motor), which also drives a kymograph drum. Both appear to rely on mechanical rather than electrical drives for their operation, and thus would seem to suffer variations in rotation speed; Schumann's device does not have this problem, because it is driven by an electric motor.

4. *Measuring reaction time.* Reaction time measurement was, at this time, often accomplished by a Hipp chronoscope, a piece of apparatus that was actually difficult to use with accuracy. The weights moved the hands at an acceptably constant speed, but the clutch that engaged the rotating dial was actuated by a battery-powered solenoid. The inconsistencies of its performance required calibration by the more constant fall time of a Wundt *Controlhammer*, a term best translated as "checking-hammer," with checking used in the sense of calibration. In 1892, Leipzig had two Hipp chronoscopes with associated electrical apparatus, while Göttingen had one.

In addition to the Hipp chronoscope, a simpler timing apparatus, devised by Schumann, was available in Göttingen. This device used a water motor (which provided more constant rotation speed than a spring motor) to turn a kymograph cylinder. On the cylinder, following the example of Donders, a 250 Hz tuning fork was used to provide the time pulses, and the number of cycles between stimulus onset and response was counted. Since such a device only depends on the accuracy of the tuning fork, it seems intrinsically superior to the Hipp chronoscope. It thus appears that Schumann's timing device, which depended on the same type of motive power (weights or a water motor) for providing speed, but which used the more constant vibration of a tuning fork for registering the time intervals, would require much less calibration.

While Wundt was aware of the relative accuracy of the two devices (for example, Wundt, 1893), the Leipzig Institute made the use of the Hipp chronoscope a standard. If Wundt, as administrator, thus opted for convenience over accuracy, this would seem to be an unacceptable solution for his students and for experimentalists in psychology. This solution is the more unacceptable since time and time differences were the key to any strategy of mental chronometry. It was only Wundt's later assistants who acquired the improved versions of these devices.

5. *Memory apparatus.* 1892 may be too early to judge the lack of memory apparatus in Leipzig, yet no Ebbinghaus-style memory studies are among the 187 dissertations Wundt directed—not surprising because of Wundt's theoretical differences with Ebbinghaus's orientation. Henri makes no mention of memory apparatus in Wundt's laboratory. Since memory apparatus was a significant innovation at the time, unlikely to

be overlooked by such an observer, we can assume that no memory apparatus was present.

For memory apparatus, there really is no comparison between Müller and Wundt, or anyone else, for that matter. Ebbinghaus had used scarcely any apparatus in his studies of learning syllables, but Müller had invented the first memory drum as an adaptation of a Ludwig-Baltzar kymograph (Haupt, in press) as well as an additional device for testing the strength of pairing used by Müller and Pilzecker (1900), which can be found in the Spindler and Hoyer catalog (1908/1921).

More than a decade later, in 1909, Wundt wrote a description of his laboratory for the 500th anniversary of the founding of Leipzig University in 1909 (Wundt, 1910). By this time, Wundt's *Assistent*, Wilhelm Wirth, had designed and used a memory apparatus. However, Wundt's description indicates that there are two apparatuses, both consisting of Wirth's improvements to the Ranschburg apparatus. While the timing control of the Ranschburg apparatus (through a metronome) seems precisely variable, the presentation of materials (from pre-printed circular cards) was restricted. Thus, aside from Wundt's coolness to Müller's procedure (Scheerer, 1980), the absence of the Müller-Schumann apparatus (1894), the Müller-Pilzecker apparatus (1900), and later devices such as the Lipmann apparatus (Sommer, 1904/1984) makes a statement about the attitude in Leipzig toward the orientation of Müller's memory research.

6. *Auditory apparatus.* Wundt had an extensive collection of auditory apparatus, including electrically driven tuning forks, and a single apparatus that can produce variable frequencies, the Appun "sound-measurer" (*Tonmesser*). What seems to be lacking are devices to produce "pure" (i.e. single-frequency) sounds which were used by Helmholtz. Moreover, Wundt's conflict with Stumpf over the Lorenz study in 1890 and 1891 (Boring, 1929) might provide some doubt about how well the auditory research from Wundt's laboratory was received by experts on audition.

Müller had no auditory apparatus, while Wundt had extensive apparatus. However, the very best auditory equipment was in Berlin in Helmholtz's lab, which would, in 1894, become Stumpf's workshop.

7. *Other equipment.* Henri concludes by noting that Müller's laboratory has, in addition, many pieces of physiological and physical apparatus, which are clearly more numerous than those in Wundt's. Thus Göttingen had a laboratory which specialized in newer apparatus and clever adaptations of basic apparatus such as the kymograph. In addition,

with a director who had a year's study of experimental physics (Müller) and a second-in-command (Schumann) with a physics doctorate, the fundamental training of the leading personnel, with regard to the precision of the instrumentation, was better than in the Leipzig Institute.

8. *A summary of the laboratory equipment.* With the exception of auditory equipment, an area of research that Müller apparently left to his colleague Stumpf (still in Munich in 1892, but soon to be made professor in Berlin), Müller's equipment appears to be consistently superior to that of Wundt in the early 1890s. If we ignore Boring's editorial emendation, it is obvious that Krohn understood this, and Henri's descriptions fully support Krohn's evaluation. And by the turn of the century Wundt was beginning to make sarcastic remarks about obsessions over apparatus precision that he perceived to be growing among experimental psychologists.

German Equipment Catalogs

The second major part of this study assesses two sets of equipment catalogs, those from the Leipzig firm of Zimmermann and the Göttingen firm of Carl Diederichs (bought by two Göttingen precision machinists, Spindler and Hoyer, in 1898, and under whose names the firm still survives today). In fact, as I discovered when preparing materials for a cyber-museum of early equipment (Haupt & Perera, 1997), the study of catalogs can provide an unexpected window into the history of psychology.

The Zimmermann Catalog

The origins of the Zimmermann firm are obscure, strangely so when Zimmermann's close association with Wundt is considered. The story begins with Gerhard Baltzar (185?–1899), first listed in the Leipzig *Adreßbuch* in 1885. He was the precision machinist for Carl Ludwig's physiology laboratory at Leipzig in the 1870s. Baltzar is not easy to trace, but he created Ludwig's new-model kymograph in the 1870s, an improvement on the Marey model. Ludwig's kymograph was the world standard until after World War I. Unlike the Marey model, the Ludwig-Baltzar kymograph could be adjusted so that its drum rotated at any speed, and it had a highly reliable spring motor. By 1887, when Müller commissioned

Baltzar to make the first memory drum, Baltzar and Schmidt had dissolved their partnership as machinists, and the Zimmermann firm was founded (Haupt, in press). Since the Ludwig-Baltzar kymographs occupy a substantial part of the Zimmermann catalog, it must be assumed that Zimmermann bought the assets of the firm of Baltzar and Schmidt and thus also had possession of the drawings that contained the specifications for the Müller memory drum.

During the period from 1887 to 1894, there are few traces of Zimmermann himself in Leipzig. During the 1880s and 1890s, he is not listed as a resident of Leipzig in the *Adreßbuch* or city directory. However, in 1894, the Zimmermann firm did publish a catalog with very brief descriptions, much smaller than the well-known 1903 catalog, available in facsimile edition (Zimmermann, 1903/1983). Although the 1903 catalog is important, it is important to note that it is primarily a catalog of physiological equipment, with psychological equipment as a secondary feature. There is no doubt, however, that Zimmermann should be considered the main equipment manufacturer for Wundt.

The 1903 Zimmermann catalog proclaims its origins and status in ways that show the context of its time. The cover displays *Jugendstil* lettering and decoration; such artistic designs, shortly after the Vienna Succession, were emblems of newness. The signature apparatus is the Ludwig-Baltzar kymograph, and in the catalog the variations on this basic model, and peripherals for it, seem to exhaust every possible modification of this device.

The Diederichs Firm

The counterpart to the Zimmermann firm in Leipzig was the Göttingen firm of Carl Diederichs (1852–1909), who specifically worked on apparatus for G. E. Müller and Friedrich Schumann. The origins of this firm and its close relationship to both men is described in a joint catalog of the exhibition of several Göttingen firms for the 1900 Paris exposition (Behrendsen, 1900).

Diederichs had been an employee, presumably a journeyman precision machinist, of the Göttingen manufacturer Meyerstein, until Meyerstein closed his workplace in 1875. Then, Diederichs and another Meyerstein employee, Bartels, set up a mechanical workshop. Presumably both had, by that time, passed the master test (*Meisterprüfung*) and could thus meet the legal requirements to form such a business in Prussia. Their partnership lasted until 1890, when Diederichs set up his own workshop at a nearby location. Diederichs's main business was the manufacture of electromechanical apparatus. However, toward the end of the 1880s, he added the apparatus that was of special interest to G. E. Müller. Behrendsen describes Müller's establishment as an Institute, although that designation, as previously noted, was not yet sanctioned by the Prussian *Kultusministerium*. In addition, Behrendsen describes G. E. Müller and his work in psychology as the "best-known representative of the newly blooming psychophysical [natural] science." (Behrendsen, 1900, p. 36).

In a personal communication, Rand Evans has informed me that Diederichs (1895, November 10) apparently published a catalog of specifically psychological equipment in 1894, the same year as the first Zimmermann list (Zimmermann, 1894). I do not believe that this Diederichs catalog has been mentioned anywhere else in the literature of the history of psychology. Evans has found, among Titchener's papers, a handwritten copy of parts of the catalog, sent to Titchener because the catalog itself was out of print at the time of the inquiry. Diederichs sent to Titchener a list of fifty or so pieces of psychological equipment, including extended descriptions of the ten pieces of apparatus about which Titchener had specifically requested information, as well as photographs of those ten pieces. By contrast to the informative Diederichs catalog, the Zimmermann catalog of 1894 gives only brief descriptions of the equipment, none of the extended descriptions, and no images of the apparatus.

Spindler & Hoyer Catalogs

Spindler & Hoyer is the successor to the firm of Carl Diederichs, and this firm still exists in Göttingen. Spindler and Hoyer acquired the Diederichs assets and continued to use his name at least until 1904; the only indication of the firm in the 1904 booklet for the first congress of *Deutsche Gesellschaft für experimentelle Psychologie* has the name of the firm as Diederichs, with Spindler and Hoyer as owners (*Inhaber*) (Sommer, 1904/1984).

Spindler and Hoyer incorporated the apparatus of Diederichs into their catalogs by 1898 (Spindler & Hoyer, 1908/1921, p. 3) and sought to expand the range of psychological apparatus (Behrendsen, 1900, p. 37). For our purposes, there are two versions of their catalog extant, the prewar one published in 1908 and the 1921 version, a slight revision of the 1908 version. These 1908 and 1921 Spindler & Hoyer catalogs, often found bound together in American libraries, show strong connections to G. E. Müller and his work. A recommendation for the catalog (p. 2) is signed by Hans Rupp, who was serving as *Assistent* to Carl Stumpf in Berlin in 1908, after he had already served as *Assistent* to G. E. Müller. (Interestingly, Rupp notes his Göttingen experience in the catalog, as former assistant there.) Since the Spindler & Hoyer catalogs can be found in several American libraries (including the Archives of the History of American Psychology in Akron), American psychologists apparently considered it important enough not only to use, but also to donate for preservation.

Determining How the Apparatus Worked

Probably the most important sources on the role of psychological laboratories and the history of experimentation are the textbooks and other writings that explain the apparatus. However, explanations given by iconic figures such as Titchener (1901; 1905) and even Woodworth (1938) can be unreliable guides. The problem with Titchener is that his student guides often talk down to the user, while the teacher's guides expect a level of sophistication and expertise which few possessed even at that time. Woodworth, surprisingly, is rather spotty in his explanations. Some topics are covered well, but others, such as constant stimuli methods, have weak presentations, as I have argued elsewhere (Haupt, 1998).

Nowadays very few people understand how early psychological apparatus was used, since few people trained after World War II learned their craft with spring-motor-driven mechanical devices and kymographs in which a stylus scratches records on blackened paper. There are still some fine collections in Germany and in East-European countries. Several years ago I visited the Leipzig Physiological Institute (now named after Carl Ludwig, the founder of the institute and the originator of the kymograph). The person who cared for its older apparatus showed me a late-model, Ludwig-Baltzar kymograph with an aluminum drum, a form of the apparatus that was standard for instruction in physiology from the 1870s until well after World War I. A relatively complete teaching laboratory, comprised of early equipment, exists in Belgrade under the watchful eye of Alexander Kostic (Kostic & Todorovic, 1997), but all the apparatus is not completely understood there, either. So there remain many gaps in our knowledge of the practices and content of early experimental psychology. A remedy might be effected if the museums of older equipment would show each piece of apparatus in connection with the important or typical experiments in which it was used; the results of such experiments should be interpreted in terms of the psychological systems of that day, as well as of the present day, when appropriate.

Unexpectedly, writing the captions for the cyber-museum of early psychological apparatus (Haupt & Parera, 1997) sensitized me to yet another way to use the catalogs as sources of historical information on early experimental psychology. These catalogs are interesting not only for understanding the studies which were carried out during early years of psychology, but also for the way in which they can reflect the conflicts which took place at that time.

Conflicts between G. E. Müller and Wundt

This paper has reviewed two contemporary accounts of the two laboratories from the early 1890s, both of which clearly indicated that the Göttingen laboratory was better for research. Such differences are also well illustrated in the catalogs of German equipment manufacturers. In the third major part of this article, I probe the conflict in German psychology between the laboratory in Göttingen that belonged to Müller and the laboratory in Leipzig that belonged to Wundt. In particular, it has become my conviction that Müller and his adherents considered Leipzig experimental work to be shoddy. Although this opinion was held most firmly in the stronghold of experimental research, Göttingen, indirectly it also reached the American psychological press. In Boring's (1950) great opus on the development of experimental psychology, however, there is scarcely a whiff of this conflict, although he makes quite a bit out of the Wundt-Stumpf controversy over Lorenz's acoustical study.

Wundt's Rejection of Müller's Memory Apparatus

Wundt, though no longer an active experimentalist himself, administrated the best financed psychology laboratory in Germany. He would seem to have had ample funds to buy the types of devices found in

Müller's laboratory. However, Wundt's very different theoretical orientation was moving away from the mechanistic associationism that Müller supported. This apparently diminished, in his view, the relevance of those devices. As previously noted, the most striking absence from Wundt's description of his laboratory (1910) was any memory equipment associated with Ebbinghaus and Müller. By then the following were available: the Müller-Schumann memory drum that is found in the 1903 Zimmermann catalog; the first paired-associate measurement device used by Müller and Pilzecker (1900, found only in the Spindler & Hoyer catalog); and the memory drum devised by Ebbinghaus's student, Otto Lipmann, in 1904 (also in the Spindler & Hoyer catalog), a major step on the way to the Gerbrands model.

The late Eckhard Scheerer has given us one explanation of Wundt's views on memory. According to Scheerer (1980, p. 139), Wundt apparently first followed a standard Herbartian associationistic theory of memory, as appeared in his earliest work, *Vorlesungen über Menschen- und Thierseele* of 1863. Yet Wundt offered his first psychological experimentation, conducted in the early 1860s, namely the "complication" experiment that began his reaction-time research program, as a rejection of the very core of Herbartian associationistic thought. Herbart's system was mechanistic to the core, whereas Wundt argued that central control processes could override associative effects. By 1892, Wundt's explanation of "associative" phenomena in psychological processes, one unique to his system, put problems of both recognition and recall under that category (Scheerer, 1980, pp. 143–144). As a result, any associative event that did not, at least initially, occur as a conscious process was not considered to be properly psychological in Wundt's theoretical system. (In most other association theories, the connection is often assumed to be unconscious.) Wundt thus found the "memorization" experiments of Ebbinghaus and Müller to be inaccurate, following the wrong lead (Scheerer, 1980, p. 147). Wundt found that any concept of memory or idea as some kind of physical entity (or engram, as it would later be called) was also theoretically questionable, and he referred to that notion as a reflection of "vulgar" thinking (in the sense of unsophisticated) (Scheerer, 1980, p. 136). Wundt's was a mentalist, non-physiological, position with respect to both mental states and memories.

While Wundt's early students were carrying out studies that reflected his core interest in central control processes (of selective attention or "apperception") and that were derivative from earlier lines of thought in

German philosophical literature, Ebbinghaus (1885/1909) was achieving recognition for establishing an entirely new area of research (not merely the first studies of learning/memory). Ebbinghaus's work was so original because his experiments created a research domain that had not been previously researched in physiology (sensory processes and capacities) or astronomy (reaction time).

Ebbinghaus's techniques resemble later serial anticipation methods. But Müller, not Ebbinghaus, set the standards for those methods (1894; see also Haupt, 1998). And while Mary Calkins introduced the method of paired associates (Madigan & O'Hara, 1992), the standards for that method were established by Müller and Pilzecker (1900). Calkins did no similar work after that. I argue that the source of an idea plays only a small role in the way the methods are later used, and verbal learning methods owe more to Müller than anyone else. Wundt approached verbal behavior from the viewpoint of linguistics research seeing the analysis of grammatical systems and other linguistics variables as the more important approach in this area.

Scheerer notes that Wundt strongly rejected the doctrine of preservation that emerged from Müller and Pilzecker's major study. Müller was a strong Herbartian in his theory. Wundt correctly found Müller's work to be a continuation of Herbart's associationist doctrines (Scheerer, 1980, p. 143). The neo-Herbartian Max Drobisch had been Müller's principal teacher of philosophy in Leipzig, and Müller was perhaps attempting to produce a *Vorstellungsmechanik* (mechanical theory of how images succeed each other in consciousness), an approach that can be identified with Herbart.

Wundt's interest in these early memory methods was only that of a critic, arguing against their importance from his theoretical positions. He sponsored no studies like those of Ebbinghaus or Müller. Nevertheless, Wundt's lab assistants and students were often given free rein, and work done in the Leipzig Institute sometimes moved in directions away from Wundt's particular theories (Scheerer, 1980, pp. 147–148). For example, the Radoslowow dissertation of 1907 and some work by Wilhelm Wirth (1902) in Leipzig may reflect memory research closer to Müller's. Wundt's student Meumann did memory studies only after moving to Zürich. Although Meumann had been Wundt's student and assistant, the memory work that he began in Zürich was part of his work in *experimentelle Pädagogik* (experimental educational psychology). He may not have initiated such work in Wundt's laboratory, both because Wundt did not support applied psychology in his Institute and because Wundt argued against Ebbinghaus's theoretical assumptions. When Meumann published his memory studies, he used Müller-style memory drums. Wirth developed a memory apparatus by 1902 (Scheerer, 1980, p. 147) and supervised memory research later (pp. 150–151), nearly ten years after Müller and Schumann's work and after Meumann had done similar work.

Two early studies, which are closely connected to problems of memory, actually were carried out in Wundt's laboratory. The Wolfe dissertation (1886; cited in Burnham, 1888–89) and the Lehmann study (1888; cited in Burnham, 1889–90) both concern recognition, rather than recall. Like that of Ebbinghaus, Wolfe's study varied the time to test (although only up to 30 seconds), and the physical difference between the auditory stimulus (to be recognized) and the test stimulus (either 2, 4, or 6 Hz; or 4, 8, or 12 Hz) depended on which of the 5 octaves the test was conducted in. Burnham (1889–90) also describes a similar study on visual recognition done by Lehmann in 1888. Both recognition studies were reported in Wundt's journal, *Philosophische Studien*. Since Wundt had about thirty potential doctoral students in his seminars at any time during the 1890s, as well as Külpe and Meumann (who later worked on memory) as his *Assistenten*, the paucity of something as important as Müller-style memory research is striking, and it was due to the theoretical predisposition of the director.

Wundt questioned nonsense-syllable learning experiments for a variety of theoretical reasons, not all of which were articulated before the completion of Müller's major works on the topic (Müller & Schumann, 1894; Müller & Pilzecker, 1900). Müller's experiments, even more than those of Ebbinghaus, required participants to learn under highly controlled and speeded conditions, and that set-up did not fit Wundt's idea of learning as an activity controlled by a process of selective attention that might involve imagery and configurational variables. For Wundt, those central mental controls regulate both the acquisition and the recall process.

Wundt's theoretical objection to serial memory experiments rested mainly on this conviction: such experiments presented to the experimental participant an "apperception" (selective attention) situation of considerable complexity. Wundt argued that any acquisition process that rapidly presents 12 syllables in 10 seconds (typical of Müller's experiments, though not as rapid as in Ebbinghaus's procedures) would require complex actions of selection, decision, and choice. Since those "apperception" conditions were not well controlled, the experiments could not show anything definite about the learning process. In addition, since the acquisition process had been compromised, the recollection could not easily be analyzed under these conditions either.

Müller, operating under assumptions that were then called "psychophysical" and that were strongly derived from Herbart's strictly associationist view, assumed that single-syllable presentations could not reflect the conditions that he considered important (i.e., the meter with which the syllables were read and the recall conditions). Müller also argued that single presentations contained random errors that had to be eliminated through repetition of the study with a single subject; single presentations could not provide what Müller wanted. Thus the theoretical and empirical purposes of memory research were very different in Leipzig and Göttingen.

Now we shall consider the catalog pages that present the first memory drum, according to Zimmermann and according to Spindler & Hoyer. The Müller-Schumann memory drum in Zimmermann's 1903 catalog is almost certainly the first illustration of this device. The illustration, however, contains an error: it shows two German words, "Blitz-Wolke" (Lightning-Cloud) being presented. This is an error on two counts. The drum was largely used for presentation of Ebbinghaus-Müller-style syllables, and it would be a mistake to try to use it for any paired-associates presentation. Apparently, subsequent changes in method for memory work do not seem to have affected Zimmermann. In 1930, the firm presents virtually the same image and text.

The comparable section in the Spindler & Hoyer catalog (1908) is much more detailed. It begins with a five-page section in which the series of apparatus solely for serial lists is described. Finally, the Müller-Schumann apparatus is shown, but with a much simpler weight motor, rather than the more expensive spring motor. In addition, there is a second version, "Simplified according to MacDougall"—a reminder that William MacDougall spent some time in Göttingen as part of a continental tour after his marriage.

In Leipzig the most common device for studying memory seems to have been the apparatus designed by the Hungarian pediatrician, Paul Ranschburg (1901). I think, however, that any comparison of Ranschburg's apparatus with Müller's apparatus makes it clear that Ranschburg's device is much less flexible than Müller's.

In the summer of 1998, I spent a few days in Budapest as the guest of Csaba Pleh, a psycholinguist there, and met with Gyorgy Kiss, who has written extensively about the history of early Hungarian psychology. From them I tried to discover what I could about Ranschburg and why Wundt might possibly have preferred to provide that apparatus to his researchers. I could only determine that Ranschburg visited Wundt several times and was on friendly terms with him. Ranschburg himself did not show sustained interest in his apparatus, since only one or two of his many publications concern its use. His publications are mainly studies of diagnosis of child psychopathology, not about experiments on memory processes.

The Ranschburg apparatus was apparently made by both firms. Again, Zimmermann gives a minimal description, while Spindler & Hoyer provides a much more detailed explanation. In fact, the Zimmermann description is rather misleading since it implies that the Ranschburg apparatus could easily be used for replication of the Müller and Pilzecker paired-associate work. While the Ranschburg apparatus would probably work for the presentation and pairing of syllables, Müller's testing apparatus (Spindler & Hoyer, 1908/1921) would be required to test the strength of associations.

Although Toronto, for example, has a Ranschburg apparatus in its collection, I started out with the impression that this apparatus was not very common. I consulted some later North American catalogs, in order to see how the different memory apparatuses were represented there. The "great" Stoelting catalog of 1930 (Stoelting, 1930–37/1997, p. 93), as it turned out, has only one memory apparatus illustrated, that of Ranschburg, and so it seems to have been influenced by the Zimmermann catalog in this regard. The catalog supplement, however, also mentions a Chicago memory drum that is reminiscent of an early Müller-Schumann model. The Stoelting catalog from 1937 also has only the Ranschburg apparatus, and still follows the pattern of the Zimmermann catalog. It includes a circuit for timing, using a metronome, similar to that in the Zimmermann catalog. The Marietta catalog (Marietta Apparatus Co., 1948) includes a classic, spring-driven Ludwig-Baltzar kymograph, with the inscription "Diel & Co." perfectly visible in the photograph, but there is no memory apparatus at all. My survey was thus fairly inconclusive with regard to memory devices, though it did show extended influence of the Zimmermann catalog in the American catalogs.

The common simple device used for memory studies in North America (and I remember it from graduate school in the early 1960s) was called the Gerbrands. This device, which is illustrated in Woodworth's textbook (1938, p. 38), should perhaps be called the Hempel/Rupp-Gerbrands, since it closely follows the pattern of the Hempel/Rupp model (Spindler & Hoyer, 1908/1921). The "Gerbrands" style was actually a simplification of the Hempel/Rupp model that had been produced through the combined work of Hans Rupp (*Assistent* to Stumpf in Berlin) and Hempel, who was a machinist for Robert Sommer, professor of psychiatry in Giessen and former student of Wundt. Gerbrands and, later, Lafayette were long associated with this type of memory drum, usually simply known as the Gerbrands style.

Many of the equipment standards for American memory research were set by John McGeoch in the University of Missouri laboratory. An example of one of these, with a sliding viewer that allows a participant to see different pairings of a list without long delays between lists, is shown in Hilgard's chapter (1951, p. 547) in Stevens's *Handbook of Experimental Psychology*. The arrangement of the multiple versions of a list of syllables to be learned is remarkably similar to that shown in the improved version of the Müller memory drum, as indicated in notes from the 1894 Diederichs catalog sent to Titchener. Albert Goss has given me information about a major set of innovations for American memory drums, especially the ones that were built for the Psychology Department at Iowa just before World War II. These devices were made in the workshop of the Physics Department of the University of Iowa and probably did not appear in any catalogs.

The firm of Lafayette Instruments still exists today, but the apparatus it builds now is more likely to be used by a clinical psychologist than an experimental one. The firm, however, has a relatively long history of supplying experimental apparatus, from the end of World War II until at least the 1980s. The impetus for the firm came from an Austrian refugee, Max Wastl, who, while still a student, had sufficient machinist's skills to build his first apparatus for Purdue University in West Lafayette, Indiana.

Lafayette catalogs from the early 1970s show the largest range of memory drums, many of which show the pattern of the Missouri drum. A Lafayette catalog of the early 1970s has a version of the Gerbrands-Lipmann apparatus that probably dates to the years right after World War II. The catalog also includes two pages of memory drums that were better suited to paired-associate work. In addition, the catalog includes something that was very up-to-date at the time, a memory drum that used lists printed on IBM line-printer paper, designed for Murray Glanzer of NYU. This innovation must have greatly facilitated the randomization and preparation of list items, just before the use of PDP-8s and TRS-80s made such arrangements unnecessary and anachronistic.

Although Wundt often ignored it, memory apparatus has played an important role in the history of experimental psychology. Now we turn to a topic that Wundt placed at the center of research in the Leipzig Institute.

Müller and Wundt on the Proper Measurement of Reaction Time

So far I have argued that Wilhelm Wundt, essentially a theoretician, was not the paradigm of laboratory precision; that characteristic should instead be associated with the North German (or Prussian) laboratories. This claim can be supported by a critical look at the Leipzig reaction time measurements. First, I will examine the relevance of reaction time for Wundt's early theoretical orientation. Then I will describe various types of apparatus for measuring reaction time that were used in the 1870s and 1880s as well as the calibration problems that arise when using those devices. Then, drawing from a variety of sources, I will consider whether Wundt was prescribing good measurement practices, even for his own time. Finally I will discuss an extensive contemporary report by the British psychologist, Edgell, and her physiologist-colleague, Symes; this is a detailed evaluation of the nature of reaction time measurement shortly after the turn of the century. Edgell's report makes it possible to understand how the goal of one-millisecond timing accuracy could be achieved in an adequately equipped laboratory. The resulting precision of measurement reached a level that, for most purposes, was maintained for about fifty years and was only superseded in the era of tube-based cascade timers and transistors.

Wundt should be recognized as promoting a program for the study of motivationally controlled processes of decision and choice. The designation of his approach as the "Voluntarist School" derives from that. Two features of research procedure were of critical importance in his studies (Benschop & Draaisma, 2000, pp. 13–14). First, each event must have full opportunity for conscious awareness during the experimental event; and second, the time for the response to each event must be measurable,

permitting an index of the mental processes involved. He argued that an
accuracy of one millisecond was more than sufficient. The Hipp chronoscope, giving measurements in milliseconds, became a totem, according
to Horst Gundlach—more a symbol of the new psychology, than the
best measurement device (Gundlach, 1996). By looking more closely at
measurements of reaction time (RT), we can determine how this "totem"
functioned.

Wundt first presented a study involving reaction time in 1862. This
short article for a popular magazine described a kind of complication
experiment (Wundt, 1862), and he wrote it while he was *Assistent* for
physiology under the supervision of Helmholtz at Heidelberg. Thus,
Wundt's interest cannot be traced solely to Donders's experiments of the
late 1860s, as Benschop and Draaisma (2000, p. 4) would have it. It seems
more likely that Wundt was making a metaphorical extension of his
supervisor's famous studies of nerve conduction time from 1850–1852. In
such an analysis, any mental process could be considered to take a specific neural route requiring a certain amount of time. Danziger (1980, pp.
106–109) emphasizes the importance of reaction time for Wundt's theory
of self-control, that is for the central control of behavior.

Wundt thus had a mentalistic orientation before he began to sponsor
dissertations in 1879 in Leipzig. And many reaction-time investigations
that were done by his students in the Leipzig laboratory, if not all of them,
must be understood or interpreted in terms of that orientation. The first
dissertation of this series, by Max Friedrich, has been partially translated
by Peter Behrens (Friedrich, 1883/1980). This report is a good example of
the type of topic and style of presentation of the Leipzig studies of reaction time. One of the surprising aspects of this study, to my mind, is that
there is no discussion of calibration of the Hipp chronoscope that they
used. If precision should have been the issue, this was an inauspicious
beginning.

By the 1870s, there were a number of methods for measuring short
intervals of time. For the very tiny intervals of transmission along the
nerve controlling the gastrocnemius muscle of the frog, Helmholtz had
used the movement of a galvanometer needle that he calibrated, following the ideas of Pouillet (1844). Charles Wheatstone invented the chronoscope in 1839, and the improvements of the clockmaker Mathias Hipp
and others made it a standard device by the 1860s. The establishment
of the kymograph as a measuring device by Ludwig in 1847 also offered
the combination of the tuning fork and the kymograph, called the

chronograph. Although Wundt and others discussed both timing instruments in their publications, there was no systematic comparison of these methods in English until Edgell published a comprehensive article in the *British Journal of Psychology* in 1906.

The Hipp chronoscope (see Robinson's chapter in this book, Figure 2) was basically an escapement-driven clock in which a tuned spring (actually similar to a tuning fork) provided a precise driving speed of 500 (and later 1000) impulses per second through an escapement for a rotary dial. The main advantage (and chief characteristic) of the chronoscope was that it had a visible dial from which the time value could be read, thus eliminating the tedious and potentially erroneous registration of another sort—for example, counting cycles on a chronograph.

Unfortunately, the chronoscope, especially in its early versions, had intrinsic problems that hindered accuracy. The mass of the dial had to be accelerated to full speed by means of the weight driving it. The tuned spring had the tendency sometimes to double or halve its characteristic frequency. Primitive relays of the time had difficulty achieving precise onsets and offsets of the mechanism. Finally, batteries were used to power the electrical parts until well after the turn of the century, and they had varying reliability. So chronoscopes, though preferred for their visible dials, were problematic for exact timing.

The second type of precision time-measuring devices, the chronograph (see Robinson's chapter in this book, Figure 1), made use of the Marey and Ludwig-Baltzar kymographs, which had recently undergone improvements in the consistency of their rotation speeds. A spring-regulated governor (called the Foucault governor) made the accurate regulation of the rotation speeds of these kymographs possible: a spring attached to the central shaft restricted the outward travel of the movable arms of the governor. The chronograph had become the standard for accurate graphical recording of time signals by the 1870s, and when the carbon-coated paper was removed from the drum and fixed in a shellac bath, it yielded a permanent and publishable record of a time signal.

The chronograph relied upon a tuning fork to provide the accurate time base. The accuracy and simplicity of the tuning fork enabled this device to avoid the Rube Goldberg character of Hipp ensembles. Piano tuners today can be prodigiously accurate, and we can presume that similar paragons staffed the tuning fork manufactures of nineteenth-century Europe. Elementary physics courses explain how tuning forks can achieve accuracy of frequency more easily than other devices. They produce the audible phenomenon of beats: two tuning forks that are very slightly different will produce a rhythmic signal of varying loudness. The (slower) frequency of this varying loudness is the difference in frequency of the two forks, thus permitting easy adjustment of the erring fork. Jules Lissajous, the French physicist, perfected an optical standard for the calibration of tuning forks; his work established the French standard for the tone A at 435 Hz (Turner, 1997, p. 33). Thus, as long as the batteries worked to move marking pens, a chronograph, the device used by Donders (1868/1969) for his pioneering reaction time studies, had only the speed of the relays as a concern for accuracy in measurement. In fact, the time path of the relay could be plotted simultaneously on the kymograph to determine calibration. Since the speed of the tuning fork was absolute, the device needed little calibration, but merely required a willingness to count accurately the number of tuning fork excursions. A tuning fork of 200 or 256 Hz could easily enable measurements to one-thousandth second. Wundt himself sponsored the creation of a large and very precise version of such an apparatus, as Benschop and Draaisma note (though these authors incorrectly suggest that the tuning fork requires calibration; Benschop & Draaisma, 1999, p. 10). The chronograph displayed in the Zimmermann catalogs may well be a copy of the device presented by Diederichs (1895) and attributed to Schumann.

A third set of devices for reaction time experiments depended on the precise measurement of the velocity of a pendulum. Since the time for a pendulum to travel from one side to another depends only on the length between the edge from which it hangs and the center of its mass, the length along a single swing of the pendulum can serve as a time measure for periods of a fraction of a second. Since a pendulum of 1 m has a period of 2 sec, a pendulum of manageable size and arc-length has the advantage that it can measure a wide variety of typical human reaction times. The difficulty comes in stopping the pendulum precisely or otherwise marking, along the arc, the location corresponding to the time when the human reaction took place.

Pendulums were adapted for time measurement in other ways as well. The American psychologist Sanford had devised a modified "vernier" pendulum in which two pendula could be set to slightly different lengths and an accurate difference of .02 sec per swing could be found. There were also devices based on pendulums that could provide accurate time bases for calibration of chronoscopes or for timing the stimulus presentation durations for other experiments.

A fourth type of time measurement was that carried out by Helmholtz in 1850. Since, as a junior member of the Königsberg medical faculty, he did not have funds to equip a physiology lab, he resorted to a galvanometer excursion to measure short times in a manner similar to Pouillet (1844). This, however, was a very difficult measurement and was best suited for very short intervals of a few milliseconds.

Thus, in spite of the availability of alternatives, the Hipp chronoscope became a signature feature of Wundt's laboratory and in many other labs around the world. This device, however, was only one of several means for the precise measurement of time; and it was a far more problematic device than has usually been portrayed in writings on history of psychology.

Calibrating the Hipp Chronoscope

The calibration of the Hipp chronoscope involved two main sources of error. These were problems created by the spring that controlled the escapement speed and by the onset and offset times provided by the simple electrical relays, which were used to engage and disengage the clutch that caused the dial to rotate.

The first fundamental problem concerned the rate of the Hipp spring oscillation. The spring that controlled the escapement frequency actually presented two sorts of problems. One, which seems not to have been much of a practical problem, was the tendency of the spring occasionally to oscillate at twice or half the nominal speed. A second problem, however, was largely unnoticed, because it provided a consistent bias: the frequency of the springs was apparently not exactly 500 or 1000 Hz. It was 512 or 1024 Hz in the early machines. This frequency presumably predominated because the springs were made by musical instrument makers, and 512 was the C below the treble clef. Musical instrument makers (such as those who made the famous Swiss music boxes) were skilled at making devices that resonate at such frequencies, and would have charged much more for special frequencies. Thus, reaction times had to be adjusted to 1.024 the measured time. This adjustment added some tedium, but it was certainly not difficult, and a mechanical multiplier or a table of equivalent times would easily produce the correct times. By the turn of the century, the rate of spring oscillation was in fact 1000 Hz, and the springs could even be adjusted to the correct frequency (Edgell & Symes, 1908, p. 282).

The second fundamental problem with the Hipp chronoscope concerned the onset and offset times. It was the most complicated problem in calibrating the chronoscope, and it involved the electrical switches or relays that controlled the clutch that engaged the dial. If you remember, as I do, what relays were like in the 1960s, you remember compact devices, tightly constructed, which had permanent magnets and whose largest problem was the tendency for the contacts to "burn" or weld themselves together. The equivalent device of the 1870s was not so neat, although the basic principal was the same. A current from a battery was allowed to flow into a coil surrounding a movable magnet. When the current reached sufficient strength, a field strong enough to move the unmagnetized soft iron bar was created, and the bar moved to force the clutch plates together. The sweep on the dial was ended when the bar moved in the opposite direction. Until about 1900, batteries provided the electrical voltages. Wundt's new laboratory in 1897 had dc-voltage sources in the walls of experimental rooms. Almost ten years later, Edgell and Symes did their work in the London University Physiological Laboratory, which had batteries as the current source. Thus, for much of the time with which we are concerned, batteries were a problem. Batteries sometimes worked, sometimes they did not work right, and they always gave less voltage as time went on. Since different battery currents gave different onset and offset times, the problem of calibration of the chronoscope was exacerbated by the use of batteries.

Even Wheatstone already recognized that a large current to close the clutch and a small current to release it provided the best result; the onset time and the offset time would be approximately equal, thus providing an unbiased result (Edgell & Symes, 1906, p. 59). Such a requirement, however, cannot be well accommodated by batteries, since a battery that produces a large current runs down much faster than one that produces a small current. The importance of making these times equal was generally recognized (Cattell, cited in Edgell & Symes, 1906, p. 60; Külpe & Kirschmann, cited in Edgell and Symes, 1906, p. 61).

One would assume that Wundt was interested in having his Hipp chronoscopes well calibrated. However, Wundt began to view the growing and consuming interests in batteries, springs, and other mechanisms as leading away from the original mission of the study of psychological processes. During a post-doctoral stint at Berlin University in 1856–57, young Wundt's laboratory activities had disappointed Emil du Bois-Reymond (Diamond, 1980, pp. 22–26). Du Bois-Reymond later assumed the chair of physiology created after the death of Johannes Müller when the teaching of anatomy and physiology was divided; he was one of the most important physiologists of the nineteenth century as well as a leader among those who adopted the physico-chemical approach to physiology, including Ludwig, Ernst Brücke, Helmholtz. Du Bois was one of the founders of the field of electrophysiology, was an experimentalist determined to see that replications always worked, was an editor of a leading journal (*Archiv für Physiologie*), was successor to Alexander von Humboldt as president of the natural science section of the Berlin Academy of Sciences, and, along with Helmholtz, was one of the experts frequently invited by the Emperor and the Crown Prince to discuss the latest results from the world of science.

In one of the many letters he exchanged with Helmholtz, du Bois made a decidedly negative comment on Wundt, who at the time was still in Heidelberg but was no longer assistant to Helmholtz. Du Bois slams Wundt's recent book on physics for physicians (1867) and recalls a revealing observation on Wundt's work in the Berlin laboratory:

> Something worse than the presentation of electricity in Wundt's *Medical Physics* is rarely to be seen. Perhaps politics is the suitable field for him. I recognized him as ungifted for the experimental direction during his days in my laboratory, when he tried to use lacquer to stick a piece of wood on wet cardboard and when he spoiled my pretty London drill press, because he turned it by hand, and overlooked or did not understand what placed it in rotation. (Hörz & Wollgast, 1986, p. 230)

While Wundt's reputation among physiologists may not be the best place to assess his view of calibration practices in psychology, we can look at the practices of the Leipzig laboratory. Errors of commission and omission can be found among the Leipzig researchers seeming to confirm du Bois's earlier opinions. Edgell and Symes (1906, p. 60) note that the early edition of Wundt's *Grundzüge* recommends the currents for onset and offset on the chronoscope be equal—a procedure that was already then known to produce different onset and offset times. As already noted, the earliest studies published out of the Leipzig laboratory did not discuss calibration at all.

Later, in 1886, Wundt's journal published a paper by his student, Ludwig Lange, describing a Leipzig-developed *Controlhammer*, or hammer-like checking device to calibrate the chronoscope (see Robinson's chapter in this book, Figures 5 and 6), but only for durations shorter than 160 ms, thus excluding much of the measurement region that interests psychologists. It was also only at this time that Wundt's journal presented the improved chronograph, which has claims to accuracy of 1/10,000 of a second. Eventually, however, Wundt (1911, p. 377) dismissed the need for calibration apparatuses, such the Lange *Controlhammer*, that used the fall of a weight to provide a time standard for calibration of the Hipp chronoscope.

Even before Ludwig Lange, another member of Wundt's research group had begun to work on calibration problems—James McKeen Cattell. Benschop & Draaisma (2000) have summarized the relevant material from Cattell's diaries, which have been so ably edited by Michael Sokal. While published reports from the Leipzig laboratory up to that time do not indicate much interest in calibration, Cattell's letters and diaries show that he obsessively controlled his personal and laboratory life in order to carry out his timing experiments as carefully and as accurately as possible. The implicit contrast between Wundt and Cattell suggests several possibilities. One possibility is simply that Wundt's practices were appropriate and Cattell was simply a young upstart, responding to the mood of the times to feign precision and gain respectability. This certainly seems to be what Lincoln Steffens thought when he visited Leipzig and met Cattell.

I think it is perhaps more likely that Cattell, who generally seems to have been acutely oriented to the value of accurate apparatus, was concerned about the appropriate use of his equipment. As he used the measurements he collected, he attempted to bootstrap his procedures toward more precise quantification of what he was measuring. In the mid-1880s only a few buildings in the world had yet been equipped with electric power. Both wet and dry cells created frequent problems and were unreliable current sources. Cattell clearly responds to this lack of reliability; he limited himself and his fellow Leipzig student and co-worker, G. O. Berger, to series of only 26 reactions before an enforced rest period. Anyone who knows laboratory technique for reaction times will understand that this precautionary measure was a powerful guarantee that there would be good attention for each response. Such procedures also provide guarantees that battery life will be preserved.

Münsterberg and RT Studies

In 1885, Hugo Münsterberg finished his doctoral dissertation under Wundt. After medical study in Heidelberg he accepted an appointment in 1887 to become *Privatdozent* at the smaller Baden university at Freiburg im Breisgau; his sponsor there was professor of philosophy Alois Riehl. Even though he had no salary and had to use his own funds, Münsterberg set up a laboratory for experimental psychology in his own house in Freiburg. From 1889 to 1892, he published four issues of *Beiträge zur experimentellen Psychologie*, which reported his own studies as well as the studies of some of his students. It is undoubtedly this initiative in creating experimental studies that brought him to the attention of William James, who annotated copies of all four issues in his personal library (now preserved in Houghton Library of Harvard University).

These early papers of Münsterberg include several extended discrimination reversal studies (switching a watch from one pants pocket to the other; switching the inkwell from left to right on the desk) which seem to be the first proactive transfer studies. While the experiments are interesting in themselves, some of Münsterberg's interpretations of them are less attractive (for example, he thought that with progressive reversals, the discrimination became weaker). A large part of Münsterberg's studies were reaction time studies which followed in the tradition of Leipzig, but which did not espouse the central cognitive processes of Wundt's program.

G. E. Müller made two public "corrections" of Münsterberg, in which he primarily discussed the inadequacy of the measurements of reaction times. The first (Müller, 1891) was simply a review of three issues of Münsterberg's *Beiträge*, while the second (Müller, 1893) concentrated on what was wrong and labeled itself a *Berechtigung* (correction). Hale (1980, pp. 24–25) gives a summary of Müller's critique, essentially that, even though Münsterberg did not follow Wundt's arguments, he was still not a very good experimenter when the design and interpretation of his experiments is considered. In particular, Müller criticized the use of the Leipzig *Controlhammer* as a calibration device, maintaining that the error would increase systematically for intervals beyond the duration that the *Controlhammer* could normally create (about 160 ms maximum), and thus all the reaction time measurements were inaccurate.

Müller was somewhat dictatorial and scolding with students; sometimes his critical remarks were excessive. Nevertheless, he valued accuracy and methodological soundness above all. The clear implication in his critique of these studies is that the flawed timing methods had been handed from Wundt to Münsterberg as from master to pupil.

In 1893, Wundt's two assistants, virtually the acting directors of his Institute at that time, published an extensive description of methods of calibrating the Hipp chronoscope (Külpe & Kirschmann, 1893). While August Kirschmann was soon to go off to Toronto and create a laboratory there, Oswald Külpe must be counted as a significant character in this story: he soon became professor in Würzburg, where he established an important psychology laboratory and later served as Beatrice Edgell's *Doktorvater*.

Külpe was personally one of Wundt's loyal students and admirers in spite of well-known debates they had concerning a number of central theoretical issues. The question of Külpe's shifting theoretical affiliations is more problematic. He studied with G. E. Müller for three semesters before taking the doctorate with Wundt and becoming his second paid *Assistent*. Müller and Külpe were in relatively frequent contact by letter during the time that Külpe was at Leipzig, from 1886 to 1894, when Külpe became *Ordinarius* for philosophy in Würzburg. In the early years of the new century, Külpe was present at the founding (1903), and a board member at the first meeting (1904), of the *Deutsche Gesellschaft für experimentelle Psychologie*, which Müller headed for 23 years and which Wundt never joined. Moreover, Müller students (for example, Lillie Martin) frequently also worked in Külpe's lab, and Külpe students (for example, Narziß Ach) sometimes habilitated in Müller's lab. For his part, Wundt sometimes sent students to Külpe, but not to Müller.

Edgell's Analysis of RT Studies

Beatrice Edgell was a remarkable woman, an early British psychologist who in 1897 was named Lecturer in Philosophy and thus became head of the Department of Mental and Moral Sciences at Bedford College, an all-female branch of London University. We know less about her than we should, but it is clear that she had strong training and made important contributions to British psychology. She was the principal teacher of psychology at Bedford College from 1898 until her retirement in 1933. Until her death in 1948, she continued to work from her retirement home and to serve as an examiner in psychology for the Royal College of Nursing, a post that she had occupied prior to her retirement.

Edgell trained in psychology in Würzburg with Külpe and presumably met Narziß Ach, a leading theorist of voluntarist psychology, during the academic year 1900–1901. She finished her doctoral dissertation in 1902, entitled "Experimentation as a border of psychology." She returned to England where she established the laboratory at Bedford College (her first grant for equipment and supplies amounted to only $25) and worked with prominent British psychologists, including Sir Frederic Bartlett, whose later work on "remembering" was much closer to Wundt's orientation that to Müller's. In the articles with Symes, she lists "Physiological Laboratory of the University of London" as her affiliation. This may reflect Symes's position there and was likely used because only that laboratory provided equipment necessary for the studies they carried out. From 1911 to 1931, she contributed to the *Proceedings of the Aristotelian Society* what were regarded as essays on philosophical aspects of mind (Valentine, in press).

One of Edgell's significant achievements was the extended paper in the second volume of the newly founded *British Journal of Psychology*, a survey of the measurement of reaction times, part of which appeared in 1906 and part in 1908. In this article, Edgell and her collaborator, W. Legge Symes (later Professor of Physiology at the Royal Veterinary College), describe measurement devices and discuss the problems of the Wheatstone-Hipp chronoscope; they refer to similar work by Narziß Ach, particularly the appendix to his 1905 book, *Über die Willenstätigkeit* (Concerning the Activity of the Will). While Ach had earlier been a student of Külpe, this book on volitional processes was the result of Ach's *Habilitation* in G. E. Müller's laboratory in Göttingen, where Ach served as *Assistent*.

The main feature of the Edgell and Symes presentation is the use of a light lever attached to the armature of the clutch that engages the moving hand of the chronoscope. The position of the armature can thus be traced on a kymograph drum that has a tuning fork of 200 Hz providing a time-base tracing (one must read the tracings to 1/5 of a cycle to attain accuracy to one millisecond). In addition, Edgell and Symes provide a baseline showing the position of the chronoscope armature when the clutch is disengaged. They provided a mark that shows when the clutch is engaged, as well as a line halfway between the two marks that shows a putative make-or-break point for the armature.

Edgell and Symes determine that the parameters that govern the time needed to make and break the chronoscope clutch contact are different. In order to determine the time to make the clutch contact, the spring tension which holds the clutch apart, the current which is allowed to flow in the coil around the magnet, and the electrical resistance of the circuit must all be known. For breaking the clutch contact, the mechanical inertia of the magnet, dependent on its mass, and the remnant magnetism of the iron bar must be known. Remnant (or remaining) magnetism of the iron bar is a problem because, when the current in a coil around a magnet is shut off, the bar temporarily retains some strength as a magnet. The more times the magnet is used or the stronger the current to make the contact, the stronger the remnant magnetism becomes. In order to eliminate this problem of progressive changes in the time to move the clutch apart, many chronoscopes were equipped with the ability to be operated by current in either direction. In order to rapidly change the direction of the dc current, a small switch, the *Pohl'sche Wippe* (Pohl's see-saw switch) had been used (see Robinson's chapter in this book, Figure 2).

In an added note, Edgell and Symes (1908) describe a new chronoscope from Peyer and Faverger, the Neuchâtel successor to Hipp. Edgell and Symes tested the new device thoroughly, determining that the frequency generator has an error of less than one percent. A failure of the equipment then sends it back to Neuchâtel. When it returns, its calibration is not so exact. However, they use methods that they have previously described and soon the chronoscope is even more accurate than before.

The Accuracy of RT Measurement

The accurate measurement of time intervals of less than one second became important for psychology when Hirsch, Donders, von Kries, and Wundt began to use such intervals to infer time characteristics of mental processes during the 1860s and 1870s. Measuring such time intervals with chronographs was not problematic, in terms of accuracy, but the use of chronoscopes was. The main error was caused by difficulties in equalizing the times to make and break the clutch contact. Equalizing these times was a complicated problem that depended on complex electromagnetic phenomena. As Wundt's career progressed, he became less involved in the equipment himself and was never the instrumentation specialist that G. E. Müller and some others were. Wundt was perhaps often not even aware of the electrical work that his assistants and students carried out in his laboratory. A lack of electrical acumen at Leipzig may have produced unresolvable errors in the reaction times that were recorded. (For example, all the fuss over "sensory" versus "muscular" reactions, starting in the late 1880s, probably only distracted from more essential work needed on accuracy of time measurement.) While some of my criticisms of Wundt are admittedly tentative, it is clear that several major papers (Külpe & Kirschmann, 1893; Müller & Pilzecker, 1900; Ach, 1905; Edgell & Symes, 1906; 1908) were required before the difficulties with the chronoscope were sufficiently identified and generally resolved. By that time relatively stable dc currents were available (Edgell and Symes used a set of 9 batteries as large as the automobile type), and the Wheatstone-Hipp chronoscope, as manufactured by Hipp's successor, Peyer et Faverger, had finally become a reliable laboratory instrument. The main line of the studies that demonstrated the necessary techniques to calibrate the chronoscope came typically not from Wundt but from G. E. Müller, Oswald Külpe (an ally of Müller on experimental matters), and their students.

One of the surprising results of studying the development of chronographs and chronoscopes is the rediscovery of several other apparatuses. Such is the case of the 1903 chronograph and Dunlap chronoscopes (1917). Edmund Delabarre (1863–1946) had his experimental training at Freiburg im Breisgau where Alois Rhiel was the *Ordinarius* concerned with experimental psychology, and Delabarre's work was supervised there by Hugo Münsterberg. Delabarre seems to have made the next logical step in improving the chronograph. He started with the problem of unequal speeds of the chronograph paper as the spring or weight motor unwound. This meant that the times required could not be obtained just by measuring the length of the line inscribed on the blackened paper of the chronograph. Delabarre made the speed equal by using a Helmholtz constant speed motor (Haupt & Perera, 1997) to move the chronograph drum.

Knight Dunlap was an important early experimental psychologist at Johns Hopkins who is scarcely remembered today. In 1917, he published a paper on a new chronoscope that made use of the recently available ac current. Dunlap utilized a synchronous motor in which the speed is controlled by the frequency of the ac voltage. To the extent that the frequency was well controlled, such a motor had the ability to use a time base at least as accurate as the spring that controlled the time base for the Hipp. With such a device, ac relays provide the equivalent of a high-voltage battery and the Pohl see-saw switch, which accommodated the problems of soft iron core relays. With such an improvement, it is surprising that psychologists did not celebrate the arrival of the Dunlap chronoscope, but continued to see the Hipp chronoscope as the standard of accuracy.

Schlosberg (1937) prepared an apparatus so that two intervals (102 and 309 milliseconds) could be compared for the Hipp chronoscope, the

Delabarre chronograph, the Dunlap chronoscope, and the much less accurate pendulum chronoscope. In this comparison the Dunlap chronoscope had the highest accuracy, defined according to the mean variation of the recorded time. The Dunlap apparatus also had a constant error or bias, which required correction. Thus, even though the Hipp chronoscope was still available, psychologists had improved alternatives, and even before Edgell reported improved calibration procedures the Delabarre chronograph was available.

There are few accounts of the early history of reaction time measurement that recognize the fact that the frequently described accuracy of one millisecond was probably not achieved until 1908, and then only in the few laboratories that had facilities equivalent to the physiological laboratory of Symes in London. To put the problem in perspective, however, accuracy of one millisecond was more accuracy than was needed (a point Wundt would harp on), since a typical study often consisted of the averaging of hundreds of individual measurements. One one-hundredth second was nearer the needed standard, easily achieved with a simple chronograph.

Nevertheless, the Hipp chronoscope was the visible standard for experimental psychology. And it is puzzling that Wundt did not require his laboratory workers to devote more effort to its calibration, since everything in Wundt's background would suggest that he should know the importance of calibration. The critique that Müller directed at Münsterberg was surely indirectly aimed at Wundt. If Wundt understood this, he never noted it; he and his followers were more concerned that Münsterberg's studies attacked Wundt's doctrine of central attentional control processes. (See Robinson's chapter in this book.) The resolution of time measurement problems was carried out, partly in Wundt's laboratory, but more thoroughly in other places closely allied with Müller's brand of experimental psychology. Wundt himself seems to have lost interest in these matters. With regard to reaction-time studies of mental processes, a topic central to his psychological system, Wundt seems to have given up the opportunity for more accurate development of the experimental precision of his work.

Evaluation of the Productivity of the Two Laboratories

The preceding sections have demonstrated that insofar as visitors' judgments, quality of equipment, or calibrated use of the Hipp chronoscope were concerned, the laboratory of G. E. Müller was the leading institution for the experimentalist movement, by the early 1890s. Are there any other grounds for considering Wundt's laboratory to be the most important to the experimentalist movement in this period?

The decade of 1890–1900 was a period of significant productivity for the Göttingen laboratory. Müller and Schumann's paper (1894) used the first memory drum, provided the first proactive and retroactive transfer studies with syllables, refuted Ebbinghaus's claim for remote associations, executed the first factorial transfer design, and showed that serial learning processes were dependent on placement of the syllable in its proper serial position, much more than on association. Jost (1897) presented evidence for Müller's forgetting theory with the demonstration of "Jost's laws." Lillie Martin did the first major independent study of Time-Order-Errors, focusing psychophysical methods on judgment processes. Laura Steffens (1900) studied the effects of time intervals on the psychophysics of weight. Lotte Steffens (1900) completed a major study of part-whole learning. Victor Henri completed a major study on the psychophysics of touch. Müller and Pilzecker (1900) established the standard procedures for paired-associate learning, wrote the book on interference theory, provided studies in which response latency as well as response correctness were recorded, and introduced the concept of consolidation. Thus the Göttingen laboratory in the 1890s provided a wide range of the important data and methodologies for an experimental psychology.

Boring writes, "Ebbinghaus had opened up a field [memory] which the patience of G. E. Müller and his associates was soon to develop . . ." (1950, p. 388) and "[Wundt's studies] made little impression as compared with the effective research upon memory by Ebbinghaus and G. E. Müller that belongs to the same period" (p. 343). Roback (1961, p. 84), a student of Münsterberg, expresses the same opinion.

In the same decade, Wundt's lab continued to use reaction-time measures for the study of mental processes, though that tradition was now beginning to wane in the face of the new research on emotion, which was so central to Wundt's voluntarist position (see Blumenthal's chapter in this book). In the area of sensory research at that time, Wundt thought well of the major auditory study by Carl Lorenz, but Stumpf, the best psychologist of audition in those days, severely criticized it. Wundt praised Meumann's work on rhythm and short time intervals, but Schumann, as a proxy for Müller, criticized both Georg Dietze's and Meumann's studies. Thus the achievements of Wundt's laboratory in the 1890s are problematic. While we cannot say much about Wundt's laboratory as an enterprise for the production of scientific knowledge in this period, Müller's lab, even with its limited personnel, developed an enviable record of new accomplishments.

One of the major differences between Leipzig and Göttingen was in the use of classroom demonstrations. Wundt, ever the dramatic lecturer, had a large amount of equipment stored in a closet adjacent to the lecture hall, and it was presumably the job of one of his institute assistants to prepare the apparatus for lecture demonstrations of psychological processes. In contrast, Müller's meager budget did not include any money for demonstration apparatus. In 1887, Müller wrote a request for funding to equip his new laboratory. Probably in his effort to conform to the Prussian bureaucratic culture that resisted such expenditures, he noted that Wundt specialized in attracting "those who need spectacle" (die Schaulustige). Müller was thus justifying the omission of demonstration equipment from his request as befitting Prussian budgetary parsimony. In 1914, when Müller was able to invite the Deutsche Gesellschaft für experimentelle Psychologie to Göttingen (Müller, 1915), he described how he was able to use the largest hall for his lectures, but that students were shown to the laboratory in small groups; demonstrations were not part of his lectures.

Wundt's reputation as a bench physiologist in the 1850s before he became a psychologist may be suspect. His brief career as a medical doctor was followed by a somewhat longer period in the physiological laboratory, but there his thoughts turned to abstract theories. In those early years, Du Bois-Reymond described accidents that Wundt created while working in the Berlin lab in the late 1850s. Wundt was also once criticized by Ewald Hering for a mathematical error in a description of the horopter (and yet Wundt later sponsored some mathematical doctorates at Leipzig).

Müller, in his doctoral studies, had successfully completed a year of experimental physics under Wilhelm Weber and had been a proud and successful officer in the Franco-Prussian War (which featured the first bolt-action rifles). He was meticulous, even overbearing, about cleanliness and order in his laboratory. In addition, Müller was capable of using hand calculations to do relaxation methods to calculate the non-linear fit to a cumulative normal distribution, and he suggested a weighting scheme based on the function minimized in such fits (1878). When he established his lab, Müller also had the capable help of Schumann, who had just

completed, after six years of study at Göttingen, a doctorate in physics
with a dissertation on electrical conduction in fluid media. Thus, while
Wundt seems to have had more resources and personnel overall, the
stricter Müller seems to have had personnel who were better qualified to
initiate psychology as a purely experimental science—something that
Wundt never advocated and that Müller did, at least implicitly.

What Remains to Be Said

Neither Krohn's paper nor Henri's description of the German laboratories gives really complete information about the institutions that
supported psychological experimentation. Some *physiological* laboratories
of the time, while certainly keen on non-psychological topics like respiration and kidney function, were also centers of sensory experimentation
and studies of muscle function. Krohn, in particular, seems to have completely neglected several important sensory physiology laboratories that
would most likely require the attention of experimental psychologists. He
had an extended stay in Freiburg im Breisgau, as the guest of Münsterberg; however, in the medical school, Johannes von Kries also had an
important sensory workplace that Krohn does not describe. In Berlin,
where Krohn seems to have spent the semester break (February to April),
there were two important laboratories, both directed by the physicist-
physiologist Arthur König, surely accessible through Ebbinghaus, König's
co-editor of the *Zeitschrift für Psychologie*. The two laboratories for which
König had responsibility were (physically) both part of the physics-
physiology-pharmacology complex that had been built on the banks of
the Spree in 1878. König was a *Privatdozent* for physics, responsible for
the work using Helmholtz sensory equipment which was housed in the
Physical Institute. In addition, in 1889, König had been appointed *außerordentlicher Professor* of physiology and director of the "physical department" of du Bois-Reymond's Physiological Institute. Both laboratories
were only a few streets from the main buildings of the university and
even less distance from Ebbinghaus's modest laboratory in the
Dorotheenstraße (Clara-Zetkin-Straße during the GDR period).

What can be said about Boring's opinion of the two labs? Clearly his
stated opinion must be discounted. A more difficult question concerns
whether he knew better. I think he did, since many of his scattered statements on Müller are very positive, consistent with the view I have

presented in this paper and in an article for the *Encyclopedia of Psychology* (Haupt, 2000). I maintain that G. E. Müller was the central figure in the experimentalization of psychology. I am thus inclined to think that Boring did know much of what I have described here, and thus his editorializing about Müller being "second" was a *willful* distortion in the text that Boring intended to be the permanent record of psychology's history. Why would Boring do this? Perhaps it was a matter of center versus periphery, and the Harvard man (Boring) ultimately had to identify with the Leipzig center (Wundt).

It is clear that the Prussian style and approaches of G. E. Müller came to dominate the experimentalist movement in psychology. It is less clear when and how that dominance occurred. This study has tried to demonstrate that, by the early 1890s, Müller had a clear lead over others in the pursuit of experimentalist attempts to create a rigorous, precise, physicalistic psychology. The tide had already turned and was going his way. I hope that the present work gives a corrective to the widely-accepted characterizations of Wundt's laboratory, but it is only a beginning toward a better understanding of the development of experimentation in psychology in the decades of the 1880s and 1890s.

References

Adreßbuch. (1885). *Adreßbuch der Stadt Leipzig*. Leipzig. (Available in Staatsarchiv Leipzig and the Reading Room of the Library of the University of Leipzig.)

Ach, Narziß. (1905). *Über die Willenstätigkeit und das Denken: Eine experimentelle Untersuchung mit einem Anhange: Über das Hipp'sche Chronoskop*. Göttingen: Vandenboeck & Ruprecht.

Albrecht, F. M. (1960). The new psychology in America 1880–1895. Doctoral dissertation, Johns Hopkins University.

Ash, M. (1980). Academic politics in the history of science: Experimental psychology in Germany, 1879–1941. *Central European History, 13*, 255–286.

Benschop, R., & Draaisma, D. (2000). In pursuit of precision: The calibration of minds and machines in late nineteenth-century psychology. *Annals of Science, 57*, 1–25.

Behrendsen, O. (1900). *Die mechanischen Werkstätten der Stadt Göttingen*. Melle in Hannover: F. E. Haag.

Brachner, A. (1986). German nineteenth-century scientific instrument makers. In P. R. De Clercq (Ed.), *Nineteenth-century scientific instruments and their makers* (pp. 117–159). Amsterdam: Rodopi.

Boring, E. G. (1929). The psychology of controversy. *Psychological Review, 36*, 97–121.

Boring, E. G. (1950). *A history of experimental psychology* (2nd ed.). New York: Appleton-Century-Crofts.

Burnham, W. H. (1888–89). [Review of Wolfe, H. K. (1886). Ueber das Wiedererkennen der Töne. *Philosophische Studien, II(I)*]. *American Journal of Psychology, 1*, 185–186.

Burnham, W. H. (1889–90). [Review of Lehmann, A. (1888). Versuch einer experimentellen Bestätigung der Theorie der Vorstellungsassociationen. *Philosophische Studien*, *V*, 96–156]. *American Journal of Psychology*, 2, 169–171.

Davis, A. B., & Dreyfuss, M. S. (1986). *The finest instruments ever made*. Arlington, MA: Medical History Publishing Associates I.

Danziger, K. (1980). Wundt's theory of behavior and volition. In R. Rieber (Ed.), *Wilhelm Wundt and the making of a scientific psychology* (pp. 89–116). New York: Plenum. Revised in this book: The unknown Wundt: Drive, apperception, and volition.

Diamond, S. (1980). Wundt before Leipzig. In R. W. Rieber (Ed.), *Wilhelm Wundt and the making of a scientific psychology* (pp. 3–70). New York: Plenum Press. Reprinted in this book.

Diederichs, C. (1895, November 10). Preisverzeichniß über wissenschaftliche Präcisions-Instrumente zu psychologischen Untersuchungenen. (Handwritten excerpts from the 1894 catalog and cover letter to E. B. Titchener, on Diederichs letterhead, Göttingen; a copy is in the possession of Rand Evans, Department of Psychology, East Carolina State University, Greenville, NC.)

Dilthey, W. (1894/1974). Ideen über eine beschreibende und zergliederende Psychologie. In G. Misch (Ed.), *Gesammelte Schriften* (Vol. 5, pp. 136–240). Leipzig: Teubner.

Donders, F. (1868/1969). On the speed of mental processes [Over de snelheid van psychische processen] (W. G. Koster, Trans.). *Acta Psychologica*, 30, 412–431.

Dunlap, K. (1917). The Johns Hopkins chronoscope. *Journal of Experimental Psychology*, 2, 249–252.

Ebbinghaus, H. (1885/1909). *Memory: A contribution to experimental psychology* (H. R. Ruger & C. Bussenius, Trans.). New York: Teachers College.

Edgell, B., & Symes, W. L. (1906). The Wheatstone-Hipp chronoscope. A note. *British Journal of Psychology*, 2, 58–88.

Edgell, B., & Symes, W. L. (1908). The Wheatstone-Hipp chronoscope. A second note. *British Journal of Psychology*, 2, 281–283.

Friedrich, M. (1883/1980). An edited translation of the first dissertation in experimental psychology by Max Friedrich at Leipzig University in Germany (P. Behrens, Trans.). *Psychological Research*, 42, 19–38.

Gordon, J., Shapley, R. M., & Israel, D. (1999). Chromatic induction is greatest at isobrightness: Evidence for Kirschmann's third law [Abstract]. *Investigative Ophthalmology and Vision Science*, 40, S-356.

Gundlach, H. (1986). *Inventarium der älteren Experimentalapparate im Psychologischen Institut Heidelberg sowie einige historische Bemerkungen* (2nd ed.). Heidelberg: The Psychological Institute of the University of Heidelberg.

Gundlach, H. (1996). The Hipp chronoscope as totem pole and the formation of a new tribe—applied psychology, psychotechnics and rationality. *Teorie & Modelli*, 1, 65–85.

Hale, M. (1980). *Human science and social order: Hugo Münsterberg and the origins of applied psychology*. Philadelphia: Temple University.

Haupt, E. J. (1998). Origins of American psychology in the work of G. E. Müller: Classical psychophysics and serial learning. In R. W. Rieber & K. Salzinger (Eds.), *Psychology: Theoretical and historical perspectives* (2nd ed., pp. 17–76). Washington DC: American Psychological Association.

Haupt, E. J. (2000). G. E. Müller. In *Encyclopedia of psychology* (Vol. 5, pp. 332–334). Washington, DC: American Psychological Association.

Haupt, E. J. (in press). The first memory drum. *American Journal of Psychology*.

Haupt, E. J., & Perera, T. B. (1997). Museum of the history of psychological instrumentation. [http://chss.Montclair.edu/psychology/museum/museum.html]

Henri, V. (1893). Les laboratoires de psychologie expérimentale en Allemagne. *Révue philosophique de France et de l'étranger, 36*, 608–622.

Hilgard, E. R. (1951). Methods and procedures in the study of learning. In S. S. Stevens (Ed.), *Handbook of experimental psychology* (pp. 387–434). New York: Wiley.

Hofstadter, D. R. (1981). Prelude . . . and fugue. In D. R. Hofstadter & D. C. Dennett (Eds.), *The mind's I* (pp. 149–190). New York: Basic Books.

Hörz, H., & Wollgast, S. (1986). *Dokumente einer Freundschaft. Briefwechsel zwischen Hermann von Helmholtz und Emil du Bois-Reymond 1846–1894*. (C. E. A. Kirsten, Ed.). Berlin: Akademie Verlag.

Jost, A. (1897). Die Assoziationsfestigkeit in ihrer Abhängigkeit von der Verteilung der Wiederholungen. *Zeitschrift für Psychologie und Physiologie der Sinnesorgane, 16*, 436–472.

Kostic, A., & Todorovic, D. (1997). *Sense, mind, and measure: Collection of old scientific instruments of the Laboratory for Experimental Psychology, University of Belgrade*. Belgrade: Museum of Science and Technology.

Krohn, W. O. (1892). Facilities in experimental psychology at the various German universities. *American Journal of Psychology, 4*, 585–594.

Krohn, W. O. (1893a). An experimental study of simultaneous stimulation of the sense of touch. *Journal of Nervous and Mental Disease, 18*, 169–184.

Krohn, W. O. (1893b). The laboratory of the Psychological Institute at the University of Göttingen. *American Journal of Psychology, 5*, 282–284.

Kuhn, T. S. (1970). *The structure of scientific revolutions* (2nd ed.). Chicago: University of Chicago Press.

Külpe, O., & Kirschmann, A. (1893). Ein neuer Apparat zur Controle zeitmessender Instrumente. *Philosophische Studien, 8*, 145–172.

Kusch, M. (1995). *Psychologism: A case study in the sociology of philosophical knowledge*. London: Routledge.

Ladd, G. T. (1887). *Physiological psychology*. New York: Charles Scribner's Sons.

Madigan, S., & O'Hara, R. (1992). Short-term memory at the turn of the century: Mary Whiton Calkins' memory research. *American Psychologist, 47*, 170–174.

Marietta Apparatus Co. (1948). *Psychological equipment. Catalog No. 48*. Marietta, OH: Marietta Apparatus Co.

Müller, G. E. (1878). *Zur Grundlegung der Psychophysik*. Berlin: Grieben.

Müller, G. E. (1887, June 13). Antrag der Professoren für ein psychologisches Laboratorium. Göttingen, Universitäts-Archiv, Akten der Kuratorium, No. 1245.

Müller, G. E. (1891, June 1). [Review of Münsterberg, "Beiträge zur experimentellen Psychologie. Hefte 1–3"]. *Goettinger gelehrte Anzeigen*, 393–429.

Müller, G. E. (1893). Berechtigung zu Münsterbergs "Beiträge zur experimentellen Psychologie." *Zeitschrift für Psychologie und Physiologie der Sinnesorgane, 4*, 404–414.

Müller, G. E., & Schumann, F. (1894). Experimentelle Beiträge zur Untersuchungen des Gedächtnisses. *Zeitschrift für Psychologie und Physiologie der Sinnesorgane, 6*, 81–190; 257–339. (This is sometimes cited as Müller & Schumann (1893), sometimes as (1894); 1894 seems most appropriate, since the year on the front page of the bound volume is 1894, while *Hefte* [issues] 2 and 4 most likely appeared late in 1893. Reprints of the combined manuscript are dated 1893.)

Müller, G. E., & Pilzecker, A. (1900). *Experimentelle Beiträge zur Lehre vom Gedächtniß*. Leipzig: J. A. Barth. (*Zeitschrift für Psychologie und Physiologie der Sinnesorgane*, Ergänzungsband 1).

Müller, G. E. (1915). Eröffnungssprache des Göttinger Lehrstuhlinhabers und Institutgründers (Gastgeber des Kongreßes). In F. Schumann (Ed.), *Bericht über dem VI. Kongress für experimentelle Psychologie* (pp. 103–109). Leipzig: Barth.

Nicholas, S. (1994). Note historique: Qui était Victor Henri (1872–1940)? *L'Année psychologique, 94*, 385–402.

Pantalony, D. W., & Creelman, D. (1997). Brass instrument psychology at the University of Toronto. [http://www.psych.utoronto.ca/museum/]

Pouillet, M. (1844, December 23). Note sur un moyen de mesurer des intervalles de temps extrêmement courts: Comme la durée du choc des corps élastiques, celle du débandement des ressorts, de l'inflamation de la poudre, etc.; et sur un moyen nouveau de comparer les intensités des courants électriques, soit permanents, soit instantanés. *Comptes Rendus des Séances de l'Académie des Sciences, Tome XIX.*

Ranschburg, P. (1901). Ein neues Apparat für Gedächtnisforschung mit Kindern. *Monatschrift für Psychiatrie und Neurologie, 10*, 321–333.

Rice, C. E. (2000). Uncertain genesis: The academic institutionalization of American psychology in 1900. *American Psychologist, 55*, 488–491.

Roback, A. A. (1961). *History of psychology and psychiatry.* New York: Citadel.

Robinson, D. K. (1987). Wilhelm Wundt and the establishment of experimental psychology, 1875–1914: The context of a new field of scientific research. Doctoral dissertation, University of California, Berkeley.

Scheerer, E. (1980). Wilhelm Wundt's psychology of memory. *Psychological Research, 42*, 135–155.

Schlosberg, H. (1937). Reaction-time apparatus. *Journal of Genetic Psychology, 50*, 47–61.

Schumann, F. (1892). Ueber die psychologische Grundlagen der Vergleichung kleiner Zeitgrössen. *Zeitschrift fur Psychologie und Physiologie der Sinnesorgane, 4*, 50.

Sommer, R. (1904/1984). *Experimentelle-psychologische Apparate und Methoden. Die Ausstellung bei dem 1. Kongress für experimentelle Psychologie 1904.* Passau: Passavia Universitätsverlag.

Spindler, & Hoyer. (1908/1921). *Apparate für psychologische Untersuchungen. Katalog 21.* Göttingen: Spindler & Hoyer.

Sprung, L., & Sprung, H. (1986). Ebbinghaus an der Berliner Universität—ein akademisches Schicksal eines zu früh Geborenen. In W. Traxel (Ed.), *Ebbinghaus-Studien*, vol. 2. Passau: Passavia Universitätsverlag.

Steffens, L(aura). (1900). Ueber motorische Einstellung. *Zeitschrift für Psychologie und Physiologie der Sinnesorgane, 23*, 241–280.

Steffens, L(otte/ottie). (1900). Experimentelle Beiträge zur Lehre vom ökonomischen Lernen. *Zeitschrift für Psychologie und Physiologie der Sinnesorgane, 22*, 321–380.

C. H. Stoelting Co. (1930–37/1997). *The great catalog of the C. H. Stoelting Company, 1930–1937: A facsimile reproduction.* Delmar, NY: Scholars Facsimiles and Reprints.

Titchener, E. B. (1901). *Experimental psychology* (Vol. 1, part 2). New York: Macmillan.

Titchener, E. B. (1905). *Experimental psychology* (Vol. 2, part 2). New York: Macmillan.

Turner, S. (1993). Consensus and controversy: Helmholtz and the visual perception of space. In D. Cahan (Ed.), *Hermann von Helmholtz and the foundations of nineteenth-century science* (pp. 154–204). Berkeley: University of California Press.

Turner, S. (1997). Demonstrating harmony: Some of the many devices used to produce Lissajous curves before the oscilloscope. *Rittenhouse, 11*, 33–51.

Valentine, E. (in press). Beatrice Edgell: An appreciation. *British Journal of Psychology.*

Verdin, C. (1890/1993). *Catalogue des instruments de précision pour la physiologie et la médecine.* Austin: BookLab, Inc. (Originally published in Paris by Charles Verdin.)

Wirth, W. (1902). Ein neuer Apparat für Gedächtnisversuche mit sprungweise fortschreitender Exposition ruhender Gesichtsobjecte. *Philosophische Studien, 18*, 701–714.

Woodworth, R. S. (1938). *Experimental psychology.* New York: Holt.

Wundt, W. (1862). Die Geschwindigkeit des Gedankens. *Gartenlaube*, pp. 263–267.

Wundt, W. (1867). *Handbuch der medicinishen Physik.* Erlangen: F. Encke.

Wundt, W. (1893). Chronograph und Chronoskop: Notiz zu einer Bemerkung J. M. Cattells. *Philosophische Studien, 8,* 653–654.

Wundt, W. (1907). *Grundriß der Psychologie* (8th ed.). Leipzig: Wilhelm Engelmann.

Wundt, W. (1910). Das Institut für experimentelle Psychologie zu Leipzig. *Psychologische Studien, 5,* 279–293.

Wundt, W. (1911). *Grundzüge der physiologischen Psychologie* (6th ed., Vol. 3). Leipzig: Engelmann.

Wundt, W. (1920). *Erlebtes und Erkanntes.* Stuttgart: Alfred Kröner.

Zimmermann, E. (1894). *Preis-Verzeichniß über Apparate zu psychologischen und physiologischen Experimenten.* Leipzig: E. Zimmermann.

Zimmermann, E. (1903/1983). *XVIII. Preis-Liste über psychologische und physiologische Apparate.* (Faksimilenachdruck 1983: FIM-Psychologie Modellversuch, Universität Erlangen-Nürnberg und Institut für die Geschichte der Neueren Psychologie, Universität Passau, in Zusammenarbeit mit den Sondersammlungen des Deutschen Museums München.) Passau: Passavia Universitätsverlag.

Zimmermann, E. (1930). *LII. Preis-Liste über psychologische und physiologische Apparate.* Leipzig: E. Zimmermann.

8

THE WUNDT COLLECTION IN JAPAN

Miki Takasuna

A Brief History of the Wundt Collection

It is not well known that many of the books, journals, and reprints, which belonged to Wilhelm Wundt (1832–1920), have been kept in Japan. In this short article, I sketch the history of how the Wundt Collection ended up in Japan and describe its current status.

The Wundt Collection has been preserved in the Main Library of Tohoku University of Sendai, which lies in the northeastern part of Japan, about 350 kilometers north of Tokyo. Tohoku University, founded in 1907, was originally named Tohoku Imperial University and was the third national university built in Japan. Tenenari Chiba (1884–1972) [Fig. 1], an associate professor at Kyoto Imperial University, resided in Europe from 1921 to 1923, mainly in Leipzig, Germany, in order to study psychology. In 1922, while he was abroad, Chiba was nominated as chair of the new Law and Literature Faculty at Tohoku Imperial University. At that time, Mr. Wiegand, the owner of Lorenz Bookstore in Leipzig, contacted Chiba about Wundt's books. In the 1920s, following World War I, inflation was at an all-time high in Germany and Wundt's family needed money, so they asked Wiegand to sell the collection. (Indeed, attempts to give current equivalents to money amounts given below are confounded by the hyperinflation of this period.) Chiba wanted to buy Wundt's books to provide the future psychology laboratory of Tohoku University with its own special feature, one that would make it unique among

251

Figure 1. Chiba Tanenari (1884–1972), the first chair of psychology at Tokoku Imperial University (1923–1940)

the other imperial universities such as Tokyo and Kyoto. Ultimately, after great effort, he procured the books and brought them back to Japan.

Chiba was diligent and seemed to like writing and drawing. In November 1923, he introduced the idea of keeping a log on a type of large notebook called *Daifuku-cho*, which was a typical old-fashioned accounting book used by Japanese merchants. He maintained this notebook in the psychology laboratory and added to it until it grew to five volumes. The middle ten pages of the first volume were written by Chiba himself at the end of June 1932. This part of *Daifuku-cho* was entitled "The Story of the Wundt Collection" and included some illustrations drawn by Chiba.

"The Story of the Wundt Collection" (An Excerpt from Daifuku-cho)[1]

"The Story of the Wundt Collection" begins with a brief description of how Chiba visited Eleonore Wundt on 2 May 1922, in Großbothen (p. 1). On the next page Chiba takes up the story in 1921. On November 19 of that year Chiba received a letter from Professor Kiba of Otani College, who was in Freiburg. Kiba wrote, "I heard that the Wundt Collection will be sold, and I would like to ask you to acquire it for Otani College" (p. 2). Chiba apparently heard of the Wundt Collection for the first time with this letter.

Next Chiba talked to "Mr. Süssmann, the father of a Japan advisor to the Chamber of Commerce and Industry" who was "familiar with Professor Driesch" so that he could "contact the professor through him"

Figure 2. The first page of *The Story of the Wundt Collection*. The calligraphy and illustrations are by Tanenari Chiba in 1932

[1]Quotations from this document are translated from Chiba's Japanese handwriting. All personal names were rendered in Japanese letters; therefore, some of the names that appear, such a Wiegand or Süssmann, might be different from their proper spellings. The same is true for Japanese names and some unidentified names, which could also be spelled differently. For this translation, I used a replica of *Daifuku-cho* that was made by the Department of Psychology at Tohoku University for the 55th Annual Meeting of the Japanese Psychological Association in 1991. The original *Daifuku-cho* is made of Japanese paper, and Professor Chiba wrote "The Story of the Wundt Collection" on it with Chinese ink.

(p. 2). A letter from Hans Driesch (22 November 1921), a philosophy professor at Leipzig University, recommended that Chiba "negotiate with Lorenz Bookstore" (p. 2). So Chiba wrote to the bookstore (25 November 1921): "If I could obtain the collection of Professor Wundt, whom I have respected for many years, for the future psychology laboratory, it would be a great honor to my university. With your introduction, I visited Lorenz a few days ago and we talked. It's reasonable to take the desires of the bereaved family of Wundt into consideration." (p. 2) Chiba was not yet appointed to the chair of a new faculty at Tohoku Imperial University, so "my university" in this letter meant either Kyoto Imperial University or Otani College (both "university" and "college" were expressed by the same word in Japanese).

Chiba received a reply from Wiegand, the owner of Lorenz Bookstore, on 28 March 1922. At that time Chiba had heard of his appointment to Tohoku Imperial University. He went to see Wiegand on March 30. Wiegand showed him the telegrams from four American universities and said that "there are several big universities, such as Yale and Harvard, that also wish to buy the collection." Chiba replied, saying, "I've heard that Leipzig University and the family of Wundt wouldn't sell to American universities, and I am sorry to hear that you might sell it to America. Somehow I would like to buy it for my university" (p. 3). After surveying the Wundt Collection in the bookstore, Chiba wrote, "The content of the collection was considerably good, but still he didn't mention its price. These books were all stored in wooden cases. It was a huge collection, including not only psychology, but also philosophy, history, law, and other disciplines. *Handapparate 8000* (a special collection of literature) was specially decorated with gold foil by Wundt himself. Most of the main journals were also included. It is needed for a newly established university at any cost. I have decided to obtain it somehow for my university!" (p. 3).

Wiegand did not determine the price of the collection until April 10. The price was "about twenty thousand yen!" (p. 4) perhaps more than $200,000 in today's currency. On April 22, after a few business talks between Chiba and Wiegand, and "after looking at the list of books and documents held in the Lorenz Bookstore, the provisional contract was finally completed!" (p. 4) Chiba had to write a few letters to people in Sendai to ask for money. In his letter on 22 April 1922, he wrote that "the money circulates temporarily, but the library is a treasure for one thousand years!" (p. 4).

While Chiba sent letters to Japan, he talked with Professor Felix Krueger, Wundt's successor, several times and learned that Krueger wished to reserve the works which Wundt had used in the Leipzig laboratory but which Krueger no longer had there; he would also like some of Wundt's books on folk psychology (p. 4). Chiba said to Krueger, "I heard that Leipzig University would like to purchase the collection, and, if that's true, I would abstain from buying it. But if you don't have any plan to buy it, I would like to obtain it for my university" (p. 5). Krueger responded: "We would like the collection, indeed. We are now pooling the money . . . We wonder how cheaply the family of Wundt would sell it" (p. 5).

As May came, Krueger could "understand well the circumstances in which the Wundt Collection would be purchased for Sendai" (p. 5). But Chiba heard nothing from Japan, and Wiegand's demand became "more and more intensive" (p. 6). On May 23, Wiegand gave Chiba "a ready consent to prolong the date of payment and to pay one quarter of the total payment first" (p. 6).

Chiba moved his residence to Königsberg at the end of May. He had postponed the move because of this negotiation, but since he did not know when it would be settled, he left Leipzig and entrusted Dr. Nishikida, another Japanese professor in Berlin, with the matter. But there was "always a demand for the payment in letters and telegrams coming all the way to Königsberg" (p. 7).

Wiegand was apparently somewhat irritated by the slow payment. On his letter to Chiba on 14 June 1922, he noted that "there are proposals from four American universities and also one from Professor Tetsujiro Inoue in Tokyo saying that they are ready to pay more for the collection" (p. 7). Chiba patiently kept negotiating with Wiegand from outside of Leipzig. He moved to Berlin at the end of September, and on October 5, he went to Leipzig to see Krueger. After confirming the titles of the books Krueger needed, Chiba donated them "on my own judgment" (p. 9).

In was November 1922 when the first money arrived to Wiegand from Japan. On November 16 Wiegand wrote to Chiba in Paris that "the money arrived in part. It cost 15 Marks to make a catalogue, and 42,000 Marks for the books you have donated to Krueger. I still need more" (p. 9). In a letter to Chiba on 30 January 1923, Wiegand wrote that "it was fourteen days late, but we received the money on January first. As we have written in the letter of November sixteenth, the books donated to Leipzig University were 42,500 Marks, about 10 dollars' worth. Please send the money" (p. 9). Chiba studied in Paris during the first half of 1923. After he left France for Japan, a letter from Wiegand, dated August 23, arrived at Paris. In the letter Wiegand wrote that he had a letter from Japan stating "that the collection has just arrived, and they finished paying the rest" (p. 10). Chiba went back to Japan without knowing if the Wundt Collection had already arrived in Japan successfully. After returning to Japan, Chiba wrote a final letter to Wiegand from Sendai:

> I have just read the letter of August twenty-third and two other letters for-
> warded from Paris. As for the account, the cost of making a catalogue was sup-
> posed to be paid by Professor Nishikida already. If it's not paid yet, please ask
> Prof. Nishikida about it. However, as for the cost of books donated to Leipzig
> University, I didn't know that you had completed the runs of the journals for
> the university. When the complete list of books arrives, those should be paid
> by Leipzig University. I never promised to donate the subscriptions of jour-
> nals and so forth. I remember you told me about it, but I did not promise. The
> office of the university might not change things as easily as you supposed. I
> cannot make this claim to Professor Hayashi, but I will tell him what you wish.
> Sincerely yours. (Nov. 10, p. 10)

The story ended with the letter.

The Current Status of the Wundt Collection

As noted in the previous section, it took a few years to finish negotiating with the owner of the German bookstore and bring the huge number
of books and journals to Japan. According to the library catalogue of the
1920s, the collection consisted of 6,762 books (including already-bound
journals) and 9,098 reprints (including private leaflets). The number of
books was huge, because the librarians apparently counted a bound
volume, or a leaflet, as one book. Today, most of the books and reprints
are still well preserved, but some books seem to be missing. The reprints
are arranged and filed in folders according to subject field, and there are
468 folders in all. Presently, there is no electronic catalogue of the Collection. As of 1 December 1999, the collection extends about 216 linear
meters. Several books with publication dates after Wundt's death also
found their way into the Collection. Apparently these books had been sent
to Wundt's home, but were of course never read by him, at least in printed
form.

Dr. Mioko Takahashi, a former professor at Senshu University, once
surveyed the books of the Collection and classified them into categories

Table 1 Categories of Books in the Wundt Collection

Category	Number of books
Philosophy	1,764
	(527 on psychology)
Religion	261
Education	58
History	123
Biography	6
Geography	62
Language	144
Literature	75
Arts	42
Law	104
Politics	30
Economics (incl. Statistics)	85
Mathematics	35
Natural Science	223
Medicine	131
Technology	4
Total	3,147
(compare to 6762, in the 1920s catalogue)	

(from Takahashi, 1983)

as shown in Table 1 (Takahashi, 1983, 1992). Among the books of philosophy, 527 books corresponded to the category of psychology. These categories and classifications were presumably made by Japanese librarians, although some books were included that didn't correspond to the category. Takahashi counted a series of volumes as just one book, and that is why the total number of books in Table 1 differs so much from the earlier tally. Among the philosophy books, works of Immanuel Kant (1724–1804) and Benedict Spinoza (1632–1677) are notable.

Those 527 books of psychology were classified further into subcategories [Table 2]. As told in "The Story of the Wundt Collection," many of the books in the field of "folk psychology" were donated to the Psychological Institute of Leipzig University at the request of its director, Professor Felix Krueger (1874–1948). Still, the collection holds many books on "folk psychology," as well as books on history, geography, and linguistics. There is a relatively large number of books written by Adolph Bastian (1826–1905) and Théodule Ribot (1839–1916) found in the section on

Table 2 Subcategories for the Section "Psychology" in the Wundt Collection

Subcategory	Number of books
1) Miscellaneous & General psychology	64
2) General psychology	171
3) Sensation & Perception	97
4) Developmental psychology	180
5) Applied psychology	10
6) Auxiliary sciences	5
Total	527

psychology. The books donated to Leipzig University were apparently destroyed during World War II (Bringmann & Ungerer, 1980). We are fortunate that Tohoku University Library in Sendai was spared such destruction during this war.

The Wundt Collection is located in a special section of the Main Library at Tohoku University. Access is restricted to the university's faculty members and graduate students. Non-members who wish to see the Collection must be accompanied by a qualified faculty member. Few working materials are allowed into the Collection's section—for example, no laptop computers. Access to the Collection is on weekdays only, from 9 a.m. until noon and 1 p.m. to 4:30 p.m. While there are many books in which the handwriting of Wundt still remains, there are also some books that Wundt apparently did not read at all. Deciphering the handwriting and making a complete electronic catalogue of the Collection are major tasks still to be done.

References, with Annotations

Bringmann, W. G. & Ungerer, G. A. (1980). An archival journey in search of Wilhelm Wundt. In J. Brozek & L. J. Pongratz (eds.), *Historiography of Modern Psychology* (pp. 201–240). Toronto: C. J. Hogrefe.

This contains an outline of the Wundt Collection. However, mainly because the authors did not see the Collection themselves and had to rely on personal communications during the late 1970s, the description contains a few mistakes and some unreliable data. Early in the 1980s, Dr. Takahashi began a survey of the Collection and found that many books were dispersed over the Tohoku University campus. For example, the whole series of *Graefe's Archiv für Ophthalmologie* (65 volumes), now back in the Collection, had previously been in the medical school laboratory. The books of the Collection are easily distinguished because all contain a special seal. Because the Collection cost so much money, Professor Sato, the head of the Faculty of Law and Literature at Tohoku Imperial University, sought financial support from Mr. Saito, a local man of wealth. Therefore, every book in the Wundt Collection was given a large seal proclaiming "Saito Foundation" to honor the benefactor (see Fig. 3).

Miyakawa, T. (1981). The Tohoku University Wundtian Collection. *Journal of the History of the Behavioral Sciences, 17,* 299.

This was the first, one-page notice of the Collection, in English.

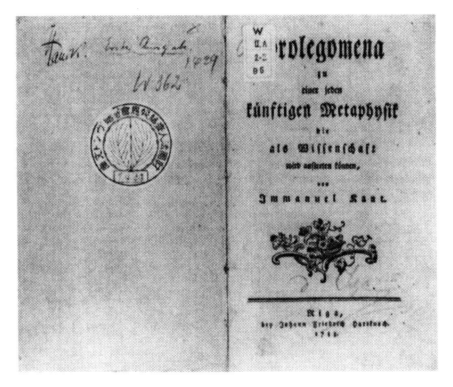

Figure 3. An example from the Wundt Collection. *Prolegomena zu einer jeden künftigen Metaphysik* von Immanuel Kant. Riga, 1783

Takahashi, M. 1983. Interim report on the Wilhelm Wundt Collection (1). *Tohoku Psychologica Folia*, *42*, pp. 1–7.

Until now, this was the most extensive report on the Collection, written in English by a Japanese. *Tohoku Psychologica Folia* is the oldest Japanese psychology journal written in English. It was founded by Chiba himself in 1933 and is still published annually by the Department of Psychology at Tohoku University. From the title, one might expect that there was a sequel; however, no sequel appeared in English. There is a leaflet in Japanese by the same author, which supplements the article:

Takahashi, M. (1992). About the Wundt Collection. *Bulletin of the Tohoku University Library*, *17*(1), 16–18. (In Japanese)

Professor Chiba also left an autobiography in Japanese, and there are several pages describing his stay in Germany. The circumstances of the Wundt Collection are just as described in the second section above. There are several Japanese psychology textbooks that refer to the Wundt Collection, but there is no need to list them here.

Chiba, T. (1972). *Following the soul [autobiography]*. In *Complete works of Tanenari Chiba*, vol. 4. Tokyo: Kyodo Shuppan. (In Japanese)

Acknowledgments

I greatly thank the people of the Main Library and Department of Psychology at Tohoku University, especially Professor Toshiteru Hatayama. Without his help, I could not have surveyed the Wundt Collection. Also, I am grateful to Dr. Mioko Takahashi for permitting me to refer to her works on the Collection.

BIBLIOGRAPHY OF WILHELM WUNDT'S WRITINGS

AS COMPILED BY ELEONORE WUNDT

Edited by David K. Robinson

It would certainly be useful to have a full, annotated bibliography of Wilhelm Wundt's writings and works about Wundt. Due to Wundt's stature as founder and long-time influence on modern psychology, however, such an enterprise would require years of work and, of necessity, a lot of selection. A great many books and articles in early psychology were, in one way or another, "about Wundt." So for this volume we offer simply the bibliography of works (nearly all of them in German language) published by Wundt during his lifetime (including a few that appeared shortly after his death in 1920).

I use the word "simply" advisedly, since the list consists of about 540 items, by the count of Meischner and Metge (1979). Nevertheless, that number would be considerably higher, if all translations and foreign editions (not to mention excerpts for textbooks) were also included. Most of the earlier translations of Wundt's writings are included in the authoritative bibliography compiled by his daughter, Eleonore Wundt (1927). In fact, what follows is essentially her list of the original publications, by year of appearance, only slightly edited.

Eleonore Wundt's bibliography was obviously a work of love by a very capable scholar, who served as her father's personal secretary and assistant for many years, and she was privy to some obscure information about her father's work (e.g., unsigned reviews). I chose not to translate anything, nor to change any of her formats, since she had achieved an economy and consistency that would be hard to match. In a few cases, I added dates (for example, when an article was to appear in an anthology later, the date of that anthology has been given). In a very few cases, I cleared up inconsistencies in form, or corrected a reference that I had verified to be faulty. Eleonore Wundt obviously made every effort to retain the original orthography of all the titles, over a period when the rules for German were changing, so I also left them as she had them. The result may not be very helpful to readers who are not proficient in German, but those people will be challenged in Wundt studies anyway; probably more of his work translated into Russian and Spanish, than into English.

The following short bibliography shows that the list of Wundt's works has been published three times, twice in recent years, but all in fairly obscure German publications. E. B. Titchener apparently made the first attempt at a Wundt bibliography, *American Journal of Psychology*, *19* (1908), 541–556, and in seven more installments in vols. 20–25, and 33. The list by Meischner and Metge (1979) was among the celebratory publications associated with the Wundt centennial in Leipzig in 1980, and Schneider (1990) duplicated their list.

Browse the list and become acquainted, not only with Wundt's writings (and their multiple editions and reprintings), but also with his reading (if we can presume that he read books he reviewed). Generally, for any given year, books appear first, followed by articles, then reviews and occasional pieces (e.g. newspaper articles). At the first mention of a new book, the subsequent editions are also given. Your own exploration will probably uncover other interesting patterns.

Wundt, Eleonore. (1927). *Wilhelm Wundts Werk: Ein Verzeichnis seiner sämtlichen Schriften* (Abhandlungen der sächsichen staatlichen Forschungsinstitute. Forschungsintitute für Psychologie, Nr. 28). Munich: C. H. Beck'sche Verlagsbuchhandlung.

Meischner, Wolfram, & Metge, Anneros. (1979). Verzeichnis sämtlicher Veröffentlichungen Wilhelm Wundts. *Wissenschaftliche Zeitschrift der Karl-Marx-Universität, Leipzig, Gesellschafts- und Sprachwissenschaftliche Reihe, 28* (2), 243–259.

Schneider, Christina Maria. (1990). *Wilhelm Wundts Völkerpsychologie: Entstehung und Entwicklung eines in Vergessenheit geratenen, wissenschaftshistorisch relevanten Fachgebietes* (Abhandlungen zur Philosophie, Psychologie und Pädagogik, 224) (Dissertation, University of Zurich, 1989). Bonn: Bouvier.

Writings of Wilhelm Wundt, by Year

1853

Über den Kochsalzgehalt des Harns. Journal für practische Chemie, herausg. von Otto Linne Erdmann und Gustav Werther. Jahrgang 1853, 59. Band, S. 354–363.

1855

Versuche über den Einfluß der Durchschneidung des Lungenmagennerven auf die Respirationsorgane. Preisarbeit. Johannes Müllers Archiv für Anatomie, Physiologie und wissenschaftliche Medicin, Jahrgang 1855, S. 269–313.

1856

Untersuchungen über das Verhalten der Nerven in entzündeten und degenerierten Organen. Inauguraldissertation. (Auch Habilitationsschr.) 26 Seiten. Heidelberg, G. Mohr.

Aus dieser Schrift ein Auszug: Archiv für pathologische Anatomie und Physiologie und für klinische Medicin, herausgegeben von Virchow, 10. Band, 1856, S. 404–407.

Über die Elasticität der thierischen Gewebe. Vortrag im naturhistorisch-medicinischen Verein in Heidelberg am 19.12.56. Verhandlungen des Vereins Bd. I, S. 9–10, und Heidelberger Jahrbücher der Literatur, Jahrgang 50 (1857), S. 249–250.

1857

Über die Elasticität feuchter organischer Gewebe. Johannes Mullers Archiv für Anatomie, Physiologie und wissenschaftliche Medicin, S. 298–308.

1858

Die Lehre von der Muskelbewegung. Nach eigenen Untersuchungen bearbeitet. Mit 22 Holzschnitten, XIV, 241 S., Braunschweig, Fr. Vieweg.

Über das Gesetz der Zuckungen und die Veränderungen der Erregbarkeit durch geschlossene Ketten. Vortrag im naturhistorisch-medicinischen Verein in Heidelberg am 12.7.58. Verhandlungen des Vereins Bd. I, S. 159–160 und Heidelberger Jahrbücher der Literatur, Jahrgang 51, S. 915–918.

Über das Gesetz der Zuckungen und die Modification der Erregbarkeit durch geschlossene Ketten. Wunderlichs Archiv für physiologische Heilkunde, N.F.II, S. 354–400.[1]

[1]Der vorige Vortrag ist hier ausführlicher ausgearbeitet. Der "nachträgliche Zusatz" im Vortragsbericht ist erst nach dieser Ausarbeitung zugefügt.

Über den Verlauf idiomuskulärer Zusammenziehungen. Vortrag auf der 34. Versammlung deutscher Naturforscher und Ärzte in Karlsruhe am 18.9.58. Amtlicher Bericht S. 200–202.

Über den Einfluss hydrotherapeutischer Einwickelungen auf den Stoffwechsel. Archiv des Vereins für gemeinschaftliche Arbeiten zur Förderung der wissenschaftlichen Heilkunde, herausg. von Vogel, Nasse und Beneke, Bd. III, S. 35–43.

Beiträge zur Theorie der Sinneswahrnehmung. I. Abhandlung: Über den Gefühlssinn mit besonderer Rücksicht auf dessen räumliche Wahrnehmungen. Henle und Pfeufers Zeitschrift für rationelle Medicin, 3. Reihe, IV, S. 229–293.

1859

Über die Geschichte der Theorie des Sehens. Vortrag im naturhistorisch-medicinischen Verein in Heidelberg am 14.2.59. Verhandlungen des Vereins Bd. I, S. 196–198 und Heidelberger Jahrbücher der Literatur, Jahrgang 52, S. 348–350.

Über die Bewegungen des Auges. Vortrag ebenda am 5.8.59. Verhandlungen des Vereins Bd. I, S. 240–245 und Heidelberger Jahrbücher der Literatur, Jahrgang 52, S. 833–835.

Beiträge zur Theorie der Sinneswahrnehmung. 2. Abhandlung: Zur Geschichte der Theorie des Sehens. Henle und Pfeufers Zeitschrift für rationelle Medicin, 3. Reihe, VII, S. 279–317.

Beiträge zur Theorie der Sinneswahrnehmung. 3. Abhandlung: Über das Sehen mit einem Auge. Ebenda S. 321–396.

Über secundäre Modification der Nerven. Reichert und Du Bois Reymonds Archiv für Anatomie, Physiologie und wissenschaftliche Medicin, Jahrgang 1859, S. 537–548.

Über den Verlauf der Muskelzusammenziehung bei direkter Muskelreizung. Ebenda S. 549–552.

1860

Über den Einfluß des Curaregiftes auf Nerven und Muskeln. Vortrag im naturhistorisch-medicinischen Verein in Heidelberg am 6.1.60. Verhandlungen des Vereins Bd. II, S. 12–13 und Heidelberger Jahrbücher der Literatur, Jahrgang 53, S. 172–173.

Über die Elastizität der organischen Gewebe. Vortrag im naturhistorisch-medicinischen Verein in Heidelberg am 11.5.60. Verhandlungen des Vereins Bd. II, S. 33–42 und Heidelberger Jahrbücher der Literatur, Jahrgang 53, S. 723–732.

Dasselbe nochmals abgedruckt und etwas erweitert in Henle und Pfeufers Zeitschrift für rationelle Medicin, 3. Reihe, VIII, S. 267–279.

Über das binoculare Sehen. 2 Abteilungen. Vorträge im naturhistorisch-medicinischen Verein in Heidelberg am 6.11 und 7.12.60. Verhandlungen des Vereins Bd. II, S. 69–72, 75–78 und Heidelberger Jahrbücher der Literatur, Jahrgang 54 (1861), S. 163–166, 169–172.

1861

Beiträge zur Theorie der Sinneswahrnehmung. 4. Abhandlung: Über das Sehen mit zwei Augen. Henle und Pfeufers Zeitschrift für rationelle Medicin, 3. Reihe, XII, S. 145–262.

Bemerkung zu dem Aufsatz des Herrn Dr. H. Munk "Über die Leitung der Erregung im Nerven II" (Reichert und Du Bois Reymonds Archiv 1861, Heft 4). Reichert und Du Bois Reymonds Archiv für Anatomie, Physiologie und wissenschaftliche Medicin, Jahrgang 1861, S. 781–783.

Über die Entstehung des Glanzes. Vortrag im naturhistorisch-medicinischen Verein in Heidelberg am 26.4.61. Verhandlungen des Vereins Band II, S. 115–118 und Heidelberger Jahrbücher der Literatur, Jahrgang 54, S. 561–564.

Über die Bewegung des Auges. Vortrag auf der 36. Versammlung deutscher Naturforscher und Ärzte in Speyer am 18.9.61. Beilage zum Tagblatt der Versammlung S. 6.

Über personliche Differenz zwischen Gesichts- und Gehörsbeobachtung. Vortrag ebenda am 28. September. Beilage zum Tagblatt S. 25.

Über die Vertheilung der Muskelkrafte am Auge. Vortrag im naturhistorisch-medicinischen Verein in Heidelberg am 29.11.61. Verhandlungen des Vereins Band II, S. 176–181 und Heidelberger Jahrbücher der Literatur, Jahrgang 55, S. 164–169.

Der Blick. Eine physiognomische Studie. "Unterhaltungen am häuslichen Herd," herausgegeben von K. Gutzkow, 3. Folge, I. Band, S. 1028–1033.

1862

Über binokulares Sehen. Poggendorffs Annalen der Physik und Chemie CXVI, 4. Stuck, S. 617–626.

Über die Entstehung des Glanzes. Ebenda S. 267–631.

Beiträge zur Theorie der Sinneswahrnehmung. 5. Abhandlung: Über einige besondere Erscheinungen des Sehens mit zwei Augen. Henle und Pfeufers Zeitschrift für rationelle Medicin, 3. Reihe XIV, S. 1–77.

Beiträge zur Theorie der Sinneswahrnehmung. 6. Abhandlung: Über den psychischen Prozeß der Wahrnehmung. Henle und Pfeufers Zeitschrift für rationelle Medicin, 3. Reihe XV, S. 104–179.

Beiträge zur Theorie der Sinneswahrnehmung. XXXII, 451 S. Leipzig und Heidelberg, C.F. Winter.[2]

Über ein künstliches Augenmuskelsystem. Vortrag im naturhistorisch-medicinischen Verein in Heidelberg am 27.6.62. Verhandlungen des Vereins Band II, S. 225 und Heidelberger Jahrbücher der Literatur, Jahrgang 55, S. 583.

Über die Bewegung des Auges. Archiv für Ophtalmologie, herausgeg. von Arlt, Donders u. Gräfe, VIII, Abt. II, S. 1–87.

---

[2]Enthält die sechs in Henle und Pfeufers Zeitschrift für rationelle Medicin erschienenen Abhandlungen unverändert.

Beschreibung eines künstlichen Augenmuskelsystems zur Untersuchung der Bewegungsgesetze des menschlichen Auges im gesunden und kranken Zustand. Ebenda S. 88–114.

Zur "secundären Modification," Reichert und Du Bois Reymonds Archiv für Anatomie, Physiologie und wissenschaftliche Medicin, Jahrgang 1862, S. 498–507.[3]

Notiz über neue Inductionsapparate. Ebenda S. 507.

Der Mund. Eine physiognomische Studie. "Unterhaltungen am häuslichen Herd," herausgegeben von K. Gutzkow, 3. Folge II, S. 505–510.

Die Zeit. Ebenda S. 590–593.

Die Geschwindigkeit des Gedankens. Gartenlaube, herausgegeben von E. Keil, Nr. 17, S. 263–265.

Aufsätze in der Volkszeitung für Süddeutschland, geleitet von Dr. Pickford, Heidelberg:[4]

Nr. 26 (31. Jan.). Eine Benefizvorstellung.

Nr. 28 (2. Febr.). Karl Freund.

Nr. 36 (12. Febr.). Robert und Bertram.

Nr. 43 (20. Febr.). Das Benefiz des Rezensenten.

Nr. 45 (22. Febr.). Zum Besten der Theaterbaukasse.

Nr. 61 (13. März). Theatralischer Unsinn.

1863

Vorlesungen über die Menschen- und Thierseele. 2 Bände. 1. Band XIV, 491 S. 2. Band VIII, 463 S. Leipzig, L. Voß.

2. Aufl. 1892 (diese und die folgenden Auflagen in einem Bande); 3. Aufl. 1897; 4. Aufl. 1906; 5. Aufl. 1911; 6. Aufl. 1919; 7./8. Aufl. 1922.

Über Dr. E. Herings Kritik meiner Theorie des Binokularsehens. Poggendorffs Annalen der Physik und Chemie CXX, 4. Reihe, 30. Band, S. 172–176.

Wie der Tod in die Welt kam. Gartenlaube, herausgegeben von E. Keil, Nr. 24, S. 383–384. (Blätter und Blüthen.) (W.W. gezeichnet.)

1864

Lehrbuch der Physiologie des Menschen. 1. und 2. Lieferung, S. 1–448. Erlangen, F. Enke.

1865

Lehrbuch der Physiologie des Menschen. 3. Lieferung, S. 449–661. Erlangen, F. Enke.

---

[3]Gegen H. Munk, Ueber Herrn Dr. Wundts Bemerkung usw. (1861), dasselbe Archiv 1862, S. 142. Auf S. 654–660 erschien von H. Munk: Ueber Dr. Wundts Replik.

[4]Alle diese Aufsätze sind ohne Namen erschienen, aber nach mündlicher Angabe meines Vaters von ihm verfaßt.

Lehrbuch der Physiologie des Menschen. Mit 137 Holzschnitten. XIII, 661 S. Erlangen, F. Enke.
    2. Aufl. 1868; 3. Aufl. 1873; 4. Aufl. 1888.
Das Gutachten des Heidelberger Arbeiterbildungsvereins über den Gewerbeschulzwang. (Gegen die Konstanzer Zeitung.) Heidelberger Journal, 5. August.

1866

Die physicalischen Axiome und ihre Beziehung zum Causalprinzip. Ein Capitel aus einer Philosophie der Naturwissenschaften. IV, 137 S. Erlangen, F. Enke.
    2. Aufl. u. d. T. Prinzipien der mechanischen Naturlehre, 1910.
Über einige Zeitverhältnisse des Wechsels der Sinnesvorstellungen. Vorläufige Mittheilung. Göschens Deutsche Klinik, XVIII, Nr. 9, S. 77–78.
Über das psychische Maaß. Ein populärer Vortrag. Ebenda Nr. 45 und 46, Feuilleton. S. 401–403, 409–412.
Besprechungen in "Kritische Blatter für wissenschaftliche und praktische Medicin," herausgegeben von Dr. A. Göschen, Berlin:
    Nr. 10, S. 93–96. Deiters, Untersuchungen über Gehirn und Rückenmark des Menschen und der Säugetiere; Setschemow [sic?] u. Paschutin, Neue Versuche am Hirn und Rückenmark des Frosches. Sanders, Geleidingsbanen in het Ruggemerg voor de Gevoelsindrukken.
    Nr. 13, S. 26–126. Pflüger, Untersuchungen aus dem physiologischen Laboratorium zu Bonn.
    Nr. 14, S. 133–134. W. Krause, Beiträge zur Neurologie der oberen Extremitäten.
    Nr. 21, S. 201–202. A. Fick, Die medicinische Physik.
    Nr. 42, S. 377–378. C.S. Cornelius, Grundzüge einer Molecularphysik.
Die folgenden nur "dt" gezeichnet:[5]
    Nr. 12, S. 113. Dr. G. A. M. Kneuttinger, Zur Histologie des Blutes.
    Nr. 12, S. 113–114. Dr. W. Kühne, Lehrbuch der physiologischen Chemie. 1. Lieferung: Die Lehre von der Verdauung.
    Nr. 19, S. 181–182. Wilhelm Müller, Über den feineren Bau der Milz.
    Nr. 20, S. 193–194. Ludwig, Die physiologischen Leistungen des Blutdrucks. Antrittsvorlesung.
    Nr. 36, S. 329–330. Dr. O. Nasse, Beiträge zur Physiologie der Darmbewegung.
    Nr. 39, S. 353. E. Ph. Bischoff, Microscopische Analyse der Anastomosen der Kopfnerven.
    Nr. 39, S. 353–354. Rauber, Vatersche Körper der Bänder und Periostnerven und ihre Beziehung zum sogenannten Muskelsinne.
    Nr. 40, S. 363. V. Kletzinsky, Mittheilungen aus dem Gebiete der reinen und angewandten Chemie.
    Nr. 40, S. 363. Al. Winter, Experimentalstudien über die Pathologie des Flügelfelles.

[5]Nach dem Register in Göschens Deutsche Klinik, Band 20, 1868, sind die "dt" gezeichneten Aufsätze von Wundt.

Nr. 42, S. 378–379. Meißner und Sheppard, Untersuchungen über das Entstehen der Hippursäure im thierischen Organismus.

Nr. 51, S. 453. Dr. W. Kühne, Lehrbuch der physiologischen Chemie. 2. Lieferung: Die Chemie der thierische Flüssigkeiten und Gewebe.

Das allgemeine Wahlrecht und die Arbeiterfrage. Heidelberger Journal, 19. und 20. Januar. (Ohne Namen.)

Vom Neckar: Badische Zustände. Beilage zur Allgemeinen Zeitung, Augsburg, 9. August. (Ohne Namen.)[6]

1867

Handbuch der medicinischen Physik. Mit 244 Holzschnitten, XVI. 555 S. Erlangen, F. Enke.

Neuere Leistungen auf dem Gebiete der physiologischen Psychologie. Vierteljahrsschrift für Psychologie, Psychiatrie und gerichtliche Medicin, herausgegeben von Leidesdorf und Meynert, Jahrgang I, S. 23–56.

Über die Physik der Zelle in ihrer Beziehung zu den allgemeinen Principien der Naturforschung. Vortrag in der 2. allgemeinen Sitzung der 41. Versammlung deutscher Naturforscher und Ärzte, Frankfurt a.M. 20. September. Tagblatt der Versammlung, S. 21–26.

Besprechung von Helmholtz, Handbuch der physiologischen Optik. (Allgemeine Encyklopädie der Physik, herausgegeben von G. Karsten, 9. Band.) Göschens Deutsche Klinik. XIX, S. 326–328.

Besprechungen in "Kritische Blatter für wissenschaftliche und praktische Medicin," herausgegben von Dr. A. Göschen, Berlin:

Nr. 2 und 5, S. 13–17, 41–45. Haeckel, Generelle Morphologie der Organismen.

Nr. 8, S. 69–70. M. Schultze, Zur Anatomie und Physiologie der Retina.

Nr. 9, S. 77–78. C. Nägeli und G. Schwendener, Das Microscop. Theorie und Anwendung.

Die folgenden nur "dt" gezeichnet:[7]

Nr. 2, S. 17. Kübler, Microscopische Bilder aus dem Leben unserer einheimischen Gewässer. Kübler und Zwingli, Microscopische Bilder aus der Urwelt der Schweiz.

Nr. 3, S. 22–23. Frey, Handbuch der Histologie und Histochemie des Menschen. Lehre von den Form- und Mischungsbestandtheilen des Körpers. —Frey, Das Microscop und die microscopische Technik. —Harting, Das Microscop.

Vom Neckar: Die Reformbedurfnisse Badens. Beilage zur Allgemeinen Zeitung, Augsburg, 4. Januar. (Ohne Namen.)

Antwort auf eine "Erklärung" badischer Ständemitglieder. Heidelberger Zeitung, 15. Mai.

---

[6]Diese und die späteren ohne Namen erschienenen Aufsätze in der Beilage der Allgemeinen Zeitung sind von meinem Vater mündlich als von ihm verfaßt bezeichnet.

[7]Vgl. Anm. 5.

Commissionsbericht über den Gesetzesentwurf, die Rechtsverhältisse der Studierenden an den beiden Landesuniversitäten betreffend. Beilage zum Protokoll der 23. öffentlichen Sitzung der 2. Badischen Kammer vom 6. November 1867. 10 S.

1868

Lehrbuch der Physiologie des Menschen, 2. völlig umgearbeitete Auflage. Mit 143 Abbildungen, XVII, 729 S. Erlangen, F. Enke.

Besprechung von Th.W. Engelmann, Über die Hornhaut des Auges. (Gez. dt.) Göschens Deutsche Klinik XX. S. 186.

Vom unteren Neckar: Die Zollparlamentswahlen in Baden. Beilage zur Allgemeinen Zeitung, Augsburg, 7. März. (Ohne Namen.)

Vom Neckar: Das provisorische Gesetz über die Militärstrafrechtspflege in Baden. Allgemeine Zeitung, Augsburg, 21. und 22. April. (Ohne Namen.)

Vom Neckar: Das badische Ministerium und die liberale Parthei. Außerordentliche Beilage zur Allgemeinen Zeitung, Augsburg, 12. Dezember. (Ohne Namen.)

1869

Über die Entstehung räumlicher Gesichtswahrnehmungen. Philosophische Monatshefte, herausgegeben von J. Bergmann, III, S. 225–247. U.d.T. "Das Raumproblem in erkenntnistheoretischer Beleuchtung," Kleine Schriften III (1921).

1870

Über die Erregbarkeitsveränderungen im Elektrotonus und die Fortpflanzungsgeschwindigkeit der Nervenerregung. Vortrag im naturhistorischmedicinischen Verein in Heidelberg am 10.6.70. Verhandlungen des Vereins Band V, S. 163–166 und Heidelberger Jahrbücher der Literatur, Jahrgang 63, S. 481–484.

Dasselbe als "Vorläufige Mittheilung" Pflügers Archiv für Physiologie, Band III, S. 437–440.

Besprechung von Harms, Philosophische Einleitung in die Encyklopädie der Physik, 1. Band. G. Karsten, Allgemeine Encyklopädie der Physik, 1. Band. Philosophische Monatshefte, herausgegeben von J. Bergmann, V, S. 253–259.

1871

Untersuchungen zur Mechanik der Nerven und Nervencentren. 1. Abtheilung: Über Verlauf und Wesen der Nervenerregung. Mit 30 Abbildungen, IX, 278 S. Erlangen, F. Enke.

Besprechungen im literarischen Zentralblatt für Deutschland:[8]

[8]Soweit es nicht besonders bemerkt ist, sind die Besprechungen im Literarischen Zentralblatt ohne Namen erschienen. Die Verfasserschaft konnte durch die Liebenswürdigkeit von

Nr. 44, Sp. 1106. Brandt, Anatomisch-histologische Untersuchungen über den Sipunculus Nudus L.

Sp. 1106–1107. Wilhelm Müller, Beiträge zur pathologischen Anatomie und Physiologie des menschlichen Rückenmarkes.

Sp. 1107. Bernstein, Untersuchungen über den Erregungsvorgang im Nerven- und Muskelsystem.

1872

Physiologie. Artikel (Nr. 8) der wissenschaftlichen Biographie "Alexander von Humboldts Wirksamkeit auf verchiedenen Gebieten der Wissenschaft," herausgegeben von K.C. Bruhns, S. 303–314.

Besprechungen im Literarischen Zentralblatt für Deutschland:

Nr. 5, Sp. 106. Henle, Anatomischer Handatlas, 1. Heft.

Nr. 8, Sp. 186–187. Aeby, Der Bau des menschlichen Körpers.

Nr. 11, Sp. 267. Preyer, Die Blutkrystalle.

Nr. 33, Sp. 383–384. Huxley, Grundzüge der Physiologie in allgemein verständlichen Vorlesungen, herausgegeben von Rosenthal.

Nr. 36, Sp. 982. Ultzmann und Hofmann, Atlas der physiologischen und pathologischen Harnsedimente in 44 chromolithographischen Tafeln.

Nr. 38, Sp. 1039–1040. Braune, Die Oberschenkelvene des Menschen in anatomischer und klinischer Beziehung.

Nr. 39, Sp. 1070–1071. 1. Henle, Handbuch der Nervenlehre des Menschen, 1. Lieferung. 2. Quains, Lehrbuch der Anatomie, bearbeitet von C.E.E. Hoffmann, 4. Lieferung: Die Lehre von dem Nervensystem und den Sinnesorganen.

1873

Lehrbuch der Physiologie des Menschen. 3., völlig umgearbeitete Auflage. Mit 164 Abbildungen, XII, 790 S. Erlangen, F. Enke.

Besprechungen im Literarischen Zentralblatt für Deutschland:

Nr. 2, Sp. 44–45. Althann, Beiträge zur Physiologie und Pathologie der Circulation. I. Der Kreislauf in der Schädelrückgratshöhle.

Nr. 3, Sp. 77. Pettenkofer, Beziehungen der Luft zu Kleidung, Wohnung und Boden. Drei populäre Vorlesungen.

Nr. 4, Sp. 108–109. Kleinenberg, Hydra. Eine anatomisch-entwicklungs- geschichtliche Untersuchung.

Nr. 6, Sp. 167–168. Henke, Beiträge zur Anatomie des Menschen mit Beziehung auf Bewegung.

Nr. 6, Sp. 168. Ceradini, Der Mechanismus der halbmondförmigen Herzklappen.

Herrn Professor Dr. Ed. Zarncke—Leipzig nach dem Handexemplar des Herausgebers fest- gestellt werden.

Nr. 6, Sp. 170–171. Wilckens, Untersuchungen über den Magen der wiederkäuenden Hausthiere.

Nr. 8, Sp. 243. Lott, Zur Anatomie und Physiologie des Cervix uteri.

Nr. 12, Sp. 357–358. Arbeiten aus der physiologischen Anstalt zu Leipzig. Mitgetheilt von C. Ludwig.

Nr. 12, Sp. 358–359. Rauch, Die Einheit des Menschengeschlechts. Anthropologische Studien.

Nr. 13, Sp. 399. Schenk, Anatomisch-physiologische Untersuchungen.

Nr. 13, Sp. 399–400. E. Hoffmann, Die Körperhöhlen des Menschen und ihr Inhalt. Nebst Anleitung zu ihrer Eröffnung und Untersuchung.

Nr. 21, Sp. 651–652. Ranke, Grundzüge der Physiologie des Menschen mit Rücksicht auf die Gesundheitspflege. 2. Aufl.

Nr. 21, Sp. 653. Müller, H., Gesammelte und hinterlassene Schriften zur Physiologie des Auges.

Nr. 24, Sp. 748. Stieda, Die Bildung des Knochengewebes.

Nr. 24, Sp. 748. Landzert, Beiträge zur Anatomie und Histologie.

Nr. 25, Sp. 775. Preyer, Über die Erforschung des Lebens (W.).

Nr. 26, Sp. 812–813. 1. Czermak, Über das Ohr und das Hören. 2. Derselbe, Über das physiologische Privatlaboratorium an der Universität Leipzig.

Nr. 26, Sp. 813. Bischoff, Anatomische Beschreibung eines microcephalen achtjährigen Mädchens Helene Becker aus Offenbach.

Nr. 26, Sp. 813. Exner, Leitfaden bei der mikroskopischen Untersuchung thierischer Gewebe.

Nr. 32, Sp. 1003. Merkel, Der Kehlkopf oder die Erkenntnis und Behandlung des menschlichen Stimmorgans im gesunden und erkrankten Zustande.

Nr. 33, Sp. 1039. Rüdinger, Topographisch-chirurgische Anatomie des Menchen. I. Band, 2. Abth. Brust und Bauch.

Nr. 33, Sp. 1039–1040. Gesellius, Die Transfusion des Blutes.

Nr. 33, Sp. 1040. Neumann, Zur Kenntniß der Lymphgefäße der Haut des Menschen und der Säugethiere.

Nr. 34, Sp. 1067–1068. Hasse, Die vergleichende Morphologie und Histologie des häutigen Gehörorgans der Wirbelthiere, nebst Bemerkungen zur vergleichenden Physiologie.

Nr. 36, Sp. 1128. Schmidt, G., Die Laryngoskopie an Thieren.

Nr. 37, Sp. 1163. Eckhard, C., Beiträge zur Anatomie und Physiologie.

Nr. 37, Sp. 1163–1164. Huxley, Handbuch der Anatomie der Wirbelthiere. Übersetzt von F. Ratzel.

Nr. 39, Sp. 1228–1229. Hyrtl, Die Corrosionsanatomie und ihre Ergebnisse.

Nr. 39, Sp. 1229. Brücke, Vorlesungen über Physiologie. 2. Band: Physiologie der Nerven und der Sinnesorgane und Entwicklungsgeschichte.

Nr. 39, Sp. 1229–1230. Heitzmann, Die descriptive und topographische Anatomie in 600 Abbildungen. 5. Lieferung: Das Nervensystem.

Nr. 51, Sp. 1617. Boll, Die Histologie und Histiogenese der nervösen Centralorgane.

1874

Grundzüge der physiologischen Psychologie. Mit 155 Abb., XII, 870 S. Leipzig, W. Engelmann.
2. Aufl. in 2 Bänden 1880. 3. Aufl. 1887. 4. Aufl. l893. 5. Aufl. in 3 Bänden 1902/3. 6. Aufl. 1908/11.

Über die Aufgabe der Philosophie in der Gegenwart. Akademische Antrittsrede in Zürich. Leipzig, W. Engelmann 21. —Stark umgearbeitet unter dem Titel "Philosophie und Wissenschaft." Essays (1885).

Besprechungen im Literarischen Zentralblatt für Deutschland:[9]

Nr. 12, Sp. 380–381. Gruber, Monographie über das zweigetheilte Jochbein os zygomatitum bipartitum bei dem Menschen und den Säugethieren und Bericht über die Leistungen der praktischen Anatomie an der medicochirurgischen Akademie in St. Petersburg.

Nr. 13, Sp. 417. His, Untersuchungen über das Ei und die Eientwicklung bei Knochenfischen; auch unter dem Titel: Untersuchungen über die erste Anlage des Wirbelthierleibes.

Nr. 19, Sp. 630. Braune und Trübiger, Die Venen der menschlichen Hand.

Nr. 22, Sp. 724–725. Gegenbaur, Grundriß der vergleichenden Anatomie.

Nr. 22, Sp. 725–726. Kölliker, Die normale Resorption des Knochengewebes und ihre Bedeutung für die Entstehung der typischen Knochenformen.

Nr. 26, Sp. 848. Jahresbericht über die Fortschritte der Anatomie und Physiologie, herausgegeben von Hofmann und Schwalbe.

Nr. 26, Sp. 848–849. Ebner, Die acinösen Drüsen der Zunge und ihre Beziehungen zu den Geschmacksorganen.

Nr. 28, Sp. 917. Fick, Compendium der Physiologie des Menschen mit Einschluß der Entwicklungsgeschichte.

Nr. 32, Sp. 1038–1039. Bain, Geist und Körper. Die Theorien über ihre gegenseitigen Beziehungen. (W.W.)

Nr. 32, Sp. 1039–1041. Preyer, Das myophysische Gesetz. (W.W.)

Nr. 36, Sp. 1206–1207. Franz Eilh. Schulze, Über den Bau von Syncoryne Sarsii lovén und der zugehörigen Meduse Sarsia Tubulosa Lesson.

Nr. 37, Sp. 1234–1235. Rüdinger, Topographisch-chirurgische Anatomie des Menschen. 3. Abth., 1. Hälfte: Der Kopf.

Nr. 39, Sp. 1301. Brücke, Vorlesungen über Physiologie. 1. Band: Physiologie des Kreislaufs, der Ernährung, der Absonderung, der Respiration und der Bewegungserscheinungen.

Nr. 41, Sp. 1357. Noel, Die materielle Grundlage des Seelenlebens. (W.W.)

Nr. 41, Sp. 1358. Strümpell, Die Natur und Entstehung der Träume (W.W.)

Nr. 42, Sp. 1396. Nägeli, Beiträge zur näheren Kenntnis der Stärkegruppe in chemischer und physiologischer Beziehung.

Nr. 42, Sp. 1397. Filehne, Über das Cheyne-Stokessche Athmungsphänomen.

Nr. 47, Sp. 1552. Bischoff, Über den Einfluß des Freiherrn Justus von Liebig auf die Entwicklung der Physiologie. (W.W.)

[9]Vgl. Anm. 8.

Besprechung von Hitzig, Untersuchungen über das Gehirn. Jenaer Literaturzeitung, S. 518–519.

1875

Die Theorie der Materie. Deutsche Rundschau, herausgegeben von J. Rodenberg, V, S. 364–386. Wenig geändert in Essays (1885).

La Mesure des Sensations. Résponse à propos du logarithme des sensations à Mr. Emile Alglave. La Revue scientifique de la France et de l'Étranger. 2. Serie, VIII, S. 1917–1918. Nochmals abgedruckt in Delboeuf, Eléments de Psychophysique générale et spéciale, 1883, S. 128–131.

Besprechungen im Literarischen Zentralblatt für Deutschland.[10]

> Nr. 4, Sp. 106. Ludwig, Über die Einbildung im Thierreiche.

> Nr. 5, Sp. 136–137. Meynert, Zur Mechanik des Gehirnbaues.

> Nr. 5, Sp. 231. Auerbach, Organologische Studien. I. Heft: Zur Charkteristik und Lebensgeschichte der Zellkerne.

> Nr. 15, Sp. 484–485. Mach, Grundlinien der Lehre von den Bewegungsempfindungen.

> Nr. 15, Sp. 485. Becker, Repetitorium der Physiologie.

> Nr. 17, Sp. 543. Kollmann, Mechanik des menschlichen Körpers.

> Nr. 18, Sp. 577–578. Gerlach, Das Verhältnis der Nerven zu den willkürlichen Muskeln der Wirbelthiere.

> Nr. 21, Sp. 676–677. Gudden, Experimentaluntersuchungen über das Schädelwachsthum.

> Nr. 22, Sp. 706–707. Rubinstein, Die sensoriellen und sensitiven Sinne.

> Nr. 32, Sp. 1035–1036. His, Unsere Körperform und das physiologische Problem ihrer Entstehung. (W.W.)

> Nr. 49, Sp. 1576. Büchner, Physiologische Bilder. (W.W.)

Besprechungen in der Jenaer Literaturzeitung, 2. Jahrgang:

> S. 841. Fritz Schulze, Kant und Darwin, ein Beitrag zur Geschichte der Entwicklungslehre.

> S. 841. J. Huber, Zur Kritik moderner Schöpfungslehren.

> S. 858. E. Hitzig, Untersuchungen über das Gehirn. Neue Folge.

> S. 858–859. J. Bernstein, Die fünf Sinne des Menschen.

> S. 859. L. Mann, Betrachtungen über die Bewegung des Stoffes.

> S. 859–860. 1. J. Spicker, Über das Verhältnis der Naturwissenschaft zur Philosophie. 2. K. Dieterich, Philosophie und Naturwissenschaft. 3. E. Hallier, Die Weltanschauung des Naturforschers.

> S. 893–894. H. Spencer, Grundlagen der Philosophie, übersetzt von B. Vetter.

> S. 911–912. A. Mayer, Die Lehre von der Erkenntnis, vom physiologischen Standpunkte allgemeinverständlich dargestellt.

---

[10]Vgl. Anm. 8.

1876

Untersuchungen zur Mechanik der Nerven und Nervencentren. 2. Abtheilung: Über den Reflexvorgang und das Wesen der centralen Innervation. Mit 41 Abb., IV, 144 S. Stuttgart, F. Enke.

Über den Einfluß der Philosophie auf die Erfahrungswissenschaften. Akademische Antrittsrede in Leipzig. 27 S. Leipzig, W. Engelmann.

Central Innervation and Consciousness. Mind, a quarterly Review of Psychology and Philosophy, ed. by C. G. Robertson, I, S. 161–178.

Besprechungen im Literarischen Zentralblatt für Deutschland:[11]

> Nr. 2, Sp. 33. Drobisch, Neue Darstellung der Logik nach ihren einfachsten Verhältnissen mit Rucksicht auf Mathematik und Naturwissenschaft. 4. Aufl. (W.W.)

> Nr. 2, Sp. 33–34. Volkmann und Volkmar, Lehrbuch der Psychologie vom Standpunkte des Realismus und nach genetischer Methode. I. Bd. (W.W.)

> Nr. 2, Sp. 44. Stieda, Über den Bau des centralen Nervensystems der Amphibien und Reptilien. (W.W.)

> Nr. 2, Sp. 45. Straßburger, Über Zellbildung und Zelltheilung.

> Nr. 2, Sp. 45–46. Wolff, Untersuchungen über die Entwicklung des Knochengewebes. (W.W.)

> Nr. 3, Sp. 83. Landois, Die Transfusion des Blutes. (W.W.)

> Nr. 3, Sp. 83–84. Müller, J. W., Transfusion und Plethora. (W.W.)

> Nr. 3, Sp. 84. Frey, H., Grundzüge der Histologie, zur Einleitung in das Studium derselben.

> Nr. 18, Sp. 591–592. Baumgärtner, Die Weltzellen. (W.W.)

> Nr. l8, Sp. 592. Lamarck, Zoologische Philosophie. (W.W.)

> Nr. 22, Sp. 716–717. Volkmann und Volkmar, Lehrbuch der Psychologie vom Standpunkte des Realismus und nach genetischer Methode. 2. Band. (W.W.)

> Nr. 25, Sp. 820. Jahresbericht über die Fortschritte der Anatomie und Physiologie, herausgegeben von Hofmann und Schwalbe, 3. Band, 1874, 2. Hälfte.

> Nr. 26, Sp. 843–844. Hazard, Zwei Briefe über Verursachung und Freiheit im Wollen, gerichtet an John Stuart Mill. (W.W.)

> Nr. 29, Sp. 949. Virchow, Über einige Merkmale niederer Menschenrassen am Schädel.

> Nr. 30, Sp. 975–976. Schmitz-Dumont, Zeit und Raum in ihren denknothwendigen Bestimmungen, abgeleitet aus dem Satz des Widerspruchs.

> Nr. 31, Sp. 1001–1003. 1. Hildebrandt, Der Traum und seine Verwerthung fürs Leben. 2. Volkelt, Die Traumphantasie. (W.W.)

> Nr. 31, Sp. 1003. Sterne, Werden und Vergehen. Eine Entwicklungsgeschichte des Naturganzen.

> Nr. 31, Sp. 1003. Hermann, Die Sprachwissenschaft nach ihrem Zusammenhang mit Logik, menschlicher Geistesbildung und Philosophie.

[11]Vgl. Anm. 8.

Nr. 31, Sp. 1014. Rosenthal, Bemerkungen über die Thätigkeit der automatischen Nervencentren, insbesondere über die Athembewegungen.

Nr. 31, Sp. 1014–1015. Preyer, Über die Grenzen der Tonwahrnehmung. (W.W.)

Nr. 33, Sp. 1081–1082. Tyndall, Das Licht. (W.W.)

Nr. 33, Sp. 1085–1085. Du Bois-Reymond, Gesammelte Abhandlungen zur allgemeinen Muskel- und Nervenphysik.

Besprechungen in der Jenaer Literaturzeitung, 3. Jahrgang:

S. 281–282. C. Radenhausen, Osiris. Weltgesetze in der Erdgeschichte.

S. 295–296. H. Spencer, Einleitung in das Studium der Sociologie. Theil 1 und 2.

S. 456–457. Fr. Kirchner, Leibniz' Psychologie. Ein Beitrag zur Geschichte der Philosophie und Naturwissenschaft.

1877

Über den Ausdruck der Gemüthsbewegungen. Vortrag in Berlin, Winter 1876/77. Deutsche Rundschau, herausgegeben von J. Rodenberg, XI, S. 120–133 Essays (1885).

Über das kosmologische Problem. Vierteljahrsschrift für wissenschaftliche Philosophie, herausgegeben von R. Avenarius, I, S. 80–136. Umgearbeitet Kleine Schriften I (1910).

Philosophy in Germany. Mind, a quarterly Review of Psychology and Philosophy, ed. by C. G. Robertson, II, S. 493–518.

Selbstanzeige: Untersuchungen zur Mechanik der Nerven und Nervencentren. 2. Abth.: Über den Reflexvorgang und das Wesen der centralen Innervation. Vierteljahrsschrift für wissenschaftliche Philosophie, herausgegeben von R. Avenarius, I, S. 156.

Einige Bemerkungen zu vorstehender Abhandlung. (K. Laßwitz, Ein Beitrag zum kosmologischen Problem und zur Feststellung des Unendlichkeitsbegriffs.) Vierteljahrsschrift für wissenschaftliche Philosphie, herausgegeben von R. Avenarius, I, S. 361–365.

Besprechungen im Literarischen Zentralblatt für Deutschland:[12]

Nr. 9, Sp. 268–269. Carneri, B., Gefühl, Bewußtsein, Wille.

Nr. 9, Sp. 269–270. Michelet, Das System der Philosophie als exakter Wissenschaft.

Nr. 10, Sp. 298. Widemann, Über die Bedingungen der Übereinstimmung des discursiven Denkens mit dem intuitiven.

Nr. 10, Sp. 298. Raith, Entdeckungen im Gebiet der geistigen Verrichtungen des Centralnervensystems.

Nr. 10, Sp. 203–204. Flechsig, Die Leitungsbahnen im Gehirn und Rückenmark des Menschen, auf Grund entwicklungsgeschichtlicher Untersuchungen dargestellt. (W.W.)

---

[12]Vgl. Anm. 8.

Nr. 10, Sp. 303. Frommann, Untersuchungen über die normale und pathologische Histologie des centralen Nervensystems.

Nr. 14, Sp. 454. Krause, A., Die Gesetze des menschlichen Herzens, wis-
senschaftlich dargestellt als die formale Logik des reinen Gefühles.

Nr. 21, Sp. 681–682. 1. Owen, Das streitige Land. 2. Psychische Studien
(monatliche Zeitschrift), herausgegeben von Aksakow.

Nr. 21, Sp. 689–690. Jahresberichte über die Fortschritte der Anatomie und
Physiologie, herausgegeben von Hofmann und Schwalbe. 4. Band.

Nr. 27, Sp. 881. Henle, Anthropologische Vorträge.

Nr. 28, Sp. 914. Witte, Zur Erkenntnistheorie und Ethik.

Nr. 30, Sp. 985–986. Schmidt, Oscar, Die naturwissenschaftlichen Grundlagen
der Philosophie des Unbewußten.

Nr. 31, Sp. 1091. Ribot, Die Erblichkeit.

Nr. 33, Sp. 1091–1092. Schellwien, Das Gesetz der Causalität in der Natur.

Nr. 52, Sp. 1713–1715. Entleuthner, Naturwissenschaft, Naturphilosophie und
Philosophie der Liebe.

Nr. 52, Sp. 1714–1715. Rée, Der Ursprung der moralischen Empfindungen.

Besprechungen in der Jenaer Literaturzeitung, 4. Jahrgang:

S. 37–38. Paul Langer, Die Grundlagen der Psychophysik.

S. 250–251. H. Spencer, System der synthetischen Philosophie. II. Die
Principien der Biologie, Bd. I. Übersetzt von B. Vetter.

1878

Lehrbuch der Physiologie des Menschen. Vierte umgearbeitete Auflage. Mit 170
Abb. XII, 851 S. Stuttgart, F. Enke.

Über den gegenwärtigen Zustand der Thierpsychologie. (Fußnote: Mit besonderer
Rücksicht auf Alfred Espinas, Les sociétés animales, étude de psychologie
comparée, Paris 1877.) Vierteljahrsschrift für wissenschaftliche Philosophie,
herausgegeben von R. Avenarius, II, S. 137–149. Umgearbeitet unter dem Titel
"Die Thierpsychologie," Essays, 1. Aufl. (1885).

Sur la Theorie des Signes locaux. Revue philosophique de la France et de
l'Étranger, VI, 3. Jahrgang, herausgegeben von Th. Ribot, S. 217–231.[13]

Besprechungen im Literarischen Zentralblatt für Deutschland:[14]

Nr. 1, Sp. 12. Luys, Das Gehirn, sein Bau und seine Verrichtungen.

Nr. 20, Sp. 674. Mihalkovics, Entwicklungsgeschichte des Gehirns.

Nr. 20, Sp. 674. Stilling, Neue Untersuchungen über den Bau des kleinen
Gehirns beim Menschen.

Nr. 22, Sp. 737–738. Kalischer, Goethes Verhältnis zur Naturwissenschaft und
seine Bedeutung in derselben.

Nr. 24, Sp. 786–787. Kirchmann, Erläuterungen zu Kants Schriften zur
Naturphilosophie.

Nr. 24, Sp. 787. Prinz, Über den Traum.

---

[13]Richtet sich gegen Lotze, Sur la Fonction de la Notion d'Espace. Ebenda 1877.
[14]Vgl. Anm. 8.

Nr. 30, Sp. 971–972. Pflüger, Die teleologische Mechanik der lebendigen Natur.

Nr. 30, Sp. 972. Huber, Das Gedächtnis.

Besprechung von Kußmaul, Störungen der Sprache, Versuch einer Pathologie der Sprache. (Ziemßens Handbuch der Pathologie und Therapie XII, 2.) Vierteljahrsschrift für wissenschaftliche Philosophie, herausgegeben von R. Avenarius, II, S. 352–368.

Besprechung in der Jenaer Literaturzeitung, 5. Jahrgang: S. 35–36. H. Spencer, System der synthetischen Philosophie. II. Die Principien der Biologie, Band 2. Übersetzt von B. Vetter.

1879

Der Spiritismus, eine sogenannte wissenschaftliche Frage. Offener Brief an Herrn Prof. Ulrici in Halle. 1. bis 4. Abdruck. 31 S. Leipzig, W. Engelmann. Essays (1885).

Über das Verhältnis der Gefühle zu den Vorstellungen. Vierteljahrsschrift für wissenschaftliche Philosophie, herausgegeben von R. Avenarius, III, S. 129–151. Unter dem Titel Gefühl und Vorstellung, Essays, 1. Aufl. (1885).

Psychologische Thatsachen und Hypothesen. Reflexionen aus Anlaß der Abhandlung von A. Horwicz "Über das Verhältnis der Gefühle zu den Vorstellungen." Vierteljahrsschrift für wissenschaftliche Philosophie, herausgegeben von R. Avenarius, III, S. 342–357.[15]

1880

Logik. Eine Untersuchung der Principien der Erkenntnis und der Methoden wissenschaftlicher Forschung. I. Band: Erkenntnislehre. XII, 585 S. Stuttgart, F. Enke.

2. Aufl. 1893, 3. Aufl. 1906, 4. Aufl. 1919, 5. Aufl. 1924.

Grundzüge der physiologischen Psychologie. 2. völlig umgearbeitete Auflage. In zwei Bänden. 1. Band mit 123 Abb., XII, 499 S. 2. Band mit 57 Abb., VIII, 472 S. Leipzig, W. Engelmann.

Gehirn und Seele. Deutsche Rundschau, herausgegeben von J. Rodenberg, XXV, 7. Jahrgang, S. 47–72. Essays (1885).

Der Aberglaube in der Wissenschaft. Nach einem am 16. Oktober 1879 im Kaufmännischen Verein in Leipzig gehaltenen Vortrag. Unsere Zeit, Deutsche Revue der Gegenwart, herausgegeben von R.v. Gottschall, I, S. 26–47. Essays (1885).

Entgegnung. (Auf A. Horwicz, Nochmals die Priorität des Gefühls.) Vierteljahrsschrift für wissenschaftliche Philosophie, herausgegeben von R. Avenarius, IV, S. 135–136.

---

[15]Ebenda IV, 1880: Horwicz, Nochmals die Priorität des Gefühls. Constatierung einiger Thatsachen in den Reflexionen des Herrn Prof. Wundt. Zur nothgedrungenen Vertheidigung.

Berichtigende Bemerkung, zu dem Aufsatze des Herrn B. Erdmann, "Zur zeit-genössischen Psychologie in Deutschland." (Dieselbe Zeitschrift, voriges Heft). Vierteljahrsschrift für wis-senschaftliche Philosophie, herausgegeben von R. Avenarius, IV, S. 137–138.

Besprechungen im Literarischen Zentralblatt für Deutschland:[16]

Nr. 2, Sp. 38–39. Haeckel, Gesammelte populäre Vorträge aus dem Gebiete der Entwicklungslehre.

Nr. 2, Sp. 39. Espinas, Die thierischen Gesellschaften.

Nr. 3, Sp. 71–72. Quatrefages, Das Menschengeschlecht.

Nr. 48, Sp. 1617. Heidenhain, Der sogenannte thierische Magnetismus.

Nr. 48, Sp. 1622–1623. Bergmann, Thesen zur Erklärung der natürlichen Entstehung der Ursprachen.

Nr. 50, Sp. 1692–1693. Strümpell, Psychologische Pädagogik.

Nr. 52, Sp. 1769. Roskoff, Das Religionswesen der rohesten Naturvölker.

1881

Besprechungen im Literarischen Zentralblatt für Deutschland:[17]

Nr. 1, Sp. 7–8. Stern, Die Philosophie und die Anthropogenie des Professor Dr. E. Haeckel.

Nr. 1, Sp. 8. 1. L. Schütz, Der sogenaunte Verstand der Thiere oder der animalische Instinkt. 2. L. Hoffmann, Thierpsychologie.

Nr. 1, Sp. 26–27. Stricker, Studien über die Sprachvorstellungen.

Nr. 3, Sp. 75. Tschofen, Die Philosophie Arthur Schopenhauers in ihrer Relation zur Ethik.

Nr. 14, Sp. 482–483. K. Lange, Über Apperception. Eine psychologisch-pädagogische Monographie.

Nr. 14, Sp. 483. C. S. Cornelius, Zur Theorie der Wechselwirkung zwischen Leib und Seele.

Nr. 46, Sp. 1570–1571. Roux, Der Kampf der Theile im Organismus.

Nr. 48, Sp. 1634. Ferd. Schultz, Erinnerung und Gedächtnis.

1882

Das Webersche Gesetz und die Methoden der Minimaländerungen. Dekanatss-chrift. Qu. 57 S. Leipzig, Edelmann. Erweitert: Philosophische Studien II, 1885.

Logische Steitfragen. 1. Artikel. Vierteljahrsschrift für wissenschaftliche Philoso-phie, herausgegeben von R. Avenarius, IV, S. 340–355.[18]

Die Aufgaben der experimentellen Psychologie. Unsere Zeit. Deutsche Revue der Gegenwart, herausgegeben von R. v. Gottschall. III, S. 389–406. Essays (1885). In der 2. Auflage (1906) umgearbeitet.

---

[16]Vgl. Anm. 8.
[17]Vgl. Anm. 8.
[18]Ein zweiter Artikel ist nicht erschienen.

Besprechungen im Literarischen Zentralblatt für Deutschland:[19]
  Nr. 46, Sp. 1540–1541. Lotze, Grundzüge der Psychologie. Dictate aus den
    Vorlesungen.
  Nr. 50, Sp. 1694–1695. Lazarus, Das Leben der Seele in Monographien über
    seine Erscheinungen und Gesetze. 3. Band.
  Nr. 51, Sp. 1732–1733. Stricker, Studien über die Bewegungsvorstellugen.
Besprechung von Joh. Rehmke, Die Welt als Wahrnehmung und Begriff. Eine
  Erkenntnistheorie. Göttingische Gelehrte Anzeigen, Stück 25.

1883

Logik. Eine Untersuchung der Principien der Erkenntnis und der Methoden wis-
  senschaftlicher Forschung. 2. Band: Methodenlehre. XIII, 620 S. Stuttgart,
  F. Enke.
  2. Auflage (beider Bände) 1893. 3. Auflage in 3 Bänden 1906–1908. 4. Auflage
    1919–1920.
Über psychologische Methoden. Philosophische Studien, herausgegeben von W.
  Wundt, I, S. 1–38.
Über die mathematische Induction. Ebenda S. 90–147. Kl. Schriften III (1921).
Über die Messung psychischer Vorgänge. Ebenda S. 251–260.
Zur Lehre vom Willen. Ebenda S. 337–378.
Weitere Bemerkungen über psychische Messung. Ebenda S. 463–471.
Die Logik der Chemie. Ebenda S. 473–494. Kl. Schriften III (1921).
Über die Methode der Minimaländerungen. Ebenda S. 556–572. Kl. Schriften III
  (1921).
Schlußwort zum 1. Band. Ebenda S. 615–617.
Über Schallstärkemessung. Annalen der Physik und Chemie, herausgegeben von
  Wiedemann, N.F. XVIII, S. 695–703.

1884

Bemerkungen zu vorstehendem Aufsatz. (Poske, Der empirische Ursprung und
  die Allgemeingültigkeit des Beharrungsgesetzes.) Vierteljahrsschrift für wissenschaftliche Philosophie, herausgegeben von R. Avenarius, VIII, S. 405–406.
Besprechung im Literarischen Zentralblatt für Deutschland:[20]
  Nr. 16, Sp. 567. Stumpf, Tonpsychologie. I. Band.

1885

Essays. IV, 386 S. Leipzig, W. Engelmann.
  2. Aufl. 1906.
  Inhalt: Philosophie und Wissenschaft, 1874. Die Theorie der Materie, 1875.
    Die Unendlichkeit der Welt. Gehirn und Seele, 1880. Die Aufgaben der
    experimentellen Psychologie, 1882. Die Messung psychischer Vorgänge,

---

[19]Vgl. Anm. 8.
[20]Vgl. Anm. 8.

Vortrag 1871/72. Die Thierpsychologie, 1878. Gefühl und Vorstellung, 1879. Der Ausdruck der Gemütsbewegungen, 1877. Die Sprache und das Denken, Vortrag, 1875/76. Die Entwicklung des Willens. Der Aberglaube in der Wissenschaft, 1880. Der Spiritismus, 1879. Lessing und die kritische Methode.[21]

Über das Webersche Gesetz. Philosophische Studien, herausgegeben von W. Wundt, II, S. 1–36.[22]

Zur Geschichte und Theorie der abstrakten Begriffe. Ebenda S. 161–193. Etwas umgearbeitet Kl. Schriften I (1910).

Erfundene Empfindungen. Ebenda S. 298–305.

Zur Kritik des Seelenbegriffs. Ebenda S. 483–494.

Kants kosmologische Antinomien und das Problem der Unendlichkeit. Ebenda S. 495–538. Umgearbeitet und sehr erweitert Kl. Schriften I (1910).

1886

Ethik. Eine Untersuchung der Thatsachen und Gesetze des sittlichen Lebens. XI, 577 S. Stuttgart, F. Enke.
>   2. Aufl. 1892. 3. Aufl. in 2 Bänden 1903. 4. Aufl. in 3 Bänden 1912. 5. Aufl. 1923/24.

Über den Begriff des Gesetzes mit Rücksicht auf die Ausnahmslosigkeit der Lautgesetze. Philosophische Studien, herausgegeben von W. Wundt, III, S. 195–215. Kl. Schriften III (1921).

Wer ist der Gesetzgeber der Naturgesetze. Ebenda S. 493–496. Kl. Schriften III (1921).

Das Sittliche in der Sprache. Deutsche Rundschau, herausgegeben von J. Rodenberg, XII, S. 70–92.

Über die physikalischen Axiome. Festschrift des historisch-philosophischen Vereins in Heidelberg zum Universitätsjubiläum, S. 87–99. (Umarbeitung eines in demselben Verein 1865 gehaltene Vortrags.)

Besprechung im Literarischen Zentralblatt für Deutschland:[23]
>   Nr. 8, Sp. 254–255. Gerber, Die Sprache und das Erkennen.

Vorwort zur französischen Übersetzung der Grundzüge der physiologischen Psychologie.

1887

Grundzüge der physiologischen Psychologie. 3. umgearbeitete Auflage, in 2. Bänden. 1. Band mit 142 Abbs., XII, 144 S. 2. Band mit 68 Abb., X, 562 S. Leipzig, W. Engelmann.

---

[21]Die Aufsätze ohne Jahreszahl und die beiden Vorträge sind hier zum erstenmal gedruckt, das Manuskript zu "Lessing und die kritische Methode" stammt in der Hauptsache schon aus den Jahren um 1880. Die Aufsätze "Die Tierpsychologie" und "Gefühl und Vorstellung" sind in der zweiten Auflage fortgefallen.

[22]Erweitert die Dekanatsschrift aus dem Jahre 1882.

[23]Vgl. Anm. 8.

Zum ethischen Evolutionismus. Eine Entgegnung. Preußische Jahrbücher, her-
ausgegeben von Treitschke und Delbrück, LIX, S. 478–485.[24]
Zur Moral der literarischen Kritik. Eine moralphilosophische Streitschrift. 77 S.
Leipzig, W. Engelmann.[25]
Zur Erinnerung an Gustav Theodor Fechner. Worte, gesprochen an seinem Sarge
am 21. November 1887. 12 S. Leipzig, Breitkopf & Härtel.

1888

Über Ziele und Wege der Völkerpsychologie. Philosophische Studien, heraus-
gegeben von W. Wundt, IV, S. 1–27.
Bemerkungen zu vorstehendem Aufsatz. (H. Neiglick, Zur Psychophysik des
Lichtsinns.) Ebenda S. 112–116.
Selbstbeobachtuung und innere Wahrnehmung. Philosophische Studien IV, S.
292–309. Kl. Schriften III (1921).
Die Empfindung des Lichts und der Farben. Ebenda S. 311–389. Kl. Schriften III
(1921).
Zur Erinnerung an Gustav Theodor Fechner. Worte am Sarge. (Unveränderter
Abdruck.) Ebenda S. 471–478.
Berichtigung. Ebenda S. 640. (Bezieht sich auf eine angebliche Schrift Fechners:
Die Auflösung der Arten durch natürliche Zuchtwahl.)

1889

System der Philosophie. X, 669 S. Leipzig, W. Engelmann.
   2. Aufl. 1897. 3. Aufl. in 2 Bänden 1907. 4. Aufl. 1919.
Über den Zusammenhang der Philosophie mit der Zeitgeschichte. Eine Centen-
narbetrachtung. Rektoratsrede. Qu. 33 S. Leipzig, Edelmann. Reden und
Aufsätze.
Über die Eintheilung der Wissenschaften. Philosophische Studien, herausgegeben
von W.Wundt, V, S. 1–55. Kl. Schriften III (1921).
Biologische Probleme. Ebenda S. 327–380. Kl. Schriften III (1921).
Vorwort des Herausgebers. (Zu Fechner, Elemente der Psychophysik, 2. unverän-
derte Auflage.) S. V–VI.

1890

Über den Zusammenhang der Philosophie mit der Zeitgeschichte. (Unveränderter
Abdruck.) Deutsche Rundschau, herausgegeben von J. Rodenberg, XVI, S.
52–71.
Bericht über das Studienjahr 1889/90. Rede als abtretender Rektor. Qu. 13 S.
Leipzig, Edelmann.

---

[24]Gegen Hugo Sommers Abhandlung "Der ethische Evolutionismus W. Wundts." Preuss.
Jahrb. LIX.
[25]Antwort auf die Erwiderung Sommers.

1891

Über das Verhältnis des Einzelnen zur Gesellschaft. Rede an Königs Geburtstag. Deutsche Rundschau, herausgegeben von J. Rodenberg, XVII, S. 190–206. Unter dem Titel: "Über das Verhältnis des Einzelen zur Gemeinschaft," Reden und Aufsätze (1913).

Zur Frage der Localisation der Großhirnfunctionen. Philosophische Studien, herausgegeben von W. Wundt, VI, S. 1–25. Kl. Schriften III (1921).

Über die Methoden der Messung des Bewußtseinsumfanges. Ebenda S. 250–260. Erweitert Kl. Schriften II (1911).

Zur Lehre von den Gemüthsbewegungen. Ebenda S. 335–393. Erweitert Kl. Schriften II (1911).

Über Vergleichungen von Tondistanzen. Ebenda S. 605–640.

Zur Erinnerung an den Heimgang Fr. Zarnckes. Rede, gehalten am Sarge, 15.10.91. Leipzig, Breitkopf & Härtel.

1892

Ethik. Eine Untersuchung der Thatsachen und Gesetze des sittlichen Lebens. 2. umgearbeitete Auflage. XII, 684 S. Stuttgart, F. Enke.

Vorlesungen über die Menschen und Thierseele. 2. umgearbeitete Auflage. XII, 495 S. Hamburg und Leipzig, L. Voß.

Hypnotismus und Suggestion. 110 S. Leipzig, W. Engelmann. 2. Auflage 1911. Kl. Schriften II (1911).

Was soll uns Kant nicht sein? Philosophische Studien, herausgegeben von W. Wundt, VII, S. 1–49. Sehr erweitert Kl. Schriften I (1910).

Zur Frage des Bewußtseinsumfanges. Ebenda S. 222–231.

Eine Replik C. Stumpfs. Ebenda S. 298–327.

Bemerkungen zur Associationslehre. Ebenda S. 329–361. Etwas erweitert unter dem Titel "Zur Assoziationslehre," Kl. Schriften II (1911).

Auch ein Schlußwort. Ebenda S. 633–636.[26]

Besprechung im Literarischen Zentralblatt für Deutschland:[27]
> Nr. 14, Sp. 474–475. Das Dasein als Lust, Leid und Liebe. Die altindische Weltanschauung in neuzeitlicher Darstellung.

1893

Grundzüge der physiologischen Psychologie. 4. umgearbeitete Auflage. In 2 Bänden. 1. Band mit 143 Abbildungen, XV, 600 S. 2. Band mit 94 Abbildungen, XII, 684 S. Leipzig, W. Engelmann.

Logik. Eine Untersuchung der Principien der Erkenntnis und der Methoden wissenschaftlicher Forschung. 1. Band: Erkenntnislehre. 2. umgearbeitete Auflage. XIV, 651 S. Stuttgart, F. Enke.

[26]Gegen ein "Schlußwort" von C. Stumpf, Zeitschrift für Psychologie und Physiologie der Sinnesorgane II.
[27]Vgl. Anm. 8.

Psychophysik und experimentelle Psychologie. In "Die deutschen Universitäten," für die Weltausstellung in Chicago, herausgegeben von W. Lexis. Band I, S. 450–457.

Hypnotismus und Suggestion. Philosophische Studien, herausgegeben von W. Wundt, VIII, S. 1–85. (Unveränderter Abdruck des 1892 separat erschienenen Aufsatzes.)

Ist der Hörnerv direct durch Tonschwingungen erregbar? Ebenda S. 641–652.

Chronograph und Chronoskop. Notiz zu einer Bemerkung J.M. Cattells. Ebenda S. 653–654.

Notiz über psychologische Apparate. Ebenda S. 655–656.

Besprechung im Literarischen Zentralblatt für Deutschland:[28]

Nr. 51, Sp. 1812–1813. Pesch, Die großen Welträtsel. Philosophie der Natur.

1894

Logik. Eine Untersuchung der Principien der Erkenntnis und der Methoden wissenschaftlicher Forschung. 2. Band: Methodenlehre. 1. Theil: Allgemeine Methodenlehre: Logik der Mathematik und der Naturwissenschaften. 2. umgearbeitete Auflage. XII, 590 S. Stuttgart, F. Enke.

Bemerkungen zu vorstehendem Aufsatz. (Cattell, Chronoskop und Chronograph.) Philosophische Studien, herausgegeben von W. Wundt, IX, S. 311–315.

Akustische Versuche an einer labyrinthlosen Taube. Ebenda S. 496–509.

Über psychische Causalität und das Princip des psycho-physischen Parallelismus. Ebenda X, S. 1–124. Umgearbeitet unter dem Titel "Über psychische Kausalität," Kl. Schriften II (1911).

Sind die Mittelglieder einer mittelbaren Association bewußt oder unbewußt? Ebenda S. 326–328.

Zur Beurtheilung der zusammengesetzten Reactionen. Ebenda S. 485–498.

1895

Logik. Eine Untersuchung der Principien der Erkenntnis und der Methoden wissenschaftlicher Forschung. 2. Band: Methodenlehre. 2. Theil: Logik der Geisteswissenschaften.

2. umgearbeitete Auflage. VII, 643 S. Stuttgart, F. Enke.

Zur Frage der Hörfähigkeit labyrinthloser Tauben. Pflügers Archiv für die gesamte Physiologie des Menschen und der Thiere. Band 61, S. 339–341.

Besprechungen im Literarischen Zentralblatt für Deutschland:[29]

Nr. 3, Sp. 83–84. Höffding, Psychologie in Umrissen auf Grundlage der Erfahrung.

Nr. 9, Sp. 283–284. De la Grasserie, De la Classification objective et subjective des arts, de la littérature et des sciences.

---

[28]Vgl. Anm. 8.
[29]Vgl. Anm. 8.

1896

Grundriß der Psychologie. XVI, 392 S. Leipzig, W. Engelmann.
   2. Aufl. 1897; 3. Aufl. 1898; 4. Aufl. 1901; 5. Aufl. 1902; 6. Aufl. 1904; 7. Aufl.
   1905; 8. Aufl. 1907; 9. Aufl. 1909; 10. Aufl. 1911: 11. Aufl. 1913; 12. Aufl.
   1914; 13. Aufl. 1918; 14. Aufl. 1920; 15. Aufl. 1922.
Über die Definition der Psychologie. Philosophische Studien, herausgegeben von
   W. Wundt, XII, S. 1–66, z.T. umgearbeitet Kl. Schriften II (1911).
Über naiven und kritischen Realismus. 1. Artikel. Ebenda S. 307–408. Kl. Schriften
   I (1910).

1897

Vorlesungen über die Menschen- und Thierseele. 3. umgearbeitete Aufl. XII, 519
   S. Hamburg u. Leipzig, L. Voß.
Grundriß der Psychologie. 2. verbesserte Aufl. XVI, 392 S. Leipzig, W. Engelmann.
System der Philosophie. 2. umgearbeitete Aufl. XVIII, 689 S. Leipzig, W.
   Engelmann.
Gutachten über das Frauenstudium. In "Die akademische Frau," Gutachten von
   Universitätsprofessoren usw. über die Befähigung der Frau zum wis-
   senschaftlichen Studium, herausgegeben von Arthur Kirchhoff. S. 179–181.

1898

Grundriß der Psychologie. 3. verbesserte Aufl. XVI, 403 S. Leipzig, W. Engelmann.
Die geometrisch-optischen Täuschungen. Abhandlungen der mathematisch-
   physischen Klasse der Königlich sächsischen Gesellschaft der Wis-
   senschaften, Band XXIV, S. 55–178, mit 65 Abbildungen. Leipzig, Teubner.
Über naiven und kritischen Realismus. 2. Artikel. Philosophische Studien,
   herausgegeben von W. Wundt, XIII, S. 1–105. Kl. Schriften I (1910).
Einige Bemerkungen zu vorstehendem Aufsatze. (Schubert-Soldern, Erwiderung
   auf Prof. Wundts Aufsatz "Über naiven und kritischen Realismus.") Ebenda
   S. 318–322.
Über naiven und kritischen Realismus. 3. Artikel. Ebenda S. 323–433. —Etwas
   gekürzt Kl. Schriften I (1910).
Bemerkung zu vorstehender Berichtigung. (Heymans, Berichtigung.)[30] Ebenda S.
   616–619.
Zur Theorie der räumlichen Gesichtswahrnehmungen. Ebenda XIV, S. 1–118. Kl.
   Schriften III (1921).

1900

Völkerpsychologie. Eine Untersuchung der Entwicklungsgesetze von Sprache,
   Mythus und Sitte. 1. Band in 2. Theilen: Die Sprache. 1. Band mit 40
   Abbildungen, XV, 627 S. 2. Band mit 2 Abbildungen, X, 644 S. Leipzig, W.
   Engelmann.
   2. Aufl. 1904. 3. Aufl. 1911/12. 4. Aufl. 1922.

[30]Bezieht sich auf eine Bemerkung in den geometrisch-optischen Täuschungen.

Bemerkungen zur Theorie der Gefühle. Philosophische Studien, herausgegeben von W. Wundt, XV, S. 149–182. Etwas umgearbeitet u.d.T. "Zur Theorie der Gefühle." —Kl. Schriften II (1911).

Zur Kritik tachistoskopischer Versuche. Ebenda S. 287–317.

Zur Technik des Complicationspendels. Ebenda S. 579–582.

Zur Kritik tachistoskopischer Versuche. 2. Artikel. Ebenda Band XVI, S. 61–70.

Besprechung von Osthoff, Vom Suppletivwesen der indogermanischen Sprachen. Anzeiger für indogermanische Sprach- und Altertumskunde, herausgegeben von W. Streitberg, Band II, S. 1–6.

1901

Grundriß der Psychologie. 4. neubearbeitete Aufl. XVII, 411 S. Leipzig, W. Engelmann.

Einleitung in die Philosophie. XVII, 466 S. Leipzig, W. Engelmann.
2. Aufl. 1902; 3. Aufl. 1904; 4. Aufl. 1906; 5. Aufl. 1909; 6. Aufl. 1914; 7. Aufl. 1918; 8. Aufl. 1920; 9. Aufl. 1922.

Gustav Theodor Fechner. Rede zur Feier seines 100. Geburtstages. Mit Beilagen und einer Abbildung des Fechnerdenkmals. 92 S. Leipzig, W. Engelmann. — Reden und Aufsätze (1913).

Sprachgeschichte und Sprachpsychologie. Mit Rücksicht auf B. Delbrücks Grundfragen der Sprachforschung. 110 S. Leipzig, W. Engelmann.

Besprechung von Thumb and Marbe, Experimentelle Untersuchungen über die psychologischen Grundlagen der sprachlichen Analogiebildungen. Anzeiger für indogermanische Sprach- und Altertumskunde, herausgegeben von W. Streitberg, Band 12, S. 17–20.

Besprechung im Literarischen Zentralblatt für Deutschland, Nr. 20, Sp. 817. Mauthner, Sprache und Psychologie.

1902

Grundzüge der physiologischen Psychologie. 5. völlig umgearbeitete Auflage. Band 1 u. 2. 1. Band mit 156 Abbildungen, XV, 553 S. 2. Band mit 153 Abbildungen, VIII, 686 S. Leipzig, W. Engelmann.

Grundriß der Psychologie. 5. umgearbeitete Aufl. XVI, 410 S. Leipzig, W. Engelmann.

Einleitung in die Philosophie. 2. unveränderte Aufl. XVIII, 466 S. Leipzig, W. Engelmann.

1903

Grundzüge der physiologischen Psychologie. 5. völlig umgearbeitete Aufl. 3. Band mit 75 Abbildungen, IX, 796 S. Leipzig, W. Engelmann. —Gesamtregister zu Band 1–3 von W. Wirth. Leipzig, W. Engelmann.

Naturwissenschaft und Psychologie. Sonderausgabe der Schlußbetrachtungen der 5. Auflage der Grundzüge der physiologischen Psychologie. I, 124 S. Leipzig, W. Engelmann.

Ethik. Eine Untersuchung der Tatsachen und Gesetze des sittlichen Lebens. 3. umgearbeitete Aufl. In 2. Bänden. 1. Band X, 524 S. 2. Band VI, 409 S. Stuttgart, F. Enke.

Schlußwort des Herausgebers. Philosophische Studien, herausgegeben von W. Wundt. XVIII, S. 793–795.

1904

Völkerpsychologie. Eine Untersuchung der Entwicklungsgesetze von Sprache, Mythus und Sitte. 1. Band: Die Sprache. In 2 Teilen. 2. umgearbeitete Auflage. 1. Band mit 40 Abbildungen, XV, 667 S. 2. Band mit 4 Abbildungen, X, 673 S. Leipzig, W. Engelmann.

Grundriß der Psychologie. 6. verbesserte Aufl. XVI, 408 S. Leipzig, W. Engelmann.

Einleitung in die Philosophie. 3. Aufl. Mit einem Anhang tabellarischer Übersichten zur Geschichte der Philosophie und ihrer Hauptrichtungen. XVIII, 471 S. Leipzig, W. Engelmann.

Über empirische und metaphysische Psychologie. Eine kritische Betrachtung. Archiv für die gesamte Psychologie, herausgegeben von E. Meumann, II, S. 333–361. —Etwas geändert Kl. Schriften II (1911).

Psychologie. Aus "Die Philosophie im Beginn des 20. Jahrhunderts." Festschrift für Kuno Fischer, herausgegeben von W. Windelband. Bd. I, S. 1–53. Heidelberg, Winter. 2. Aufl. 1907. U.d.T. "Die Psychologie im Anfang des 20. Jahrhunderts." Reden und Aufsätze (1913).

1905

Völkerpsychologie. Eine Untersuchung der Entwicklungsgesetze von Sprache, Mythus und Sitte. 2. Band: Mythus und Religion. 1. Teil. Mit 53 Abbildungen. XII, 617 S. Leipzig, W. Engelmann.

Weitere Auflagen u.d.T. "Die Kunst": 2. Aufl. 1908; 3. Aufl. 1920; 4. Aufl. 1923.

Grundriß der Psycholgie. 7. verbesserte Auflage. Mit 23. Abbildungen. XVI, 414 S. Leipzig, W. Engelmann.

Antwort auf die Enquête der Zeitschrift L'Européen, Courier internationale hebdomadaire: "La France est-elle en Décadence?" Nr. 122, 2. April 1904.

1906

Völkerpsychologie. Eine Untersuchung der Entwicklungsgesetze von Sprache, Mythus und Sitte. 2. Band: Mythus und Religion. 2. Teil. Mit 8 Abbildungen. VIII, 481 S. Leipzig, W. Engelmann.

Weitere Auflagen als 4. Band, Mythus und Religion. 1. Teil: 2. Aufl. 1910; 3. Aufl. 1920; 4. Aufl. 1926.

Logik. Eine Untersuchung der Prinzipien der Erkenntnis und der Methoden wissenschaftlicher Forschung. 1. Band: Allgemeine Logik und Erkenntnistheorie. 3. umgearbeitete Auflage. XIV, 650 S. Stuttgart, F. Enke.

Vorlesungen über die Menschen- und Tierseele. 4. umgearbeitete Auflage, mit 53
    Abbildungen, XIV, 547 S. Hamburg und Leipzig, L. Voß.
Einleitung in die Philosophie. 4. Auflage. XVIII, 471 S. Leipzig, W. Engelmann.
Essays. 2. Auflage. Mit Zusätzen und Anmerkungen. IV, 440 S.[31]
Vorwort des Herausgebers. Psychologische Studien, herausgegeben von W.
    Wundt, I, S. 1–3.
Kleine Mitteilungen: "Über den Begriff des Glücks." Darwinismus contra
    Energetik. Ebenda S. 173–177.
Kleine Mitteilungen: Die dioptrischen Metamorphopsien und ihre Ausgleichung.
    Ebenda S. 494–497.

1907

Logik. Eine Untersuchung der Prinzipien der Erkenntnis und der Methoden
    wissenschaftlicher Forschung. 2. Band: Logik der exakten Wissenschaften. 3.
    umgearbeitete Auflage. XV, 653 S. Stuttgart, F. Enke.
System der Philosophie. 3. umgearbeitete Auflage. In 2 Bänden. 1. Band: XVIII,
    436 S. 2. Band: VI, 302 S. Leipzig, W. Engelmann.
Grundriß der Philosophie. 8. verbesserte Auflage. Mit 23 Abbildungen, XVI, 414
    S. Leipzig, W. Engelmann.
Kleine Mitteilungen: Ist Schwartz eine Empfindung? Psychologische Studien,
    herausgegeben von W. Wundt, II, S. 115–119.
Kleine Mitteilungen: Die Projektionsmethode und die geometrische-optischen
    Täuschungen. Ebenda S. 493–498.
Die Anfänge der Gesellschaft. Eine völkerpsychologische Studie. Ebenda III, S.
    1–48.
Über Ausfrageexperimente und über die Methoden zur Psychologie des Denkens.
    Ebenda S. 301–390. —Kl. Schriften II (1911).
Psychologie. Aus "Die Philosophie im Beginn des 20. Jahrhunderts," Festschrift
    für Kuno Fischer, herausgegeben von W. Windelband. 2. Auflage.
Schallnachahmungen und Lautmetaphern in der Sprache. Beilage zur Allge-
    meinen Zeitung, München, Nr. 40, S. 313–316.
Metaphysik. Aus "Die Kultur der Gegenwart," herausgegeben von P. Hinneberg,
    I. Band, Abt. 6, S. 103–137. Leipzig, Teubner.
    2. Aufl. 1908; 3. Aufl. 1921. Unter dem Titel "Die Metaphysik in Vergangen-
        heit und Gegenwart." Reden und Aufsätze (1913).
Die Anfänge der Philosophie. Internationale Wochenschrift für Wissenschaft,
    Kunst und Technik, herausgegeben von P. Hinneberg. I, col. 935–940.
Vorwort des Herausgebers. (Fechner, Elemente der Psychophysik, 3. unveränderte
    Auflage.) S. V–VI.
Besprechung von Böckel, Psychologie der Volksdichtung. Hessische Blätter für
    Volkskunde, herausgegeben von Helm und Hepding, Bd. VI, S. 197–198.

---

[31]Inhalt s. 1885. In der zweiten Auflage sind fortgelassen: "Die Tierpsychologie" und "Gefühl
und Vorstellung."

1908

Logik. Eine Untersuchung der Prinzipien der Erkenntnis und der Methoden wissenschaftlicher Forschung. 3. Band: Logik der Geisteswissenschaften. 3. umgearbeitete Auflage. XII, 692 S. Stuttgart, F. Enke.

Grundzüge der physiologischen Psychologie. 6. umgearbeitete Auflage. 1. Band. Mit 161 Abbildungen, XV, 725 S. Leipzig, W. Engelmann.

Völkerpsychologie. Eine Untersuchung der Entwicklungsgesetze von Sprache, Mythus und Sitte. 3. Band: Die Kunst. 2. neu bearbeitete Auflage. Mit 59 Abbildungen, X, 564 S. Leipzig, W. Engelmann.

Kritische Nachlese zur Ausfragemethode. Archiv für die gesamte Psychologie, herausgegeben von Meumann u. Wirth, XI, S. 445–459.

Märchen, Sage und Legende als Entwicklungsformen des Mythus, Archiv für Religionswissenschaft, herausgegeben von A. Dietrich, XI, S. 200–222.

Metaphysik. Aus "Die Kultur der Gegenwart," herausgegeben von P. Hinneberg, 1. Abt. V, S. 66–118. 2. durchgesehene Auflage.

1909

Völkerpsychologie. Eine Untersuchung der Entwicklungsgesetze von Sprache, Mythus und Sitte. 2. Band: Mythus und Religion, 3. Teil. XII, 792 S. Leipzig, W. Engelmann.

Weitere Auflagen als 5. und 6. Band: Mythus und Religion, 2. und 3. Teil, 2. Aufl. 1914/15; 3. Aufl. 1923.

Grundriß der Psychologie. 9. verbesserte Auflage. XVI, 414 S. Leipzig, E. Engelmann.

Einleitung in die Philosophie. 5. Auflage. XVIII, 471 S. Leipzig, W. Engelmann.

Festrede zur fünfhundertjährigen Jubelfeier der Universität Leipzig. Mit einem Anhang: Die Leipziger Immatrikulationen und die Organisation der alten Hochschule. I, 83 S. Leipzig, W. Engelmann. Unter dem Titel "Die Leipziger Hochschule im Wandel der Jahrhunderte," Reden und Aufsätze (1913).

Das Institut für experimentelle Psychologie. Festschrift zum 500-jährigen Jubiläum der Universität. 16 S.

Die Anfänge der Philosophie und die Philosophie der primitiven Völker. Aus "Die Kultur der Gegenwart," herausgegeben von P. Hinneberg, 1. Teil, Abt. V, S. 1–31. Leipzig, Teubner.

2. Aufl. 1913. Unter dem Titel "Die Philosophie des primitiven Menschen," Reden und Aufsätze (1913).

1910

Grundzüge der physiologischen Psychologie. 6. umgearbeitete Auflage. 2. Band. Mit 167 Abbildungen. VIII, 782 S. Leipzig, W. Engelmann.

Völkerpsychologie. Eine Untersuchung der Entwicklungsgesetze von Sprache, Mythus und Sitte. 4. Band: Mythus und Religion, 1. Teil. 2. neu bearbeitete Auflage. XII, 587 S. Leipzig, W. Engelmann.

Die Prinzipien der mechanischen Naturlehre. Ein Kapitel aus einer Philosophie der Naturwissenschaften. 2. umgearbeitete Auflage der Schrift: Die physikalischen Axiome und ihre Beziehung zum Kausalprinzip (1866). XII, 217 S. Stuttgart, F. Enke.

Kleine Schriften, 1. Band. VIII, 640 S. Leipzig, W. Engelmann.

(Inhalt: Über das kosmologische Problem, 1877. Kants kosmologische Antinomien und das Problem der Unendlichkeit, 1885. Was soll uns Kant nicht sein? 1892. Zur Geschichte und Theorie der abstrackten Begriffe, 1885. Über naiven und kritischen Realismus, 1896/98. Psychologismus und Logizismus, 1910.)[32]

Über reine und angewandte Psychologie. Psychologische Studien, herausgegeben von W. Wundt, V, S. 1–47. Etwas umgearbeitet Kl. Schriften II (1911).

Das Institut für experimentelle Psychologie. Ebenda S. 279–293.

Logik und Psychologie. Zeitschrift für pädagogische Psychologie, Pathologie und Hygiene, herausgegeben von Brahn, Deuchler und Scheibner. Band XI, S. 1–18. Kl. Schriften III (1921).

1911

Grundzüge der physiologischen Psychologie. 6. umgearbeitete Auflage. 3. Band. Mit 71 Abbildungen, XI, 810 S. Leipzig, W. Engelmann.

Naturwissenschaft und Psychologie. Sonderausgabe des Schlußabschnitts der Grundzüge der physiologischen Psychologie, 2. Aufl. 124 S. Leipzig, W. Engelmann.

Völkerpsychologie. Eine Untersuchung der Entwicklungsgesetze von Sprache, Mythus und Sitte. 1. Band: Die Sprache. 1. Teil. 3. neubearbeitete Auflage. Mit 40 Abbildungen, XV, 695 S. Leipzig, W. Engelmann.

Vorlesungen über die Menschen- und Tierseele. 5. Auflage. Mit 53 Abbildungen. XVI, 558 S. Hamburg und Leipzig, L. Voß.

Grundriß der Psychologie. 10. verbesserte Auflage. Mit 23 Abbildungen. XVI, 414 S. Leipzig, W. Engelmann.

Probleme der Völkerpsychologie. VII, 120 S. Leipzig, E. Wiegandt.

2. Aufl. 1921.

Einführung in die Psychologie. 1. und 2. Abdruck. (1.–13. Tausend.) Ordentliche Veröffentlichung der pädagogischen Literaturgesellschaft "Neue Bahnen." VIII, 129 S. Leipzig, R. Voigtländer.

3. Abdruck 1913. 4. Abdruck 1918.

Kleine Schriften. 2. Band, VII, 496 S. Leipzig, W. Engelmann.

(Inhalt: Über psychische Kausalität, 1894. Die Definition der Psychologie, 1896. Über psychologische Methoden: Die Methoden der Messung des Bewußtseinsumfanges, 1891. Zur Assoziationslehre, 1892. Zur Theorie der Gefühle, 1900. Über Ausfrageexperimente und die Methoden der Psychologie des Denkens, 1907. Reine und angewandte Psychologie, 1910. Empirische und metaphysische Psychologie, 1904. Zur Lehre von den Gemütsbewegungen, 1891. Hypnotismus und Suggestion, 1892.)

---

[32]Der letzte Aufsatz ist hier zum erstenmal gedruckt.

Hypnotismus und Suggestion. 2. durchgesehene Auflage. 69 S. Leipzig, W. Engelmann.

Sprachwissenschaft und Völkerpsychologie, Indogermanische Forschungen, herausgegeben von Brugmann und Streitberg, XXVIII, S. 205–219.

Antwort auf die Rundfrage der Deutschen Juristenzeitung, Berlin, über der Beibehaltung der Todesstrafe. XVI. Jahrgang, S. 18.

Zur Psychologie und Ethik. 10 ausgewählte Abschnitte, herausgegeben und eingeleitet von J.A. Wentzel. Leipzig, Reclam.

(Inhalt: Der Ursprung der Sprache, Völkerpscyhologie. Psychologische Kunstbetrachtung, Völkerpsychologie. Das Märchen, Völkerpsychologie. Die Aufgabe der experimentellen Psychologie, Essays. Über eudämonistische Moralsysteme, Ethik. Die sittlichen Normen, Ethik. Das Recht, Ethik. Der Beruf, Ethik. Der Staat als Gesellschaftseinhalt, Ethik. Der wirtschaftliche Völkerverkehr, Ethik.)

1912

Völkerpsychologie. Eine Untersuchung der Entwicklungsgesetze von Sprache, Mythus und Sitte. 2. Band: Die Sprache. 2. Teil. 3. neubearbeitete Auflage. Mit 6 Abbildungen, X, 678 S. Leipzig, W. Engelmann.

Elemente der Völkerpsychologie. Grundlinien einer psychologischen Entwicklungsgeschichte der Menschheit. XII, 523 S. Leipzig, A. Kröner.

Ethik. Eine Untersuchung der Tatsachen und Gesetze des sittlichen Lebens. 4. umgearbeitete Auflage. In 3. Bänden: 1. Band: XII, 304 S.; 2. Band: IV, 306 S.; 3. Band: IV, 360 S. Stuttgart, F. Enke.

Die Entstehung der Exogamie. Archiv für Rechts- und Wirtschaftsphilosophie, herausgegeben von Kohler und Berolzheimer. V. Band, S. 1–40.

Die Bedeutung der akademischen Seminarien für die Geisteswissenschaften. Handbuch der Politik, herausgegeben von Berolzheimer u.A. 2. Band, S. 586–587.

2. Auflage 1921.

Nachruf auf Paul Richter. Gedächtnisbuch S. 38–43.

Antwort auf die Rundfrage des Leipziger Tageblatts "Über das Frauenstimmrecht." 7. Juli.

1913

Grundriß der Psychologie. 11. Auflage. Mit 23 Abbildungen, XVI, 414 S. Leipzig, A. Kröner.

Einführung in die Psychologie. 3. Abdruck (14.–18. Tausend.) VIII, 129 S. Leipzig, Voigtländer.

Reden und Aufsätze. VII, 397 S. Leipzig, A. Kröner.

(Inhalt: Über den Zusammenhang der Philosophie mit der Zeitgeschichte, 1889. Über das Verhältnis des Einzelnen zur Gemeinschaft, 1891. Die Metaphysik in Vergangenheit und Gegenwart, 1907. Die Philosophie des primitiven Menschen, 1909. Die Psychologie im Anfang des 20.

Jahrhunderts, 1904/07. Gottfried Wilhelm Leibniz, 1902.[33] Gustav
Theodor Fechner, 1901. Die Leipziger Hochschule im Wandel der
Jahrhunderte, 1909.)

Die Psychologie im Kampf ums Dasein. 38 S. Leipzig, A. Kröner. –Kl. Schriften III
(1921).

Die Anfänge der Philosophie und die Philosophie der primitiven Völker. Aus "Die
Kultur der Gegenwart," herausgegeben von P. Hinneberg. 2. Auflage, Band
I, Abt. V, S. 1–29. Leipzig, Teubner. –Reden und Aufsätze (1913).

Gutachten über die Dresdner Universitätsfrage. Leipziger Neueste Nachrichten,
29. April.

Erklärung über Gerhard Hauptmanns Jahrhundertfestspiel, Leipziger Tageblatt,
1. Juli.

1914

Völkerpsychologie. Eine Untersuchung der Entwicklungsgesetze von Sprache,
Mythus und Sitte. 5. Band: Mythus und Religion, 2. Teil. 2. neubearbeitete
Auflage. XIII, 494 S. Leipzig, A. Kröner.

Sinnliche und übersinnliche Welt. VIII, 423 S. Leipzig, A. Kröner. –2. Aufl. 1923.

Einleitung in die Philosophie. 6. Auflage. XVIII, 448 S. Leipzig, A. Kröner.

Totemismus und Stammesorganization in Australien. Anthropos, Internationale
Zeitschrift für Völker- und Sprachenkunde, herausgegeben von P.W. Schmidt.
Band IX, S. 13–39.

Kleine Mitteilungen: Zur Frage der umkehrbaren, perspektivischen Täuschungen.
Psychologische Studien, herausgegeben von W. Wundt, IX, S. 272–277.

Über den wahrhaften Krieg. Rede vom 10. September. 40 S. Leipzig, A. Kröner.

England und der Kreig. Internationale Monatsschrift für Wissenschaft, Kunst und
Technik, herausgegeben von M. Cornicelius, 9. Jahrgang, Sp. 121–128.

Gutachten über den Schutz des Kunstbesitzes in Feindesland. Deutsche Kunst
und Dekoration, Novemberheft.

1915

Völkerpsychologie. Eine Untersuchung der Entwicklungsgesetze von Sprache,
Mythus und Sitte. 6. Band: Mythus und Religion, 3. Teil. 2. neubearbeitete
Auflage. XII, 564 S. Leipzig, A. Kröner.

Die Nationen im Spiegelbild ihrer Philosophie. Österreichische Rundschau, herausgegeben von Chlumecky, Glossy und Oppenheimer. Band: Liebesgaben
aus dem deutschen Volk, S. 127–134.

Deutschland im Lichte des neutralen und des feindlichen Auslandes. Scientia,
Band XVII, S. 71–85.

Die Nationen und ihre Philosophie. Ein Kapitel zum Weltkrieg. VII, 146 S. Leipzig,
A. Kröner.

An der Bahre Karl Lamprechts. Akademische Rundschau III, S. 1–6.

---

[33]Akademischer Vortrag in Anwesenheit König Georgs, hier zuerst gedruckt.

Karl Lamprecht. Ein Gedenkblatt von W. Wundt und Max Klinger. 18 S. Leipzig, Hirzel.

Zur Erinnerung an Ernst Meumann. Zeitschrift für pädagogische Psychologie und experimentelle Pädagogik, herausgegeben von Meumann und Scheibner, Band XVI, S. 211–214.

Besprechung im literarischen Zentralblatt für Deutschland: Nr. 46, Sp. 1131–1137: Bönke, Plagiator Bergson.

Eine Berichtigung. (Gegen das Buch von Stanley Hall, Die Begründer der modernen Psychologie.) Literarisches Zentralblatt für Deutschland: Nr. 48, Sp. 1080.

1916

Die Nationen und ihre Philosophie. Taschenausgabe. 154 S. Leipzig, A. Kröner.

Völkerpsychologie und Entwicklungspsychologie. Psychologische Studien, herausgegeben von W. Wundt, X, S. 189–239. –Probleme der Völkerpsychologie, 2. Aufl (1921).

Gottfried Wilhelm Leibniz zum Gedächtnis. Rede am 14. November. Bericht der mathematisch-physischen Klasse der kgl. sächsischen Gesellschaft der Wissenschaften, Band LXVIII, S. 255–266. Deutsche Revue, herausgegeben von R. Fleischer, S. 248–254.

Zur Lage. Polnische Blätter, Zeitschrift für Politik, Kultur und soziales Leben, herausgegeben von W. Feldman, Band V, S. 99–101.

Noch einmal die Volksausschüsse. Erwiderung auf W. Goetz. Leipziger Tageblatt, 11. Oktober.

Über die Lage. Interview der Leipziger Abendzeitung.

1917

Völkerpsychologie. Eine Untersuchung der Entwicklungsgesetze von Sprache, Mythus und Sitte. 7. und 8. Band: Die Gesellschaft. 1. Teil: VIII, 438 S.; 2. Teil: VI, 344 S. Leipzig, A. Kröner.

Leibniz. Zu seinem 200jährigen Todestag. III, 132 S. Leipzig, A. Kröner.

Chauvinismus und Militarismus. Kulturrundschau der Leipziger Illustrierten Zeitung, Band 148, 1 Februar.

Luther als deutscher Mensch. Kunstwart (Deutscher Wille), herausgegeben von F. Avenarius. 1. Novemberheft, S. 99–100.

Die formale Abschluß. Gutachten über Abschaffung der Reifeprüfung. Berliner Tageblatt, 25 Dezember.

1918

Völkerpsychologie. Eine Untersuchung der Entwicklungsgesetze von Sprache, Mythus und Sitte. 9. Band: Das Recht. XVIII, 484 S. Leipzig, A. Kröner.

Einleitung in die Philosophie. 7. Auflage. VI, 448 S. Leipzig, A. Kröner.

Grundriß der Psychologie. 13. Auflage. VI, 414 S. Leipzig, A. Kröner.

Einführung in die Psychologie. 4. Abdruck (19.–23. Tausend). VI, 123 S. Leipzig, Dürr.

Deutsche Träumer vergangener Zeiten. Aus "Die deutschen Träumer," Süddeutsche Monatshefte, April, S. 12–13.[34]

Die Zeichnungen des Kindes und die zeichnende Kunst der Naturvölker. Festschrift zu Johannes Volkelts 70. Geburtstag, S. 1–24. Probleme der Völkerpsychologie, 2. Auflage (1921).

Schlußwort des Herausgebers. Psychologische Studien, herausgegeben von W. Wundt, X. S. 571–572.

Stimmen führender Männer zur Not der Zeit. Nr. 6 der Veröffentlichungen der Gesellschaft für staatsbürgerliche Erziehung.

Geschichte der Universität. Aus Stätten der Bildung: Bd. 1 "Leipzig." Herausgegeben von Rektor und Senate der Universität. S. 28–35.

1919

Völkerpsychologie. Eine Untersuchung der Entwicklungsgesetze von Sprache, Mythus und Sitte, 3. Band: Die Kunst. 3. neubearbeitete Auflage. Mit 59 Abbildungen. XII, 624 S. Leipzig, A. Kröner.

Logik. Eine Untersuchung der Prinzipien der Erkenntnis und der Methoden wissenschaftlicher Forschung. 1. Band: Allgemeine Logik und Erkenntnistheorie. 4. neubearbeitete Auflage. XVI, 654 S. Stuttgart, F. Enke.

System der Philosophie. 4. umgearbeitete Auflage, in 2 Bänden. 1. Band: XVI, 436 S. 2. Band: VI, 304 S. Leipzig, A. Kröner.

Vorlesungen über Menschen- und Tierseele. 6. neubearbeitete Auflage. Mit 53 Abbildungen, XVI, 579 S. Leipzig, L. Voß.

Offener Brief an den Leipziger evangelischen Pfarrerverein über Abschaffung des Religionsunterrichts. In vielen Zeitungen.

Dem Bund der Frontsoldaten. Akademische Nachrichten und Leipziger Studentenzeitung, 1. Jahrgang, Nr. 6.[35]

Das Land Baden im Kriegsjahr 1866. Den Mitgliedern des Leipziger Bibliophilenabends.[36]

1920

Völkerpsychologie. Eine Untersuchung der Entwicklungsgesetze von Sprache, Mythus und Sitte. 10. Band: Kultur und Geschichte. IX, 478 S. Leipzig, A. Kröner.

Die Zukunft der Kultur. Schlußkapitel aus Band 10 der Völkerpsychologie. 54 S. Leipzig, A. Kröner.

Völkerpsychologie. Eine Untersuchung der Entwicklungsgesetze von Sprache, Mythus und Sitte. 4. Band: Mythus und Religion. 1. Teil, 3. Auflage. XII, 587 S. Leipzig, A. Kröner.

Grundriß der Psychologie. 14. Auflage. XVI, 414 S. Stuttgart, A. Kröner.

Einleitung in die Philosophie. 8. Auflage. XVIII, 448 S. Stuttgart, A. Kröner.

[34]Abdruck aus "Erlebtes und Erkanntes" (1920).
[35]Abdruck aus "Die Zukunft der Kultur" (1920).
[36]Abdruck aus "Erlebtes und Erkanntes" (1920).

Logik. Eine Untersuchung der Prinzipien der Erkenntnis und der Methoden wissenschaftlicher Forschung. 2. Band: Logik der exakten Wissenschaften. 4. neubearbeitete Auflage. XV, 671 S. Stuttgart, F. Enke.

Erlebtes und Erkanntes. XII, 399 S. Stuttgart, A. Kröner.

Die Weltkatastrophe und die deutsche Philosophie. Veröffentlichungen der Deutschen Philosophischen Gesellschaft, 6. Beiheft. 16 S.[37]

1921

Logik. Eine Untersuchung der Prinzipien der Erkenntnis und der Methoden wissenschaftlicher Forschung. 3. Band: Logik der Geisteswissenschaften. 4. umgearbeitete Auflage.[38] XII, 693 S. Stuttgart, F. Enke.

Erlebtes und Erkanntes. 2. Auflage. XII, 399 S. Stuttgart, A. Kröner.

Kleine Schriften. 3. Band. VI, 549 S. Stuttgart, A. Kröner.

(Inhalt: Über die Einteilung der Wissenschaften, 1889. Über die mathematische Induktion, 1883. Die Logik der Chemie, 1883. Über die Methode der Minimaländerungen, 1883. Biologische Probleme, 1889. Die Empfindung des Lichts und der Farben, 1888. Zur Theorie der räumlichen Gesichtswahrnehmungen, 1888, Anhang: Das Raumproblem in erkenntnistheoretischer Beleuchtung, 1869. Selbstbeobachtung und innere Wahrnehmung, 1888. Zur Frage der Lokalisation der Großhirnfunktionen, 1891. Über den Begriff des Gesetzes mit Rücksicht auf die Ausnahmslosigkeit der Lautgesetze, 1886. Wer ist der Gesetzgeber der Naturgesetze, 1886. Logik und Psychologie, 1910. Die Psychologie im Kampf ums Dasein, 1913.)

Probleme der Völkerpsychologie. 2. vermehrte Auflage. VI, 217 S. Stuttgart, A. Kröner.

Metaphysik. Aus "Die Kultur der Gegenwart," herausgegeben von P. Hinneberg, 1. Band, 6. Teil, 3. Aufl. S. 98–134. Leipzig, Teubner.

Die Bedeutung der akademischen Seminarien für die Geisteswissenschaften. Handbuch der Politik, 2. Aufl. Band III, S. 276–278.[39]

1922

Vorlesungen über die Menschen- und Tierseele. 7. und 8. mit der 6. übereinstimmende Auflage. Leipzig, L. Voß.

Völkerpsychologie. Eine Untersuchung der Entwicklungsgesetze von Sprache, Mythus und Sitte. Band 1. und 2: Die Sprache, 1. und 2. Teil. 4. unveränderte Auflage. Stuttgart, A. Kröner.

Einleitung in die Philosophie. 9. unveränderte Auflage. Leipzig, A. Kröner.

Grundriß der Psychologie. 15. Auflage. Mit Ergänzungen zur Literatur von Prof. Dr. W. Wirth. VI, 431 S. Leipzig, A. Kröner.

---

[37]Mit einigen Zusätze und Abkürzungen aus "Erlebtes und Erkanntes" (1920).
[38]Bis S. 100 durchgearbeitet.
[39]Gegenüber der 1. Auflage (1912) etwas erweitert.

1923

Völkerpsychologie. Eine Untersuchung der Entwicklungsgesetze von Sprache, Mythus und Sitte. 3. Band: Die Kunst. 4. Auflage. Leipzig, A. Kröner.

Völkerpsychologie. Eine Untersuchung der Entwicklungsgesetze von Sprache, Mythus und Sitte. 5. und 6. Band: Mythus und Religion, 2. und 3. Teil. 3. Auflage. Leipzig, A. Kröner.

Ethik. Eine Untersuchung der Tatsachen und Gesetze des sittlichen Lebens. 1. Band. 5. Auflage. Stuttgart, F. Enke.

Sinnliche und übersinnliche Welt. 2. unveränderte Auflage. Leipzig, A. Kröner.

1924

Ethik. Eine Untersuchung der Tatsachen und Gesetze des sittlichen Lebens. 2. und 3. Band. 5. Auflage. Stuttgart, F. Enke.

Logik. Eine Untersuchung der Prinzipien der Erkenntnis und der Methoden wissenschaftlicher Forschung. 1. Band: Allgemeine Logik und Erkenntnistheorie. 5. Auflage. Stuttgart, F. Enke.

1926

Völkerpsychologie. Eine Untersuchung der Entwicklungsgesetze von Sprache, Mythus und Sitte. 4. Band: Mythus und Religion. 1. Teil, 4. Auflage. Leipzig, A. Kröner.

NAME INDEX

SUBJECT INDEX

hypnosis   19 - look up - summary very confused
                  88 - good

p 22   scientific knowledge + philosophical
       knowledge are one - Wundt accused
       of mysticism

37 - The Complication experiment - here, one
      sense modality competing against another -
      fore - runner of Stroop?
      -- see also 44 + 46

141 - Automatization frees up mental
energy

148 - Francis Wayland as Y pioneer in US

149 - American dream responsible
for the quick acceptance of mesmerism

Printed in the United States
71884LV00002B/203